RE-INTERPRETING BLACKSTONE'S *COMMENTARIES*

This collection explores the remarkable impact and continuing influence of William Blackstone's *Commentaries on the Laws of England*, from the work's original publication in the 1760s down to the present. Contributions by cultural and literary scholars, and intellectual and legal historians trace the manner in which this truly seminal text has established its authority well beyond the author's native shores or his own limited lifespan.

In the first section, 'Words and Visions', Kathryn Temple, Simon Stern, Cristina S Martinez and Michael Meehan discuss the *Commentaries*' aesthetic and literary qualities as factors contributing to the work's unique status in Anglo-American legal culture.

The second group of essays traces the nature and dimensions of Blackstone's impact in various jurisdictions outside England, namely Quebec (Michel Morin), Louisiana and the United States more generally (John W Cairns and Stephen M Sheppard), North Carolina (John V Orth) and Australasia (Wilfrid Prest). Finally Horst Dippel, Paul Halliday and Ruth Paley examine aspects of Blackstone's influential constitutional and political ideas, while Jessie Allen concludes the volume with a personal account of 'Reading Blackstone in the Twenty-First Century and the Twenty-First Century through Blackstone'.

This volume is a sequel to the well-received collection *Blackstone and his Commentaries: Biography, Law, History* (Hart Publishing, 2009).

Re-Interpreting Blackstone's *Commentaries*

A Seminal Text in National and International Contexts

Edited by
Wilfrid Prest

OXFORD AND PORTLAND, OREGON
2017

Hart Publishing
An imprint of Bloomsbury Publishing Plc

Hart Publishing Ltd
Kemp House
Chawley Park
Cumnor Hill
Oxford OX2 9PH
UK

Bloomsbury Publishing Plc
50 Bedford Square
London
WC1B 3DP
UK

www.hartpub.co.uk
www.bloomsbury.com

Published in North America (US and Canada) by
Hart Publishing
c/o International Specialized Book Services
920 NE 58th Avenue, Suite 300
Portland, OR 97213-3786
USA

www.isbs.com

HART PUBLISHING, the Hart/Stag logo, BLOOMSBURY and the
Diana logo are trademarks of Bloomsbury Publishing Plc

First published in hardback, 2014
Paperback edition, 2017

© The editor and contributors severally 2017

The editor and contributors have asserted their right under the Copyright, Designs and Patents Act 1988, to be identified as the Authors of this work.

All rights reserved. No part of this publication may be reproduced or transmitted in any form or by any means, electronic or mechanical, including photocopying, recording, or any information storage or retrieval system, without prior permission in writing from the publishers.

While every care has been taken to ensure the accuracy of this work, no responsibility for loss or damage occasioned to any person acting or refraining from action as a result of any statement in it can be accepted by the authors, editors or publishers.

All UK Government legislation and other public sector information used in the work is Crown Copyright ©. All House of Lords and House of Commons information used in the work is Parliamentary Copyright ©. This information is reused under the terms of the Open Government Licence v3.0 (http://www.nationalarchives. gov.uk/doc/open-government-licence/version/3) except where otherwise stated.

All Eur-lex material used in the work is © European Union,
http://eur-lex.europa.eu/, 1998–2017.

British Library Cataloguing-in-Publication Data
A catalogue record for this book is available from the British Library.

ISBN: HB: 978-1-84946-538-0
PB: 978-1-50991-386-2

Typeset by Compuscript Ltd, Shannon
Printed and bound in Great Britain by
Lightning Source UK Ltd

To find out more about our authors and books visit www.hartpublishing.co.uk. Here you will find extracts, author information, details of forthcoming events and the option to sign up for our newsletters.

Preface

Since first appearing in print nearly two and a half centuries ago, the reputation of William Blackstone's *Commentaries on the Laws of England* has waxed and waned and waxed again. Today the remarkable intellectual and literary qualities of Blackstone's masterwork, as also its extensive and surprisingly durable influence, are widely—if not quite universally—acknowledged. But much remains to be discovered about the different agendas, messages and purposes with which the *Commentaries* has been associated over the years, as well as the changing composition of its international readership and the various sources of its appeal to those readers.

The present volume seeks to advance discussion and exploration of these themes. It is derived from papers presented to a symposium convened at the University of Adelaide on 6 December 2012, together with additional chapters written after the event by John Orth and the editor. Responses from Ruth Paley, Stephen Sheppard and Simon Stern as invited commentators on the papers of John Cairns, Paul Halliday and Kathryn Temple now provide codas to their respective chapters. This symposium was the second in what threatens to become a series. The first, in 2007, on 'William Blackstone: Life, Thought, Influence', generated *Blackstone and his* Commentaries: *Biography, Law, History* (Hart Publishing 2009; 2014). Planning is currently underway for a third Adelaide symposium in December 2015 on 'Blackstone and his Critics'.

While other combinations and permutations might be possible, the following chapters are arranged under three main subject headings. The first, 'Words and Visions', brings the insights of literary criticism and art history to bear on our reading of the *Commentaries* as text; the second, 'Beyond England', looks at the dissemination and impact of that text in various parts of North America and the South Pacific; finally 'Law and Politics' discusses aspects of Blackstone's political thought and legal doctrines in the context of his own time, the subsequent centuries and our present day.

It is a pleasure to acknowledge the assistance of my Adelaide colleague David Lemmings in co-convening the 2012 symposium, of Janet Hart in facilitating arrangements and of the Australian Research Council for funding (under DP 120101749) that helped make possible the attendance of Dr Paley and Prof Stern. My thanks also go to Paul Wilkins of the Barr Smith Library for smoothing our access to the Ira Raymond Room and to the office staff of the Law School and the School of History and Politics (notably Greta Larsen and Moira Groves), who provided much kind help before, during and after the symposium, not least in the process of converting papers to chapters. Other Adelaide colleagues and friends in Law and History have been generous with their assistance, as was my former Baltimore colleague Jack P Greene. Philip Schofield kindly verified two quotations from the Bentham papers at University College London, while Sabina Flanagan has once again helped bring an editorial project to fruition. Finally, I owe heartfelt thanks for forbearance and support to my fellow contributors, as well as to Richard Hart, Rachel Turner and their colleagues at Hart Publishing.

Wilfrid Prest

Contents

Preface	*v*
List of Contributors	*ix*
List of Illustrations	*xi*
List of Figures and Tables	*xii*
List of Abbreviations	*xiii*

I WORDS AND VISIONS

1. Blackstone's 'Stutter': the (Anti)Performance of the *Commentaries*   3
   Kathryn Temple
   William Blackstone: Courtroom Dramatist?   21
   Simon Stern
2. Blackstone as Draughtsman: Picturing the Law   31
   Cristina S Martinez
3. Blackstone's *Commentaries*: England's Legal Georgic?   59
   Michael Meehan

II BEYOND ENGLAND

4. Blackstone in the Bayous: Inscribing Slavery in the Louisiana *Digest* of 1808   73
   John W Cairns
   Legal Jambalaya   95
   Stephen M Sheppard
5. Blackstone and the Birth of Quebec's Distinct Legal Culture 1765–1867   105
   Michel Morin
6. Blackstone's Ghost: Law and Legal Education in North Carolina   125
   John V Orth
7. Antipodean Blackstone   145
   Wilfrid Prest

III LAW AND POLITICS

8	Blackstone's King *Paul D Halliday*	169
	Modern Blackstone: the King's Two Bodies, the Supreme Court and the President *Ruth Paley*	188
9	Blackstone's *Commentaries* and the Origins of Modern Constitutionalism *Horst Dippel*	199
10	Reading Blackstone in the Twenty-First Century and the Twenty-First Century through Blackstone *Jessie Allen*	215

Index 239

Contributors

Jessie Allen, Assistant Professor in the Law School, University of Pittsburgh, authors the blog *Blackstoneweekly*.

John W Cairns is Professor of Civil Law at the University of Edinburgh.

Horst Dippel is Professor Emeritus of British and American Studies at the University of Kassel.

Paul D Halliday is Julian Bishko Professor of History and Professor of Law at the University of Virginia.

Cristina S Martinez lectures in the School for Studies in Art and Culture, Carleton University.

Michael Meehan, Emeritus Professor in the School of Communication and Creative Arts at Deakin University, has published novels in Australia, Britain and the United States.

Michel Morin is Professor of Law at the University of Montreal.

John V Orth holds the William Rand Kenan Jr Chair of Law at the University of North Carolina, Chapel Hill.

Ruth Paley is editor of both the forthcoming volume on the House of Lords 1660–1832 for the History of Parliament Trust and of Book IV of Blackstone's *Commentaries* for Oxford University Press.

Wilfrid Prest is Professor Emeritus in History and Law, University of Adelaide.

Stephen M Sheppard is William H Enfield Distinguished Professor of Law, University of Arkansas.

Simon Stern, Associate Professor of Law and Graduate Faculty in English, University of Toronto, is editing Book II of the *Commentaries* for the Oxford Variorum edition.

Kathryn Temple is Associate Professor and Head of the Department of English at Georgetown University.

Illustrations

Chapter 2, Figure 1	The Five Orders: 'Elements of Architecture' (1747)
Chapter 2, Figure 2	Title Page: 'Elements of Architecture' (1747)
Chapter 2, Figure 3	Staircases: 'Elements of Architecture' (1747)
Chapter 2, Figure 4	St Paul's Cathedral: 'Elements of Architecture' (1747)
Chapter 2, Figure 5	Chapter One, p 4: 'Elements of Architecture' (1747)
Chapter 2, Figure 6	'Chapter IX': 'An Abridgement of Architecture' (1743)
Chapter 2, Figure 7	'Analysis of this Abridgement': 'An Abridgement of Architecture' (1743)
Chapter 2, Figure 8	'Contents of this Analysis', *An Analysis of the Laws of England* (Oxford, 1771)
Chapter 2, Figure 9	Table of Consanguinity: *Commentaries on the Laws of England* vol 2 (Oxford, 1776) facing p 203
Chapter 2, Figure 10	Table of Descents: *Commentaries on the Laws of England* vol 2 (Oxford, 1766) between pp 241 and 242
Chapter 2, Figure 11	Table of Descents: *An Analysis of the Laws of England* (Oxford, 1771) between pp 166 and 167
Chapter 2, Figure 12	Thomas Rowlandson (Detail), *Billy Lackbeard and Charley Blackbeard Playing at Football* (1784)
Chapter 6, Figure 1	Title Page: *The Tree of Legal Knowledge* (1838)
Chapter 6, Figure 2	'Rights of Things', ibid.
Chapter 6, Figure 3	'Public Wrongs' (detail), ibid.
Chapter 7, Figure 1	Stained Glass Window (Detail), Clayton and Bell (1857–58), Great Hall, University of Sydney.
Chapter 7, Figure 2	Law School Entrance, Forgan Smith Building (1940), University of Queensland

Figures and Tables

Chapter 4, Appendix I   Table and Figure: Citations to Blackstone's *Commentaries* or *Reports* in Louisiana Reported Opinions 1781–1980

Chapter 4, Appendix II   Table and Figure: Citations to Blackstone's *Commentaries* or *Reports* in Selected US State Courts 1781–1980

Chapter 6, Appendix II   Table: Blackstone's *Commentaries* correlated with Manning's *Commentaries*

Chapter 6, Appendix III   Table: Blackstone's *Commentaries* correlated with Mordecai's *Law Lectures*

Chapter 10, Figure 1:   Counsels' and Justices' Citations of Blackstone's *Commentaries* in US Supreme Court 1801–2012

Chapter 10, Table 1:   Citations of Blackstone's *Commentaries* in Opinions of US Supreme Court 1920–2012

Abbreviations

BL	British Library
Commentaries	W Blackstone, *Commentaries on the Laws of England* (Oxford, 1765–69; facsimile edn, Chicago IL, 1979)
Eller	CS Eller, *The William Blackstone Collection in the Yale Law School Library: A Bibliographical Catalogue* (New Haven CT, 1938)
Letters	WR Prest (ed), *The Letters of Sir William Blackstone 1744–1780*, Selden Society, Supplementary Series vol 14 (London, 2006)
Lockmiller	DA Lockmiller, *Sir William Blackstone* (Chapel Hill NC, 1938)
Nolan	DR Nolan, 'Sir William Blackstone and the New American Republic: a Study of Intellectual Impact' (1976) 145 *New York University Law Review* 731–68
Prest (ed) Commentaries	W Prest (ed), *Blackstone and his Commentaries: Biography, Law, History* (Oxford, 2009, 2014)
Prest, *William Blackstone*	W Prest, *William Blackstone: Law and Letters in the Eighteenth Century* (Oxford, 2008, 2012)

Quotations from primary sources retain original spelling and capitalisation but punctuation is modernised.

I
Words and Visions

There is no simple explanation for the resounding success of Blackstone's *Commentaries*. This is not because it is difficult to find reasons for the overwhelmingly favourable reception which greeted the four volumes on their first publication between 1765 and 1769. The impressive scope of Blackstone's undertaking to deliver a coherent, comprehensive and intellectually respectable account of English law and government, and the careful polishing of his text over 13 years of lectures delivered to a fee-paying Oxford student audience, provide two obvious leading candidates. But from the start readers and reviewers recognised that this book's appeal and impact also had something to do with how it was written, with matters of approach, expression and style as distinct from content or copy-editing.[1]

The following section offers four different perspectives on Blackstone's creative imagination as it is manifested in the *Commentaries*. Kathryn Temple's opening chapter explores the striking contrast between our author's well-attested and indeed self-admitted deficiencies as a public speaker (at least in his native tongue) and the smooth harmonic flow of language which characterises his written text. At the risk of distorting or at least flattening her complex argument, Blackstone's displays of apparent oral 'dysfluency' may express his lack of sympathy towards any hint of artifice or the theatrical in forensic oratory, together with a decidedly modern preference for print over speech as the source of law and justice. Simon Stern extends the discussion by distinguishing between various modes of legal rhetoric and doctrinal analysis, while further elaborating upon the controverted issues at stake in the political libel case *Onslow v Horne* (1770), for which we have what purports to be a verbatim shorthand record of Justice Blackstone's oral interventions in courtroom debate, with particular reference to the legal significance of a miniscule variation in a copy document tendered by the plaintiff.

From words, spoken, printed and written, we move to visions, pictures in the mind and on the page. Whereas Temple highlights some affective

---

[1] On Blackstone's style, *cf* AV Dicey, 'Blackstone's Commentaries' (1932) *Cambridge Law Journal* 4, 286–307 and KM Parker, 'Historicising Blackstone's *Commentaries on the Laws of England*' in A Fernandez and MD Dubber (ed), *Law Books in Action: Essays on the Anglo-American Legal Treatise* (Oxford, 2012) 22–37.

and emotional aspects of Blackstone's way with words, Cristina Martinez analyses the visual dimension of his sensibility, in terms both of overall conceptual design and detailed graphic execution, not least the use of carefully drafted charts, diagrams and figures to convey his meaning to the reader. She concludes by pointing to an intriguing parallel between Blackstone's treatment of equity in relation to the common law and Sir Joshua Reynolds's account of the role of genius in artistic composition. Lastly Michael Meehan relates what he terms the 'rich metaphoric visualisations' of the *Commentaries* to the early Hanoverian literary vogue for the neo-Virgilian georgic, an extended poetic exposition of human achievement in harmonious relation with the world of nature. In their different ways all four essays exemplify the illuminating additional insights that arise when Blackstone's book is viewed as an artefact (if not indeed a work of art) generated within a quite specific cultural and historical setting.

1

Blackstone's 'Stutter': The (Anti)Performance of the Commentaries

KATHRYN TEMPLE

It almost seems that legal performance is a legal embarrassment.

Bernard J Hibbitts[1]

DURING THE VERY period when theatre dominated English culture and actors became cultural icons for the first time, William Blackstone took his place on the national cultural stage, first with his Vinerian lectures, and later with the publication of the *Commentaries on the Laws of England*. As is well known and was brilliantly argued by Daniel Boorstin in 1941, Blackstone offered a comprehensive restatement of English law framed by Enlightenment philosophical and aesthetic values and famed for its commitment to reason and historical method.[2] But reason and history alone do not explain his unique achievement. While assuming the voice of reason and claiming historical accuracy as the source of his authority, all in the service of presenting a clear and comprehensive, yet portable and easily assimilated guide to English law, Blackstone was also deeply invested in affects related to law and justice. Highlighting affect allows us to see how Blackstone placed what might seem to be a purely rational approach in an affective frame, thus allowing his readers to *feel* rather than reason their way towards justice.[3] That *feeling* element in the

---

[1] BJ Hibbitts, http://faculty.law.pitt.edu/hibbitts/describ.htm.
[2] DJ Boorstin, *The Mysterious Science of Law: An Essay on Blackstone's Commentaries* (Chicago IL, 1941). For my analysis of Blackstone's speech patterns, I am grateful to Jay Fliegelman's work on Jefferson, *Declaring Independence: Jefferson, Natural Language, and the Culture of Performance* (Stanford CA, 1993). The literature on affect is large; *cf* M Gregg and GJ Seigworth (ed), *The Affect Reader* (Durham NC, 2010).
[3] For the relationship between affect and reason in the legal context and in eighteenth-century thought, see TA Maroney, 'The Persistent Cultural Script of Judicial Dispassion'

Commentaries is the key to what might be called its 'binding' power, the power that attracted both readers and non-readers to the *Commentaries* and made it an icon for English justice.[4]

Surprisingly, the *Commentaries* is framed in affective terms; it engages an abstracted rational process only reluctantly. Consider, for instance, the opening chapter where Blackstone lays out the relationship between justice, law and reason. Because man has no direct access to the law of nature in every particular, 'it is still necessary to have recourse to reason'.[5] But Blackstone never offers an enthusiastic endorsement of reason as the crystalline guide to right action that one might expect. Instead 'reason is corrupt, and ... understanding full of ignorance and error'.[6] As Blackstone sees it, 'the only true and natural foundations of society are the wants and the fears of individuals', wants and fears Blackstone expresses both directly and indirectly in the *Commentaries*, but wants and fears that have seldom been emphasised by later readers. It is no accident or mere literary convention, then, that Blackstone further frames the *Commentaries* by offering an affective commentary on its narrator as characterised by 'great diffidence and apprehensions'.[7] In introducing his monumental work in such personalised, affective terms, Blackstone recognises emotions as, in Martha Nussbaum's words, 'upheavals of thought', and marks (again in Nussbaum's words) not only the 'importance ... of things [people] do not fully control', but also 'their neediness before the world and its event'.[8]

This framing device intersects with the biographical and critical commentary on Blackstone's personal 'diffidence' to suggest that we look more carefully at other examples of such 'diffidence', at moments when he seems to stumble, lose control or exhibit anxiety. Looking for such moments reveals a significant gap between Blackstone the writer and Blackstone the speaker. As a writer, Blackstone was known for his style, which was described as 'pleasing' by Mansfield, 'luminous'[9] by James Sedgwick and most interestingly as 'correct, elegant, *unembarrassed*'[10] by Bentham.[11] This elegant smoothness, or 'unembarrassed' quality—which in other work I have argued is related to Blackstone's allegiance to eighteenth-century poetic theory—is

---

(2011) 99 *California Law Review* 629; GL Clore, 'For Love or Money: Some Emotional Foundations of Rationality' (2005) 80 *Chicago-Kent Law Review* 1151; ML Frazer, *The Enlightenment of Sympathy* (Oxford, 2010).

[4] See P Goodrich (ed), *Law and the Unconscious: A Legendre Reader* (New York NY, 1997) 25.
[5] *Commentaries* vol 1, 41: 'Introduction: of the Nature of Laws in general'.
[6] Ibid.
[7] *Commentaries* vol 1, 3: 'Introduction: on the Study of Law'.
[8] M Nussbaum, *Upheavals of Thought: The Intelligence of Emotions* (Cambridge, 2001) 22.
[9] Quoted in Lockmiller, 163.
[10] JH Burns and HLA Hart (ed), J Bentham, *A Fragment on Government* (London, 1776; Cambridge, 1998) 23 (emphasis added).
[11] See Prest, *William Blackstone* 218ff, for the reception of the *Commentaries*.

characteristic of the *Commentaries*.[12] For the *Commentaries* was devoted to an Enlightenment version of what has been called 'harmonic justice', an idea Blackstone may have cobbled together from classical sources, from Jean Bodin's political theory and from his own extensive reading of poetry. In the *Commentaries* Blackstone smoothed out and, in effect, harmonised English law with an elegance that gained almost universal admiration. As many commentators noted, each sentence, paragraph, chapter, book and volume re-imagined English legal history as expressing a harmonic, balanced order unknown in earlier attempts to summarise English law.

While harmony characterised the *Commentaries*, disharmony and discordance, or what specialists call 'dysfluency', characterised Blackstone's oral style. Anything but an orator, said to fall silent when called upon to speak, to evince embarrassment while on the bench, even to be a graceless lecturer, though he made his reputation by giving lectures (albeit read from a carefully prepared text), he was notoriously ashamed of public performance. His discomfort manifested itself differently at different stages of his career—it appeared whether lecturing, attempting to practise law or serving on the bench at Westminster Hall. Bentham, for instance, found the delivery of the lectures 'formal, precise, and affected', the work of a man uneasy with extemporaneous speech.[13] Regarding his appearances at the bar, Blackstone's brother-in-law James Clitherow noted that he was 'not … happy in a graceful Delivery or a flow of Elocution (both which he much wanted)'.[14] The poet Richard Graves, a friend and mentor, noted that he 'lacked that plausible superfluity of words, which gives some pleadings a show of eloquence'. Graves seems to have seen the problem as one involving a lack of filler phrases and expressions that allowed other more accomplished speakers to fill in gaps:

> [He] never used those supplementary phrases, of I humbly apprehend; and I beg leave to insist on it; or I can take it upon me to prove; with all imaginable ease and facility, to the perfect satisfaction of your lordship and the court, & c.[15]

Others were overtly unkind, suggesting that his deficits were so great that he should have avoided becoming 'a Pleader at the Bar'.[16] Blackstone himself was under no illusions: as he put it, 'there are certain Qualifications for being a public Speaker, in which I am very sensible of my own deficiency'.[17]

---

[12] Not everyone liked Blackstone's style and some even critiqued the *Commentaries* as if it were a clever performance meant to deceive the public regarding English law; *cf* E Kadens, 'Justice Blackstone's Common Law Orthodoxy' (2009) 103 *Northwestern University Law Review* 1566, n 63.
[13] JH Burns and HLA Hart (ed), *The Works of Jeremy Bentham* (London, 1997) vol 1, 45.
[14] Prest, *William Blackstone* 6.
[15] Quoted in W Prest, *Blackstone as a Barrister* (London, 2010) 15.
[16] Quoted in Kadens (n 12) 1562, n 50.
[17] *Letters* 29.

Even those who praised him damned him: As Prest notes, a Rev W Palmer found that Blackstone 'spoke reasonably well … in a manner much like that of reading a lecture in college'.[18] Summing up, Emily Kadens concludes that Blackstone was a 'fussy, by-the-book pedant', ill-spoken and perhaps actually ill-mannered.[19]

Diffident, dysfluent, pedantic: these evaluative judgements clash with Blackstone's judicial philosophy, with the desire evinced in his poetry and in the *Commentaries* for a justice imagined neither as hesitant or uncertain, nor as angry, vindictive or punishing, but as harmoniously interweaving a culture and its history just as God had woven all of nature together into one harmonious whole. Various explanations for his inability to express these harmonies in speech have been offered, including an innate shyness that may even have resulted in a near breakdown after he gave his first lecture as Vinerian Professor.[20] Perhaps Blackstone's humble origins and the loss of his father before he was born had thrown his confidence. Bad experiences at school may also have contributed to his 'later self-consciousness'.[21] Here, though, I focus not on his personal psychology but on how these representations of Blackstone as an embarrassed, dysfluent public speaker operate to suggest a legible affective sign that we can read not only as a symptom of intense discomfort, whether personal or cultural, with what had become a highly theatricalised legal environment at Westminster Hall, but also and perhaps more importantly as a performative rejection of orality in favour of the book and the priority of writing. In other words, Blackstone's embarrassment marks not so much his own deficits, but the shift from a no-longer-effective oral culture of law to the culture of the book and particularly to the primacy of the *Commentaries*.

I EMBARRASSMENT, 'DIFFIDENCE' AND PERFORMANCE

To understand this legible affective sign we need to know a little about how 'diffidence' or embarrassment works, for embarrassment turns out to be a crucially important affect for understanding social relations, one intimately related to how we understand justice. Embarrassment is one of the moral emotions that occur only in social situations and only when engaging in a behaviour thought, at least by the embarrassed one, to be improper or a violation of social norms. As anyone who has ever cringed alongside an embarrassed speaker knows, it is highly communicative. In its essence, it marks breaches in civility, whether those of the embarrassed or of those

---

[18] Prest *William Blackstone* 201.
[19] Kadens (n 12) 1604.
[20] Prest, *William Blackstone* 153.
[21] Ibid 22.

who have created embarrassment. It interrupts the smooth flow of discourse and the genial celebration of communal agreement through the creation of a non-violent but aggressive, visible and sometimes auditory, punctuation.[22] To serve its social functions, embarrassment must be manifested broadly, must be visible and easily recognised. Thus, from the first moment of cognition, of the recognition that one has deviated from social norms and been observed, one begins to exhibit symptoms such as restlessness, abrupt gestures and even stuttering.[23] Where the 'stutter' or 'stammer' appears in eighteenth-century plays, novels and biographical accounts it manifests not so much as a medical problem, but rather as an awkwardness of expression. We see this in the *Aberdeen Magazine* account of those who, when introduced to the king, become 'so much abashed … as to stammer in their speech, look foolishly, and bow awkwardly'.[24] Such dysfluency is often associated with lawyers. The 'stuttering lawyer' in the farce *Jacques Splin* presented at Cambridge in 1798 offers one instance,[25] while for a better-known example, we have only to read Samuel Foote's *The Orators* (1762) with its lengthy section on dysfluent lawyers.[26]

To make Blackstone's embarrassment speak we can rely partly on the reports of his contemporaries while positioning it in its performative context, as a 'performance' at Westminster Hall, as anti-performative as that might seem. For these interruptive dysfluencies do have a performative value: through a very particular type of performance of the natural, they call the opposition between theatricality and the natural into question. More specifically, a dysfluent, halting, stuttering or oppositional 'by the book' style pushes observers into impatience, into desire for the unimpeded word, away from courtroom theatrics and towards the certainty and security of the book. This is how Blackstone's dysfluency worked: His 'over-expression' of affective discomfort highlights the comforts offered by the *Commentaries*, comforts sorely needed as Blackstone's 'harmonic' idealisation of justice, his 'natural law' bent, was colliding with the commercial, statutory law of a rapidly developing culture. It speaks to the new priority of the book; going forward, print, not men with their ephemeral performances, whether good or bad, would play starring roles in Anglo-American law.

---

[22] See JL Tracy, RW Robins, JP Tangney (ed), *The Self-Conscious Emotions: Theory and Research* (London, 2007).
[23] RS Miller, 'Is Embarrassment a Blessing or a Curse?' in ibid 248.
[24] *Aberdeen Magazine* (1788–1790) vol 1, 3.
[25] J Patrat, *Le Fou raissonable, ou l'Anglais* (Paris, 1781). George Colman's version, first performed at Covent Garden on 24 April 1798, was adapted in turn for the version titled 'Jacques Splin' performed at Cambridge on 21 June 1798. I wish to thank Simon Stern for this reference.
[26] MC Murphy (ed), *Samuel Foote's Taste and The Orators: a Modern Edition with Five Essays* (Annapolis MD, 1982).

II THIS LEARNED THEATRE OF LAW

By 1770, when Blackstone became a judge, eloquence was expected, but anything too obviously oratorical might be criticised. Under such scrutiny, anxiety ran high, both among practitioners and judges. As Bentham was to argue, this was an age that brought home the idea that 'Publicity is the very soul of justice ... It keeps the judge himself, while trying, under trial'.[27] Westminster Hall had become a highly theatricalised environment and both justices and lawyers were evaluated for their performative potential just as actors were.[28] Perhaps an 1825 description of Lord Mansfield best reveals both the minute level of inspection justices endured and the blurring of lines between the court and the theatre:

> This nobleman was now in the decline of his life ... but the roses and lilies had not yet forsook his cheeks, and the lustre of his complexion was augmented by means of eyes that seemed to sparkle with genius. His person, if somewhat below the exact standard of beauty, was yet exquisitely formed; his motions were graceful ... He also possessed a voice replete with music in all its various modulations.[29]

The description focuses on the theatricalised operations of the judicial body, its cheeks and eyes (and through its eyes, its living brain and soul), its complexion with its visible blood, its motions and vocal modulations, all within the space of Westminster Hall, reminding us that legal decisions were made in a physical context by real human beings who were observed by other human beings to be breathing, speaking and feeling. It also speaks to the theatricalisation of the juridical world, a theatricalisation that emphasised the 'charms of sound' and 'music' of the law as much as its visual aspects. Such a theatrical, emotional and visceral display made justice and the law come alive to an audience.

But theatricalisation was a double-edged sword; it could easily be overdone. A highly theatrical oratorical style could be equated with inauthenticity as is clear in journalistic responses to both the Duchess of Kingston and Warren Hastings trials.[30] Given the connections between theatricality

---

[27] J Bentham, *Draught of a new plan for the organisation of the judicial establishment in France: proposed as a succedaneum to the draught presented, for the same purpose, by the Committee of Constitution, to the National Assembly, December 21st, 1789* (London, 1790) 25–26.

[28] See J Fawcett, 'The Overexpressive Celebrity and the Deformed King: Recasting the Spectacle as Subject in Colley Cibber's *Richard III*' (2011) 126 *Proceedings of the Modern Language Association* 950. See also JR Roach, *Cities of the Dead: Circum-Atlantic Performance* (New York NY, 1996) 73–118; C Rojek, *Celebrity* (London, 2004); C Wanko, *Roles of Authority: Thespian Biography and Celebrity in Eighteenth-Century Britain* (Lubbock TX, 2003).

[29] [Anon], *Westminster Hall: or Professional Relics and Anecdotes of the Bar, Bench, and the Woolsack* (London, 1825) vol 2, 87.

[30] See JS Peters, 'Theatricality, Legalism, and the Scenography of Suffering: The Trial of Warren Hastings and Richard Brinsley Sheridan's Pizarro' (2006) 18 *Law and Literature* 15.

and instability, disguise and false appearances, theatricality could tarnish the juridical world 'with the artifice, dissimulation, effeminacy, and luxury' popularly associated with the theatre.[31] Critiques span the century, with Pope's 1727 *Peri Bathous* proposing sarcastically that Westminster Hall be turned into a massive theatre with room for 10,000 (including the judges), while a 1794 advertisement mocked the 'grand display' of 'astonishing and magnificent deceptions' to be held at the 'grand Hall of Exhibitions at Westminster'. These were to include 'an enchanted drum', which, rather than promoting harmony, would 'set all the company a fighting, for the avowed purpose of order and tranquillity'.[32]

The stakes for public oratory were also under radical revision that reflected changes occurring in the theatre. Beginning in the middle of the eighteenth century, the old 'formal' acting style lost its effectiveness and began to be replaced by what was thought of as a 'natural' style. A challenging double bind evolved as orators came to be closely scrutinised for their 'natural' expression of feelings. As Jay Fliegelman points out, oratorical texts read like instructions to actors while actors, as they adopted a more 'natural' style (most obviously exemplified by Garrick), began to seem more like orators. James Burgh's *Art of Speaking*, first published in 1764 and frequently reprinted during Blackstone's career, is 'nothing less than a theatrical text committed to the physiognomy and tonal semiotics of over 76 passions'.[33] According to Burgh, the best natural and spontaneous public speaking could have a profound impact on the listener through its extraordinary qualities: 'Like irresistible beauty, it transports, it ravishes, it commands the admiration of all, who are within its reach ...'. And yet because it subordinated reason to affective presentation, it revealed 'the nakedness of truth, a true beauty, a self-evidence that required no judgment'.[34] One can well imagine the stress resulting from an attempt to speak 'naturally' while drawing on a memorised performance of over 76 passions. This emphasis on the truth value of fine oratory, on the ability of oratory to stand in for evidence and eliminate the need for judgment, raised the stakes even higher: as the author of *Deiology* opined, 'The perfection of speech depends upon beauty of thought and beauty of expression. As the excellence of speech is thought, so the value of thought is truth'.[35]

Adding to the pressure for oratory to signify 'truth' was Blackstone's status as first an academic lecturer on the law and later, by the time he was

See also MJ Kinservik, *Sex, Scandal and Celebrity in Late Eighteenth-Century England* (New York NY, 2007).

[31] Fliegelman (n 2) 90.
[32] *Wonderful Exhibition* (London 1794).
[33] Fliegelman (n 2) 31.
[34] Ibid 31–32.
[35] Ibid 1.

on the bench, the author of the *Commentaries*. For as much as his person, his works were on display when he sat in Westminster Hall, with all who came to observe ready to critique the consistency of his opinions with the *Commentaries*. Even before Blackstone became a judge, he had been attacked in Parliament for espousing a position which seemed at odds with the *Commentaries*. Blackstone's response suggests the extreme discomfort accompanying such an attack:

> Instead of defending himself upon the spot, he sunk under the charge, in an agony of confusion and despair. It is well known that there was a pause of some minutes in the house, from a general expectation that the Doctor would say something in his own defence; but, it seems, his faculties were too much overpowered to think of those subtleties and refinements, which have since occurred to him.[36]

The very idea of a print representation of the law seems to have been on trial here; much of the conversation around the importance of oratory made unfavourable comparisons to writing. Did Thomas Sheridan have Blackstone in mind when he complained that 'Our greatest men have been trying to do that with the pen, which can only be performed with the tongue'?[37] Sheridan certainly reinforced the dichotomy when he asserted that 'all writers seem to be under the influence of one common delusion, that by the help of words alone, they can communicate'.[38]

Truth, the natural, and oratory were all conflated in the public mind with a highly desirable 'harmony', thought to be natural, but also ideal. In reading Fliegelman's description of the purposes of late eighteenth-century elocution and its relationship to 'harmony', one is reminded of the harmony Blackstone associated with an idealised form of justice and tried to explicate in the *Commentaries*.[39] But harmonising texts and voices created a disharmonising disjunction of its own, as it reinforced differences between text and body, between the natural body and the body that lived only to be interpreted for its authentic—or inauthentic—expression of feelings. Both *embodied*—in that self and body were held to be identical—and *disembodied*—in that the surface of the body became a textual surface subject to interpretation, the speaking body of a prominent justice in Westminster Hall must have been under considerable pressure.[40] That Blackstone seemed to have been afflicted with some form of dysfluency, that his utterances were interruptive if not precisely abrasive, seems particularly unfortunate given his commitment to the smooth, harmonious representation of English law, but also particularly evocative. His dysfluency suggests

---

[36] Prest, *William Blackstone* 244.
[37] Quoted in Fliegelman (n 2) 26.
[38] Quoted in ibid 30.
[39] Ibid 64–65.
[40] See ibid 130, for a discussion of this dichotomous relationship between embodiment and disembodiment, self as self and 'self reduced to evidence of itself'.

an anti-performance as performative in its own way as any oratorically sophisticated performance could have been. To make Blackstone's dysfluency speak—rather than to pathologise it or dismiss it as incidental—is to begin to understand the complex relationship between legal orality and print culture during his time.

III ON NOT KNOWING WHERE TO STOP

In Samuel Foote's *The Orators*, an extremely successful play, performed 39 times in 1762 and on numerous occasions in 1765 and 1766 just as the *Commentaries* was coming out, all sorts of ill-speakers find themselves under review.[41] The play satirises *both* the overly eloquent, overly theatrical new oratory with its supposedly 'natural' style *and* what we might call the dysfluent or 'stuttering' style—a style that we think of as truly natural in that it seems to be seamlessly integrated with the body. In the first act of the play, Foote hammers Thomas Sheridan and his oratorical movement. As Murphy explains it, in Foote's view this new oratorical movement 'overemphasized voice and gesture and appealed to the imagination and the passions rather than to the understanding'.[42] But in Act II, Foote turns to a 'Hall of Justice', obviously Westminster Hall, where he mocks the 'stuttering' style, one which he denaturalises with his stage directions and over-the-top dialogue. The players are admonished to remember 'your proper pauses, repetitions, hums, has, and interjections: now seat yourselves and you the counsel remember to be mighty dull, and you the justice to fall asleep'.[43] The actual dialogue is so interrupted as to be painful to read. One lawyer speaks as follows:

> I have an objection to make, that is—hem—I shall object to her pleading at all.—hem—it is the standing law of this country—hem—and had—hem—always been so allow'd, deem'ed, and practis'd that—hem—all criminals should be try'd *per pares*, by their equals—hem—that is—hem—by a jury of equal rank with themselves.[44]

Here Foote turns what we commonly think of as the natural on itself, making of it an artificial performance subject to mockery. The connections he creates between halting and yet repetitive speech and 'the standing law of this country,' as well as the inclusion of the Latin phrase, speak to issues of literacy and writing, if not print. Thus, halting and repetitive speech marks more than the stupidity or awkwardness of the speaker; in *The Orators*, interruptive dashes, the unnecessary piling on of multiple synonyms, the repetitive

---

[41] Murphy (n 26) 53–55.
[42] Ibid xlix.
[43] Ibid 77.
[44] Ibid 78.

'hems' of a speaker who makes a speech out of multiple dysfluencies, rather than signs of the natural, mark an adherence to precedent and history, to a particular kind of highly theorised affectation.

By the middle of the eighteenth century, the use of the new natural style was linked by many to ideas of natural law. Fliegelman has pointed to the mid-century development of the idea that one could find a 'natural spoken language that would be a corollary to natural law'.[45] Paradoxically, however, making natural speech represent natural law created an equal if not greater need for theatricality. Over time, the natural became not only as frustratingly artificial as the artificial had been, but also far more difficult to perform.[46] Given the twisting meanings of natural and artificial in this context, it seems important to focus on Blackstone in all his particularity, on the performative nature of his anti-performative style. For when associated with the author of the *Commentaries*, an anti-performative performance must have taken on a very specific meaning. We have evidence for four kinds of dysfluency that Blackstone exhibited: first, the strange formality with which he presented the lectures; second a reticence or 'stammer' while attempting to develop his practice at Westminster Hall; third a paralysis of articulation when challenged in Parliament; and fourth a sort of oppositional dysfluency while on the bench. Such dysfluencies—what I call his 'stuttering' style—mark his performance as both memorable and undesirable, as uncomfortable, and as anti-performative. When we read of Blackstone's 'diffidence', his silence when challenged, his formality, we can imagine both his own embarrassment and observers becoming impatient and embarrassed, even wishing for an escape from orality into writing. Blackstone's style interrupted proceedings, and called into question the oratorical smoothness of public juridical performances.

Such seems to have been the case in *Onslow v Horne* (1770), a case which Kadens draws on to demonstrate Blackstone's desire 'to avoid exercising discretion' while on the bench.[47] True, this libel action did showcase Blackstone's adherence to a precedent that may have seemed overly precious, embodying the requirement that a print libel be reproduced in the pleadings exactly, to the letter, as it had appeared in its original publication. But while Kadens focuses on Blackstone's preoccupation with precedent, a closer look at her examples reveals that print and precedent are often conflated. As she puts it, Blackstone came to the bench with a reputation for his 'knowledge of black letter law … primarily from books'.[48] This bookish orientation, the faith in the power of print that had motivated him to publish the *Commentaries*, underlies most of Kadens' examples. She notes

---

[45] Ibid 1–2.
[46] See generally Peters (n 30).
[47] Kadens (n 12) 1592.
[48] Ibid 1576.

that in the case of *Perrin v Blake* (1772), Blackstone preferred the exact words of a testator's will over his expressed oral intent; that in an assault case, Blackstone 'quoted Bracton and Coke regarding the nature of the fear demanded ...'; that on occasion he quotes directly from the *Commentaries*; that he frequently lighted on 'authoritative medieval texts'; and that in one case, he sought not legal precedents, but print evidence from 'the book of rates attached to the Statute of Tunnage and Poundage', deciding in the end that there was not enough 'authority in print' to make a just decision.[49] It seems clear that although Blackstone valued precedent—as he indicates not only in most of these examples, but also in *Onslow*—it was precedent preserved in print that he relied on.

In fact, a closer look at *Onslow v Horne* reveals it as an extraordinarily condensed representation of anxieties related to oral, manuscript and print cultures, all in the context of public embarrassment and dysfluent, disruptive speech. That these anxieties were contained under the umbrella of a libel case is itself suggestive, for libel is in its essence interruptive of social norms. As Blackstone put it, libel has a tendency 'to disturb the public peace', causing breaches in social relations and potentially leading to violence.[50] More commonly, libel causes embarrassment through loss of reputation (as in *Onslow*), a dynamic uncomfortably close to Blackstone's own issues with embarrassment and reputation. Here Blackstone's 'diffidence' reverberates with the embarrassment of the libelled plaintiff, while Blackstone's dysfluent assertions, efforts to assert the primacy of text, interrupt the eloquent efforts of counsel to subordinate text to oral interpretation.

The case itself was highly politicised, almost guaranteeing that it would become at least a minor media event, exposing Blackstone to scrutiny beyond the confines of Westminster Hall. Horne was a well-known political agitator who over his long life took on many political battles.[51] By the late 1760s he had developed a reputation for providing 'counsel to every man who thought himself capable of being made an object of public commiseration'.[52] Apparently this was the role he took on for a Mr Burns, whom he believed to have been cheated by George Onslow, MP for Surrey. In the April 1770 case that Blackstone presided over, Horne was accused of libelling Onslow in a letter published in the *Public Advertiser*.[53] As a libel case, *Onslow* was bound to bring at least some issues of speech, writing and print into play, but the case is notable for the range of expressive forms it brought to the bench: first, a speech by Horne, overheard and repeated

---

[49] Ibid 1553, 1558.
[50] *Commentaries* vol 4, 150: 'Of Public Wrongs: of Offences Again[s]t the Public Peace'.
[51] MT Davis, 'John Horne Tooke [*formerly* John Horne] (1736–1812)', C Matthew and B Harrison (ed), *Oxford Dictionary of National Biography* (Oxford, 2004) vol 55, 7–15.
[52] Quoted ibid 9.
[53] Ibid.

by witnesses who may or may not have been reliable; second, two letters in manuscript, which may or may not have been written by Horne, one of which remained available while the second was accidentally destroyed by the printer; third, those letters reprinted in the *Public Advertiser*, purportedly as written and yet with at least one error; fourth, other letters written by those implicated in Horne's letters, now read into the record and reprinted in the 'transcript' of the case; fifth, a letter written by Onslow, the plaintiff; sixth, Horne's letters reprinted in the record, incorporating several misprints including the word '11th' for '11'; seventh, testimony by various witnesses as to the provenance of these letters; and finally, the 'transcript' of the case itself entitled

> The Whole Proceedings in the Cause on the Action Brought by The Rt.Hon. GEO. ONSLOW, Esq. Against The Rev. Mr. HORNE ... for a DEFAMATORY LIBEL, Before the Right Honourable Sir WILLIAM BLACKSTONE, Knt. ... Taken in Short-hand (by permission of the Judge). By JOSEPH GURNEY.

Much of the case 'transcript' records concerns about the status of these documents, their reliability, their meaning, and the accuracy of their transcriptions, concerns which will ironically reappear here in my discussion of the potential inaccuracies of the very trial 'transcript' we rely on for analysis.

Kadens calls on the case as a rare opportunity 'to listen to Blackstone as he struggled spontaneously with a legal problem'.[54] And if Joseph Gurney's transcription is accurate, the case also offers a rare opportunity to analyse Blackstone's 'performance' on the bench. That accuracy is impossible to judge; court reporting during this period was an uneven business.[55] In fact, a comparative examination of other records demonstrates the unlikelihood of Gurney's claims to accuracy. When one reads other cases that he reported, one discovers that almost everyone in Gurney's world speaks rather eloquently; even the rape victim is well spoken in *The Trial of Frederick Calvert, Esq; Baron of Baltimore* (1768).[56] Applying a similar comparative method to what we might call part two of the *Onslow* case, we find that when these facts were revisited in August 1770, Mansfield presided and it appears that someone other than Gurney, listed as 'anonymous' on the title page, transcribed the case. One is surprised to see here that Mr Serjeant Leigh, so eloquently well spoken the first time around, has suddenly taken to blurting out run-on, ungrammatical sentences.[57] Given the

---

[54] Kadens (n 12) 1553.
[55] Ibid 1580, n 139.
[56] *The Trial of Frederick Calvert, Esq; Baron of Baltimore in the Kingdom of Ireland* (London, 1768).
[57] [J Gurney] *The Whole Proceedings in the Cause on the Action Brought by The Rt. Hon. Geo. Onslow, Esq. against The Rev. Mr. Horne* (London, 1770); *The Genuine Trial between The Rt. Hon. Geo. Onslow, Esq; and The Rev. Mr. John Horne, tried at Guildford the 1st of August, 1770* (London, 1770).

vagaries of eighteenth-century legal transcription, what can be learnt then from a 'record' of the case? While we can know little of the actual facts, of what really was said and how it was said, we can learn much about how Blackstone was represented to the larger world, by examining the record, such as it is, for what it has to tell us about representation rather than about the 'real'. Was Blackstone *really* embarrassed or literally (a weighted word in this context) stuttering or searching for words? It is difficult to tell. Certainly, he sounds hesitant when the issue of the two letter mistake first arises: to Leigh's confident 'it is not necessary that it should have *th* over it', he replies, 'In common understanding it is not necessary'.[58] It is only after 10 lines of back and forth between the lawyers that he finally says he does 'really think' the variance is fatal.[59] From this point on in the Gurney transcript, his assertions become more forceful and assertive and begin to elicit impatient responses from his interlocutors. To read this transcript at a bit of a slant, for its performative value, is to notice the impatience Blackstone evoked in others and to recognise the ways Blackstone's style caught them up short and interrupted the oratorical smoothness of on-the-bench performances.

This case was complex, mired in the interpretive issues that plague the oral–literate continuum, involving the identity and intent of the letter writer; the differences between accusing someone of taking bribes and asking someone in a public forum whether or not he had taken a bribe; the question of whether or not letters actually ever 'speak for themselves'; the importance of stories; and even the question of whether certain rhetorical ploys were honest or more typical of the notorious 'Jonathan Wild'.[60] But in the end, Blackstone's decision to non-suit the case was predicated on a simple rule of libel law that required a print libel to be reprinted in the pleadings with minute accuracy. The mistake here was indeed minute, so minute that in print it could barely be seen. It consisted of the substitution of 'July 11th' for 'July 11', a difference of 'two insignificant letters' as the plaintiff's junior counsel put it.[61] While this mistake did not result in any interpretive confusion, it was a sticking point for Blackstone as well as an interruptive moment in a case that had largely consisted of lengthy, eloquent speeches until the last few pages. Here, as Simon Stern points out below,[62] Blackstone is legally correct as well as quick to correct others. But one sees a shift to short queries, interrogatories, exhortations and expressions of disbelief in all the speakers just as the issue of the 'letter' or the

---

[58] [Gurney] (n 57) 44–45.
[59] Ibid.
[60] Ibid 22.
[61] Ibid 45.
[62] S Stern, 'William Blackstone: Courtroom Dramatist' pp. 28–29.

literal adherence to it is raised. The number of times Blackstone references text and textuality is itself striking:

— 'We are not to conclude ... what he writes must be strictly grammatical: he might mean to write July *eleven*. Dates are written differently. Some put the figures before the name of the month, some after; and in describing the year, the Scotch write, that such a thing happened in *the* 1770, not in 1770, as we do'.[63]
— 'You ought to prove it *literatim* in the words, letters, and figures; it strikes me as being so'.[64]
— 'Your argument would have done better, if in the record they had wrote it *eleven* in letters; for 11 in figures, and *eleven* in letters, certainly read both alike. But they have wrote the figures, and put the *th* over it; which alters the reading and the grammar'.[65]
— 'Your solution then is, that these are two different marks to signify the same word; one mark is used in the printed letter, another in the record; in the letter two units, in the record two units and *th*; but the word so signified is the same'.[66]
— 'If I admit the variation of a single letter, I don't know where to stop'.[67]
— 'It must appear to be literally and numerically the same ... you ought to have copied it exactly'.[68]
— 'Had it been a record of the crown-office, it would have been sent down more correct'.[69]
— 'I ... should be glad if you could draw me a line, to get rid of so minute a nicety; but I take the law to be so settled ...'.[70]
— 'If you can draw me any rational line, at which I can stop, consistently with the rules of law, I would not consent to non-suit a plaintiff'.[71]

Blackstone's responses are both repetitive and as interruptive as the line he wishes someone would draw, making much of an issue that Onslow's lawyers thought insignificant. The interruptive theme repeats at the level of the sentence: with hardly any clause going over 10 words, every sentence is sprinkled with semicolons and comma breaks. Repeating his point again and again underscores the poignancy of his plaintive, 'If I admit the variation of a single letter, I don't know where to stop'—indeed, he seems not to know when to stop. And although it is difficult to interpret either his tone or the tone of those who respond, the tendency of his remarks is oppositional,

[63] [Gurney] (n 57) 46.
[64] Ibid 44.
[65] Ibid 44–45.
[66] Ibid 45.
[67] Ibid.
[68] Ibid 47.
[69] Ibid.
[70] Ibid.
[71] Ibid.

an interruptive force in what might otherwise have been the smooth and collegial operations of the court.

Ironically, Blackstone's interruptive moments induce interruptive responses in others: the possibly irritated responses of the generally genial and long-winded Cox and Leigh, including Cox's 'it is only two letters; it must amount to a word; it is two insignificant letters', almost call out for explanation marks. But Blackstone sticks to his point, revealing what Kadens rightly argues is a didactic loyalty to precedent, but also to text. His rejection of 'the variation of a single letter' corresponds to his rejection of any departure from what he understands to be the law. The sacred nature of text in a libelled letter, reflected in the principle of exactitude that he adheres to, points directly to the *Commentaries* and to his insistence on the importance of the system he had 'methodised' over expedience. His purpose, though expressed through discordance, is to seek a larger harmony, as he points out when he says, 'I'm afraid that would not do. That would let in a hundred altercations'. (Note that he is interested in reducing *altercations* as well as alterations.) Through creating discord then, Blackstone points towards the idealised harmonies of the law as represented in the book. While Kadens sees this as a negative ('Whereas the other judges ... accepted the limits of the ideal, [Blackstone] ... did not accept that law in practice did not fit into his neat theories'), one might just as easily read it as 'pushback', as loyalty to principle, to a system that Blackstone had spent many years perfecting and one that many had praised for its beauty.[72] By over-expressing interruptive opposition and calling attention to the importance of the word, even the letter of the law, Blackstone urged observers towards the perfections of the *Commentaries*.[73]

IV BLACKSTONE'S DYING WORDS: BE FIRM IN YOUR OPINION

Ephemerality is the greatest enemy of law in any society.

J Bernard Hibbitts [74]

In an anecdote recorded in 1792, Blackstone was reportedly asked on his deathbed his opinion as to a decision involving penitentiary house management. As the story goes, he responded in favour of firmness, leading the

---

[72] Kadens (n 12) 1605.

[73] Simon Stern helpfully complicates these issues in his response below at S Stern, 'William Blackstone: Courtroom Dramatist,' pp 21–29. In the larger project from which this chapter is drawn, I elaborate on Blackstone's rhetorical use of emotive moments in the *Commentaries* themselves.

[74] BJ Hibbitts, 'Coming to Our Senses: Communication and Legal Expression in Performance Cultures' 41 *Emory Law Journal* 4 (1992) 960.

biographer to remark, 'Mr. Justice Blackstone's dying words, *be firm in your opinion*, seem to me the most important direction for our conduct'.[75] These words may as well have been directed to the English legal system as to any one person, for they mandate a consistency that Blackstone associated with the book, one that he had attempted to memorialise in the *Commentaries*. Thus, to condemn Blackstone as a poor speaker, whether embarrassed or irascible or inflexible, does not tell the whole story, or at least does not reveal in full what he valued in his own time. Blackstone's terse last words reflect a lifetime of adherence to principle, not so much to abstract principle, but to the principle of the text. For how could one be 'firm in your opinion' if opinions were based only in memory or shifted with every shift of eloquent expression? Seen in the hindsight filtered through these words, Blackstone's frequent and dysfluent insistence on the text over the word suggests the oratorical over-expression of anti-oratorical fervour that in itself elaborates a performance.

Let me explain: Jessie Allen has noted the occasional twenty-first-century use of what she calls a 'naturalistic drama': 'so unstudied … [but] much more heavily masked than a formal legal ritual, whose artifice is readily apparent'.[76] As Allen suggests, an 'unstudied' performance can sometimes be the most effective of all. But Blackstone over-expresses this anti-performative, unstudied style, over-performing the 'naturalistic drama', his diffidence and halting expression so marked as to become the subject of spectatorial comment and critique. Blackstone's over-expressive performance thus draws attention to its own 'naturalness' while avoiding accusations of theatrical falsity. Perhaps the problem here is what Joseph Roach has referred to as an anxiety of authenticity, an 'anxiety generated by the process of substitution'.[77] In Roach's schema, actors are 'surrogated doubles', performing as surrogates for the 'thing', person, idea or, in Blackstone's case, book that is represented. Their self-representation hovers in a space between 'body politic and body natural'.[78] In Blackstone's case, this surrogated double is actually a sort of quintuple surrogate: Blackstone on or off the bench stands in for the *Commentaries* and the *Commentaries* stands in for the law of England while the law of England stands in for natural justice and finally for the harmonic justice that Blackstone idealised. Much mediated then, the relationship between Blackstone's body and the abstraction he called justice is an attenuated one, one that is both represented and protected by his hesitant, pedantic elaboration. Like Pope, who

---

[75] [Anon], *The Beauties of Biography, a Selection of the Lives of Eminent Men* (London, 1792) vol 2, 35.
[76] J Allen, 'Theater of the Invisible', *Blackstone Weekly* (23 May 2011): www.blackstoneweekly.wordpress.com.
[77] Roach (n 28) 3ff.
[78] Ibid 79.

contrasted his deformed body to his perfectly formed poetry, Blackstone contrasts his less than fluent speech to the perfections of writing and thus to the new dominance of print as its own sort of performance, one that made the *Commentaries* not only a best-seller, but the primary conduit for the transmission of English legal principles to Britain's colonies.[79]

Turning to Samuel Johnson's definition of performance, as 'to execute, to do, ... to achieve an undertaking, to accomplish, completion of something designed', we can reinterpret Blackstone's performance as a lecturer, barrister and on the bench as successful.[80] His dysfluency marked his dissension from the usual way of doing things, from everyday practice at Westminster Hall, and led observers away from performance and towards the sophisticated print texts that were to become the norm. Meanwhile, this strategy, if we can call it that, undid the distinction between the natural and the artificial, even as it underscored both the authority of the book and the machinations of juridical oratory. In some ways, it celebrated the book as *more* authentic, more reliable than any performance on the bench. Thus, Blackstone's mode of affective embodiment communicated the decline of one system and the rise of another.

Books, as Milton asserted, have a 'potencie of life' and 'contain the pretious life-blood of a master-spirit'.[81] As we have seen, Blackstone rejected traditionally understood theatricality and performance in favour of what might be called the performance of the book. Instead of performing oratorically, he performed the necessity of the book as a method of access to law—and implicitly of access to justice. His public self-representations paradoxically promoted the book, encouraging a readership that lasted for generations and made the *Commentaries* into an iconic cultural monument, a representative of what Frye termed 'the authority of tradition', similar to other iconic texts such as the Bible or, more on point, the Declaration of Independence. Yet, the *Commentaries*, like the Declaration, had the potential for permanence, for influence that went beyond that of any single physical object, precisely because as a print production, it could be easily replicated, distributed and preserved. As its endlessly proliferating copies were annotated, discussed, read again and again, never read at all but carried about, and collected purely for their historical value, they transcended monumental status, and became absorbed into Anglo-American legal culture. As Hibbitts has said, 'We might "performatize" certain legal texts by ... reconsidering them as instruments of performance rather than

---

[79] See H Deutsch, *Resemblance and Disgrace: Alexander Pope and the Deformation of Culture* (Cambridge MA, 1996) for a discussion of the relationship between body and text in Pope's career.
[80] S Johnson, *A Dictionary of the English Language* (London, 1755).
[81] J Milton, 'Areopagitica' in DM. Wolfe (ed), *Complete Prose Works of John Milton* (New Haven CT, 1953–82) vol 2, 493.

documentary ends in themselves'.[82] In this sense the *Commentaries* need not even be present to perform its mission; mere citation, even when cited by those who have never read it, operates as a sign of Blackstone's long-standing influence and of the victory of print over performance that has dominated the modern period.

---

[82] http://faculty.law.pitt.edu/hibbitts/describ.htm.

William Blackstone: Courtroom Dramatist?

SIMON STERN

KATHRYN TEMPLE'S OBSERVATIONS about legal 'dysfluency' raise a host of questions about legal performance in the courtroom and about the ways in which a printed text can serve as a legal performance. In this response, I propose to consider the meanings of legal fluency and dysfluency by inquiring into the occasion of the lawyer's performance. This concept is most conventionally associated with the work of the trial lawyer, particularly as it involves the careful orchestration of facts and evidence so as to persuade a jury. The understanding of law as a rhetorical activity, however, also includes another sense of legal argumentation as performance, centring on the analysis and summation of doctrine. Criticisms of Blackstone's courtroom presence, I will argue, conceive of performance as a persuasive activity aimed at jurors and the court of public opinion more generally. The commendation of Blackstone's writing style, by contrast, speaks to a textual performance associated with doctrinal explication. Just as the prevailing styles of theatrical and public oratory may influence perceptions about a lawyer's effectiveness in court, the conventions of doctrinal analysis also change over time—and indeed, Blackstone's style of explanation in the *Commentaries* may have helped to alter them in the course of the eighteenth century, providing a model not only for legal writing but also for the forensic cadences of the figure whose expertise is the hallmark of the 'consummate lawyer'.[1]

To understand the place of the natural and the artificial in legal performance, then, it is not enough to appeal to contemporaneous thinking about acting and oratory. In addition, we might ask: Who is speaking—a witness, a lawyer, a judge? Who is the audience—a jury, a judge, the public, the press? What is the subject—the prosecution's motives, the defendant's alibi, the plaintiff's conduct, the majesty of the common law, an abstract

---

[1] J Clitherow, 'Preface' to *Reports of Cases ... Taken and Compiled by ... Sir William Blackstone* (1781) vol 1, 1.

doctrinal point? A stammer prompted by amazement at an opponent's insolence, a pause to ensure that the audience takes in the full implications of a new legal proposition, may be very different from a hesitant, halting, elliptical exposition of a doctrinal point. To be sure, legal doctrines can also evoke emotional responses from lawyers and judges. The question, however, is not simply about where emotion enters into legal argument, but where it is perceived to be appropriate in legal argument, when it is permissible to give explicit attention to emotional impulses.

In Blackstone's time, the stammering lawyer was a common exemplar of legal ineptitude. English instances include the ironically named Counsellor Smooth in Charles Johnson's *The Successful Pyrate* (1713), Serjeant Target in Richard Steele's *The Conscious Lovers* (1722), Feignwell (who impersonates a lawyer) and Justice Lovelaw in Edward Phillips's *The Mock Lawyer* (1733), the repeatedly self-interrupting 'Counsellor' in Samuel Foote's *The Orators* (1762), and Stutter in *The Lawyer's Panic* (1785).[2] This character evidently enjoyed a certain degree of popularity, but one may doubt that he tells us much about contemporaneous perceptions of lawyers. Unlike the overly histrionic lawyers of the early nineteenth century, discussed below, this figure is mocked not because he has mastered the wrong skills, but because he has not mastered any. His plosive confusions would furnish just as much amusement if he were a politician or a hawker of quack medicines. While the stuttering lawyer is particularly eligible for ridicule because he is supposed to be nimble and alert, his profession merely supplies an additional excuse for laughing at a trait that was already regarded as hilarious by eighteenth-century audiences.[3] The forms of legal fluency and dysfluency become clearer when we turn to instances that do not simply exhibit a speech impediment as an amusing spectacle in itself, but instead show how a particular use of language and diction may be effective even if the speaker's presentation is studied and might be seen as artificial.

Numerous discussions of courtroom argumentation have considered the ways in which a lawyer's presentation of facts, examination of witnesses, and summation of the applicable law should be modulated to influence the perceptions of the judge and jury.[4] Because the lawyer's choreography of

---

[2] These figures have not received much critical attention. On the lawyers in Johnson's play, see G Windmüller, *Rushing into Floods: Staging the Sea in Restoration and Early Eighteenth-Century English Drama* (Goettingen, 2012) 133–35. Steele's lawyer is discussed in S Dickie, *Cruelty and Laughter: Forgotten Comic Literature and the Unsentimental Eighteenth Century* (Chicago IL, 2011) 63. For Phillips's characters, see W Prest, 'Lay Legal Knowledge in Early Modern England' in JA Bush and A Wijffels (ed), *Learning the Law* (London, 1999) 303–14, esp 304–08.

[3] Dickie (n 2) 62–63.

[4] For some overviews, see RA Mead, '"Suggestions of Substantial Value": A Selected, Annotated Bibliography of American Trial Practice Guides' (2003) 51 *University of Kansas Law Review* 543; HA Anderson, 'Changing Fashions in Advocacy: 100 Years of Brief-Writing Advice' (2010) 11 *Journal of Appellate Advocacy and Process* 1.

these details is so visibly driven by the aim of persuading an audience, ideas of natural and unnatural performance, of legal fluency and dysfluency, find a ready place in discussions of trial advocacy, and the emphasis on proper modulation makes the point that speed and smoothness do not always yield the most effective argument. A lawyer speechifying on behalf of an unpopular client might do well to seem passionate and extemporaneous, taken aback by powerful machinations conspiring to commit an injustice. That application of the Stanislavski method, in which the counsel strives almost literally to represent the client, is particularly appropriate when the venue is a jury trial, with public onlookers. Popular views about acting, oratory, and authenticity seem to have particular importance to this role, which requires the lawyer to understand what audiences expect from a performance. What sounds natural, compelling, and accomplished in one era may seem stilted, dull or perplexing in another.

If we consider the question of 'natural' courtroom performance in relation to James Burgh's important treatise on oratory, *The Art of Speaking* (1761), it becomes apparent that his comments apply most readily to a trial lawyer arguing about the justice of his client's case. Burgh explains:

> True eloquence does not wait for *approbation*. Like irresistible *beauty*, it *transports*, it *ravishes*, it *commands* the *admiration* of all, who are within its reach. If it allows *time* to *criticize*, it is not *genuine* ... The hearer finds himself ... unable to *resist* ... His *passions* are no longer *his own*. The *orator* has taken *possession* of them; and, with superior power, *works* them to whatever he *pleases*.[5]

Burgh describes the kind of trial oratory that attracted large audiences and served as a kind of public theatre in England and America in the late eighteenth century and early nineteenth century. Indeed, Burgh observes, a dozen pages later, that

> [t]he *pleader* at the bar, if he lays before the judges and jury, the *true state* of the *case*, so as they may be most likely to see where the *right* of it lies, and a just decision may be given, has done his duty.[6]

While the sweeping, all-absorbing declamation that takes possession of the audience, and allows no time to criticise, might have made for a stellar performance when arguing to a jury, it would hardly have suited the needs of an argument with the bench about doctrinal matters, in anticipation of the consequences for future cases. The aesthetic that Burgh advocates, though evidently popular at the time, would itself give way, in the legal context, to an aesthetic of calm, rational, coherent exposition, associated with the primacy of the book, and exemplified by the expository style we find in the *Commentaries*.

---

[5] J Burgh, *The Art of Speaking* (London, 1761) 29.
[6] Ibid 40.

Similarly, when commentators drew on the language of theatricality to single out lawyers for praise, during this period, the reference was typically to the lawyers' talents to move juries and other public observers, imagined as part of larger jury. Thomas Erskine, seen as 'the exemplar of the ideally "patriotic" barrister' near the end of the eighteenth century, was admired for his ability to 'make the sympathies of his audience subservient to his purpose' and for his use of body language to 'enforce the passions which his language was exciting', precisely insofar as those skills helped to 'lead to the conviction of the jury in favour of his client'.[7] William Garrow's performances in jury trials garnered similar praise: a contemporary called him 'an actor as well as an advocate', noting that 'when silent, he ceased not to address the jury by the change of his features'.[8] In the proceedings against Warren Hastings, Sheridan won the applause of 'The *Gallery folk*' who '[c]onceived 'twas a *Play-House*',[9] precisely because the event took the form of a trial, revolving around matters that engaged the attention of a wide audience. James Epstein observes that at this time, 'Trials possessed many of the attributes of theater', in part because '[t]here was an audience; indeed, there were a number of audiences ranged both within and outside the courtroom'.[10] The significance of this point gains additional force when we note that 'the court of public opinion' (or 'bar of public opinion') was beginning to come into currency in the 1790s, as a way of talking about the wider audience outside the courtroom.[11]

---

[7] PC Scarlett, *A Memoir of the Right Honourable James, First Lord Abinger* (London, 1877) 66; quoted in DF Lemmings, *Professors of the Law* (Oxford, 2000) 307. Similarly, according to JC Jeaffreson, 'Erskine was a perfect master of dramatic effect, and much of his richly-deserved success was due to the theatrical artifices with which he played on the passions of juries': *A Book about Lawyers* (London, 1867) vol 2, 47.

[8] 'Amicus Curiæ' (pseud. of JP Collier), *Criticisms on the Bar; Including Strictures on the Principal Counsel Practising in the Courts* (London, 1819) 55. Collier's book is full of similar examples in which jury trials provide the context for evaluating lawyers' theatrical powers; see, eg, 37–38, 169, 228. On Garrow, and Collier's evaluation of him, see also S Devereaux, 'Arts of Public Performance: Barristers and Actors in Georgian England' in D Lemmings (ed), *Crime, Courtrooms and the Public Sphere in Britain, 1700–1850* (Farnham, 2012) 93–118, esp 99–100.

[9] [Ralph Broome], *Letters from Simpkin the Second ... Containing an Humble Description of the Trial of Warren Hastings* (London, 1789) 33; for further discussion, see G Ridley, 'Sheridan's Courtroom Dramas: The Impeachment of Warren Hastings and the Trial of the *Bounty* Mutineers', in JE DeRochi and DJ Ennis (ed), *Richard Brinsley Sheridan: The Impresario in Political and Cultural Context* (Lewisburg PA, 2013) 177–90, esp 185.

[10] JA Epstein, *Radical Expression: Political Language, Ritual, and Symbol in England, 1790–1850* (New York NY, 1994) 33.

[11] See, eg, 'Catiline', 'To the Honorable the Court of Public Opinion in the State of Connecticut', *Hartford Gazette*, 9 October 1794, 3; [W Penn], *Vindiciæ Britannicæ* (London, 1794) 30; [Anon], *Letters in Answer to the Earl of Carlisle ... on the Administration and Conduct of Earl Fitzwilliam* (London, 1795) 30; [Anon], 'Proceedings of the Whig Club' (1798) 1 *The Anti-Jacobin; Or Weekly Examiner* 201; [Anon], *A Letter to the Hon. Charles-James Fox* (London, 1799) 6; 'Bathylus', 'Miscellanies', *Green Mountain Patriot* (Peacham VT), 14 September 1803, 1.

Some contemporaries, however, objected the theatrical analogy; thus, for example, Henry Crabb Robinson observed that 'the Barrister, tho' he acts *before* the public, does not act *for* the public' and should not be classified with '[a]ctors [and] public performers'.[12] By the 1830s the assumption that juries were to be swayed by histrionics had evidently become so widespread, and so unthinkingly adopted, that one commentator could criticise 'young and inexperienced barristers' who stormed about the courtroom, 'making outrageous demands on the sympathy of a jury', only to find their efforts 'successfully met and opposed by the adverse party casting ridicule on their extravagance'.[13] The enthusiasm for high-flown courtroom oratory seems to have diminished by the mid-century, requiring lawyers to develop other skills if they wanted to cultivate an impressive courtroom presence.

Predominant among these skills were the orderly and enumerative methods of the lawyer who is well versed in precedent and can bring it to bear at a moment's notice. The lawyer who studies oratory textbooks to learn about new trends in acting styles will misunderstand what is required to exhibit this kind of fluency. A strict set of conventions about ordering and relevant detail govern the tempo and structure of a lawyerly presentation of doctrine, and although for laypersons the effect might seem stilted, observing these conventions is the only way to demonstrate fluency among professionals. Robert Ferguson, describing an argument before the US Supreme Court in the 1840s, observes that Daniel Webster, a 'master orator' in the style of the early nineteenth century, 'evok[ed] applause and even tears from [his] immediate audience but [not] from the bench', whereas his opponent, Horace Binney, prevailed with an argument resembling 'a modern legal brief'.[14] Nor were the judges the only observers to prefer Binney's citation-heavy mode of presentation: a contemporary also characterised his oral performance as a kind of text, saying that he 'unfolded [a] masterly treatise on charitable uses', and a journalist who found the argument 'as dry as the African deserts' nevertheless acknowledged that Binney had given a 'slow, cautious, logical analysis ... a perfectly well constructed, highly polished law argument, calculated to rivet a lawyer ... but rather caviare to the multitude'.[15] Webster's mistake was to persist in an oratorical mode that could impress jurors, but would not sway a bench focused on doctrinal matters.

---

[12] HC Robinson, diary entry for 17 October 1818 (commenting on Collier, *Criticisms* (n 8)) quoted in A Freeman and JI Freeman, *John Payne Collier: Scholarship and Forgery in the Nineteenth Century* (London, 2004) vol 1, 82.

[13] [Anon], 'Expression', *The Athenæum*, 21 September 1833, 635–36. Perry Miller observes that Joseph Story was similarly unimpressed with a style of advocacy prevalent around this time among American lawyers, who 'played shamelessly to the galleries' when 'putting on exhibitions of forensic melodrama which rivaled the splendiferous performances of the theater': P Miller, *The Life of the Mind in America* (New York NY, 1965) 151.

[14] R Ferguson, *Reading the Early Republic* (Cambridge MA, 2004) 246, 243. The case was *Vidal v. Girard's Executors*, 43 U.S. 127 (1844).

[15] Ibid 244, quoting HA Wise, *Seven Decades of the Union* (Philadelphia PA, 1872) 218 and 'The Great Girard Will Case', *New York Herald*, 10 February 1844, 2.

The distinction also appears in commentaries on advocacy from the late eighteenth century. An account of prominent lawyers and jurists published in 1790 could praise Sir John Scott in terms that make him sound like the oral edition of a treatise:

> His Speaking, is of that subtle, correct, and deliberate kind, that has more the appearance of written than of oral Eloquence. He branches forth his Arguments into different Heads and Divisions; and pursues the respective Parts through all their various Ramifications, with such methodical Accuracy, that Argument seems to rise out of Argument, and Conclusion from Conclusion, in the most regular and natural Progression.[16]

Here is a speaker who might, one imagines, have developed his style through extensive study of the *Commentaries*. Scott's speciality, the authors noted, was in Chancery pleading: 'Mr. SCOTT is little known *out* of the Metropolis, or *in* it, but as a Chancery pleader—The Subtlety of his Metaphysical Reasonings are admirably adapted to the Practice of this Court'.[17]

William Garrow, mentioned earlier as a brilliant trial lawyer, was also praised by Collier for his talent in adopting a meticulous and disciplined mode when explaining legal doctrine: '[H]e never ventures upon a point of law, of which he himself is not only completely master, but of which he does not make his hearers completely master'.[18] Again, in describing the abilities of Sir Arthur Piggott, Collier remarked that in the equity courts, where there was no jury,

> all that is very important to an advocate is a knowledge of his business, a distinct mode of detailing facts, and a perspicuous manner of stating arguments founded upon them: eloquence, or any attempts beyond a clear uninterrupted flow of words and thoughts, would ... be wasted. The counsel do not address a jury of twelve men upon matter with which their individual feelings may be connected.[19]

The same distinction explained why Sir Francis Buller excelled as a judge, though not as a trial lawyer. Because he had not sufficiently 'direct[ed] his attentions to the embellishments of oratory', and 'had little success in his address to the passions', he 'could not ... be eminent in his appeal to a Jury'. On the bench, however, his rhetorical talents found their natural place:

> It is the *general*, as it is the *just* professional character of this great lawyer, that he states his arguments with the utmost accuracy and precision, reasoning logically, and in a style, which may be deemed the true eloquence of law.[20]

---

[16] [LT Rede and E Wynne], *Strictures on the Lives and Characters of the Most Eminent Lawyers of the Present Day* (London, 1790) 203; see also R Melikan, *John Scott, Lord Eldon, 1751–1838* (Cambridge, 1999) 9.

[17] Rede and Wynne (n 16) 205.

[18] [Anon], 'The Law Student' (1811) 1 *The Reflector* 374, 377.

[19] Collier (n 8) 87. Again, Collier could write (ibid 133–34) that Serjeant John Lens was 'most impressive' even though 'his voice is rather too monotonous'—a trait that made his 'stile ... much better adapted to a continued legal argument, than to an address to a jury'.

[20] Rede and Wynne (n 16) 106, 108.

The declamatory mode was not the preferred means of explaining legal doctrines and concepts in Blackstone's time, and while passion would continue to have a place in legal advocacy, the measured cadences of the legal expert would become increasingly pronounced, even in trial courts, as the nineteenth century wore on.[21] Just as perceptions about 'natural' styles of acting vary from one era to the next, the conventions of doctrinal analysis also change over time, as we may see by studying judgments and legal texts from the early eighteenth century, which rarely exhibit the attributes for which Buller was praised. These attributes are, however, abundantly visible throughout Blackstone's *Commentaries*, and while he can hardly be hailed as a pioneer for using stylistic techniques that appear in the works of writers such as Samuel Johnson, Edmund Burke, and Adam Smith, nevertheless Blackstone was among the first to attempt a sustained exposition of legal doctrine in language (and a more general structure) organised by features such the use of balance, antithesis, and enumeration. These are the features that explain why his style was so widely praised, not only for being 'correct' and 'elegant', but also for being 'easy' and 'intelligible'—that is, for presenting legal concepts in a way that made them easily comprehensible for readers.[22] Blackstone's writing style, of course, may have been very different from the manner of speech he used as a judge. Perhaps the mode of delivery Bentham characterised as 'formal, precise, and affected'[23] was the sound of Buller's 'accuracy and precision' to an ear unreceptive to this style, or perhaps Blackstone's oral efforts at precision took on a pedantic and laboured tone that is not apparent to the reader of the *Commentaries*. If his courtroom delivery was irritating and hard to follow, however, these effects are not apparent from Joseph Gurney's transcript of the trial arguments in *Onslow v Horne*.

Gurney's shorthand report shows no sign of the hesitations, stutters, or other interruptions that supposedly punctuated Blackstone's speech. Perhaps Gurney simply did not bother to record such details. But whether or not those paralinguistic elements were originally part of the interchange, the point of contention in the arguments between counsel and bench—and the issue that has been highlighted as evidence of Blackstone's dysfluency—turned on a dispute about the way in which the defendant's statement was recorded in the plaintiff's evidence. Onslow proffered a document purporting to give a

---

[21] For a helpful discussion of this trend, as evidenced by changing assumptions about linguistic precision in judgment writing, see P Tiersma, 'The Textualization of Precedent' (2007) 82 *Notre Dame Law Review* 1187.

[22] [J Touchet], Review of *Reports of Cases ... Taken and Compiled by ... Sir William Blackstone* (1782) 67 *Monthly Review* 1, 5; JB Trotter, *Memoirs of the Latter Years of ... Charles James Fox*, 3rd edn (London, 1811) 512 (letter of 28 October 1802); 23 *Hansard* 1083 (Lord Ellenborough, Lords, 17 July 1812); T Ruggles, *The Barrister, Or, Strictures on the Education Proper for the Bar*, 2nd edn (London, 1818) 199.

[23] J Bentham, *Memoirs*, in J Bowring (ed), *Works of Jeremy Bentham* (1843) vol 10, 45. For further discussion of this characterisation, see Prest, *William Blackstone* 114.

verbatim transcript of a letter by Howe, with a small variation in the written form of the date ('11' versus '11th').[24] Blackstone concluded that any variation, no matter how minor, precluded the use of the transcript as evidence, and on that ground he non-suited the plaintiff. When the plaintiff moved for a new trial, Blackstone's position was rejected, and the case proceeded on the merits.[25]

Nevertheless, Blackstone's objections are well-considered and forceful. He does not grope feebly for rationales; he supplies them immediately. He sets out a bright-line rule: 'If I admit the variation of a single letter, I don't know where to stop'.[26] Though not the only plausible view to take, this represents a cogent position, which he defends ably. When offered the case of *R v Drake* in rebuttal, Blackstone parries it rapidly, observing that the plaintiffs have 'undertaken to prove the *tenor*'—that is, that it is not just a question of meaning, but of the precise form in which the meaning is conveyed.[27] When answered with a distinction between civil and criminal law, he does not take the blandly obstructionist route of simply failing to see the significance, but instead responds with a legal observation that dismantles the distinction: 'This is an action founded upon a supposed crime'.[28] When the counsel give their version of a bright-line rule ('The true line is, where there is an alteration of the sense'), he has an immediate answer: 'That would let in a hundred altercations, whether the sense is or is not altered, and leave too much in the discretion of the judge: *tenor* and *purport* would then signify exactly the same'.[29] Again, his rationale may be timorous and over-precise, but it reflects a plausible view that he defends according to a well-accepted mode of argument.

Indeed, even if Blackstone were merely seeking to test the argument, rather than taking a certain position, his objections would be readily familiar to most lawyers as the kind of devil's advocacy that judges often pursue to clarify their own thoughts—and far from registering as awkward or impaired, the practice is typically seen as a sign of agility. According to the judicial philosophy implicit in his comments, it is possible to eradicate judicial discretion and as a result the law will gain more predictive value. This view may be misguided, or may be misapplied here, but if so, that does nothing to alter the fluency of Blackstone's responses.

---

[24] [J Gurney] *The Whole Proceedings in the Cause on the Action Brought by The Rt. Hon. Geo. Onslow, Esq. against the Rev. Mr. Horne* (London 1770) 43–45. On the trial and its aftermath, see also Prest, *William Blackstone* 269.

[25] *The Genuine Trial between the Rt. Hon. Geo. Onslow, Esq; and the Rev. Mr. John Horne, Tried ... before the Right Honourable Lord Mansfield* (1770). Onslow prevailed at trial but on appeal the judgment was arrested: *Onslow v Horne* (1771) 2 Bl W 750, 96 ER 439.

[26] [Gurney] (n 24) 45.

[27] Ibid 47. See *R v Drake* (1706) 2 Salk 660, 91 ER 563.

[28] [Gurney] (n 24) 47.

[29] Ibid.

If we consider the question of legal dysfluency as a matter of argumentative and analytical facility, rather than as a question of diction, then binaries such as *closed/open*, *formal/informal*, and *antagonistic/receptive* are unlikely to map readily onto the contrast between fluency and dysfluency, because the first term in each pair may comport with a legally agile performance. What makes for an effective legal argument is a question of the occasion and the subject, and in *Onslow v Horne*, the subject is a legal point, not a factual point. The question is not whether the transcript has '11' or '11th', but whether that difference matters legally. Turning the positions around, if Blackstone had favoured a more discretionary approach and it had been the defendant's counsel who argued for the bright-line rule (that any variation in a single letter misstates the alleged libel), Blackstone would have appeared no less obstructionist and resistant from their perspective.

Gurney's transcript, of course, cannot prove that lawyers and spectators did not find Blackstone's courtroom manner grating and cumbersome. Perhaps Blackstone was unable to produce spontaneously the kind of tidy analysis for which Buller was admired, or the 'methodical accuracy' that Scott displayed in following arguments out to their conclusions. But as Wilfrid Prest notes, whatever failings Blackstone may have had as an orator at the bar, he proved 'highly effective when speaking from a prepared text, presenting his carefully arranged material in an accessible and polished fashion'.[30] Indeed, given that the *Commentaries* reflected and facilitated a shift towards an orderly and methodical style of legal explication that would become an essential feature of lawyers' oral arguments, it is notable that on one occasion, Blackstone's speech was literally displaced by his text. When the great copyright case of *Donaldson v Beckett* came before the House of Lords in 1774, 10 judges read their views from the bench, but Blackstone, who was that day 'confined by the gout', sent in a very brief set of answers to the questions put to the bench, and the published reports of the judgments opted instead to 'substitute his *printed* Opinion'—that is, to reprint, nearly verbatim, two paragraphs from the second volume of the *Commentaries*.[31] It is appropriate that in a decision about the legality of reprinting, Blackstone's own text should be taken as the preferable expression of his views. The episode might serve as an emblem of the process by which the written word, with all its deliberation and formality, came increasingly to provide the paradigmatic form of legal expression and to define the basis of legal elegance.

---

[30] Prest, *William Blackstone* 114.
[31] *The Cases of the Appellants and Respondents in the Cause of Literary Property* (London, 1774) 36.

2

Blackstone as Draughtsman: Picturing the Law

CRISTINA S MARTINEZ

But if architecture gave birth to painting and sculpture, conversely it's to these two arts that architecture owes its great perfection, and I advise you to be suspicious of any architect who's not also a fine draftsman. Where would such a man have educated his eye? Where would he have acquired a refined feeling for beautiful proportions? Where would he have developed his ideas of grandeur, simplicity, nobility, heaviness, lightness, stylishness, solemnity, elegance, and seriousness?

Denis Diderot[1]

IF DRAWING IS how an architect educates his eye and develops his ideas, as Diderot claimed, Blackstone's practice as a draughtsman constitutes an important means to investigate how that architect of the common law studied, conceived and ultimately systematised his subject. More than any other English jurist, Blackstone tried to delineate the law as a complete system. This chapter examines how Blackstone used the principles of drawing and design to give form to his thoughts and to elaborate upon them in the *Commentaries* and how that book's illustrative images allowed a richer and fuller understanding of his ideas.

I am here concerned with Blackstone's artistic instincts as well as the visual dimensions of his thought.[2] Blackstone, I argue, had a complete design mapped out in his mind and was applying a form of generalisation or idealisation that had a direct parallel to artistic formulations. He worked

---

[1] D Diderot, 'Notes on Painting' in *Diderot on Art* (tr) J Goodman (New Haven CT, 1995) vol 1, 233.
[2] My aim is not to examine the role that architecture and spatial metaphors played in Blackstone's systematic exposition of English law. Recent work on Blackstone's architectural interests and activities has been published by W Prest, 'Blackstone as Architect: Constructing the Commentaries' (2003) 15 *Yale Journal of Law & the Humanities* 103–34 and C Matthews, 'A "Model of the Old House": Architecture in Blackstone's Life and Commentaries' in Prest (ed), Commentaries 15–34. I have also delved into the subject in 'Art and Law: Disciplines Intertwined in Eighteenth-Century England' (PhD thesis, University of London, 2007).

to refine the law and was determined to find the most beautiful way to present it. Blackstone's visual approach, which aimed to create order and incite pleasure in the reader, differed from Sir Edward Coke's unsystematic exposition intended to preserve law's varied historical foundations. The chapter concludes with a parallel between Blackstone's conception of equity and Sir Joshua Reynolds's interpretation of genius. Reynolds was the first President of the Royal Academy of Arts and England's leading portrait painter. As will be shown, Blackstone viewed a pleasing and orderly exposition of English law as necessary and, like Reynolds in art, endeavoured to find a proper structure for the presentation of its principles.

Blackstone's interest in and knowledge of architectural theory is demonstrated by his remarkable compilation in 1743 of a treatise entitled 'An Abridgement of Architecture' (now at the Getty Research Institute, Los Angeles), and in the preparation, in 1746 and 1747, of a revised and improved version, 'Elements of Architecture' (held by the Codrington Library of All Souls College, Oxford). These works were the precursors to the grand conception of English law upon which Blackstone was to build his system in later years. The 'Abridgement' contains no illustrations except for a tabular diagram, although reference is made to numbered figures, for example in Chapter Five 'Of the Walls of Muring' and other sections of the text. Carol Matthews, in her study of Blackstone and architecture, notes 14 stubs where pages have been torn from the manuscript. It is presumed that these missing pages were illustrations.[3] The second treatise, 'Elements of Architecture', much more systematic and polished, is illustrated with 23 drawings. Extending over 137 pages, it opens with a short preface, followed by a table of contents, introduction, 29 substantive chapters and a well-ordered index. A short introduction on the art of drawing is followed by a basic definition of architecture and a brief survey of the several characteristics of a good building. The treatise includes observations on the role of the architect, structure and materials, the classical orders, ornament, and other basic concepts. Blackstone's interest in architecture was not unusual among the nobility and gentry. In the eighteenth century it was thought proper to have some knowledge of architecture 'but to have too much', as Lord Chesterfield cautioned, was 'lowering'.[4] Blackstone used his artistic and architectural skills in the design and building of a number of projects in Oxford and Wallingford.[5] Architecture was one of his many interests but far from a full-time career. In fact most English architects had a training in other arts or were professionals in other fields. Thus John Shute, Inigo Jones and Balthazar Gerbier were painters by training; Sir Christopher Wren was a mathematician and astronomer; Colen Campbell, a lawyer; William Winde, a military engineer; and Sir Henry Wotton, a diplomat and scholar.

[3] Matthews (n 2) 17.
[4] B Kaye, *The Development of the Architectural Profession in Britain* (London, 1960) 66.
[5] See Prest (n 2) 117–18.

There were hardly any English architects who, as R Campbell declared in 1747, 'have had an education regularly designed for the profession'.[6]

Blackstone came to architecture by way of mathematics.[7] He was careful to note in his preface to the 'Elements of Architecture' that he had completed his treatise 'at leisure Hours',[8] thus confirming that this was a diversion for him. Blackstone also took a special interest in drawing, the primary and most pertinent medium of expression for architects.[9] The practice of drawing was promoted in amateur drawing manuals such as Henry Peacham's *Gentleman's Exercise* and increasingly taught in private academies and secondary schools.[10] John Locke in *Some Thoughts Concerning Education* recommended 'insight into *Perspective*, and skill in *Drawing*',[11] but also advised the young not to devote themselves exclusively to these activities. The refinement and exploration of an artistic ability would indicate long and hard labour, a factor which could compromise social status. Continuing a long-established tradition, the English generally held the artist in low esteem; lawyers were designated as 'Gentlemen' but not painters. ''Tis true,' Jonathan Richardson observed, 'the Word *Painter* does not generally carry with it an Idea equal to what we have of other Professions'.[12]

Blackstone's drawings in pen and ink are rendered copies or adaptations of printed illustrations found in treatises such as Fréart de Chambray's *Parallèle*. His drawing of the five Column Orders (see Figure 1), one of the primary subjects of architectural literature in the Renaissance and following periods, was an adaptation of Claude Perrault's design, which, according to Blackstone, 'can never be enough commended, for cutting off all Uncertainties, by reducing the Orders, and each of them, to a settled Measure; by taking the Medium of the varying Proportions we find in Ancient Examples, and Modern Writers'.[13]

In Blackstone's opinion, Perrault's plan should be followed, with the exception of 'a few Particulars, especially in the Height of his Columns'.[14]

---

[6] R Campbell, *The London Tradesman* (1747), quoted in G Holmes, *Augustan England. Professions, State and Society, 1680–1730* (London, 1982) 26.

[7] Lockmiller 10.

[8] W Blackstone, 'Elements of Architecture', preface: MS 333 Codrington Library, All Souls College, Oxford.

[9] Baldassare Castiglione, the sixteenth-century nobleman and author, advocated drawing and painting as activities worthy of the courtier. His *Book of the Courtier* appealed to readers all over Europe and had been influential in England since Elizabethan times: *cf* P Burke, *The Fortunes of the Courtier. The European Reception of Castiglione's Cortegiano* (Cambridge, 1995).

[10] See K Sloan, '"The Draughtsman's Assistant": Eighteenth-Century Drawing Manuals' in *The Line of Beauty. British Drawings and Watercolors of the Eighteenth Century* (New Haven CT, 2001) 187–90.

[11] J Locke, *Some Thoughts Concerning Education* (London, 1693) in JL Axtell (ed), *The Educational Writings of John Locke* (Cambridge, 1968) 265.

[12] J Richardson, *An Essay on the Theory of Painting* (London, 1725; Menston, 1971) 31.

[13] Blackstone (n 8) 32. 'By an Order', Blackstone explained (ibid 26), 'is meant a System of the several Members, Proportions and Ornaments of a Column; or as some will have it, A Column, Supported by a Pedestal, and charged with an Entablature'.

[14] Ibid 32.

Figure 1. The Five Orders: 'Elements of Architecture' (1747)
The Codrington Library, All Souls College, Oxford. Courtesy of the Warden and Fellows.

Blackstone's illustration of the Orders is technical rather than artistic in nature and aims to convey practical information about proportions and calculations. In comparison with the exceptional architectural drawings that survive from the Renaissance, the drawings are clearly the work of an amateur. Even so, Blackstone's approach to the subject matter is extremely orderly and his command of theoretical architectural principles is impeccable. It is in the artistic detail that the amateur appears.

Nowhere is this more obvious than in the lettering of the title on the cover of the manuscript (see Figure 2). A trained eye and skilled hand could readily fit the word 'Architecture' evenly across the page, however

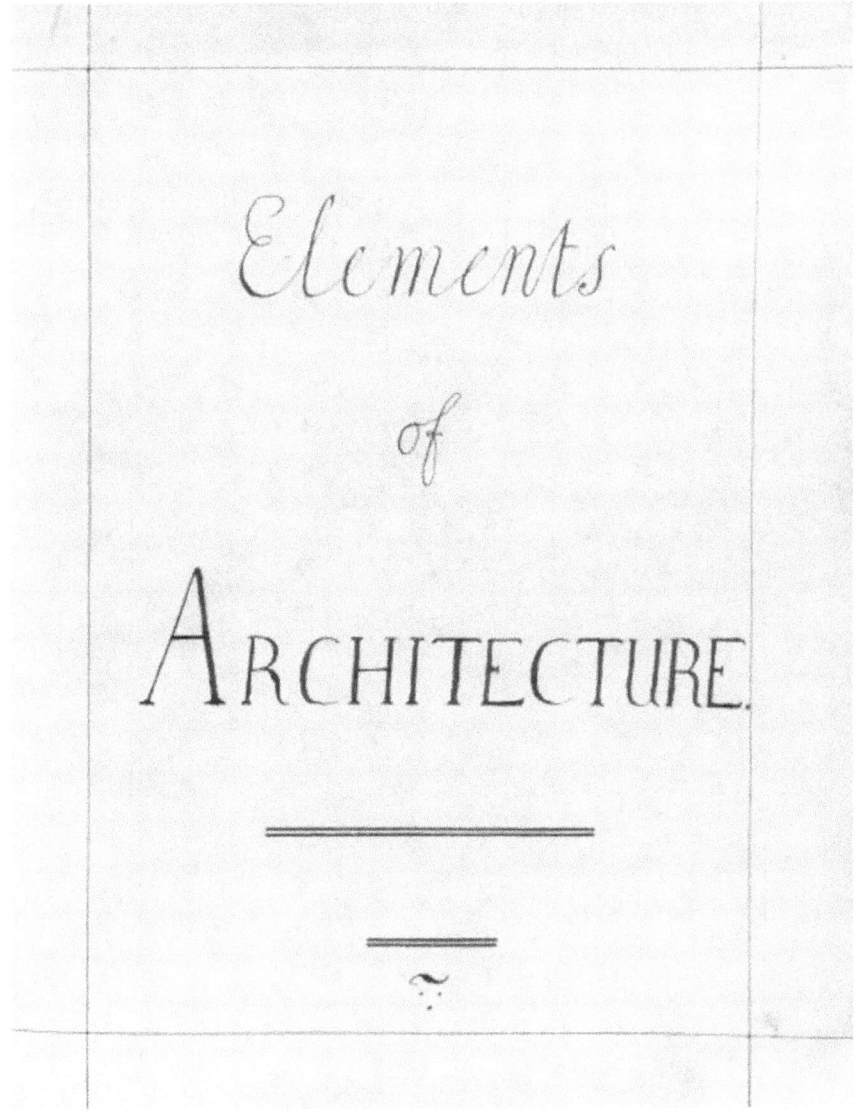

Figure 2. Title Page: 'Elements of Architecture' (1747)
The Codrington Library, All Souls College, Oxford. Courtesy of the Warden and Fellows.

Blackstone does not accomplish that feat. The letters remaining after the second 'T' are compressed—more closely leaded than those preceding it—in order to fit the word within the ruled lines. Here, order triumphed over beauty in the most obvious manner.

In drawings such as his thorough illustration of the varieties of staircases (see Figure 3), Blackstone exhibited meticulous precision and an acute concern with taxonomies.

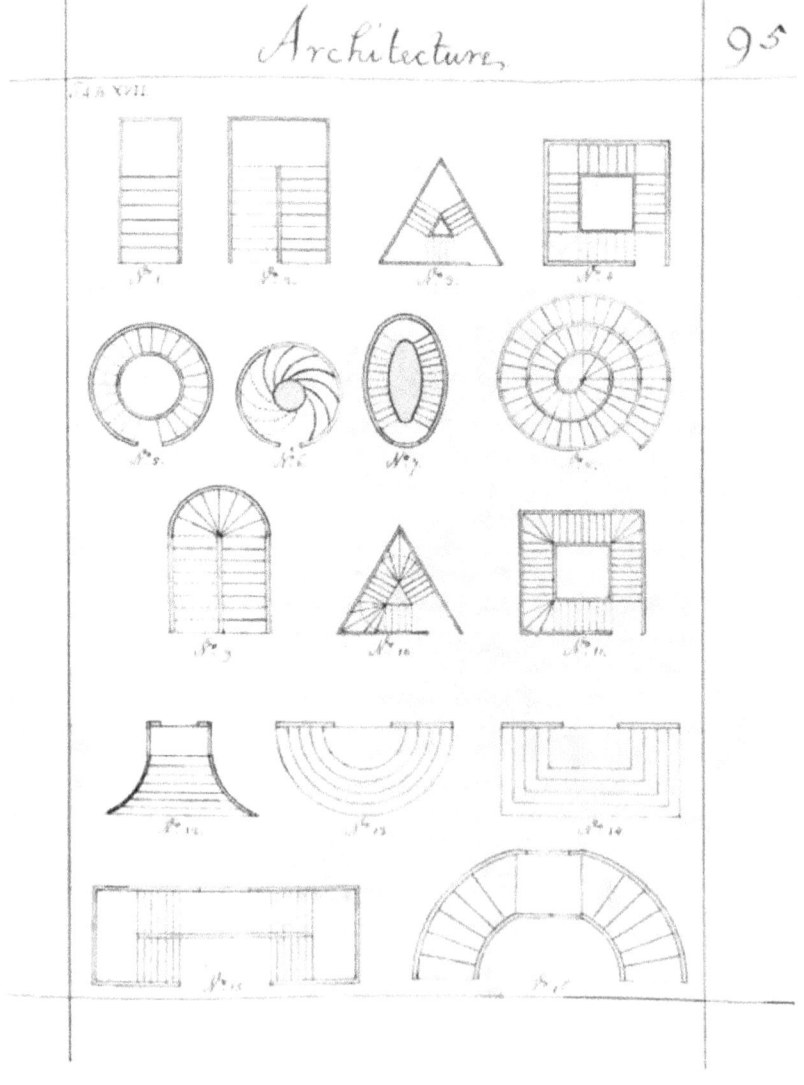

Figure 3. Staircases: 'Elements of Architecture' (1747)
The Codrington Library, All Souls College, Oxford. Courtesy of the Warden and Fellows.

A sense of order and an intense spirit of classification dominated the period. The empirical nature of eighteenth-century thought brought with it the rise of systematic and taxonomic order. Architecture, in particular, was the subject of systematic understanding, schematic organisation and typological display.[15] Blackstone's small drawings (16 variations in total) are rendered with great rigour and carefully numbered and arranged. Was Blackstone's intention to make drawings in a pure outline style to avoid the reputation of a mechanical artist? Or did his drawing skills improve substantially with practice over time, as the accomplished drawing of St Paul's Cathedral (see Figure 4), the last illustration in the manuscript, may suggest? For this drawing is of a much higher quality and more artistically rendered than his previous work. Applying a significantly more sophisticated technique, Blackstone creates light and shade effects and demonstrates that he could take his skill to another level.

Although he seems to have attached importance to drawing and to have made an effort to preserve his architectural treatises, he never mentions his drawings or architectural interests in his writings. The concern for acquiring 'a fine Taste of Music, Painting and Architecture' led one commentator in the *London Journal* to declare:

> I would not be understood to condemn or despise those polite Arts and Sciences; but give me leave to say, they ought not to posses the first Place in a Man's Mind; they are at best but ornamental Qualities, and therefore only secondary to such as are usual. To say otherwise, would be in effect to affirm, that the *Professors* and *Connoisseurs* of them, are Characters of equal Dignity with the Givers and Teachers of Laws; and, ridiculous Comparison, that *Palladio, Da Vinci* and *Corelli*, are Authors more excellent and more useful, than *Coke, Selden*, or *Hale*.[16]

Drawing played a decisive role in the transformation of the artist from mere craftsman to creative and learned individual. From the Renaissance onwards, the relationship between drawing and thinking was a frequent subject of inquiry. Giorgio Vasari in the *Lives of the Painters, Sculptors and Architects* declared that '*disegno* is nothing else than an apparent expression and declaration of the *concetto* that is held in the mind, and of that which also is imagined in the mind and fabricated in the *idea*.'[17] '*Disegno*' here incorporates both the initial mental composition of a work of art (design) and its practical execution (drawing). With Vasari's definition in mind, the English encyclopaedist Ephraim Chambers noted that 'Design, or *Draught*, with regard to the Arts and Sciences, signifies the Thought, Plan, Geometrical Representation, Distribution, and Construction of a Painting,

---

[15] See M Foucault, *The Order of Things. An Archaeology of the Human Sciences* (London, 1970).
[16] *London Journal*, 21 May 1726.
[17] D Summers, *Michelangelo and the Language of Art* (Princeton NJ, 1981) 519 n 49.

Figure 4. St Paul's Cathedral: 'Elements of Architecture' (1747)
The Codrington Library, All Souls College, Oxford. Courtesy of the Warden and Fellows.

Poem Book, or Building'.[18] It is this aspect, the planning or outline of a scheme prior to execution, which Blackstone mastered. In his preface to the *Analysis of the Laws of England*, he acknowledged the favourable

---

[18] E Chambers, *Cyclopaedia: Or, An Universal Dictionary of Arts and Sciences* (London, 1728) vol 1, 191.

reception of his work, attributing its success 'entirely to the Propriety of the Design, and not to the Manner of its Execution'.[19] His efforts to 'render this Attempt more extensively useful' included as a first step 'to mark out a Plan of the Laws of England, so comprehensive, as that every Title might be reduced under some or other of its general Heads, which the Student might afterwards pursue to any Degree of Minuteness; and at the same time so contracted, that the Gentleman might with tolerable Application contemplate and understand the Whole'.[20]

The practice that Blackstone undertook in the composition of his architectural treatises laid the groundwork for his greatest achievement, which was to 'draw' the common law's intricate complexities. The manuscript of Blackstone's first architectural treatise, *An Abridgement of Architecture*, reveals something of the design process that contributed to the clear, concise, well-ordered expression which distinguishes his later writings on the law. Unlike the very clean and much shorter manuscript of 'Elements of Architecture', this earlier document is littered with second thoughts and reconsiderations in the form of marginal notes, deletions of words and paragraphs, and substituted words and phrases. An extensive addendum shows Blackstone in the act of systematising, contriving and imposing his own structure on the subject matter he openly ascribed to others. The overall visual presentation of the first treatise is less contrived, less self-consciously structured. For example, the ruled lines that frame the text on every page of the 'Elements of Architecture' (Figure 5) and the lines offsetting the chapter headings, are notably absent in the 'Abridgement' (see Figure 6). Thus comparison of the two documents yields a glimpse of Blackstone's progression from development of the system to refinement of the presentation of the system. If in the 'Abridgement' the concepts and ideas are sketched, in the 'Elements' they are carefully rendered, condensed and embellished with drawings.

Specifically, Blackstone used tables and charts to map out his ideas and compose his texts. In both 'An Abridgement of Architecture' and *An Analysis of the Laws of England*, he prefixed tabular diagrams which summed up in one view both the whole and the necessary relation of the parts (see Figures 7 and 8).[21]

---

[19] W Blackstone, *An Analysis of the Laws of England* (Oxford, 1771) iv.
[20] Ibid.
[21] Such tabular schemes were not altogether uncommon. As Alan Watson has pointed out, Dionysius Gothofredus (1549–1622), editor of the *Corpus Juris Civilis*, set out his analysis of Justinian's *Institutes* in tabular form: A Watson, 'The Impact of Justinian's *Institutes* on Academic Treatises: Blackstone's *Commentaries*' in *Roman Law & Comparative Law* (Athens GA, 1991) 176–77.

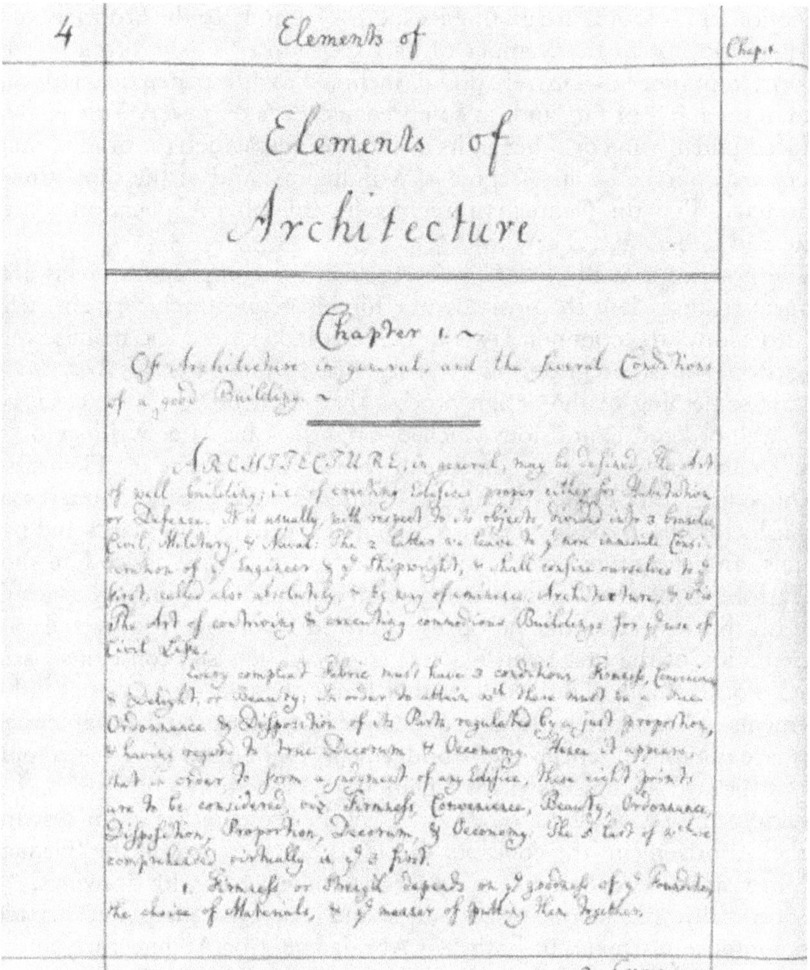
4 Elements of Chap. 1

Elements of Architecture

Chapter 1.

Of Architecture in general, and the several Conditions of a good Building.

ARCHITECTURE, in general, may be defined, the Art of well building; i.e. of erecting Edifices proper either for Habitation or Defence. It is usually, with respect to its objects, divided into 3 branches, Civil, Military, & Naval: The 2 latter we leave to ye more immediate Consideration of ye Engineer & ye Shipwright, & shall confine ourselves to ye first, called also absolutely, & by way of eminence, Architecture, & is the Art of contriving & executing commodious Buildings for ye use of Civil Life.

Every compleat Fabric must have 3 conditions Firmness, Convenience & Delight, or Beauty: in order to attain wch there must be a due Ordonnance & Disposition of its Parts, regulated by a just proportion, & having regard to true Decorum & Oeconomy. Hence it appears, that in order to form a judgment of any Edifice, these eight points are to be considered, viz. Firmness, Convenience, Beauty, Ordonnance, Disposition, Proportion, Decorum, & Oeconomy. The 5 last of which are comprehended virtually in ye 3 first.

1. Firmness or Strength depends on ye goodness of ye Foundation, the choice of Materials, & ye manner of putting them together.

2. Convenience

Figure 5. Chapter One, p 4: 'Elements of Architecture' (1747)
The Codrington Library, All Souls College, Oxford. Courtesy of the Warden and Fellows.

While the diagrams are a useful visual aid to the reader, their role may have been even more important for the author. They expose choices and decisions, and so encapsulate and define the thinking process behind the final work. Blackstone's interest in tables and classification had a notable precedent in the tabular schemes of civilian jurists and the work of the English jurists Henry Finch and Matthew Hale. The first manuscript version of Finch's law treatise *Nomotechnia*, later printed in French (1613) and translated into

Chap. IX
Of yͤ Pedestal, Column, & Entablature.

An Order, as was before observed, consists of a Pedestal, Column, & Entablature, of all which in order, & first of yͤ Pedestal.

The Pedestal is yͤ lowest part of an Order, serving by way of foot or stand to support a Column (TAB. II. fig. 1.) so called from Pes a Foot, & Stare, to Stand: it is also named Stylobates & Stereobates, as being a solid prop, or prop of a Column: Though some will have Stereobates to signify what yͤ French call Soubassement, & we yͤ Basement or Continued Socle, which is a kind of stand or continued Pedestal, running round yͤ whole Building, though without either Base or Cornice. The Pedestal consists of three Parts: 1st, yͤ Base; 2dly yͤ Dye, so called from its cubic figure; as it is also Trunco, Dado, Pillow, & Poggio, & 3dly yͤ Cap, called also Cornice & Coronix, as crowning yͤ Pedestal. Their particular Proportions shall be assigned under their several Orders; the general Proportion is this, that yͤ Pedestal shall be one fifth of yͤ height of yͤ whole Order. That of yͤ several Parts is this, Divide yͤ height of yͤ Pedestal into eight parts, of w͡ch yͤ Base shall be two, yͤ Dye five, & yͤ Cap one, & yͤ Plinth of yͤ Base shall be two thirds of yͤ Base itself. The Projecture of yͤ Base is one third of its height, & that of yͤ Cap equal to that of yͤ Base. They Face of yͤ Dye projects equally w͡th yͤ Plinth of yͤ Column. The Antients seldom used Pedestals at all, so that it is rather an Appendage than essential to a Column, tho' Le Clerc is of a different Opinion. A Double Pedestal (TAB. II fig. 2.) is that which supports two Columns, and a continued Pedestal (TAB. II. fig. 3.) is that which supports a row of Columns without Break or Interruption & differs from what we called Scamilli impares by being proportioned to its Order; whereas those Scamilli are no more than certain Blocks serving to raise yͤ whole Order, or any of its Members from being lost out from yͤ sight, when it must of necessity be placed below their Horizon, that is, beneath yͤ eye, when it must of necessity hide them, without yͤ help of these Scamilli, any projecture that must unavoidably hide them, without yͤ help of these Scamilli to elevate & support them; which is an agreeable Reconciliation of Opticks and architectonical Proportions.

The Column is yͤ Second or middle part of an Order, so called as being yͤ common or Support of a Building (TAB. II. fig 4.) It also consists of three parts, first yͤ Base ... also Spira, because it somewhat resembles yͤ folds or Spires of a Serpent laid at rest. The height of yͤ Base is always yͤ Semidiameter of yͤ Column. Next comes yͤ Shaft, so called from its straitness, as likewise truncus as representing yͤ Body of a Tree, Fust, from its roundness resembling a Cask, as yͤ French word literally signifies; Scapus, Tige, & The Naked, all is that cylindrical part which makes yͤ Body of a Column exclusive of yͤ Base & Capital. It is always round & strait; for twisted, or torsed, wreathed, & yͤ like Columns are abuses crept into Architecture, whose chief end being firmness, can never admit of any appearing Weakness or Shrinking, such as those Extravagancies seem to have. On yͤ contrary true & regular Architecture aims at yͤ Greatest appearance of Stability, which is yͤ Reason of yͤ Diminution generally used in Columns which is a contraction of yͤ upper part of a Column whereby its diameter is made less than that of yͤ lower part. It is also partly meant to represent yͤ natural tapering of Trees, whereof yͤ first Columns were formed. By this Diminution Pillars are distinguished from Columns; those being perfect Cylinders, without

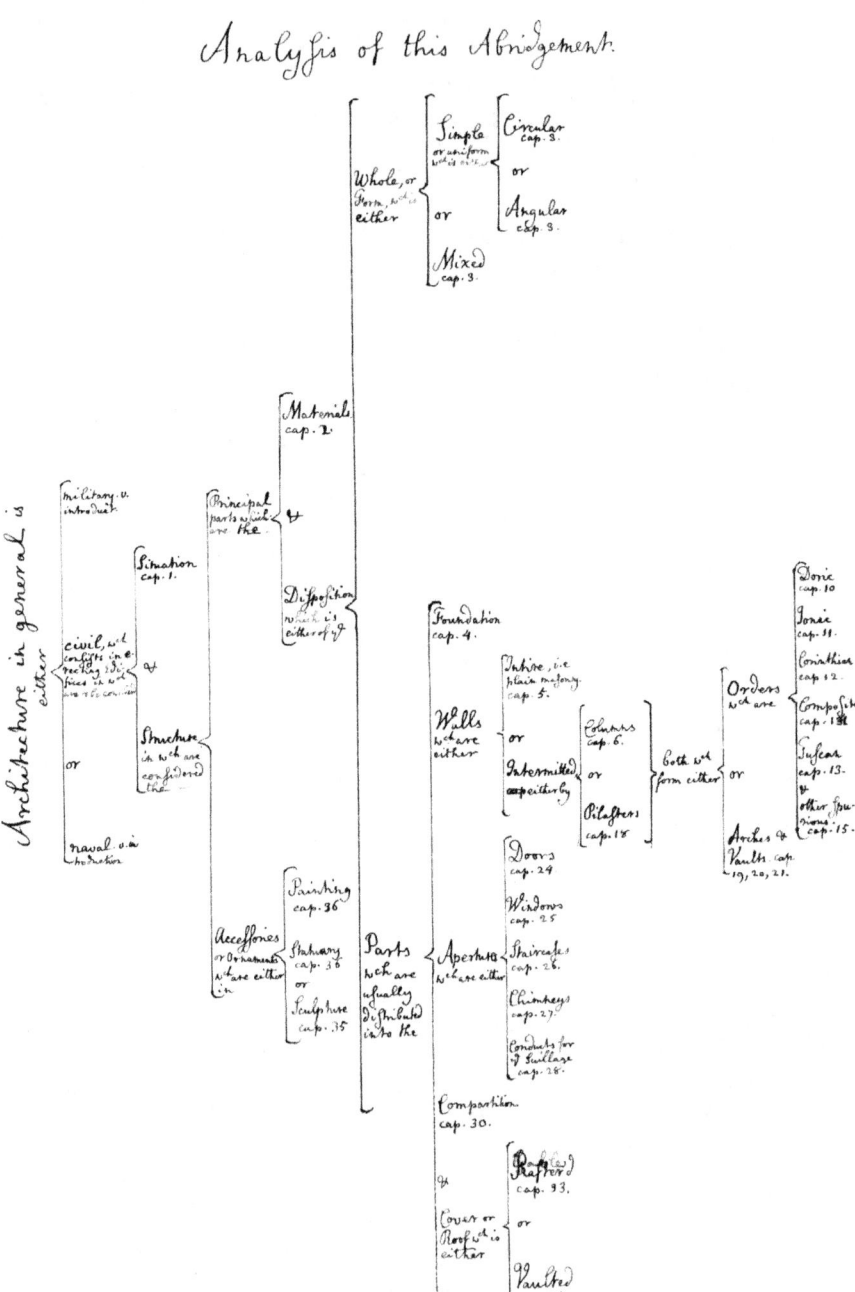

Figure 7. 'Analysis of this Abridgement': 'An Abridgement of Architecture' (1743) The Getty Research Institute, Los Angeles (90-A13).

CONTENTS

OF THIS

ANALYSIS.

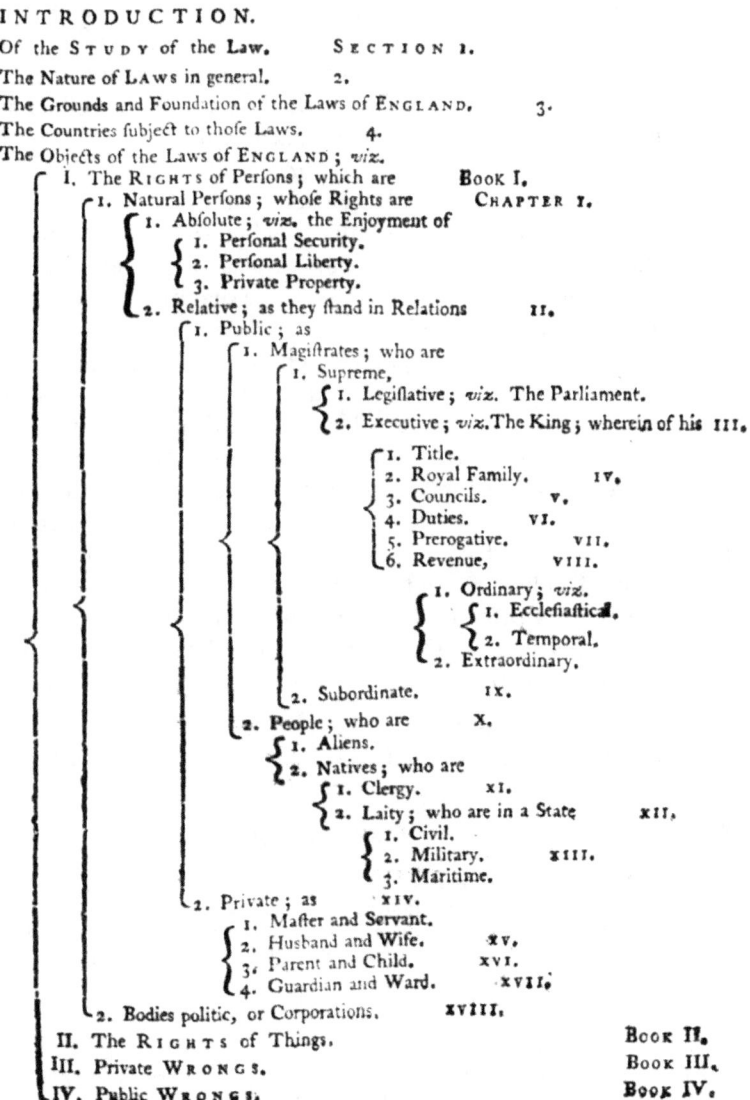

Figure 8. *'Contents of this Analysis'*, An Analysis of the Laws of England *(Oxford, 1771)* Rare Book Collection, Lillian Goldman Law Library, Yale Law School.

English in 1759, was abridged in a diagrammatic 'Short table of the common law'.[22] Hale assisted his friend John Wilkins, Bishop of Chester, in his efforts to draw a classification of law for his *Essay Towards a Real Character and a Philosophical Language*.[23] The emphasis in Hale and Wilkins's rhetorically oriented scheme, however, is placed upon the classification of legal terms and the thorough exposition of many subcategories. Hale, in fact, admitted in his *Analysis of the Law* (1713) that he had tried to systematise the law without success: the law is 'so various', he stated in his Preface, 'that I cannot reduce it to an exact *Logical Method*', but 'it is not altogether impossible, by much Attention and Labour, to reduce the Laws of *England* at least into a tolerable *Method* or *Distribution*'.[24] He thought it would give him, as well as others, the opportunity 'to rectify, and to reform what is amiss in this ... whereby, in Time a more *Methodical System* or *Reduction* of the Titles of the Law, under Method, may be discovered'.[25] Blackstone seizes the opportunity to advance Hale's method, stating that 'of all the Schemes hitherto made public for digesting the Laws of England, the most natural and scientifical of any, as well as the most comprehensive, appeared to be that of Sir Matthew Hale, in his posthumous Analysis of the Law'.[26]

Hale had some interest in building, although unlike Blackstone his knowledge of architecture was 'rudimentary' and 'there is no indication that he had any interest in the visual arts'.[27] This is significant, for although the work of both Hale and Blackstone was born of an orderly, logical approach, Blackstone understood law from an architectural point of view and likened its rules to building blocks 'so nicely constructed and so artificially connected together, that the least breach in any of them disorders for a time the texture of the whole'.[28] English law had not generated a single text in the form of an orderly exposition of its principles. Its several parts had not been gathered in a systematic manner.[29] In 1743 the author of *A Calm Examination into the Causes of the Present Alarm in the Empire* commented upon the law:

> Our jurisprudence is enveloped in a fog impenetrable to the eye of Reason—this is a grievance of frightful magnitude;—our statutes are in many cases contradictory,

---

[22] See W Prest, 'The Dialectical Origins of Finch's *Law*' (1977) 36 *Cambridge Law Journal* 332–34.

[23] J Wilkins, *An Essay Towards a Real Character and a Philosophical Language* (London, 1668) 270–75. I am grateful to Marty Slaughter for this reference.

[24] M Hale, *The Analysis of the Law: being a Scheme, or Abstract, of the several Titles and Partitions of the Law of England, Digested into Method* (London, 1713) preface.

[25] Ibid.

[26] Blackstone (n 19) vii–viii.

[27] E Heward, *Matthew Hale* (London, 1972) 10, 23.

[28] *Commentaries* vol 2, 376.

[29] AWB Simpson, 'The Rise and Fall of the Legal Treatise: Legal Principles and the Forms of Legal Literature' (1981) 48 *University of Chicago Law Review*, 632–79. DJ Seipp, 'The Structure of English Common Law in the Seventeenth Century' in WM Gordon and TD Fergus (ed), *Legal History in the Making. Proceedings of the Ninth British Legal History Conference* (London, 1991) 61–83.

and so numerous, that they cannot be contained in one hundred volumes folio. Then is it not highly injurious to the subject, that he has not the power of decyphering or knowing what is law and what is not? A revision or interpolation of our governing rules is indispensably necessary; it would do immortal honor to any, who influenced by a regard for unoffending ignorance, would fulfill this common desire.[30]

Sir Edward Coke's *Institutes of the Laws of England*, written in four parts, was criticised for its obscurity and disorganised style. Blackstone described Coke as 'greatly defective in method'[31] and Lord Keeper North commented that it 'is the confusion of a student and breeds more disorder in his brains than any other book'.[32] Whereas the legal texts of 'our ancient writers', Blackstone observed, revealed a 'very immethodical arrangement', the special 'endeavour' of the *Commentaries* was 'to examine [the law's] solid foundations, to mark out its extensive plan, to explain the use and distribution of its parts, and from the harmonious concurrence of those several parts to demonstrate the elegant proportion of the whole'.[33] Blackstone's quest for systematisation drew on aesthetic considerations, as one commentator noted:

> It is not to be denied, but that many law-writers have before wrote treatises, which were very much to the purpose; their institutes, their abridgements, and their dictionaries, have all their use. But Mr. Blackstone is the first who has treated the law of England as a liberal science. His commentaries besides affording equal instruction, are infinitely better calculated to render that instruction agreeable.[34]

In four volumes the law was defined, divided and subdivided with logical consistency. Volume 1, 'Of the Rights of Persons', includes 'absolute rights' such as rights of personal security and liberty, and 'relative rights', these being rights in either public or private relations. Volume 2, 'Of the Rights of Things', deals with the 'law of property', both real and personal, and the 'law of contract,' dealing with formal contracts and the so-called simple or parole contracts. Volume 3, 'Of Private Wrongs', summarised the law of civil offences and civil procedure and was balanced with Volume 4, 'Of Public Wrongs', a lucid survey of crimes and criminal procedure, concluding with a chapter on 'the Rise, Progress and gradual Improvements, of the Laws of England'.

---

[30] 'A Friend to his King and Country', *A Calm Examination into the Causes of the Present Alarm in the Empire* (London, 1743) 46.
[31] *Commentaries* vol 1, 73.
[32] R North, *A Discourse on the study of the Laws* (London, 1824) 22. The American jurist Joseph Story is said to have 'wept bitterly' after trying to work his way through Coke's first book. WW Story (ed), *The Miscellaneous Writings of Joseph Story* (Boston MA, 1852) 20.
[33] *Commentaries* vol 3, 265; vol 4, 436.
[34] *The Annual Register ... For the Year 1767* (London, 1768) 287.

Blackstone's artistic approach and use of visual aids gave his work much of its strength and appeal. He explains in the preface of the *Analysis* that 'an Appendix, consisting of such Tables, Copies of Instruments, and Forms of judicial Proceedings' was essential 'for explaining certain Principles, and Matters of daily Practice; of which it was however impracticable to convey any adequate Idea by verbal Descriptions only'.[35] Blackstone's words bear an interesting resemblance to those of the Italian architect Francesco di Giorgio, who reproached the authors of architectural treatises who did not use drawings to illustrate their arguments and thus obliged the reader 'to rely on his own idea of what is being described'.[36] In his exposition of the law of inheritance, Blackstone resorted to visual aids, which as the legal historian SFC Milsom has noted, enabled Blackstone 'to compress into a single chapter the mass of detailed rules which would in every possible case identify who a man's heir was'.[37] In the *Analysis* and also in the *Commentaries*, Volume Two, Chapter 14, Blackstone included a Table of Consanguinity to fully illustrate the different methods by which canon and civil law calculated the degrees of lineal and collateral consanguinity (see Figure 9).

This table had appeared earlier in *An Essay on Collateral Consanguinity, Its Limits, Extent, and Duration*, first published in 1750. Blackstone stated in the *Analysis* that the subject 'is sufficiently obvious upon mere Inspection of the Table'.[38] Identified as 'the *Arbor Consanguinitatis* usually printed with the Bodies of civil and canon Law',[39] the Table uses Roman numerals to express the degrees of relationship by the civil law, and Arabic figures to express those of the canon law and common law. Blackstone's table served to graphically illustrate complex concepts and has influenced the work of later legal scholars. For example, the American lawyer and anthropologist Lewis Henry Morgan states that one of his drawings

> is not in the form of that used by the civilians. It is framed in accordance with the form adopted by Blackstone for the purpose of showing the several persons in the lineal and collateral lines, who stand at equal distances in degree from their respective common ancestors, in the same horizontal plane. Since the movement downward is with equal step in each of the lines, the common law method has an

---

[35] Blackstone (n 19) ix–x.
[36] F di Giorgio, *Trattato di architettura civile e militare* (c 1470), as cited in R Zwijnenberg, *The Writings and Drawings of Leonardo da Vinci* (tr) Caroline A van Eck (Cambridge, 1999) 44. Drawings, di Giorgio wrote, are necessary to any discourse: 'anyone who reflects on how useful and necessary it is for every human activity, whether for the process of invention or for the exposition of ideas, whether for working purposes or for art—and whoever considers too how closely related it is with geometry, arithmetic, and optics—will easily judge that drawing is a necessary means in all knowledge and work regarding things doable, with right reason'.
[37] SFC Milsom, *The Nature of Blackstone's Achievement* (London, 1981) 5.
[38] Blackstone (n 19) 163.
[39] Ibid 164.

Blackstone as Draughtsman 47

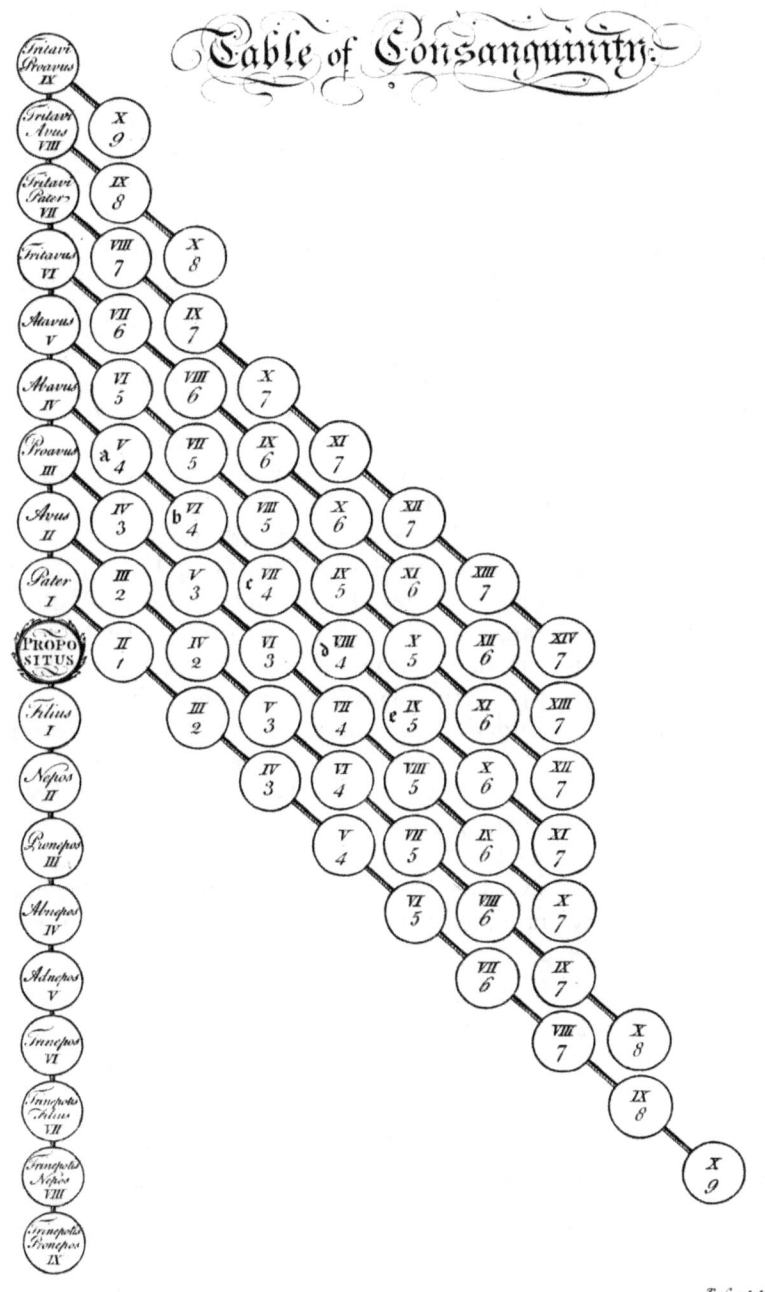

Figure 9. Table of Consanguinity: **Commentaries on the Laws of England** *vol 2 (Oxford, 1776) facing p 203*
Rare Book Collection, Lillian Goldman Law Library, Yale Law School.

advantage over that of the civil law in illustrating to the eye the relative position of consanguinei.[40]

Like Blackstone, Coke used a diagram to visually explain the degrees of parentage and consanguinity, but his illustration stresses the patriarchal power of the father and lacks the immediacy and clarity of Blackstone's diagram. It should further be noted that Coke admitted that he 'had once intended for the ease of our student to have made a Table to these Institutes, but when [he] considered that Tables and abridgements are most profitable to them that make them, [he has] left that worke to every Studious Reader'.[41]

Blackstone's creative visual approach is further manifested in the 'Table of Descents' 'intended to exhibit, to the Eye of the Student, the successive Order, in which he must search for the Heir of a Person' (see Figure 10).[42]

Here Blackstone used squares, circles and octagons to represent and visually distinguish categories of people. Marriages are indicated through the representation of handshakes and lines of relation are shown with intricately drawn ropes. In the version found in the *Analysis* (see Figure 11), the intersections of the ropes are further embellished with bows.

Legal texts were often illustrated in the medieval period, but it became the modern practice to exclude images and ornamental details.[43] Besides the use of schematic diagrams, Blackstone strove to render law's connections visible, connections which, to this point, had remained mostly hidden or unseen. The law of real property, Blackstone explained, 'in this country wherever its materials were gathered, is now formed into a fine artificial system, full of unseen connexions and nice dependencies; and he that breaks one link of the chain, endangers the dissolution of the whole'.[44] Blackstone's starting point was to provide 'a general map of the law' from which its principles could be 'explained'; their history 'deduced' and 'their changes and revolutions observed'.[45] A general map of the law facilitated a richer and fuller understanding of the law but 'no map can show everything', as Denis Wood explains:

> Could it, it would ... *no more than reproduce the world*, which, without the map ... *we already have*. It is only its *selection* from the world's overwhelming richness that justifies the map; it is only its selectivity, its attention, its focus on

---

[40] LH Morgan, *Systems of Consanguinity and Affinity of the Human Family* (1868) in *Smithsonian Contributions to Knowledge* (Washington DC, 1871) vol 17, 23.

[41] E Coke, *The First Part of the Institutes of the Laws of England: Or A Commentary Upon Littleton* in S Sheppard (ed), *The Selected Writings and Speeches of Sir Edward Coke* (Indianapolis IN, 2003) vol 2, 744.

[42] Blackstone, (n 19) 165.

[43] See SL Engle and R Gibbs, *Illuminating the Law. Legal Manuscripts in Cambridge Collections* (London, 2001).

[44] F Hargrave, *Collection of Tracts*, cited in D Lieberman, *The Province of Legislation Determined. Legal Theory in Eighteenth-Century Britain* (Cambridge, 1989) 140.

[45] *Commentaries* vol 1, 35–36.

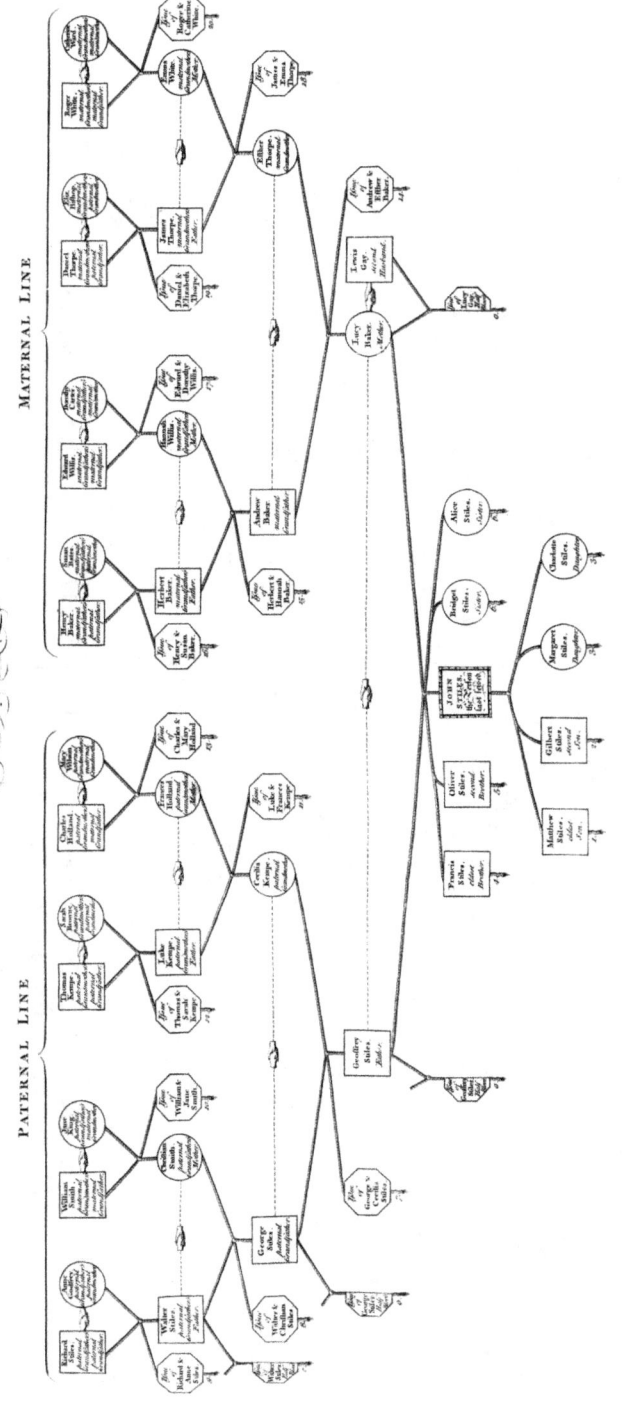

Figure 10. Table of Descents: Commentaries on the Laws of England *vol 2 (Oxford, 1766) between pp 241 and 242* Rare Book Collection, Lillian Goldman Law Library, Yale Law School.

50 Cristina S Martinez

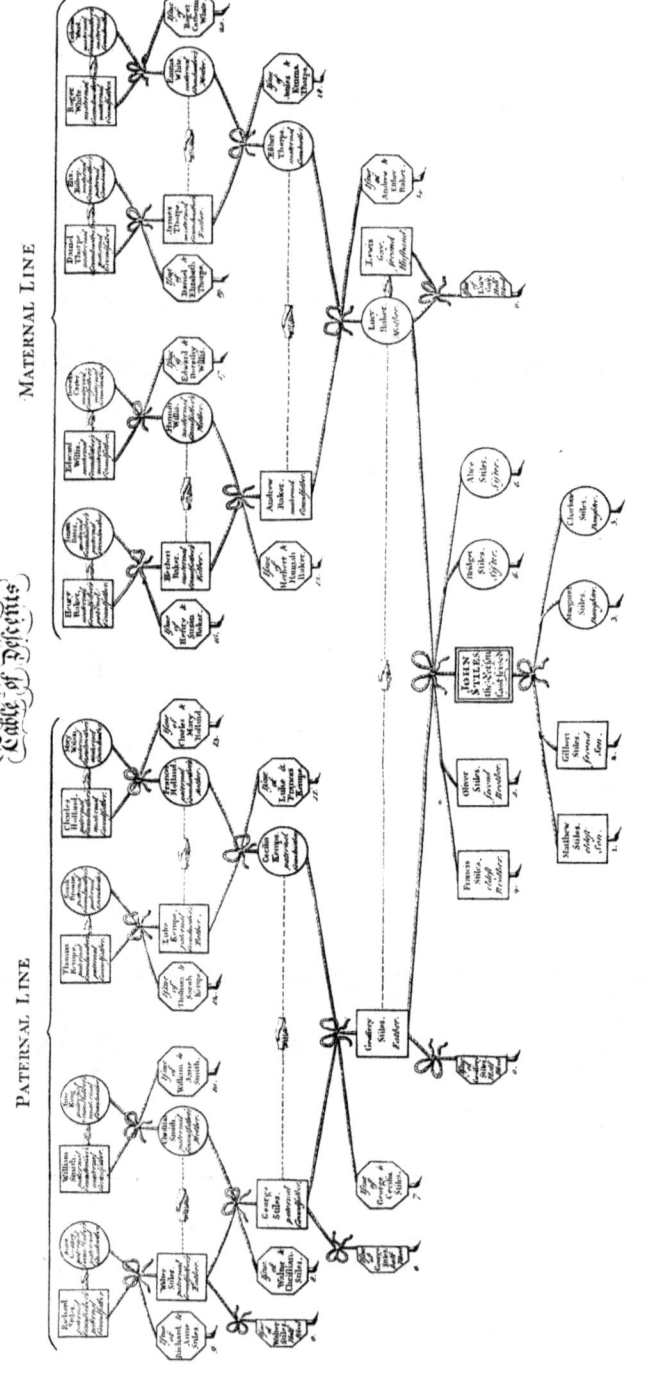

Figure 11. Table of Descents: An Analysis of the Laws of England (Oxford, 1771) between pp 166 and 167 Rare Book Collection, Lillian Goldman Law Library, Yale Law School.

this at the expense of that, its enthusiasm, ... that distinguishes the map from the world it represents.[46]

In his efforts to delineate the law, Blackstone recognised rules and elements which interfered with one another. He simplified, classified and emphasised, and suppressed details. He faced numerous difficulties in reconciling the particularity of the common law and the generality of a system of principles, theoretical and abstract in nature. Equity, which Blackstone had practically left untouched and treated with no more than brief remarks in the first volume, was the most telling example of 'the inevitability of variety and disorder in adapting the law to changing needs'.[47] It was defined by Bentham as 'that capricious and incomprehensible mistress of our fortunes, whose features neither our Author, nor perhaps any one is well able to delineate'.[48] Still, Blackstone tried to fit it into his system, and began by ascribing to Grotius's Aristotelian definition of equity 'the correction of that, wherein the law (by reason of its universality) is deficient'.[49] Blackstone, however, acknowledged the imprecise quality of equity and referred to it as '[this mighty river] which in the course of a century ... hath imperceptibly shifted its channel'.[50]

Blackstone's struggle with equity can be traced throughout his work and is consonant with the struggle that his contemporary, the celebrated painter Sir Joshua Reynolds, underwent to fit the concept of genius into his *Discourses on Art*.[51] There is in genius and equity a tendency towards the idiosyncrasies of individual judgement. Genius is inventive, and equity presupposes innovation. They both have an arbitrary or discretionary element that undermines the foundation of both Blackstone's and Reynolds's work. The difficulties lie in the creative impulse in art, and in the unforeseen case in law. To see art and law as essentially particularistic and undergoing constant change conflicted with the notion of a complete system.

In the *Commentaries* Blackstone began by relegating equity to a clearly subordinate position. He ends his introductory section 'Of the Nature of

---

[46] D Wood, 'The Interest the Map Serves Is Marked' in D Wood and J Fels, *The Power of Maps* (New York NY, 1992) 86–87.
[47] DJ Boorstin, *The Mysterious Science of the Law. An Essay on Blackstone's Commentaries* (Chicago IL, 1941; 1996) 218 n 75.
[48] JH Burns and HL Hart (ed), J Bentham, *A Fragment on Government* (London, 1776; Cambridge, 1988) 5.
[49] *Commentaries* vol 1, 61.
[50] Ibid vol 3, 440.
[51] Reynolds's ideas on art are expressed most clearly and systematically in his monumental *Discourses*, a compilation of the 15 speeches he delivered at the Academy's annual award ceremonies over a span of 20 years. These speeches, to an audience of students, patrons and fellow artists, interpreted the rules of art and emphatically restated his philosophy that painting, given a theoretical foundation, could be elevated to a liberal art and in turn the artist would be acclaimed as a practitioner not of a craft, but of a discipline based squarely on the rules and noble traditions of past masters: RR Wark (ed), J Reynolds, *Discourses on Art* (London, 1975).

Laws in General' with a few statements on equity, notable for their strong caution against carrying too far the equitable consideration of 'the particular circumstances of each individual case', since this would 'destroy all law, and leave the decision of every question entirely in the breast of the judge'.[52] Blackstone recognised the priority of law over the special circumstances of individual cases, just as Reynolds in his early *Discourses* placed the observance of rules over genius, admitting that

> the arts would lie open for ever to caprice and casualty, if those who are to judge of their excellencies had no settled principles by which they are to regulate their decisions, and the merit or defect of performances were to be determined by unguided fancy.[53]

Reynolds could not, however, escape genius, a concept he used frequently in his *Discourses on Art* with diffidence. He hesitated 'to enter into metaphysical discussions on the nature or essence of genius'[54] and, with few exceptions, employed the concept with no elaboration of its meaning.

Reynolds did not ignore the extraordinary nature and creative power of genius but very early rejected the possibility that genius was exempt from rules:

> The artist who has his mind thus filled with ideas, and his hand made expert by practice, works with ease and readiness; whilst he who would have you believe that he is waiting for the inspirations of Genius, is in reality at a loss how to begin; and is at last delivered of his monsters, with difficulty and pain.[55]

Reynolds maintained further that:

> Genius, begins, not where rules, abstractedly taken, end; but where known vulgar and trite rules have no longer any place. It must of necessity be, that even works of Genius, like every other effect … must likewise have their rules.[56]

Equity no less than genius was subject to rules. It appealed to a higher justice, divine in origin, and followed the dictates of honesty and conscience but its exercise, at first restricted to the king and chancellor, became less arbitrary and equitable and more regulated. As Blackstone explained, the system of the courts of equity had turned into a 'regular science', which could not 'be attained without study and experience, any more than the science of law'.[57] Blackstone commented upon its early elasticity and later fixity:

> [I]f a court of equity were still at sea, and floated upon the occasional opinion which the judge who happened to preside might entertain of conscience in every

---

[52] *Commentaries* vol 1, 61–62.
[53] Reynolds (n 51) 123.
[54] Ibid 35.
[55] Ibid 37.
[56] Ibid 97.
[57] *Commentaries* vol 3, 440–41.

particular case, the inconvenience, that would arise from this uncertainty, would be a worse evil than any hardship that could follow from rules too strict and inflexible. Its powers would have become too arbitrary to have been endured in a country like this, which boasts of being governed in all respects by law and not by will.[58]

Although the comparison between equity and genius is only in a limited way appropriate, it demonstrates that Blackstone found himself in precisely the same predicament as Reynolds. Like Reynolds, who had quite distinct, and possibly conflicting, conceptions of genius, Blackstone had different perspectives on equity and found great difficulty in reconciling its principles with his own theory of law. He was ambivalent on the subject, partly because, as Holdsworth observed, he failed to distinguish between equity as a method of interpreting laws and equity as the practice of the English equity courts.[59] Thus, in the first volume of the *Commentaries* Blackstone maintained that 'there can be no established rules and fixed precepts of equity laid down, without destroying its very essence, and reducing it to a positive law'.[60] But in the final chapter of Book Three, he stated that 'the system of our courts of equity is a laboured connected system, governed by established rules, and bound down by precedents, from which they do not depart, although the reason of some of them may perhaps be liable to objection.'[61] Equally important is Blackstone's treatment of equity in his earlier Oxford lectures, which was markedly different from that contained in the *Commentaries*, where he accepted and adopted Lord Mansfield's views and pronouncements. In Chapter 27 of Book Three, 'Of Proceedings in the Courts of Equity', Blackstone remarked that he had 'formerly touched upon it [equity], but imperfectly' and that it deserved 'a more complete explication'.[62] Like Mansfield, he criticised the complexities which resulted from separation of the courts of law and equity and, in the interest of the uniform development of English law, advocated the fusion of the two:

> the very terms of a court of *equity* and a court of *law*, as contrasted to each other, are apt to confound and mislead us: as if the one judged without equity, and the other was not bound by any law. Whereas every definition or illustration to be met with, which now draws a line between the two jurisdictions, by setting law and equity in opposition to each other, will be found either totally erroneous, or erroneous to a certain degree.[63]

---

[58] Ibid 440.
[59] WS Holdsworth, 'Blackstone's Treatment of Equity' (1929) 43 *Harvard Law Review* 3.
[60] *Commentaries* vol 1, 61–62.
[61] Ibid vol 3, 432.
[62] Ibid 429.
[63] Ibid 429–30. The fusion of equity and common law was brought about by the Judicature Act of 1873. See F Pollock, 'The Law of England I-L Victoriae' (1887) 3 *Law Quarterly Review* 345–46.

Blackstone believed that law and equity were 'equally artificial systems, founded in the same principles of justice and positive law'.[64] He admitted that these courts had different ways of proceeding but, as Daniel J Boorstin has pointed out:

> So eager was he to show the coherence of the whole system that instead of accepting the more usual view that equity was supplemental to the law, the *Commentaries* treated law and equity as theoretically one,—simply different qualities of the same essence.[65]

The concept of the 'supplemental' in regard to Blackstone's treatment of equity is important. Jacques Derrida suggested that a supplement 'harbors within itself two significations whose cohabitation is as strange as it is necessary'.[66] His American follower, Jonathan Culler, explained that 'The supplement is an inessential extra, added to something complete in itself, but the supplement is added in order to complete, to compensate for a lack in what was supposed to be complete in itself'.[67] While Blackstone accepted the common view of equity as supplementary in his earlier lectures, his *Commentaries* present a more carefully considered view that rejects the implication that there was an inherent lack or absence in the common law, that law itself was not a self-sufficient whole and needed equity as a supplement to complete it. Similarly, Reynolds's earlier writings, composed long before the *Discourses*, present a more spontaneous appreciation of genius. 'If a man,' Reynolds said, 'has nothing of that which is called genius, that is, if he is not carried away (if I may say so) by the animation, the fire of enthusiasm, all the rules in the world will never make him a painter'.[68] The problem with this view was that genius, however important, could never form the basis for art education, just as equity, in the *Commentaries*, could never form a foundation for education in the common law.

Blackstone sought to draw lines that would fully contain the law, envisioning a structure of fixed and immutable principles. Karl Marx's famous comparison between 'the worst architect and the best of bees' is useful here since, as Marx explains, what distinguishes them is that 'the architect raises his structure in imagination before he erects it in reality'.[69] Like an architect who designs before he builds, Blackstone had a plan in mind. Equity,

---

[64] *Commentaries* vol 3, 434.

[65] Boorstin (n 47) 98.

[66] J Derrida, *Of Grammatology* (tr) GC Spivak (Baltimore MD, 1997) 144.

[67] J Culler, *On Deconstruction. Theory and Criticism after Structuralism* (New York NY, 1982) 103.

[68] Reynolds's manuscript notes and memoranda, quoted by J Northcote, *The Life of Sir Joshua Reynolds* (London, 1818) vol 1, 95–96.

[69] K Marx, *Capital. A Critical Analysis of Capitalist Production* (ed) F Engels, (tr) S Moore and E Aveling (London, 1971) 157.

however, defied planning. It posed a serious impediment to Blackstone's whole design, undermining it with its constant flux, while at the same time sustaining it by allowing new light to flow through. Blackstone attempted to describe the structure of the English legal system and to formulate its main principles, but this led to some distortion of the law as it really was. In the *Commentaries*, Blackstone went so far as to reject some parts of law because they did not fit into his structure. In the first volume, he stated that martial law was 'in truth and reality no law' because it was 'built upon no settled principles'.[70] Rather than or as well as looking at the law like a lawyer, he saw law's principles and rules with the 'dilated eye'[71] of the artist, seizing the general effect while subordinating and sacrificing some detail. His division into four volumes reflected the fundamental structure of Justinian's *Institutes* into four books.[72] It is interesting to note that the quadripartite structure was the preferred framework adopted by the prominent Italian architect Andrea Palladio in his treatise *Quattro libri dell'architettura*.[73] Blackstone attempted to create for the law a text no less complete, no less systematic, and no less imposing than that classic architectural treatise.

In order to execute his design, Blackstone faced the need to build anew. In the time of Littleton, Blackstone explained, the common law 'resembled a regular Edifice', but over the years it was 'altered and mangled by various contradictory Statutes, &c ... according to Whim or Prejudice, or private Convenience of the Builders' and in its present condition 'remains a huge, irregular Pile, with many noble Apartments, though awkwardly put together, and some of them of no visible Use at present'.[74] Blackstone's design conflicted with the traces of diverging architectural styles and its builders' unequal degrees of skill. He admired the common law's ancient origins and national distinctiveness, but looked for a strong impression

---

[70] *Commentaries* vol 1, 400.
[71] Reynolds (n 51) 194.
[72] See JW Cairns, 'Blackstone, An English Institutist: Legal Literature and the Rise of the Nation State' (1984) 4 *Oxford Journal of Legal Studies* 318–60. The question of numbering in the structuring of a cohesive subject, it should be noted, had been raised by Plato and was regularly adopted in architectural treatises. Vitruvius not only divided his work into 10 books but also invoked Pythagorean maxims for presenting ideas according to 'cubical' principles, which, he noted, arose from things originally observed by 'our ancestors'. Vitruvius, *The Architecture of M. Vitruvius Pollio* (tr) W. Newton (London, 1791) vol 1, 92. Blackstone favoured four, the number of cosmic order used by Marcus Terentius Varro (the prolific Roman writer named by Vitruvius as mentor) as his preferred framework for systematising information. Like 10, four had been understood by the Pythagoreans to be a key number of the order of nature: IK McEwen, *Vitruvius. Writing the Body of Architecture* (Cambridge, 2003) 46, 325 n 156.
[73] See V Hart and P Hicks (ed), *Paper Palaces. The Rise of the Renaissance Architectural Treatise* (London, 1998) 232–46.
[74] William Blackstone to Seymour Richmond, 28 January 1746: *Letters* 4.

of visual unity and simplicity. He moved from the old architecture of the Middle Ages, where elements were oddly mingled, to the new Palladian order, inspired by the buildings of ancient Rome. Tellingly, Blackstone ended his second architectural manuscript with a drawing of the old Gothic cathedral of St Paul, which Christopher Wren remodelled, based on Roman structures under the influence of Palladio's classical style. As Blackstone's illustration demonstrates, Wren raised 'another structure over the first cupola; and this was a cone of brick, so built as to support a stone lantern of an elegant figure, and ending in ornaments of copper, gilt'.[75] Similarly, Blackstone's task was to superimpose over law's traditions and feudal past the rules of order and classical proportion.

If Blackstone might be compared to an architect who sought a Palladian building in accordance with Roman classical principles, Coke worked more as an engineer, aiming to preserve the law in its original Norman character. Coke was proprietor of the notable manor house of Minster Lovell Hall and acquired land in a historical site at Castle Acre, Norfolk, which he worked to conserve.[76] As a restorer of buildings, Coke's preoccupation was with potential threats to the integrity of the common law. He likened 'the Kingdom and commonwealth to a fair field and a pleasant garden' that if 'not tilled' could be overrun by weeds or infested by a plague of insects.[77] Like an engineer, Coke thought of the jurisdiction of courts as a system of rivers and predicted danger if the streams were to diverge from their channels.[78] Coke understood the complex operations of structures and mechanisms. He also viewed the law courts as clocks with many wheels and observed that any failing of their motions would cause entire mechanisms to collapse.[79] Blackstone's adherence to the harmonious simplicity of classical architecture and his appreciation for the Roman institutional tradition influenced his idealised conception of the common law just as Coke's special love for ruins became manifest in his legal writing.

Jeremy Bentham shared Blackstone's interest in the 'business of *arrangement*', a difficult enterprise in which, he admitted, Blackstone surpassed 'any thing in that way that has hitherto appeared'[80] but believed that his artistic perspective left too much to the imagination of the reader. He

---

[75] As cited in T Allen, *The History and Antiquities of London, Westminster, Southwark, and Parts Adjacent* (London, 1839) vol 3, 315.

[76] Castle Acre, Norfolk, was 'one of the earliest instances of conservation work on a secular ruin by a private individual': see AD Boyer, *Sir Edward Coke and the Elizabethan Age* (Stanford CA, 2003) 135.

[77] Coke, 'Speeches in Parliament' in *Selected Writings* (n 41) vol 3, 1205.

[78] SD White, *Sir Edward Coke and the 'Grievances of the Commonwealth' 1621–1628* (Chapel Hill NC, 1979) 64 n 96.

[79] Coke, 'The Fourth Part of the Institutes' in *Selected Writings* (n 41) vol 2, 1065.

[80] Bentham (n 48) 25.

regarded Blackstone's creation as an unworthy structure to be demolished and hoped for a better architect:

> Jurisprudence [wants] an Architect to build up for it a competent suite of terms and expressions, to lodge separately those meanings which as yet are either absolutely without a mansion, or else huddled up by half-dozens together in the obscure and ambiguous abodes which the current Nomenclature affords.[81]

Bentham did not rise to the challenge himself. His disjointed and incomplete codes, plans and drafts are difficult and lack a cohesive structure.[82] Blackstone's work, in contrast, became recognised as 'an essential part of every Gentleman's Library' and rapidly gained a staggering reputation and authority.[83] Its clear outline and carefully developed structure made the law accessible to a wide audience. The Duchess of Kingston, on the occasion of her bigamy trial in 1776, referred to 'Doctor Blackstone, whose works are as entertaining as they are instructive'.[84] Blackstone's beautiful presentation and intellectually daring approach were intended to make an impact. The *Commentaries* not only provided a means to navigate the intricacies of the common law, they became a symbol of the prestige of learning. In the 1780s, their popularity can be seen in Thomas Rowlandson's representation of an open book inscribed with 'Blackstone' and suggestively placed on a pedestal as a means to indicate William Pitt's legal training (see Figure 12). The author of the *Commentaries* had become synonymous with the law.

The law is an ever-changing organism that continues to evolve. Blackstone wanted to create a complete picture of the law, but encountered law's unfinished condition. Although he did not create an exact representation of the law, he succeeded in producing a new way of looking at it. His progression, according to a pre-arranged plan, made the English legal system a much more uniform system than it might otherwise have been. Drawing was an important means Blackstone used to explore, visualise and organise the common law's numerous statutes, rules and procedures. The study of the law, which Blackstone had described in his youth as 'hazardous or discouraging',[85] underwent a profound transformation. The *Commentaries*, illustrated with two diagrams, was the first textbook to give students, in a compact and manageable form, a clear and visible statement of the law. It was the best evidence of what the law was and ought to be and formed the groundwork of the English university legal education. No other work in English law had ever before been so influential or

---

[81] University College London Library, Bentham Papers, Box lxix, fo 182.
[82] See SR Letwin, *The Pursuit of Certainty* (Cambridge, 1965) 177. See also JH Burns, 'Bentham and Blackstone: A Lifetime's Dialectic' (1989) 1 *Utilitas* 22–40.
[83] Lieberman (n 44) 31.
[84] CHS Fifoot, 'Blackstone—Outside the Commentaries' (1937) 141 *Fortnightly Review* 723.
[85] As cited in Lockmiller 16.

succeeded in turning a fragmentary tradition into a coherent representation that was as persuasive as it was instructive and cohesive. It was here, for the first time, that the common law was neatly delineated and presented, to please the eye.

Figure 12. Thomas Rowlandson (Detail), **Billy Lackbeard and Charley Blackbeard Playing at Football** *(1784)*
Courtesy of The Lewis Walpole Library, Yale University.

3

Blackstone's Commentaries: England's Legal Georgic?

MICHAEL MEEHAN

THE ROLE AND the forms of literary influence are complex and varied. As scholars we look for evidence; quotations, verbal echoes, borrowed themes or ideas, recognisable formal properties, explicit confessions or admissions on the part of the author, or even, as is the case with Sir William Blackstone and Virgil's *Georgics*, a telling epigraph, of a kind to affirm the presence of influence and affiliation.[1] In reality, influence often exerts itself in more subtle and shadowy ways, many of which may be hidden even to the author of the derivative or heavily influenced text. Preceding or even contemporaneous texts may exert an intellectual and aesthetic gravitational field, bending the text and its content in elusive but powerful ways, determining a certain way of seeing and a way of writing, authorising inclusions and dictating exclusions, and in general, providing a form, a framework and a perspective that licenses inventive combinations and facilitates and furthers their reception.

It is not the intention of this chapter to argue that Blackstone's *Commentaries on the Laws of England* represent yet another English georgic, along with the work of his contemporaries and near contemporaries, in *Cyder, Windsor Forest, Public Virtue: Agriculture, The Hop-Garden, The Fleece, Sugar Cane, The Chase*, and many others. What is suggests, though, is that the culture which, in John Phillips, Alexander Pope, John Dyer, Christopher Smart, James Grainger, Robert Dodsley, John Armstrong and others, spawned the early and mid-century English georgic—the curious admixture of political, historical, legal, commercial and aesthetic factors which underwrote the efflorescence of these sometimes eccentric Virgilian adaptations, these long poetic expositions on hop gardening, sheep raising, sugar cane growing, human hygiene, hunting and the like—also

---

[1] See Prest, *William Blackstone* 46. Prest draws attention to Blackstone's use of an epigraph from Virgil's *Georgics* '*Sanctos ausus recludere fontes*': 'daring to reveal the sacred fountains' on the title page of his first published work.

supported and informed the writing of the *Commentaries*.[2] It suggests that the distinctive literary qualities of the work, much praised by Blackstone's contemporaries, if sometimes in disparagement of its genuine legal content, are best appreciated not just as particular devices, or as specific affective inputs, but rather as part of a broader writerly agenda which was shared by many others, and surfaced in a range of textual forms. It is suggested that the broad inclusiveness of the *Commentaries*—the mixing of legal taxonomy, philosophic reflection, historical retrospect and legal mythology, bound together in rich metaphoric visualisations—found inspiration and support in the georgic, and that the lawyer had not, in fact, said 'farewell to his Muse', to quite the degree that the younger Blackstone insisted.[3] Most literary genres support specific modes of resolution and finality, deeming particular forms of closure or completeness adequate and appropriate, and it is further suggested that there are aspects of 'everything is as it should be' Blackstone's heady but complacent vision both of the steady workings through of the law through English history and of the 'Glory' of the present establishment, which take both inspiration and readerly support from the poetic culture that forged the English georgic.

The English georgics largely appeared in a context of patriotism, discovering an Augustan peace and stability in the aftermath of Glorious Revolution and, after the Act of Union, new nationhood. The georgic, thus adapted, offered a poetic medium characterised by a radical inclusiveness, where the broad survey of agricultural activity and animal husbandry mixed in with poetic, political and philosophic reflection seemed to license an ever-widening survey of human industry and ingenuity. In this sense, an extension into the domain of law took it little further beyond the boundaries of the original genre than did the survey of health and hygiene, in the work of Armstrong, of hunting in Somerville, or even the training of slaves, in Grainger's *Sugar Cane*. In all, the georgic offered a timely and flexible poetic vehicle in which the sometimes divergent claims of Nature and Culture appeared effectively reconciled, a mode which moved beyond both pastoral dreaming and post-pastoral lamentation towards visions of the achievements, present and prospective, of human art and labour in a

---

[2] J Chalker, *The English Georgic: A Study in the Development of a Form* (London, 1969) 45 noted how these poems were then generally seen as 'faintly absurd and sterile offshoots of Augustan orthodoxy'. Since then, however, the English georgics have attracted much serious scholarly attention, both for the density of their political engagements and negotiations, as recently in P Rogers's 'John Phillips, Pope and the Political Georgic' (2005) 66 *Modern Language Quarterly* 411–42, and for their complex mediation of literary influences and analogues, as in D Fairer's 'Persistence, Adaptation and Transformation in Pastoral Georgic Poetry' in J Richetti (ed), *The Cambridge History of English Literature 1660–1770* (Cambridge, 2005), 259–86.

[3] See M Mauger, '"Observe how parts with parts unite/In one harmonious rule of right": William Blackstone's Verses on the Laws of England' (2012) 6 *Law and Humanities* 179–96, on Blackstone's early venture into legal verse.

cooperative and nurturing relationship, premised on peace and political stability, with the natural world.

> 'Tis art and toil
> Gives Nature value, multiplies her stores,
> Varies, improves, creates; it's art and toil
> Teaches her woody hills with fruits to shine,
> The pear and tasteful apple, decks with flow'rs,
> And foodful pulse the fields that often rise,
> Admiring to behold their furrows wave
> With yellow corn. What changes cannot Toil,
> With patient Art, effect?
>
> John Dyer, *The Fleece* (1757) 2:183–90

How far does the tracing of such literary influence risk reducing the *Commentaries* to the status of a mere literary text? How far does it risk vindicating Jeremy Bentham's caustic attacks, or John Austin's later jibe, that the work succeeded only by a 'paltry but effectual artifice'?[4] As a preliminary step, that 'mere literary text' might be restored to something closer to its eighteenth-century status. The *Commentaries*' contemporary reputation, as well as its enduring influence, had as much to do with what was literary as it had to do with what was strictly 'legal', with even Bentham, for all that he might have listened to Blackstone with 'rebel ears',[5] complimenting the work in this regard, as 'correct, elegant, unembarrassed'.[6] Attempts to divide form and content—to split embellishment and legal substance, aesthetic form and legal content—distort what Blackstone was actually seeking to do, in writing for amusement and pleasure as much as for instruction, and indeed, distort the way he and his contemporaries conceived of literature and the aesthetic, in an era long preceding that in which these various elements were packed up into their modern disciplinary boxes.[7] It is worth recalling how Blackstone's near contemporary, David Hume, described himself as pursuing a career in 'literature'—clearly invoking the word in the widest sense—and we might further recall Lord Mansfield's injunction, when asked as to how a student of law should be educated, that he [sic] should translate Cicero's works into English, and from there, translate them back into Latin, for comparison with the Latin original. After several years of engaging in this exercise, the student would, Lord Mansfield argued, be ready to be a lawyer.[8]

---

[4] Quoted in AV Dicey, 'Blackstone's *Commentaries*' (1932) 4 *Cambridge Law Journal* 287.
[5] J Bowering (ed), *The Works of Jeremy Bentham* (Edinburgh, 1838–43) vol 1, 249.
[6] JH Burns and HLA Hart (ed), J Bentham, *A Fragment on Government* (London 1776; Cambridge, 1988) 23.
[7] *Commentaries*, vol 2, 382, vol 4, 435.
[8] For Mansfield's commendation of Cicero's 'mellifluous periods' as the first concern of the student of law—'He should translate and re-translate him; write him as well as read him'— see *A Treatise on the Study of the Law, Containing Directions to Students, Written by those*

Much of the stature, and even the continuing legal authority of the *Commentaries*, inheres in its literary properties as much as in the domain of substantive law. It lies in its metaphorical density, its diverse narrative momentums, its fictionalisations and its insistent investing of its subject, English law, with its 'order', its 'symmetry', its 'connexions' and its 'proportions', and in general, with all the attributes and allure of a late-Augustan work of art. The rich metaphoric dimension of the *Commentaries* has now been well explored and articulated, in explorations of his use of powerful visualisations and organising metaphors—map, the tree, the pathway, the landscape, the ancient castle, and, in the context of the georgic, his 'marking out the shape of the country'.[9] Common law thinking often proceeds more by incantation than by logic, with those incantations deriving strong support from powerful and historically resonant imagery. Many of the innovative strengths of Blackstone's undertaking were both masked and enriched by his adaptation and expanding of metaphors and phrasings already embedded in that tradition. Sir William was in this regard a brilliant and highly strategic mimic, with the sheer familiarity and apparent impersonality of his rhetorical devices—all traditional, all sourced from elsewhere—offering his work a special air of cultural centrality, a sense of its being inextricably (and thus unassailably) woven into the fabric both of existing literature and of existing law. All of which steeply enhanced its authority, with even Sir William Jones, in his lively *Essay on Bailments*, while suggesting that reading the *Commentaries* 'alone will no more form a lawyer, than a general map of the world, however accurately and elegantly soever it may be delineated, will make a geographer', happy to commend 'our excellent Blackstone' for his 'most beautiful outline', his literary ingenuity and elegant and persuasive style.[10]

How far though, beyond the exposition of these specific literary qualities, might we claim the impress of a particular genre, and specifically the Virgilian georgic and its English adaptations, as a deeper 'gravitational field', shaping the character and objectives of the work? How far might the georgic have provided a model, an inducement, an inspiration for the wider undertaking? It is easy enough to list shared characteristics, as the *Commentaries*—in terms of its wider content, if not of specific poetic form—reproduces virtually every characteristic of the georgic in its English form. The *Commentaries*, like the georgics, offers patriotism, now in a Whiggish vein, in celebrations of post-revolution stability. Like the georgic, it offers a post-pastoral vision of the world in which nature must be enhanced and

---

Lawyers, Orators and Statesmen, the Lords Mansfield, Ashburton and Thurlow, in a Series of Letters to their Respective Young Friends: with Notes and Additions by the Editor (London, 1797) 16.

[9] *Commentaries* vol 1, 35.
[10] W Jones, *Essay on the Law of Bailments* (London, 1781) 3–4.

only fully 'possessed' through human labour, and through an extension of knowledge. It continues the deeply organic vision of the georgic, offering reconciliations of tradition and innovation in a strong historical retrospect charting a process of organic growth, disruption and restoration, which builds on the even earlier Hesiodic model of fall and redemption, with the 'iron times' of a fallen world restored through the centuries-long labour of the Law, effectively configured in the terms Pope used in *Essay on Man*, as our 'Second Providence'. As with the georgic, the *Commentaries* thrives on a rich eclecticism, a medley of philosophic and historical reflection, which intervenes in and offers texture and context to the more practical aspects of exposition. Recent commentators on the English georgic have noted its emphasis on organic links and 'connectedness', suggesting that the great strength of the genre lay in its liberal inclusiveness and its exploration of 'connexions', laying out fragments and linking them in stages that run towards a comprehensive overview as 'parts with parts unite' and an optimistic vision of the redemptive power of an expanded understanding.[11]

> Ye noble few! who here unbending stand
> Beneath life's pressure, yet bear up a while.
> And what your bounded view, which only saw
> A little part, deem'd Evil is no more:
> The storms of Wintry Time will quickly pass.
> And one unbounded Spring encircle all.
>   James Thomson, *Winter*, ll 1056–1071

Rich texts offer us the possibility of absorption—an absorption in a textual world that feels complete. In its literary context, the successful text, the engaging story, evokes a world that feels somehow seamless and entire, with the microcosm of the text and the apparent inclusiveness of its narrative instilling a confidence in a wider totality of order and comprehensibility, in the world that lies beyond the text. Much of the pleasure in reading, and even much of our necessity to read, derives from our need, in a 'real world' that is fragmented and uncertain, to sustain ourselves by the textual sensation and reassurance of a microcosmic text which in some sense manages to encompass and to tell what seems to be a whole truth.

The literary scholar Judith Roof thus writes:

> Narrative constantly reproduces the phantom of a whole, articulated system ... As a pervasive sense of the necessary shape of events and their perception and as process by which characters, causes and effects combine into patterns recognised as sensical, narrative is the informing logic by which individuality, identity and

---

[11] See, in particular, M Genovese, '"An Organic Commerce": Sociable Selfhood in the Eighteenth Century Georgic' (2013) 46 *Eighteenth Century Studies* 197–220.

ideology merge into a cooperative and apparently unified version of the truths of existence.[12]

The early-century call for order and system—for 'perspective' and the Vinerian 'distant Prospect'—and even the call for 'pathways' through the disorderly 'Heap of good Learning' that was English law, was a call for textual totality.[13] The appeal for more practical forms of legal ordering was also insistent, and was in some measure answered in the plethora of legal compendiums, legal 'pocket guides', 'compleat' handbooks, laymen's guides, and lawyers' companions that formed so large a portion of legal publication through the early decades of the eighteenth century. The appeal in writers such as Thomas Wood, though, was for something far more emblematic, something more like a coherent image and appreciable representation of the totality of English law rather than simply a 'pocket guide'. Wood, in seeking a pathway through the 'Dark and Rugged' country of English law, called not just for 'Method', but also for 'Beauty'.[14] The call for a *readable* system of law' by Lord Ashburton, and his appeal to other national developments in the Arts and Sciences as a leading model for law, also suggests a call for a more readerly, and even a more contemplative process, more closely akin to aesthetic appreciation and patriotic deep absorption—closer indeed, to 'amusement and pleasure'—than it was merely to the practical business of daily legal affairs.[15] These calls—for legal 'system', for 'order', 'pathways' and even 'boundaries'—were evidence, it is suggested, of a desire to live beyond fragmentation. In response, the projection of totality—of 'fullness' and 'comprehensiveness'—was perhaps the most seductive illusion underpinning the *Commentaries*' enduring authoritative power. That fullness, it is suggested, was again deeply underwritten by the culture of the georgic, the quest for that 'one unbounded spring', and redemption, in effect, from the fallen world of ignorance and fragmentation.

Blackstone's pursuit of this 'phantom of totality' in the *Commentaries* proceeds along two lines. The first is the synchronic view, the 'distant Prospect' as commended by Viner, articulated in the prefatory lecture and repeatedly reinforced, almost as a leitmotif thereafter and the map, showing the extent and the 'connexions' of the whole. This was an undertaking

---

[12] From *Come As You Are: Sexuality and Narrative* (New York NY, 1996), collected in M McQuillan (ed), *The Narrative Reader* (New York NY, 2000) 213.

[13] T Wood, *Some Thoughts Concerning the Study of the Laws of England Particularly in the Two Universities* (London, 1727) i.

[14] Ibid ii.

[15] Lord Ashburton, quoted in *A Treatise* (n 8) 62. For Ashburton, Blackstone's *Commentaries* did not answer to the need, and his success was undeserved, with the *Commentaries* offering 'no invention, no philosophy, no erudition; it may instruct a country gentleman, but lawyers receive no benefit from it'.

institutist in character,[16] but always, in Blackstone, with its own deeply aesthetic tinge, with a resort, not to the language of legality, but to that of contemporary aesthetics, in 'order', 'symmetry', 'harmony', and above all, with an appeal to the imagination, as the primary foundation of legal understanding, and indeed, as the faculty most susceptible to these wider apprehensions of totality.

The word 'imagination' occurs in the *Commentaries* more frequently than in almost any other text of the period; more, indeed, than in most that were more specifically concerned with matters aesthetic. Blackstone promoted imagination as the faculty through which we might most strongly comprehend and appreciate the law, and rise—in the manner of the Shaftesburyan ascent through the broadening of our perception—to visualise its full extent and 'connexions', the symmetry and harmony of the whole. In this context should be noted the importance Blackstone gave to what he called 'attentive contemplation', to a form of legal meditation much in the Shaftesburyan vein.[17] There is also the dark side: Blackstone writes, too, of the dangers of 'fertile imagination', where in place of attentive contemplation of the present excellence, the mind begins, in Blackstone's words, an active and reckless 'new fangling', and 'contrivance'.[18] Imaginative response should be passive and contemplative rather than the source of legal 'novelties', 'embellishments' and 'chicaneries', and in this carefully guarded sense the *Commentaries* is replete with reference to the 'noblest faculties of the soul', to 'the affections', to the 'cardinal virtues of the heart', and to the aesthetic instincts in general, as the highest and the most appropriate *locus* of legal imaginative response, especially where 'attentive contemplation' of the 'present Glory' is concerned.[19]

The second aspect in this pursuit of totality—a rather more phantom-like, and indeed, an even more richly imaginative device—derives from Blackstone's evocation of the 'voice' of English law. Through this device, Blackstone cleverly links the present and the past in a dynamic and organic relationship, which further provides a special assurance of totality in that the demonstrated 'system' and even the 'present Glory' will always be supported and completed by mysterious supplement. In ways more akin to established English legal thinking, and certainly more poetically, more imaginatively intrepid, that sense of 'totality' could thus also be created through enriched organic metaphor, and specifically, through the device of personification. English law, in the *Commentaries*, in at the very centre, is a voice, a living and creating entity, one that is coherent and fully articulate,

---

[16] See JW Cairns, 'Blackstone, an English Institutist: Legal Literature and the Rise of the Nation State' (1984) 4 *Oxford Journal of Legal Studies* 313–60.
[17] *Commentaries* vol 2, 78; vol 4, 436.
[18] Ibid vol 1, 329; vol 2, 344; vol 4, 86.
[19] Ibid vol 1, 27.

finally, in the 'restored' environment of post-revolution Britain. The most developed metaphor in the *Commentaries* is that of personification, and the ways in which Blackstone, as author, positioned himself as speaking for, about and *on behalf of*, the Law, is a device so familiar from even our most contemporary legal discourse, that it is practically invisible; in the everyday discourse of judgment, we still read of the body, the hand, the finger, the mind, the thinking, the heart, the soul and the spirit of the Law.[20] In Blackstone, the metaphor was more richly and more strategically sustained, and through the *Commentaries* we find the Law as variously 'anxious', 'cautious', 'tender' and 'solicitous', as gifted with 'wisdom' 'foresight', 'humanity' and 'parental solicitude'.[21] Thus equipped, the Law moves in ghostly but benign form through the full length of the *Commentaries*, as the ultimate designing force and true authorial voice, struggling through the miswritings, the 'chicanes and subtleties'[22] and 'specious embellishments and fantastic novelties'[23] that history has presented, towards clear and untrammelled articulation in the 'excellence of our present establishment'.[24]

Thus personified, the Law is a living entity, and as such, is necessarily and organically complete in itself, holding the whole system together against the prospect of fragmentation, either on the synchronic plane, through intrusion of legislation and an excess of 'fertile' legal imagining, or on the diachronic plane, through the various disruptions and distractions of English legal history, as with the intrusion of Norman 'chicaneries, subtleties and embellishments'. It is the unity, the 'wisdom' and final comprehensive clarity of the 'voice', striving towards full articulation in the 'present Glory', which affirms and encourages in that process of patriotic absorption and deep reassurance that is the prime source of 'amusement and pleasure' in the *Commentaries*. Through the device of personification Blackstone not only weaves his work most deeply into the common law tradition, but also most effectively narrativises the law, in the totalising sense that Judith Roof suggests. Through personification, through tracing the voice of the law through its various tribulations, Blackstone effectively turns legal history into a form of legal biography, with that voice, muffled and fragmented by various historical delinquencies but surviving towards rich articulations in the 'present Glory' of the English legal establishment.

So how far, finally, can we take Blackstone's own suggestion that he was writing for amusement and pleasure? How far is the *Commentaries on the Laws of England*, in the end, a significant literary work, as well as—and

---

[20] For an account of the pervasiveness and function of personification in modern legal discourse, see M Meehan, 'An Anatomy of Australian Law' in JN Turner and P Williams (ed), *The Happy Couple: Law and Literature* (Sydney, 1994) 376–91.
[21] *Commentaries* vol 3, 422–23.
[22] Ibid vol 4, 410.
[23] Ibid vol 1, 10.
[24] Ibid vol 4, 49.

not in place of—being one of the most significant contributions to English legal writing? How far can we hope to retrieve, through a close reading of the *Commentaries*, an understanding of affective and not simply intellectual modes of legal appreciation? How far, indeed, is Blackstone's Law—variously 'wise', 'anxious', 'solicitous', 'tender' and 'humane'—one of the great characters of eighteenth-century English literature?

Decades before the first publication of the *Commentaries*, Thomas Wood commended English law for the ways in which it was 'twisted and interwoven almost into all manner of Discourse and Business'.[25] It is clear that for Blackstone's readers though, one man's meat was another man's poison, and there is a curious way in which the powerful blend of form and content in Blackstone's *Commentaries* is most strongly evidenced in the furious attempts by his critics to target exactly this area; to separate, to 'disentangle' and deconstruct, and to expose just how much of the ostensibly solid content of the work was actually form—and literary rather than legal form, at that. Perversely, it was Blackstone's sternest critics who discerned most clearly the literary power of the *Commentaries*, who saw that the best way of edging 'the learned panegyrist', the 'learned commentator'[26] off his perch would be to drive a wedge between the literary and the legal, to expose the rhetorical, fictional and metaphorical aspects of his work, and then, very specifically in the case of Bentham, to pitch metaphor against metaphor, narrative against narrative, and finally, fiction against fact.

The reassuring totality as envisaged by 'everything as it should be' Blackstone was, in his critics' eyes, spurious, the product of blindness rather than comprehensive vision. Blackstone, Bentham wrote, 'makes men think they see, in order to prevent their seeing'[27] with so much of the blinding, so much of Blackstone's 'nonsense on stilts', deriving from his aesthetic aptitude, his marshalling of all the aesthetic affections, and his insistence on the English legal system, in its 'present Glory', with all its 'connexions', 'symmetries' and 'proportions', as akin, again, to an Augustan work of art, offering the blandishments of amusement and pleasure at the real cost of genuine instruction.

As such, the critique that Blackstone evoked, in these later years, is neatly inverse to the fortunes of the English georgic. Both Sir William Jones and Jeremy Bentham suggest that Blackstone presented as a practical and even scientific text what was actually a literary undertaking, and an exercise, in effect, in smoke and mirrors. The georgic, on the other hand, came by implication under heavy fire in Wordsworth and Coleridge's 1800 *Preface to the Lyrical Ballads*, for presenting as a literary undertaking, as poetry, what was in fact merely practical and distinctly unpoetical content, dressed

---

[25] Wood (n 13) 14.
[26] Bentham (n 6) vol 6, 99n; vol 3, 14.
[27] Ibid, vol 10, 141 and see also vol 7, 242n.

up in 'poetic diction', 'arbitrary, and subject to infinite caprices'.[28] In both instances, though, and even from these two highly divergent directions, what we are actually seeing is the disintegration of a distinctive Augustan and late-Augustan authorial culture, where the 'aesthetic affections' could be called on not simply in the business of art—describing 'human passions, characters and incidents'—but as an active and affective mode of understanding, a form of understanding deemed redemptive—in a far more disparate range of human activity, supplementing rather than being displaced by 'enlightenment' models in analysis and representation.

In terms of literary form, the *Commentaries* clearly does not stand on all fours with the Virgilian georgic and its English counterparts. What can be asserted though, is that the status, authority, popularity and rhetorical seductiveness of the *Commentaries* can be sheeted back to Blackstone's artful 'twisting and interweaving' of his legal taxonomy with other forms of discourse, and in particular, in his tapping and reproducing within the *Commentaries* virtually all the properties, the key characteristics, interests and 'plaguy prejudices', the rich inclusiveness and eclecticism, the culture of deep 'connectedness' and the redemptive possibilities of the comprehensive overview, that evoked and supported this curious eighteenth-century English genre. Many years ago Henry Knight Miller wrote of the 'Whig Interpretation of literary history', exposing the 'fallacies of premature teleology' that distorted the history of eighteenth-century literature in favour of any sign of incipient Romanticism.[29] Blackstone is susceptible to similar distortion, with the corresponding allure of 'Enlightenment' deflecting attention from his deeper sources and influences. The persuasive power of the *Commentaries* derives as much from creative retrospect as it does from intellectual prescience, a retrospect which reflects not only English writing on the common law, but also Blackstone's deep immersion in the classical tradition, and in particular, in the Virgilian vision of nature's transformation and the redemptive power of a broad eclectic review.

In this specific domain of comprehensiveness—in what I have called Blackstone's pursuit of the 'phantom of totality'—it was again Bentham who saw most clearly, and who sought to prick the bubble—or better, perhaps, to engage in a bit of ghost-busting. 'Hide the ends of a fishpond', he wrote, 'and you will imagine it a mighty river'.[30] What Blackstone proposed as a mighty river—a dynamic history feeding 'present Glory'—was for Bentham a mere fishpond, its limits masked and hidden by 'childish fictions' at one end—that 'Voice' which speaks 'from a time whereof the

---

[28] 'Preface to the Lyrical Ballads' in DJ Enright and E de Chickera, *English Critical Texts* (London, 1962) 177.
[29] (1972) 6 *Eighteenth Century Studies* 60–84.
[30] University College London, Bentham Papers, Box 27, fo 123. I am grateful to Philip Schofield and his colleagues at the Bentham Project for this reference.

memory of man runneth not to the contrary'[31]—and by heady but largely vapid patriotic and Whiggish panegyric at the other. For all Bentham's cleverness, though, for all his deconstructive ingenuity in disentangling the taut legal woof and poetic weft of Blackstone's legal discourse, it is finally Blackstone, not Bentham, who continues to be quoted, repeatedly and respectfully and at great length, in the courts. There is a curious way, in the former colonial jurisdictions at least, in which Blackstone, in the *Commentaries*, has become the source text, the point beyond which further legal exploration is deemed unnecessary, with Blackstone himself acceding to the status of his own personification, as that Voice which speaks with authority, encapsulating, articulating and passing forward that which lies long beyond living legal memory.[32] It is a remarkable legal achievement. It is a remarkable literary achievement. For all Blackstone's caution about the toll of the 'fertile imagination', his own *Commentaries on the Laws of England* is, first and foremost, one of the greatest imaginative monuments of the British eighteenth century.

---

[31] *Commentaries* vol 1, 67 and 76.
[32] On the 'biblical' authority of Blackstone in the colonial courts, see T Anthony, 'Blackstone on Colonialism: Australian Judicial Interpretations' in Prest (ed), Commentaries 133.

II

Beyond England

Adapted and appropriated for use in contexts far removed in both time and place from its mid-eighteenth-century English origins, the *Commentaries on the Laws of England* has exercised a remarkably wide influence beyond its author's native land. Tracing the dissemination, reception and impact of Blackstone's work within and beyond England, inside and outside the common law world, presents a scholarly challenge of massive proportions. While a start has been made, much remains to be done by way of mapping the extensive global dimensions and varying configurations of the influence exercised by the *Commentaries* over the past two and a half centuries. The following chapters demonstrate that there is a good deal still to be learnt about even the nature and role of 'American Blackstones', notwithstanding the considerable attention which has already been devoted to Blackstone's North American manifestations.[1]

Particular interest attaches to the place of the *Commentaries* in civil law or mixed jurisdictions. The contributions of John Cairns, Stephen Sheppard and Michel Morin take up the case of two former French colonies, Louisiana (or the Territory of Orleans) and Quebec, the former New France and later Lower Canada. As Cairns points out, some aspects of the use of the *Commentaries* by the drafters of the first Louisiana Civil Code or *Digest* of 1808 have previously been recognised. But Cairns now provides a comprehensive, detailed and specific account of how and why the *Commentaries* were employed, in what he terms a 'coalescing' rather than a clash of legal traditions. Having endorsed the conclusion that Blackstone was a central influence on the Louisiana drafters (and through them, on subsequent Latin American legal codes), Sheppard goes on to show that judicial citation of Blackstone in Louisiana's superior courts during the nineteenth and twentieth centuries followed a broadly similar pattern to

---

[1] See M Hoeflich, 'American Blackstones' in Prest (ed) Commentaries 171–84; *cf* Nolan; DJ Boorstin, *The Mysterious Science of the Law: An Essay on Blackstone's Commentaries* (Cambridge MA, 1941; Chicago IL, 1996); CE Klafter, 'The Americanization of Blackstone's *Commentaries*' in EA Cawthon and DE Narrett (ed), *English Law and the American Experience* (College Station TX, 1994) 42–65; A Fidler, '"A Dry and Revolting Study": the Life and Labours of Antebellum Law Students' in WW Pue and D Sugarman (ed), *Lawyers and Vampires: Cultural Histories of Legal Professions* (Oxford, 2003) 86–98; EH Pearson, *Remaking Custom: Law and Identity in the Early American Republic* (Charlottesville VA, 2011).

that found in other US jurisdictions over the same period, notwithstanding the orthodox view of Louisiana law as quite exceptional, on account of its predominantly civilian character. Michel Morin provides an equally novel reinterpretation of Blackstone's influence in Quebec during the first century of British rule, employing a wide range of sources (including library catalogues and newspaper reports) to illustrate the diffusion of his works, both in the original language and French translations, as standard sources on criminal law and parliamentary or public law, even for francophone lawyers.

The other two chapters in this section treat Blackstone's role in wholly common law jurisdictions. John V Orth traces the remarkable salience of the *Commentaries* in North Carolina from the 1770s to the present day. While no longer essential reading for would-be lawyers, as it had been until at least the 1930s, the work's influence continues to mould that state's uncodified criminal law, which is still largely defined in terms set out in Blackstone's fourth volume. Finally Wilfrid Prest looks at Blackstone in Australia and New Zealand. There the *Commentaries* seem never to have figured quite so prominently in legal culture as they did in North America, and their presence was even less evident in New Zealand than Australian law school curricula. But Blackstone still continues to be cited in the Australian High Court and New Zealand Court of Appeals, if by no means as frequently as in the US Supreme Court. And throughout Australasia, until at least the mid-twentieth century, the *Commentaries* provided policy-makers and commentators on public issues of all kinds with an invaluable resource, as an authoritative and comprehensive compendium of constitutional and legal information.

4

Blackstone in the Bayous: Inscribing Slavery in the Louisiana Digest of 1808

JOHN W CAIRNS*

WILLIAM BLACKSTONE'S *COMMENTARIES on the Laws of England* exerted significant influence outwith England. Its impact in Britain's North American colonies and the fledgling United States of America has often been noted.[1] It is easy to understand the success. In four volumes, the author gave a general overview of the British constitution and placed his pragmatic and historical exposition of the laws of England in an appropriate framework of natural law.

Blackstone's *Commentaries* is not usually described as a central Enlightenment text; but this is surely what it is.[2] The fourth edition appeared in French translation in 1774–76.[3] This gave it a wider currency in the most significant language for dissemination of Enlightenment learning. It allowed the work to be read and praised by the Empress Catherine of Russia.[4] The translator, Auguste-Pierre Damiens de Gomicourt, had already included occasional extracts from the *Commentaries* in his *L'Observateur français à Londres*.[5] The first two volumes of the translation were reviewed in the *Leipziger Gelehrte Zeitungen* towards the end of 1774.[6] In 1776 the Abbé Gabriel-François Coyer published a translation of the fourth book

---

* I am grateful to Georgia Chadwick, Director, Law Library of Louisiana, for her generous help with materials not obtainable in Edinburgh, and to Mike Widener for advice on the bibliography of Blackstone. Paul du Plessis and Michel Morin helped with suggestions.
[1] Nolan; AW Alschuler, 'Rediscovering Blackstone' (1996) 145 *University of Pennsylvania Law Review* 1–55; M Hoeflich, 'American Blackstones' in Prest (ed) Commentaries 171–84.
[2] Prest, *William Blackstone* 308–09; *cf* J Rudolph, *Common Law and Enlightenment in England, 1689–1750* (Woodbridge, 2013).
[3] *Commentaires sur les loix angloises, de M. Blackstone, traduits de l'Anglois par M. D. G***, sur la quatrieme édition d'Oxford* (Brussels, 1774).
[4] M Raeff, 'The Empress and the Vinerian Professor: Catherine II's Projects of Government Reforms and Blackstone's *Commentaries*' (1974) 7 ns *Oxford Slavonic Papers* 18–41.
[5] J Emerson, 'Did Blackstone get the Gallic Shrug?' in Prest (ed) Commentaries 186.
[6] H Dippel, 'Blackstone in Germany', in Prest (ed) Commentaries 199–200.

as *Commentaire sur le code criminel d'Angleterre*.[7] His aim was, through the translation, to contribute to the debate on crime and punishment that so marked the Enlightenment.[8] These translations were later criticised; Blackstone typically was himself more generous.[9]

This chapter explores the influence of Blackstone's *Commentaries* in Louisiana, which, in the later eighteenth century, was very much part of the French and Spanish Atlantic worlds, and increasingly of the Anglo-American—the last development confirmed by the Louisiana Purchase of 1803. Louisiana provided a space, where, for a while, the Spanish, French, and English Atlantic legal worlds met, perhaps collided, and certainly, to some extent, coalesced. Out of these circumstances came the first Louisiana Civil Code, more properly entitled *The Digest of the Civil Laws Now in Force in the Territory of Orleans* (here referred to as the *Digest of Orleans*). This was enacted in 1808 by the legislature of the Territory of Orleans. Established after the Purchase as an administrative area prior to statehood (which came in 1812), carved out of the vast area acquired, the Territory of Orleans covered the district roughly corresponding to the modern state of Louisiana, though some important parts of the future state as yet remained Spanish territory.[10]

Louisiana is often rather loosely described as a 'civil law' state, or as having the 'Napoleonic code'.[11] Like most broad generalisations, this carries an element of truth. But such remarks underplay the extent to which the meeting of three Atlantic colonial worlds ensured that Louisiana has a particularly complex and fascinating legal history. This reflects the economic and strategic importance of the Mississippi valley to various colonial powers, including the United States.[12] Part of that Atlantic cultural history is the use made of Blackstone by the drafters of the *Digest of Orleans*. That the codifiers drew on the text of the *Commentaries* to compose the text of individual articles of the *Digest* has been recognised for some 40 years. Thomas Tucker pointed to the drafters' use of Blackstone in the title of the *Digest* 'Of Master and Servant'.[13] Rodolfo Batiza claimed that 30 articles of the *Digest* were influenced by the wording of the *Commentaries*, classing the influence from 'partial' and 'substantial' through to 'almost verbatim'.[14]

---

[7] G-F Coyer, *Commentaire sur le code criminel d'Angleterre* (Paris, 1776).

[8] Emerson (n 5) 186–87.

[9] Ibid 187; W Blackstone to Unknown, 25 May 1775, in *Letters* 152.

[10] See the map reproduced in G Dargo, 'The Digest of 1808: Historical Perspectives' (2009) 24 *Tulane European and Civil Law Forum* 1–30, 11.

[11] MG Puder, 'Did you Ever Hear of the Napoleonic Code, Stella? A Mixed Jurisdiction Impact Analysis from Louisiana's Law Laboratory' (2011) 85 *Tulane Law Review* 635–75, 636–37.

[12] RW van Alstyne, 'The Significance of the Mississippi Valley in American Diplomatic History, 1686–1890 (1949) 36 *Mississippi Valley Historical Review* 215–38.

[13] TW Tucker, 'Sources of Lousiana's Law of Persons: Blackstone, Domat, and the French Codes' (1970) 44 *Tulane Law Review* 264–95.

[14] R Batiza, 'The Louisiana Civil Code of 1808: Its Actual Sources and Present Relevance' (1971) 46 *Tulane Law Review* 4–165, 45, 51, 53–54, 61–62.

More recently Alejandro Guzmán Brito has examined the intellectual context of the codifiers' use of Blackstone in the preliminary title to the *Digest*.[15] But Blackstone also influenced the structure of the first book of the *Digest of Orleans*. This relationship was first identified some 30 or so years ago; but further study shows that use of Blackstone allowed the codifiers to resolve some problems in organising their first book.[16]

The *Commentaries* was the central legal text—and Blackstone a pivotal figure—in law and governance in the eighteenth-century North Atlantic world. This chapter examines the reasons underlying the use of Blackstone and the significance of his impact on the structure of the *Digest*—an influence that, through the *Digest*, affected other civil codes even further afield.[17]

I COLONIAL LOUISIANA: FRANCE AND SPAIN

Louisiana was claimed for France in the late seventeenth century.[18] Established as a proprietary colony in the last years of Louis XIV, by 1731, when it reverted to the Crown, it had a developing slave-based plantation economy and a well-situated trading and administrative centre at New Orleans.[19] Like that of other French colonies, the law in Louisiana was in theory the same as practised in the city of Paris and Île de France, namely, the *Coutume de Paris*, royal legislation to 1717 (when the colony was granted to the *Compagnie des Indes*), and subsequent royal legislation specifically extended to the colony, as well as any local regulation.[20] Legal matters were handled by the Superior Council.[21] France's colonial legislation on slavery, the *Code Noir* of 1685, was introduced into Louisiana in 1724.[22]

The Seven Years War involved Britain and the Bourbon powers of France and Spain in significant colonial fighting. By the Treaty of Fontainebleau

---

[15] A Guzmán Brito, 'Las fuentes de las normas sobre interpretación de las leyes del "Digest des lois civiles" ("code civil") de la Luisiana (1808/1825)' (2009) 31 *Revista de estudios histórico-jurídicos* 171–95.

[16] JW Cairns, 'The 1808 Digest of Orleans and 1866 Civil Code of Lower Canada: An Historical Study of Legal Change' (PhD thesis, University of Edinburgh, 1980) 559.

[17] R Knütel, 'Influences of the Louisiana Civil Code in Latin America' (1996) 70 *Tulane Law Review* 1445–80.

[18] M Giraud, *Histoire de la Louisiane française* (Paris, 1953–74) vol 1, 3–56.

[19] *Lettres patentes*, 24 September 1712, August 1717, in *Publications of the Louisiana Historical Society, Vol IV* (New Orleans LA, 1908) 13–20, 43–61; TN Ingersoll, *Mammon and Manon in Early New Orleans: The First Slave Society in the Deep South, 1718–1819* (Knoxville TN, 1999) 3–33; J Pritchard, *In Search of Empire: The French in the Americas, 1670–1730* (Cambridge, 2004) 139.

[20] HW Baade, 'Marriage Contracts in French and Spanish Louisiana: A Study in "Notarial" Jurisprudence' (1978) 53 *Tulane Law Review* 1–92, 9–13.

[21] JA Micelle, 'From Law Court to Civil Government: Metamorphosis of the Superior Council of French Louisiana' (1968) 9 *Louisiana History* 85–107; JD Hardy, 'The Superior Council in Louisiana' in JF McDermott (ed), *Frenchmen and French Ways in the Mississippi Valley* (Urbana IL, 1969) 87–101.

[22] R Chesnais, *L'Esclavage à la Française: Le Code Noir (1685 et 1724)* (Paris, 2005) 55–69; VV Palmer, *Through the Codes Darkly: Slave Law and Civil Law in Louisiana* (Clark NJ, 2012) 3–41.

(1762), France ceded Louisiana to Spain. But when Britain acquired Florida in 1763, Spanish Louisiana, with the exception of the Île d'Orléans on which New Orleans stood, began west of the Mississippi.[23]

Spain first attempted to occupy its new territory in 1766, when Don Antonio de Ulloa was sent as governor. He was expelled in an uprising at the end of October, 1768.[24] A new governor, Don Alejandro O'Reilly, was appointed in 1769.[25] He sailed from Havana with over 2,000 troops, took possession of the colony, and arrested those who had led the revolt.[26] O'Reilly embarked on a series of reforms that integrated Louisiana into the Viceroyalty of New Spain.[27] The Superior Council was replaced with a *Cabildo* modelled on the city councils found in other Spanish colonies.[28] In place of the French laws came those of the Spanish Indies. The *Leyes de las Indias* had a default provision that, in the absence of relevant colonial enactment, the law of Castile was to be applied.[29] These changes were effective.[30] The Spanish colonial law on slavery came into use.[31]

During the 1790s a significant unofficial trade developed between the United States and Louisiana.[32] This was regularised in 1795 by the Treaty of San Lorenzo (Pinckney's Treaty), which granted free navigation of the Mississippi to the United States, together with the privilege of depositing goods at New Orleans for re-export without payment of duty.[33] But in pursuit of a strategic plan to create a buffer zone to protect the other Spanish colonies, on 1 October 1800 Spain agreed to cede Louisiana to France.[34]

---

[23] AS Aiton, 'The Diplomacy of the Louisiana Cession' (1931) 36 *American Historical Review* 701–20.

[24] JP Moore, *Revolt in Louisiana: The Spanish Occupation, 1766–1770* (Baton Rouge LA, 1976) 1–20, 143–64; RE Chandler, 'Ulloa's Account of the 1768 Revolt' (1986) 27 *Louisiana History* 407–37; CA Brasseaux, *Denis-Nicolas Foucault and the New Orleans Rebellion of 1768* (Ruston LA, 1987). On the legal position, see Baade (n 20) 30–35.

[25] B Torres Ramírez, *Alejandro O'Reilly en las Indias* (Seville, 1969) 15–94.

[26] Ibid 97–114; JDL Holmes, 'Alexander O'Reilly Colonial Governor, 1769–1770' in JG Dawson III (ed), *The Louisiana Governors: From Iberville to Edwards* (Baton Rouge LA, 1990) 49–52, 49; Baade (n 20) 35–36.

[27] Holmes (n 26) 50–52; Torres Ramírez (n 25) 116–17.

[28] GC Din and JE Harkins, *The New Orleans Cabildo: Colonial Louisiana's First City Government, 1769–1803* (Baton Rouge LA, 1996) 38–55.

[29] *Recopliación de leyes de los reynos de las Indias*, 4th edn (Madrid, 1791) II.i.2.

[30] See HW Baade, 'The Formalities of Private Real Estate Transactions in Spanish North America: A Report on Some Recent Decisions' (1978) 38 *Louisiana Law Review* 655–745; Baade, 'Marriage Contracts' (n 20); HW Baade, 'The Form of Marriage in Spanish North America' (1975) 61 *Cornell Law Review* 1–89.

[31] HW Baade, 'The Law of Slavery in Spanish Luisiana' in EF Haas (ed), *Louisiana's Legal Heritage* (Pensacola FL, 1983) 43–86.

[32] CR Arena, 'Philadelphia-Spanish New Orleans Trade in the 1790s' (1961) 2 *Louisiana History* 429–45.

[33] JG Clark, *New Orleans, 1718–1812: An Economic History* (Baton Rouge LA, 1970) 205–12.

[34] Din and Harkins (n 28) 295.

This move alarmed the United States.[35] So reneging on his promise to Spain not to cede Louisiana to a third party, Napoleon agreed to sell the vast territory to the United States in negotiations concluded in April 1803.[36]

Meanwhile, the newly appointed French *préfet* of Louisiana had already arrived to accept delivery of the colony from the Spanish governor.[37] When he finally took possession on behalf of France on 30 November 1803, it was only to hold it until the Americans came to take possession for the United States. He nevertheless embarked on a number of reforms.[38] On 17 December 1803, three days before transfer to the United States, he issued a proclamation reintroducing the Louisiana *Code Noir* of 1724. He later explained his actions as a response to local pressure.[39]

II TERRITORIAL LOUISIANA: THE MOVE TO CODIFY

The delivery of Louisiana to the United States was accepted by WCC Claiborne, Governor of the Mississippi Territory, and General James Wilkinson.[40] Claiborne issued a proclamation promising protection of the 'liberty, property, and the religion' of the inhabitants, and declaring 'that all laws and municipal regulations which were in existence at the time of the late government remain in full force'.[41]

Congress next divided the new acquisition into two at the 33rd parallel—the District of Louisiana to the north and the Territory of Orleans to the south.[42] The legal histories of the two areas now diverged, as the states eventually formed out of the District of Louisiana all went on to adopt

---

[35] R King to J Madison, 29 March, 1 June 1801, in *State Papers and Correspondence Bearing upon the Purchase of Louisiana* (Washington DC, 2001) 3–4.

[36] Alexander DeConde, *This Affair of Louisiana* (Baton Rouge LA, 1976) 161–75.

[37] GC Din, 'Francisco Bouligny, Marqués de Caso-Calvo, Manuel Juan de Salcedo, Pierre Clément, Baron de Laussat, Colonial Governors, 1799–1803' in Dawson III (ed) (n 26) 74–79, 78–79.

[38] EG Brown, 'Law and Government in the "Louisiana Purchase": 1803–1804' (1956) 2 *Wayne Law Review* 169–89, 186–87; Din and Harkins (n 28) 297–300; A Levasseur (with V Feliú), *Moreau Lislet: The Man Behind the Digest of 1808* (Baton Rouge LA, 2008) 31–32; A Lafargue, 'Pierre Clément de Laussat, Colonial Prefect and High Commissioner of France in Louisiana: His Memoirs, Proclamations, and Orders' (1937) 20 *Louisiana Historical Quarterly* 159–82.

[39] Baade (n 31) 70–72.

[40] See WCC Claiborne and J Wilkinson to J Madison, 20 December 1803, in *State Papers and Correspondence* (n 35) 286–88. For their authority and commissions, see *The Territorial Papers of the United States. Volume IX. The Territory of Orleans 1803–1812*, ed CE Carter (Washington DC, 1940) 89–90, 94–95.

[41] Proclamation, 20 December 1803, in *State Papers and Correspondence* (n 35) 288–89. See also the enabling Act of Congress 31 October 1803, s 2 in *Territorial Papers* (n 40) 89–90 on maintaining the laws in force.

[42] 'Act Erecting Louisiana into Two Territories, and Providing for the Temporary Government Thereof', 26 March 1804, s 1, in *The Statutes at Large of the United States of America* (Boston MA, 1845) vol 2, 283–89.

Anglo-American common law. The District of Louisiana was meanwhile placed under the authority of the governor and judges of the Indiana Territory.[43]

The Territory of Orleans was granted a legislative council and a governor, both to be appointed by the president; courts were created, with typical common law protections for the citizen. Once more the existing laws were stated to be preserved. But the importation into Louisiana of slaves from outside the United States was prohibited, as was that from inside the United States of any slaves who had been imported into the United States after May 1798.[44] Claiborne was appointed governor of the Territory of Orleans, taking the oaths of office on 3 October.[45]

President Jefferson had sought information in advance on what exactly were the laws now declared to remain in force. His most accurate respondent stated that:

> [T]he province is governed entirely by the laws of Spain, and ordinances formed expressly for the colony; it is believed that no correct code can possibly be procured; excepting only a few ordinances promulgated and printed by order of General O'Reilly, respecting principally the laws of inheritance and rights of dower.[46]

Other informants also reported the same problem of access to the sources of the law.[47]

Both Jefferson and Claiborne initially hoped for a reception of Anglo-American common law in Louisiana.[48] For the inhabitants, such ambitions were alarming, viewed as potentially threatening their land titles and other property rights. Restrictions on the importation of slaves were seen to imperil the flourishing plantation system. These anxieties led to a series of debates over preservation of the law.[49] But the greatest tension was

---

[43] Act 26 March 1804 (n 42), s 12; MS Arnold, *Unequal Laws unto a Savage Race: European Legal Traditions in Arkansas, 1696–1836* (Fayetteville AR, 1985) 130–208; S Banner, *Legal Systems in Conflict: Property and Sovereignty in Missouri, 1750–1860* (Norman OK, 2000) 85–151.

[44] Act 26 March 1804 (n 42), ss 2–6, 8–11.

[45] WCC Claiborne to J Madison, 3 October 1804 in *The Official Letter Books of W. C. C. Claiborne, 1801–1816*, ed D Rowland (Jackson MS, 1917) vol 2, 345–46. On attitudes to Claiborne, see RR Couch, 'William Charles Coles Claiborne: An Historiographical Review' (1995) 36 *Louisiana History* 453–65.

[46] See 'Condition of Louisiana in 1803' in JW White, *A New Collection of Laws, Local Charters and Local Ordinances of the Governments of Great Britain, France and Spain, Relating to the Concessions of Land in their Respective Colonies* (Philadelphia PA, 1839) vol 2, 690–98, 692–93. (I am grateful to Professor JW McKnight for bringing this to my attention.)

[47] WCC Claiborne to T Jefferson, 24 August 1803 in *Territorial Papers* (n 40) 19; D Clark to J Madison, 8 September 1803: ibid 35.

[48] G Dargo, *Jefferson's Louisiana: Politics and the Clash of Legal Traditions*, rev edn (Clark NJ, 2009) 85–86, 188–90, 193–94, 199–200, 223.

[49] RH Kilbourne, *A History of the Louisiana Civil Code: The Formative Years, 1803–1839* (Baton Rouge LA, 1987) 1–43; Dargo (n 48) 185–266.

probably over the trade in slaves; this became explicit in the 'Louisiana Remonstrance' of late 1804, seeking admission to the Union, and reversal of the restrictions on importation.[50] Congress responded in March by granting a more democratic constitution to the Territory; but it did so in a way that heightened anxieties about the prevailing laws, since its Act also applied to the Territory provisions of the Northwest Ordinance of 1787, which could be seen as introducing common law.[51] It is questionable whether there was any real threat to the existing law, which had been continuously applied.[52] But next year, JB Prevost, the sole Territorial judge in post, ruled that this provision had not in any way allowed for the replacement of the law in force, so that the Territory's body of private law remained based on its Roman, Spanish, and French foundations.[53]

Even before Congress's Act, the Legislative Council had established a committee to draft civil and criminal codes.[54] A statute on criminal law and procedure followed on 4 May 1805. It provided that all specified crimes 'be taken, intended and construed, according to, and in conformity with, the common law of England'. Reflecting the problem of poor access to legal material, the Act authorised the governor to provide an exposition setting out the details of individual crimes.[55] Claiborne's appointee, Lewis Kerr, had completed the task by the new year.[56]

Probably because of Claiborne's distrust of the men likely to be chosen to do the work, a civil code was not drafted.[57] Instead, on 22 May 1806 the new legislature passed 'An Act declaring the laws which continue to be in force in the Territory of Orleans, and authors which may be recurred to as authorities within the same'. The preamble noted that because of the repeated changes of government, the law was 'wrapped in obscurity': it was therefore necessary to give guidance on the laws until the 'Legislature may

---

[50] Louisiana Remonstrance, in App to *The Debates and Proceedings in the Congress of the United States* (Washington DC, 1852) 1598–1608; WCC Claiborne to T Jefferson, 27 October 1807, in *Territorial Papers* (n 40) 314.

[51] ES Brown, *The Constitutional History of the Louisiana Purchase, 1803–1812* (Berkeley CA, 1920) 154–62; 'Act Further Providing for the Government of the Territory of Orleans', 2 March 1805 in *Statutes at Large* (n 42) vol 2, 322; Dargo (n 48) 223–24.

[52] Kilbourne (n 49) 44–60; MF Fernandez, *From Chaos to Continuity: The Evolution of Louisiana's Legal System, 1712–1862* (Baton Rouge LA, 2001) 25–28.

[53] Kilbourne (n 49) 10–12, 20–22; Dargo (n 48) 230, 264.

[54] WCC Claiborne to J Madison, 6 February 1805, in *Territorial Papers* (n 40) 390; *Acts Passed at the First Session of the Legislative Council of the Territory of Orleans ... One Thousand Eight Hundred and Four* (New Orleans LA, 1805) 458–61.

[55] 'An Act Providing for the Punishment of Crimes and Misdemeanors', c 50 in *Acts* (n 54) 416–53.

[56] See WCC Claiborne to L Kerr, 12 August 1805 and L Kerr to WCC Claiborne, 1 January 1806 in L Kerr, *An Exposition of the Criminal Laws of the Territory of Orleans* (New Orleans LA, 1806) [iv]–[xiii]; WM Billings, 'A Neglected Treatise: Lewis Kerr's *Exposition* and the Making of Criminal Law in Louisiana' (1997) 36 *Louisiana History* 261–86; WM Billings, 'Origins of the Criminal Law in Louisiana' (1991) 31 *Louisiana History* 63–76; Kilbourne (n 49) 29.

[57] J Brown to J Breckinridge, 17 September 1805, in *Territorial Papers* (n 40) 506–13.

form a civil code for the Territory'. The first section accordingly explained 'the laws which remain in force' as the sources of Roman law—the foundation of that of Spain—'aided by the authority of the commentators of the civil law, and particularly by Domat', and the main sources of Spanish law, 'the whole aided by the authority of the reputable commentators admitted in the courts of Justice'.[58] Claiborne vetoed this measure—ascribed to the 'French Lawyers'—on 26 May.[59]

Protests followed: a motion to dissolve the legislature;[60] a 'Manifesto' in the *Telegraphe*;[61] and finally a Resolution to 'appoint James Brown and Moreau Lislet ... to compile and prepare, jointly, a Civil Code for the use of this territory'. Working in consultation with a committee of both houses of the legislature, Brown and Moreau were instructed to 'make the civil law by which this territory is now governed, [*lois civiles qui régisse actuellement*] the ground work of said code'. This time Claiborne did not exercise his veto.[62]

The meaning of the Resolution has been debated: were Moreau and Brown meant to found the new Code on the Spanish law in force? In fact, the *Digest* is modelled on the French *Code civil* of 1804 and its *Projet* of 1800, from which many of its specific articles are also drawn. Some therefore argue that the *Digest* is primarily Spanish law put into French form; others maintain that it is basically French.[63] In fact, the *Digest* is eclectic. Whatever may have been the intention of the legislature, Moreau and Brown interpreted their instructions in a broad way, if within the spirit of the aim expressed that the Code should be based on the civil law: after all, one of the main legislative objectives was creating accessible law. And they had the riches of three Atlantic legal worlds to draw on. Blackstone's *Commentaries*, a paradigmatic text of the common law, was an available source incorporating many universal rules.

III MOREAU, BROWN, AND BLACKSTONE

To understand the use made of Blackstone by the codifiers, it is important to say a little about the two men. Louis Moreau Lislet was one of the many

---

[58] Quoted in EG Brown, 'Legal Systems in Conflict: Orleans Territory 1804–1812' (1957) 1 *American Journal of Legal History* (1957) 35–75, 47–48; Levasseur (n 38) 54–57, n 71.
[59] WCC Claiborne to J Madison, 22 May 1806, in *Letter Books* (n 45) vol 3, 305–06; 'Message to the Legislative Council, and to the House of Representatives', in ibid vol 3, 313.
[60] WCC Claiborne to J Poydras, 26 May 1806, in *Letter Books* (n 45) vol 3, 315.
[61] WCC Claiborne to J Madison, 3 June 1806, *Territorial Papers* (n 40) 642–57.
[62] Resolutions [Résolution à la formation d'un Code Civil] in *Acts Passed at the First Session of the First Legislature of the Territory of Orleans ... One Thousand Eight Hundred and Six* (New Orleans LA, 1807) 214–19.
[63] JW Cairns, 'The de la Vergne Volume and the Digest of 1808' (2009) 24 *Tulane European and Civil Law Forum* 31–81, 35–38.

refugees from St Domingue who came to Louisiana.[64] After legal study in Paris, he had practised law in his home island; the slave rebellion and other upheavals led him to flee to Cuba, where he lived for a year, before arriving as a refugee in New Orleans, probably a year or so after the US takeover.[65] By 1806 he had already held a number of offices, including as translator; indeed he had provided the translation of Lewis Kerr's *Exposition*.[66] If he had not been so before, this certainly would have made him familiar with Blackstone's work, which was cited and quoted by Kerr.[67]

James Brown is the more interesting choice, as he had once been in favour of some measure of reception of common law.[68] Virginian by birth, he had attended Liberty Hall (later Washington and Lee University) and, briefly, the College of William and Mary, before practising as a lawyer in Kentucky, where he served as secretary to the governor. He moved to the Territory of Orleans in 1804. Initially appointed secretary to the Territory, he became US District Attorney. With a knowledge of French and Spanish, he had also successfully practised before the Louisiana courts. His training in law will have made him familiar with Blackstone. Much better connected than the outsider Moreau, he enjoyed the patronage that facilitated his more distinguished political career. He served twice as senator for Louisiana after statehood in 1812; from 1823 to 1829 he was US minister to France.[69]

IV ACCESSIBLE TEXTS OF BLACKSTONE

Michael Hoeflich has rightly pointed out that there were many *Commentaries*.[70] Which edition was used in producing the *Digest*? Guzmán Brito has shown that, as well as the *Commentaries* themselves, Edward Christian's 'Notes' to Blackstone's text were utilised.[71] (Kerr had also used these.[72]) Christian's notes were first found in the 12th edition of Blackstone, published by Cadell in London in 1793–95. The subsequent London editions of 1800 and 1803 also included them. Indeed their inclusion became standard.[73] There is no reason to believe that in drafting the *Digest* the redactors relied on a single edition of the *Commentaries*; but

---

[64] N Dessens, *From Saint-Domingue to New Orleans: Migration and Influences* (Gainesville FL, 2007) 6–21.
[65] See Levasseur (n 38) 95–113.
[66] Ibid 114–16; the French title page of the *Exposition* (n 56) states that the *Explication des lois Criminelles* was 'traduit en français par L. Moreau Lislet'.
[67] See, eg, Kerr, *Exposition* (n 56) 12–13, 18–19, 20–21, 22–23, 24–25, and *passim*.
[68] J Brown to J Breckinridge, 17 September 1805, in *Territorial Papers* (n 44) 506–13, 507.
[69] JW Bradley, 'James Brown' in JW Bradley (ed), *Interim Appointment: W.C.C. Claiborne Letter Book, 1804–1805, with Biographical Sketches* (Baton Rouge LA, 2002) 258–65.
[70] Hoeflich (n 1) 171.
[71] Guzmán Brito (n 15) 185.
[72] Kerr, *Exposition* (n 56) 10 note*.
[73] Eller 10–13; MH Hoffheimer, 'The Common Law of Edward Christian' (1994) 53 *Cambridge Law Journal* 140–63, 146.

if they did, the earliest that could have been used, because of the notes, was that of 1793–95. There had been a number of American editions to 1800 without Christian's notes, though these were published separately in 1801, as the fifth volume of the Boston duodecimo edition of 1799.[74] An important American edition was published in Philadelphia in five volumes by St George Tucker in 1803.[75] It also retained many of Christian's notes, including that identified by Guzmán Brito as drawn on in the *Digest*.[76] Any of these editions could have been used; minute study of variations and correspondences in punctuation does not provide reliable evidence. The inventory of Moreau's property at his death lists 'Blackstone's Commentaries 5 in 12'.[77] The duodecimo format of the five volumes suggests it was probably the Boston edition of 1799 with its extra volume of 1801.[78] But there is no way to know when he acquired this set, so it is impossible to take this inquiry further.[79]

Was use made of the French translation of 1774? The inventory of Moreau Lislet's property at his death lists 'Commentaires de Blackstone 6 [in 12]'.[80] The listing of six volumes indicates that this was either the French translation of 1774, or the new French translation of 1822–23 by NM Chompré, both of which were in six volumes.[81] Neither was a duodecimo in format; but the identification is certain, and the listing of the format is probably a clerical error, as the entry is in the middle of a sequence of books in duodecimo. Again, there is no way of knowing when Moreau acquired this, even if it was the edition of 1774.

The only way to know whether the French translation was used is through examination of the texts. Comparison of the French text of every article of the *Digest* in which Batiza suggested there was influence from the text of Blackstone with the corresponding French text of 1774 reveals only two articles in which there are strong similarities. Both are in the preliminary title.

---

[74] Eller 37–42.

[75] StG Tucker (ed), *Blackstone's Commentaries: With Notes of Reference, to the Constitution and Laws, of the Federal Government of the United States; and of the Commonwealth of Virginia* (Philadelphia PA, 1803).

[76] Hoffheimer (n 73) 146; Eller 42–43; *Blackstone's Commentaries* (n 75) vol 1, 59 note*.

[77] Act No 1,185, 19 December 1832, by Notary LT Caire, Notarial Archives, New Orleans. M Franklin, 'Libraries of Edward Livingston and of Moreau Lislet' (1941) 15 *Tulane Law Review* 401–14, 408 does not list the format. From context it is unlikely, though just possible, that 'in 12' means bound in 12 volumes.

[78] Eller 41–42.

[79] We do not know which edition of the *Commentaries* the compilers used, although it must have been the 12th English edition or later, since that was the first with Christian's notes. However, because the wording of the relevant passages is essentially unchanged in later editions, references below are to the first edition of 1765–69.

[80] Act No 1,185, 19 December 1832 (n 77); Franklin (n 77) 406.

[81] *Commentaires* (n 3); *Commentaires sur les lois anglaises, par W. Blackstone, avec des notes de M. Ed. Christian; Traduits de l'anglais sur la quinzième édition par N.-M. Chompré* (Paris, 1822–23).

First, French Blackstone:

> Les mots doivent être entendus dans le sens le plus connus & le plus usité; c'est-à-dire, en faisant plus d'attention à l'usage général & populaire, qu'à la propriété grammaticale ...[82]

Digest:

> Les termes d'une loi doivent être généralement entendus dans leur signification la plus connue et la plus usitée, sans s'attacher autant aux raffinemens des règles de la grammaire, qu'à leur acceptation générale et vulgaire.[83]

English Blackstone:

> Words are generally to be understood in their usual and most known signification; not so much regarding the propriety of grammar, as their general and popular use.[84]

Digest:

> The words of a law are generally to be understood in their most known and usual signification, without attending so much to the niceties of grammar rules as to their general and popular use.[85]

Secondly, French Blackstone:

> Le moyen enfin le plus universel & le plus efficace pour découvrir le véritable sens d'une Loi, lorsque les mots sont douteux, est d'en considérer la raison & l'esprit; c'est-à-dire, le motif qui l'a fait faire.[86]

Digest:

> Le moyen enfin le plus universel et le plus efficace pour découvrir le véritable sens d'une loi, lorsque les expressions en sont douteuses, est de considérer la raison et l'esprit de cette loi, ou la cause qui a déterminé la Législature à la rendre.[87]

English Blackstone:

> [T]he most universal and effectual way of discovering the true meaning of a law, when the words are dubious, is by considering the *reason* and *spirit* of it; or the cause which moved the legislator to enact it.[88]

Digest:

> The most universal and effectual way of discovering the true meaning of a law, when its expressions are dubious, is by considering the reason and spirit of it, or the cause which induced the legislature to enact it.[89]

---

[82] *Commentaires* (n 3) vol 1, 86.
[83] *Digest*, art 14 (p 5) (*Tit Prél* 14).
[84] *Commentaries* vol 1, 59.
[85] *Digest*, art 14 (p 4) (Prel Tit 14).
[86] *Commentaires* (n 3) vol 1, 88.
[87] *Digest*, art 18 (p 7) (*Tit Prél* 18).
[88] *Commentaries* vol 1, 61.
[89] *Digest*, art 18 (pp 4–6) (Prel Tit 18).

These—particularly the second—are sufficiently close that it is improbable that the similarities are the result of random chance in translating.[90] It is likely that whoever translated the draft articles from English, aware of the use of Blackstone, utilised the French translation—in itself a perfectly sensible thing to do. That this happened only twice probably reflects the rather free quality of the French translation.

What this confirms, however, is that the redactors worked primarily from an English-language edition of the *Commentaries*, with which they would both have been perfectly familiar. Indeed, Moreau Lislet had translated passages from it for his version of Kerr's *Exposition*.[91] The actual translator of the draft articles was neither Moreau Lislet nor James Brown. The Territorial Legislature made special provision to pay 'the two [unnamed] translators' in 1807.[92]

V WHY USE BLACKSTONE?

The only evidence of the codifiers' purpose in consulting Blackstone is the actual use they made of the *Commentaries* in the *Digest*. It is unnecessary to examine every article in which the wording is drawn from its text.[93] The redactors used it as the foundation for the drafts of articles in the Preliminary Title and in three titles of Book One ('Of Persons'): 'Of Master and Servant', 'Of Parent and 'Child', and 'Of Communities and Corporations'.

Two articles from the Preliminary Title have already been examined. In all, four are drawn from Blackstone.[94] Quoting another merely confirms what is already obvious.

Digest:

> Where the words of a law are dubious, their meaning may be sought by examining the context, with which the ambiguous words, phrases and sentences may be compared in order to ascertain their true meaning.[95]

---

[90] *Commentaires* (n 3) vol 2, 209–10 in some respects resembles *Digest*, art 16 (p 91) (*Communautés*, art 16), but the differences are enough to make me cautious.

[91] Comparison of translated passages shows he is not using the 1774 French translation. Compare, eg, the lengthy passage in Kerr, *Exposition* (n 56) 75–77 with *Commentaires* (n 3) vol 5, 364–65. Moreau's translation is rather better.

[92] 'An Act to fix the compensation to be allowed to the two Jurisconsults, appointed to prepare a civil code ... and to the translators of the said code', 14 April 1807, ch 31, s 2, in *Acts Passed at the Second Session of the First Legislature of the Territory of Orleans* (New Orleans LA, 1807) 190–92, 191–92.

[93] I do not accept Batiza's claim of 30: see below for instances.

[94] A fifth recognised by Batiza as 'partially influenced' by Blackstone is in fact drawn from Christian's Notes: Guzmán Brito (n 15) 185.

[95] *Digest*, art 16 (p 4) (Prel Tit 16).

Blackstone:

> If words happen to be still dubious, we may establish their meaning from the context; with which it may be of singular use to compare a word, or a sentence, whenever they are ambiguous, equivocal, or intricate.[96]

As Guzmán Brito's study shows, the provisions from Blackstone in the preliminary title all concern interpretation and are immediately rooted in a natural law tradition that may be traced back to Pufendorf and Grotius.

Batiza identified three articles in the title 'Of Father and Child' as originating in the *Commentaries*. Two of these, articles 50 and 60, seem linguistically too remote from the text of Blackstone, though described by Batiza as a 'substantial influence', for it to be their likely textual source, though the same—perfectly common—idea is expressed.[97] The remaining article states:

> Fathers and mothers may justify themselves in an action began against them, for assault and battery, if they have acted in defence of the persons of their children.[98]

Blackstone:

> A parent may also justify an assault and battery in defence of the persons of his children …[99]

While not perhaps 'almost verbatim', it is probable that the redactors were here drawing on the language of the *Commentaries*.[100] But again there is nothing remarkable or unique in the text, which also reflects a provision in Kerr's *Exposition*.[101] The last part of the 39th article of this title states that parents of a child under the age of puberty 'have a right to correct him or her, provided it be done in a reasonable manner'.[102] This seems influenced by the wording of Blackstone: 'He may lawfully correct his child, being under age, in a reasonable manner'.[103] Neither Batiza nor Tucker noticed this influence. Both French and Castilian law had provisions on chastisement, which were potentially rather more extensive. But Blackstone's language has here been drawn on as providing a useful expression of a desirable rule.[104]

Greater use was made of Blackstone in the sixth title, 'Of Master and Servant'. Batiza claims that Blackstone is a source of the second, third

---

[96] *Commentaries* vol 1, 60.
[97] *Digest*, arts 50 and 60 (pp 54, 56) (I.vii.50, 60); *Commentaries* vol 1, 434–37.
[98] *Digest*, art 56 (p 54) (I.vii.56).
[99] *Commentaries* vol 1, 438.
[100] Batiza (n 14) 54.
[101] Kerr, *Exposition* (n 56) 16–17.
[102] *Digest*, art 39 (p 52) (I.vii.39).
[103] *Commentaries* vol 1, 440.
[104] Cairns (n 16) 299–302.

and eighth articles of the title;[105] I doubt this for the second; but it may be that his text inspired aspects of the third and the eighth. The language is too remote for certainty, given the very general content of the provisions.[106] The 10th, 11th and 12th articles of the title definitely draw on the *Commentaries*.[107] The example of article 11 may be given:

> The master may bring an action against any man for beating or maiming his servant, but in such case, he must assign as a cause of action his own damage arising from the loss of his service and this loss must be proved upon the trial.[108]

Blackstone:

> A master also may bring an action against any man for beating or maiming his servant: but in such case he must assign, as a special reason for so doing, his own damage by the loss of his service; and this loss must be proved upon the trial.[109]

Again there is nothing particularly unusual about the text in juridical terms.[110] Batiza and Tucker also consider the *Commentaries* as the source of articles 13 and 14.[111] The first is linguistically remote.[112] The second enunciates a version of the Praetorian *actio de effusis vel deiectis*. Blackstone does set out a version of this, even referring to the Roman law; again, his passage is relatively remote in wording, but given that the redactors are using Blackstone extensively here, it may be that he has inspired both this and the preceding article, if not providing directly usable text.[113] As with the other uses of Blackstone, all these provisions on 'Master and Servant' draw on the general European tradition in this area of the law.

The first chapter of the title 'Of Communities or Corporations' has a number of articles in which Blackstone may have exercised a general influence, but it is once more difficult to pinpoint direct influence from his wording.[114] In the next chapter, the same may be said of articles 7, 15, and 22 (although there may be more influence on the latter).[115] Article 9 is even more clearly influenced by Blackstone.[116] There are also a number

---

[105] Batiza (n 14) 51.
[106] Cairns (n 16) 518–19, 526–27.
[107] Batiza (n 14) 51; Tucker (n 13) 280 n 84; Cairns (n 16) 528–31.
[108] *Digest*, art 11 (p 38) (I.vi.11).
[109] *Commentaries* vol 1, 417.
[110] Cairns (n 16) 528–30.
[111] Batiza (n 14) 51; Tucker (n 13) 280 n 84.
[112] Cairns (n 16) 532.
[113] Ibid 532–34.
[114] Batiza (n 14) 61.
[115] *Digest*, arts 7, 15, 22 (pp 88–92); *Commentaries* vol 1, 462, 464–65, 472–73. Batiza (n 14) 62 states art 19 is 'substantially influenced' and art 21 'partially influenced' by Blackstone. But though these provisions are compatible with the English author's views, I do not see this so clearly.
[116] *Digest*, art 9 (p 88) (I.x.9); *Commentaries* vol 1, 474.

of articles where the text of the *Commentaries* has exercised discernible influence on the wording. Thus the *Digest*:

> Communities or corporations must not only be authorised by the legislature, but a name must be given to them; and it is in that name they must sue or be sued, and do all their legal acts, although a slight alteration in this name be not important.[117]

Blackstone:

> When a corporation is erected, a name must be given it; and by that name alone it must sue and be sued, and do all legal acts; though a very minute variation is not material.[118]

But two further articles very directly draw on the wording of Blackstone. *Digest*:

> In the same manner, a community or corporation cannot bring an action for assault and battery or for other like injuries; for a corporation can neither beat nor be beaten in its political capacity.[119]

Blackstone:

> It can neither maintain, or be made defendant to, an action of battery or such like personal injuries: for a corporation can neither beat nor be beaten, in its body politic.[120]

Digest:

> A corporation cannot commit the crime of treason or any other crime or offence in its political capacity, although its members may be guilty of those crimes in their individual and respective capacities.[121]

Blackstone:

> A corporation cannot commit treason, or felony, or other crime, in its corporate capacity: though its members may, in their distinct individual capacities.[122]

Putting aside small points of detail, the passages adopted from Blackstone deal with the essential nature of a corporation as a legal person.

Examination of the articles shows there was no intention to use the *Commentaries* to incorporate specific or peculiar rules of English law into the civil law of Louisiana in a random or unprincipled way. The articles derived from Blackstone all embodied commonplaces or standard

---

[117] *Digest*, art 6 (p 88) (I.x.6).
[118] *Commentaries* vol 1, 462.
[119] *Digest*, art 17 (p 90) (I.x.17).
[120] *Commentaries* vol 1, 464.
[121] *Digest*, art 18 (p 90) (I.x.18).
[122] *Commentaries* vol 1, 464.

provisions of law or a rule the redactors thought desirable and compatible with their Code. In this respect it is important to recall Guzmán Brito's demonstration that rules on interpretation incorporated into the *Digest* derived from the English author's study of Pufendorf.[123] Blackstone was used when he provided a neatly turned, borrowable expression in English of a general rule embodying universal practice. He was not being used to express Spanish law in English dress! He was seen as a source of both *ius naturale* and *ius gentium*, with transplantable texts.

VI THE DIGEST AND BLACKSTONE'S LEGAL TAXONOMY

Moreau Lislet and Brown drew on the structure of the French *Code civil* and its *Projet* for the structure of the *Digest*. Each has a preliminary title or book;[124] all three are then divided into a book on persons, a book on property, and a book on acquisition of property. But the adoption of the French structure is at its most obvious in the second and third books of the *Digest*.

The first book of the *Digest*, '*Des Personnes*', varies quite significantly from the two French models. It consists of 10 titles: I: 'Of the Distinction of Persons, and the Privation of Certain Civil Rights in Certain Cases'; II: 'Of Domicil and the Manner of Changing the Same'; III: 'Of Absent Persons'; IV: 'Of Husband and Wife'; V: 'Of the Separation from Bed and Board'; VI: 'Of Master and Servant'; VII: 'Of Father and Child'; VIII: 'Of Minors. Of their Tutorship, Curatorship and Emancipation'; IX: 'Of Persons Insane, Idiots, and Other Persons Incapable of Administering Their Estate'; X: 'Of Communities or Corporations'. This contains some noticeable differences from the French *Code civil*, which also has 10 titles. Most obviously the latter has no equivalent to the titles 'Master and Servant' and 'Corporations'; correspondingly the *Digest* has no equivalent to the *Code*'s 'Enjoyment and Deprivation of Civil Rights' and 'Acts of Civil Status'.[125] There are other more subtle differences. Thus, while the French Code has a title 'Du

---

[123] Guzmán Brito (n 15) 178.

[124] The *Code civil* has a short preliminary title of six articles. The *Projet* has an extensive *Livre préliminaire* of 49 articles, divided into six titles. The *Digest* has a preliminary title of 24 articles divided between five chapters. In some ways it resembles a compromise between the two models.

[125] *Code civil des français*: '*Titre préliminaire*'; Book I: 'De la jouissance et de la privation des droits civils'; II: 'Des actes de l'état civil'; III: 'Du domicile'; IV: 'Des absens'; V: 'Du marriage'; VI: 'Du divorce'; VII: 'De la paternité et de la filiation'; VIII: 'De l'adoption et de la tutelle officieuse'; IX: 'De la puissance paternelle'; X: 'De la minorité, de la tutelle et de l'émancipation'; XI: 'De la majorité, de l'interdiction et du conseil judiciaire'; *Projet* of 1800: Livre préliminaire: 'Du droit et des lois'; Bk 1: I: 'Des personnes qui jouissent des droits civils, et de celles qui n'en jouissent pas'; II: 'Des actes destinés à constater l'état civil'; III: 'Du domicile'; IV: 'Des absens'; V: 'Du mariage'; VI: 'Du divorce'; VII: 'De la paternité et de la filiation'; VIII: 'De la puissance paternelle'; IX: 'De la minorité, de la tutelle et de l'émancipation'; X: 'De la majorité et de l'interdiction'.

marriage', the *Digest* has 'Of Husband and Wife'; likewise, for the *Code civil*'s 'De la paternité', the *Digest* has 'Of Father and Child'. The French *Code* has given the material a more abstract feel.

The French *Code*'s focus is on *'Personnes'* as citizens; this is not the case for the *Digest*. The former's titles on enjoyment and deprivation of civil rights and acts of civil status deal with issues of acquisition of citizenship and its loss, and the documentation of citizens through the registration of the formal acts marking birth, marriage and death. These provisions were simply inappropriate for Louisiana. It is true that the *Digest*'s first title does cover 'Privation of Certain Civil Rights in Certain Cases'; what it deals with, however, are issues of the restricted capacity of minors, the insane and slaves, while the French *Code*'s 'privation des droits civils' concerns the loss of civil rights through loss of citizenship or criminal condemnation.

If the *Code civil* and its *Projet* have provided inspiration for the structure of the *Digest*, the variations in the first book are derived from the redactors' study of Blackstone. The first 13 chapters of the first book of the *Commentaries* can be classed—if crudely—as dealing with constitutional law: in reality they are dealing with this material relating to persons using categories of duties drawn from natural law. But if we look at the 14th to 18th chapters we find the following: 'Of Master and Servant'; 'Of Husband and Wife'; 'Of Parent and Child'; 'Of Guardian and Ward'; 'Of Corporations'. I do not think it is too much to suggest that the redactors of the *Digest* have copied Blackstone's wording here for the name of the titles on 'Husband and Wife' or 'Parent and Child'. Be that as it may, there can be little doubt that the *Commentaries* provided the inspiration behind the inclusion of titles on corporations and master and servant.

A supporting influence encouraging the adoption and adaptation of a structure from Blackstone probably derived from the redactors' reading of the *Livre Préliminaire* to Jean Domat's important treatise, *Les Loix civiles dans leur ordre naturel*, first published in 1689.[126] Domat reorganised the civil law, structuring it according to a natural law scheme, which founded all law in a divine natural law.[127] After a brief introduction, Domat had divided the short title discussing persons in his *Livre Préliminaire* into two sections: 'De l'état des personnes par la nature'; 'De l'état des personnes par les Loix civiles'. Each section had its own introduction before being divided into numbered paragraphs. The *Digest* follows this model, with two chapters: 'De la Distinction des Personnes telle qu'elle est établie par la Nature'; 'De la Distinction des Personnes telle qu'elle est établie par la Loi'.

---

[126] J Domat, *Les Loix civiles dans leur ordre naturel; le droit public, et legum delectus* ed L de Héricourt (Paris, 1735) 10–15 (Liv Prél Tit II).

[127] See eg D Gilles, 'Les *Lois civiles* de Jean Domat, prémices à la Codification. Du Code Napoléon au *Code Civil du Bas Canada*' (2009) 43 ns *Revue juridique Thémis* 1–49, 12–23; B Edelman, 'Domat et la naissance du sujet de droit' (1994) 39 *Archives de philosophie de droit* 389–419.

Of course, such a division was commonplace in natural law theorising; but here the redactors were undoubtedly following Domat. The 12 articles of the first chapter are very closely derived from Domat's first section.[128] The 13th article, first of the second chapter of this title of the *Digest* states:

> L'esclave est celui qui est sous la puissance d'un maître et qui lui appartient; de sorte que le maître peut le vendre et disposer de sa personne, de son industrie et de son travail, sans qu'il puisse rien faire, rien avoir, ni rien acquérir qui ne soit à son maître.[129]

As Batiza pointed out, this is drawn 'verbatim' from Domat.[130] It is then followed by another six articles covering freed and free-born individuals, as well as children in power, and those under tutorship or curatorship. All these articles are closely based on the text of Domat's second section.[131] Domat's own analysis, however, extended beyond this. He also mentioned prodigals, the status of subjects of the king and of foreigners, civil death, the position of those who professed religion as monks, ecclesiastical persons, and ecclesiastical and lay corporations.[132] Overall, the topics dealt with here by Domat have a resemblance to those dealt with by Blackstone in his first book, and may have encouraged reliance on the latter.

Probably again influenced by Domat's analysis, the redactors copied Blackstone by ending their book 'Of Persons' with a title on 'Communities and Corporations'; Blackstone also exercised influence on some of its articles. Though the French *Code civil* did not deal with artificial persons, it may have seemed good to the redactors to include them, since there already were quite a number in the Territory, such as the religious orders. Further, unlike the *Code civil*, the *Digest*'s focus was on 'persons' in a traditional sense, not on citizens.

The *Civil Code of Lower Canada* of 1866 also concludes its first book with a title on corporations. The members of the Codification Commission of Lower Canada noted that this title was not found in the French Code, in which corporations were mentioned only incidentally; they then cited Saint-Joseph's *Concordance* as stating that corporations were not properly part of the civil law.[133] The Commission disagreed, writing:

> It is true corporations owe their existence to the public authority (royal or legislative). Once created ... they become artificial persons, capable of certain rights

---

[128] Batiza (n 14) 46.
[129] *Digest*, art 13 (p 11); in English (p 10): 'A slave is one who is in the power of a master and who belongs to him in such a manner, that the master may sell him, dispose of his person, his industry and his labor, and who can do nothing, possess nothing, nor acquire any thing, but what must belong to his master.'
[130] Domat (n 126) 14 (Liv Prél Tit Sect 2, no I); Batiza (n 14) 46.
[131] Batiza (n 14) 46–47.
[132] Domat (n 126) 15 (Liv Prél Tit Sect 2, nos 10–15).
[133] *Reports of the Commissioners Appointed to Codify the Laws of Lower Canada in Civil Matters*, 2nd edn (Quebec, 1865) vol 1, 229 (Second Report); A de Saint-Joseph, *Concordance entre les codes civils étrangers et le Code Napoléon*, 2nd edn (Paris, 1856) vol 2, 477.

and privileges and bound by certain duties and obligations; but these rights and these duties are not in all respects those of ordinary persons; the very nature of corporations, their object and destination, are the necessary causes of several of these differences, while others proceed from precautions which public interest has caused to be taken ...[134]

The Commission suggested that the omission of such a title from the French Code was probably due to the slight attention paid to corporations in France before the Revolution of 1789 because of the role of the Crown. They had decided to remedy this deficiency and provide a title 'in imitation of that to be found in the code of Louisiana'.[135] It is likely that similar thinking motivated the redactors of the *Digest*. Corporations—like slavery—needed particular treatment, as Blackstone had shown.

VII THE DIGEST, SLAVERY AND BLACKSTONE

The *Digest* was drafted during a complex period of shifting political and legal circumstances concerning slavery and the slave trade. In 1794, following the slave revolt in Moreau Lislet's St Domingue, slavery had been abolished in the French colonies.[136] In 1802 Napoleon sent an army to restore French authority in the island. A brutal, essentially racial, war resulted, with the colony ultimately becoming independent under the name Haiti.[137] Slavery was reintroduced in French colonies; but, since it was supposedly not found in France itself, the *Code civil* could ignore it.[138]

Since St Domingue had been a major producer of sugar, the revolt and wars dramatically affected the world's sugar market. The sugar industry now developed into a major driver of the economy in the lower part of Louisiana. Sugar cultivation made intensive use of slave labour, which encouraged the thriving slave trade to New Orleans.[139] This explains the opposition to Congress's attempts to restrict the further importing of slaves into the Orleans Territory. The revolt and war also scattered refugees—and their slaves and free black servants—around the Caribbean, resulting in

---

[134] *Reports of the Commissioners* (n 133) vol 1, p 229 (Second Report).
[135] Ibid 231.
[136] S Peabody and K Grinberg, *Slavery, Freedom, and the Law in the Atlantic World: A Brief History with Documents* (Boston MA, 2007) 57–62; L Sala-Molins, *Le Code Noir ou le calvaire de Canaan* (Paris, 2006) 261–74.
[137] PR Girard, 'Liberté, Égalité, Esclavage: French Revolutionary Ideals and the Failure of the Leclerc Expedition to Saint-Domingue' (2005) 6 *French Colonial History* 55–77; PR Girard, 'Caribbean Genocide: Racial War in Haiti, 1802–4' (2005) 39 *Patterns of Prejudice* 138–61.
[138] Sala-Molins (n 136) 274–75; Palmer (n 22) 123–25.
[139] A Rothman, *Slave Country: American Expansion and the Origins of the Deep South* (Cambridge MA, 2005) 73–95; Ingersoll (n 19) 181–209.

some complex questions about the legal status of the servants, given the earlier emancipation decrees.[140]

In 1806 almost half the population of the parish of New Orleans consisted of black slaves; 'free blacks' made up another 14 per cent.[141] The Territorial Legislature was dominated by planters—the very planters who had been keen to get the French *préfet* to replace the Spanish slave law with that of France, even if his proclamation seems to have been ignored.[142] In the same year the Legislature enacted an extensive 'Black Code' to regulate slavery.[143] This was partly influenced by the provisions on slavery found in other southern jurisdictions of the United States, particularly the law of South Carolina. The Black Code also had a few provisions on the position of 'free persons of color', given what some have seen as Louisiana's 'three-caste society'.[144] Though the place of such individuals was recognised to some extent in the *Digest*, its provisions on slavery and freedom were mainly 'colour-blind'.[145]

As Vernon Palmer has pointed out, there was no particular desire for the law on slavery to be either Spanish or French—it simply had to be effective, giving the planters the authority they considered they needed, making them feel secure.[146] The last must have been a very significant issue, after the recent horrors in St Domingue, from where so many recent immigrants had come to Louisiana.[147] Slave rebellion was always a real threat.[148] And in

---

[140] There have been a number of recent specific studies: MS Jones, 'The Case of Jean Baptiste, un créole de Saint-Domingue: Narrating Slavery, Freedom, and the Haitian Revolution in Baltimore City' in B Ward, M Bone and WA Link (eds), *The American South and the Atlantic World* (Gainesville FL, 2013) 104–28; GT Nessler, '"They always knew her to be free": Emancipation and Re-Enslavement in French Santo-Domingo' (2012) 33 *Slavery and Abolition* 87–103; RJ Scott, '"She ... Refuses to Deliver Herself up as the Slave of Your Petitioner": Émigrés, Enslavement, and the Louisiana Digest of the Civil Laws' (2009) 24 *Tulane European and Civil Law Forum* 115–36.

[141] Ingersoll (n 19) 247–48.

[142] JK Schafer, *Slavery, the Civil Law, and the Supreme Court of Louisiana* (Baton Rouge LA, 1994) 3.

[143] 'An Act Prescribing the Rules and Conduct to be Observed with Respect to Negroes and Other Slaves of this Territory' (c 33), in *Acts Passed at the First Session of the First Legislature* (n 62) 150–212. See also 'An Act to Regulate the Conditions and Forms of the Emancipation of Slaves' (c 10), and 'An Act to Amend the Act Entitled "An Act Prescribing the Rules and Conduct to be Observed with Respect to Negroes and Other Slaves of this Territory"' (c 30), in *Acts* (n 92) 82–88, 186–90.

[144] KS Hanger, *Bounded Lives, Bounded Places: Free Black Society in Colonial New Orleans, 1769–1803* (Durham NC, 1997); PF Lachance, 'The Formation of a Three-Caste Society: Evidence from Wills in Antebellum New Orleans' (1994) 18 *Social Science History* 211–42.

[145] 'Colour' is relevant in *Digest*, art 8 (p 24), art 30 (p 50) which discriminate among free people on the grounds of colour.

[146] Palmer (n 22) 115–23.

[147] Dessens (n 64) 22–45.

[148] JH Dormon, 'The Persistent Specter: Slave Rebellion in Territorial Louisiana' (1977) 18 *Louisiana History* 389–404; GC Din, 'Carondelet, the Cabildo, and Slaves: Louisiana in 1795' (1977) 38 *Louisiana History* 5–28.

1811 the largest slave rebellion in US history arose in the sugar parishes of the 'German Coast' of the Mississippi above New Orleans. James Brown's plantation was one of the centres of the revolt.[149]

What this indicates is that the *Digest*, unlike the *Code civil*, had to deal with slavery. The institutional tradition inherited from Rome had treated slavery as part of the law of persons, even though slaves were property. For the Romans, who had not developed modern ideas of legal personality, there was no contradiction, though it seems inconsistent to the modern mind. As Palmer has pointed out, this is also found in the Castilian law.[150] Domat's analysis of 'Personnes' in his *Livre Préliminaire* had sufficient similarity with the structure of the titles of the first book of Blackstone's *Commentaries* for Moreau and Brown to have felt quite comfortable in adopting aspects of Blackstone to develop the structure of the first book of the *Digest*. Blackstone provided a way to incorporate slavery into the *Digest*, through his inclusion of his *Commentaries* of a title on 'Of Master and Servant'. Here he even discussed slavery relatively extensively, in a passage on 'the several sorts of servants';[151] slightly relocated, this title fitted into the first book of the *Digest*, with some of his text adapted to fit the second chapter of the title.

VIII CONCLUSION

Moreau and Brown were both slave-owners.[152] Neither opposed slavery.[153] After the revolt of 1811, the heads of a number of Brown's slaves were stuck on pikes along the levee.[154] The codifiers in Brazil apparently encountered difficulty in drafting a civil code when slavery still existed in law.[155] Moreau and Brown had no such problem; for them the law on persons was not linked to citizenship and if it suited them they categorised slaves as 'persons'.[156] When the first book of the French *Code civil* proved insufficient for what was wanted, Blackstone's *Commentaries*, familiar to both of them, showed how to incorporate slavery (and corporations) into the *Digest*. Underlying the structures of the *Code civil*, the *Digest*

---

[149] Rothman (n 139) 106–17.
[150] Palmer (n 22) 125–26.
[151] *Commentaries* vol 1, 411–13. See also ibid 123.
[152] Levasseur (n 38) 283–91.
[153] Ibid 147.
[154] D Rasmussen, *American Uprising: The Untold Story of America's Largest Slave Revolt* (New York NY, 2012) 151–57.
[155] K Grinberg, 'Slavery, Liberalism, and Civil Law: Definitions of Status and Citizenship in the Elaboration of the Brazilian Civil Code (1855–1916)' in S Caulfield, SC Chambers and L Putnam (ed), *Honor, Status, and Law in Modern Latin America* (Durham NC, 2005) 109–127.
[156] *Digest*, art 47 (p 66), art 105 (pp 230–32), art 24 (p 264).

and Blackstone is the structure of Justinian's *Institutes*, drawing on a variation of the Gaian scheme dividing all law into that relating to persons, things and actions. The *Commentaries* belonged to the European genre of institutional writing—this made their structure easy to adapt for the *Digest* and their specific provisions potentially influential or transplantable.[157]

But Blackstone, like Domat, may have held other attractions for the redactors. The *Code civil*, with its legislative positivism and focus on citizenship and registration of civil acts, was less appealing than Blackstone's natural law approach with its more traditional focus on 'Persons': hence their preference for Blackstone's headings 'Husband and Wife' and 'Father and Child' over the more abstract 'Du mariage' and 'De la paternité et de la filiation'.

The explanation given here of the use of Blackstone has focused on the need to incorporate slavery into the *Digest*. Blackstone himself explained that he discussed master and servant where he did because he was turning to consider the 'rights and duties [of persons] in private *oeconomical* relations'.[158] For Blackstone, servants were concerned with households: hence their appearance in this part of his *Commentaries*. Other institutional works mentioned servants where Justinian's *Institutes* had discussed slavery.[159] So the *Commentaries* provided an obvious template for the redactors of the *Digest*. Once a decision was made to deal with slavery in the *Digest*, it became necessary to find a way to implement it; Blackstone showed how.

The redactors of the *Digest* of 1808 found Blackstone's *Commentaries* valuable not because of their discussions of the English common law, but because the English scholar and judge had composed an institutional work, heavily influenced by natural law, comparable to many continental ones. The parallels between Domat and Blackstone made this obvious. Though Blackstone drew heavily on the institutional scheme of his predecessor, Thomas Wood, an English civilian, he also used a natural law analysis—adapted to an English governmental structure—to develop a version of the institutional structure.[160] In Louisiana, the redactors used aspects of Blackstone that were essentially universal rather than 'English'.

The use of Blackstone in Territorial Louisiana demonstrates the coalescing rather than the clash of the three Atlantic legal traditions involved. A universal Enlightenment treatise, the *Commentaries* could be used for ends that would have surprised the author.

---

[157] JW Cairns, 'Blackstone, an English Institutist: Legal Literature and the Rise of the Nation State' (1984) 4 *Oxford Journal of Legal Studies* 318–60.
[158] *Commentaries* vol 1, 410
[159] See JW Cairns, 'Blackstone, Kahn-Freund and the Contract of Employment' (1989) 105 *Law Quarterly Review* 300–14.
[160] See Cairns (n 157) 343–52.

Legal Jambalaya

STEPHEN M SHEPPARD[*]

LOUISIANA IS PROUD of its eccentricities. Though many places in the United States were subject to continental rule before Anglo-American sovereignty, Louisiana's idiosyncratic mix of French and Spanish, Creole and Cajun customs yields a heritage unusually, and generally consciously, synthesising a host of traditions. Some Louisiana traditions influence wider American culture: French Quarter music and Cajun food have done well quite beyond their cribs. Others remain objects of distant fascination, only thriving along the bayou: Louisiana voodoo and Louisiana law might fall into this category.

Having grown up near the swamps of Louisiana, as a child I knew many of these customs. This way of life seemed, as locals tend to see it, like a gumbo—a single stew that (if made properly) results not so much from recipe or any prior intent as from accidents of the larder and plain old serendipity. The key to gumbo is that each ingredient keeps its own taste but still affects all the others; it isn't a chorus but a medley. In this way Louisiana law is a bit like Louisiana cooking, each source of law has its own effects but influences our engagement with the whole.

So it is easy to compare the Louisiana Code to the gumbo, remembering that the gumbo is made from pretty much what one has to hand, though with a few perpetual staples in a Louisiana kitchen, especially cayenne and paprika, but also peppers, onions, and probably celery. One could look this all up in a cookbook, but the locals tend not to do that, and there are at least twice as many gumbo recipes as there are cooks.

In the light of Professor Cairns's chapter, it becomes clear, however, that Louisiana law is not so much like gumbo as it is like another local dish. It is much more like jambalaya. Jambalaya is the Louisiana form of paella, the side dish (or sometimes an entree) of rice and meats, concocted with a performance art similar to gumbo creation.

---

[*] I am grateful to Wilf Prest and David Lemmings for their kind invitation to attend the Blackstone Symposium in Adelaide, and to John Cairns for the thoughtful work from which this minor extension is derived. Thanks, too, to Amos Gregory and to Coalt.

What locals know is that there are two families of jambalaya—red and brown. Red jambalaya, or Creole jambalaya, is made with tomatoes. Brown jambalaya, Cajun jambalaya, has no tomatoes.[1] There are, of course, countless variations of each (though cayenne and paprika are not considered optional for either in polite society). Owing to the centuries of mistrust between the bayou Cajuns, and the urban Afro-Franco-Anglo-Spaniards, there are still fierce local debates about which is the true jambalaya. Yet, from a distance, this intramural fight among Louisianans is unknown. Most Americans make jambalaya from a mix that might be red or brown but that is often labelled 'Creole' or 'Cajun' willy-nilly, and without much resort to its actual origin.

How does Blackstone fit into all this? In his Adelaide paper, now a chapter, on the origins of the 1808 *Louisiana Digest*, Professor Cairns revisited the comparative question of his youth. He raised the question, cast in culinary terms, of whether Blackstone was a principal ingredient or merely a garnish in cooking up the Louisiana Code. He then resolved, and has now more fully demonstrated, that the *Commentaries* were a core ingredient, like cayenne, rather than just an optional spice, like bay leaf. His arguments—that Moreau Lislett, James Brown, and their fellow travellers employed Blackstone's texts not only for answers to specific questions of family law and criminal law, but also for the structure needed to elaborate a law of persons more fully than had been done in Napoleonic France—are state of the art.

His contentions about the meaning of Blackstone's works for Louisiana jurists are, I think, compelling. He articulates two reasons—one cultural and one jurisprudential—for the Louisiana jurist to employ the common law Blackstone, despite the civilian's supposed antipathy towards common law sources. Culturally, plantation Louisiana needed the law to have tools with which to regulate slavery. Jurisprudentially, Blackstone's institutional style was generally acceptable, incorporating as it did many universal and natural principles that were consonant with the Spanish law long accepted in the Territory and with the French law recently imported to it.

To these points we may add one more, a reason for Blackstone to influence the *Louisiana Digest* that Cairns nicely chronicles but does not reprise: it might also have been good politics. Though we cannot be sure (at least at this stage in the historical study) that the Anglo population, or the

---

[1] These divisions between peoples might not be clear to a distant observer. 'Creole' in Louisiana usually refers to the people and the culture of the city, the mixed race inhabitants of old New Orleans. (There are other groups of Louisiana Creoles.) See S Kein, *Creole: The History and Legacy of Louisiana's Free People of Color* (Baton Rouge LA, 2000). 'Cajuns' are descendants of the French Canadians (or 'Arcadians') who settled in the swamps and bayou country west of the city. Henry Wadsworth Longfellow's poem *Evangeline* (1847) is the classic Cajun chronicle. See WF Rushton, *The Cajuns: From Acadia to Louisiana* (New York NY, 1979).

common-law-loving Territorial Governor William Claiborne, were aware of the Blackstonian ingredients in the cooking of the Code, they certainly would not have hurt in the later debate on its adoption. The incorporation of some common law ideas into the civilian enterprise would very likely have reassured the Anglophilic American southerners who had migrated to Louisiana. It might, indeed, have been some reassurance to the federal masters of Territorial fates, in the distant and infrequent reviews of Territorial affairs. Yet this would have been true only if that influence were indeed known, and I am not so sure that it was.

Back in Louisiana, Cairns has gone further than this, at least in looking into the role of Blackstone's writings as a source of law for the other significant community of lawmakers—the judges. In research conducted for his chapter in this (though not published here), he examined Blackstone's employment in several early cases, which were argued by Listlet and Brown, the two principal drafters of the Code, who used Blackstone's text to support their argument for a point of general law. For several reasons, I am curious about the same question, and I have rather shallowly but persistently examined the role lawyers and judges have assigned to Blackstone as authority in Louisiana appellate arguments over a longer time. That inquiry supports John's views rather nicely.

The 1809 term of the Superior Court of the Territory of Orleans commenced, of course, after the promulgation of the *Digest*. In the case John discusses from that year, *Folk v Solis*,[2] lawyers, notably John Brown, invoked Blackstone among other sources to argue successfully that a defendant in libel was not subject to arrest or to bail. In the opening argument, as reported, Brown and his colleagues moved for release of the defendant, starting with the proposition that 'The order [requiring bail] is unsupported by any principle of the laws of the United States, the acts of the territory, or the civil, or Spanish law, the only sources from which the court can derive any legitimate authority'. Yet they then freely refer to Blackstone's *Commentaries* for propositions narrated as civilian in origin ('[in the] civil law bail is only required in civil cases, for injuries accompanied with force. 3 Bl. Com., 280, 281.'); as a general principle of law ('An action for a libel is not instituted to recover damages for an injury to the property of the plaintiff, and there exists a clear distinction between injuries to the person and injuries to the property. 3 Bl. Com., 123. 144.'); and as a general principle of law in the demarcation of sources between common and statutory law ('If it be the practice in some of the states to require bail, in an action for a libel, it must have been introduced by statute. It is not demandable by the common law. Tidd., 13, 67. Blackstone, 3 Com., 281.').

---

[2] 1 Mart.(o.s.) 64, 1809 WL 950 (La.Terr. Super Ct. Orleans, 1809).

This case is far from unusual. Indeed earlier in the same term, none other than John Prevost, at last released from his judicial labours, argued from Blackstone that a partnership renders each partner liable to a creditor of the partnership for the whole debt.[3] As Brown and his colleagues did in the *Solis* case, Prevost and his colleagues employed Blackstone and other common law sources indiscriminately alongside civilian sources in support of his point, which was not precisely delineated in the 1808 *Digest*.[4]

Indeed this pattern of advocates' reliance on Blackstone as a source of authority in argument persists. Over time, such judicial reliance and citation became more common. It is tempting to say that both became more prevalent as the *Digest* matured, though whether this is cause or effect is hard to say. Thanks to the facility of computer-aided research, a decennial survey of Blackstone references in Louisiana appellate cases over the last centuries yields a rough outline of Blackstonian influence. Appendix I collects the volume of citations to arguments and opinions in the Louisiana reports, appellate reports, and trial records, collected in Westlaw's Louisiana cases database (La-cs), categorised decennially.

Far from waning as the corpus of local case law filled gaps and established principles, it increased, though it never approached ubiquity. From 1811 to 1820, Blackstone's writings were cited 26 times. The use of Blackstone as an authority in Louisiana opinions reached its high water mark in the 1840s. Citation in the 1840s increased considerably, most likely in part owing to the inclusion of Book Four of the *Commentaries* on the reading list issued by the state supreme court in 1840 for students seeking admission to the Louisiana bar.[5] Chancellor Kent's *Commentaries*, influenced as they were by Blackstone but tailored to an American audience, had been relied on in earlier Louisiana opinions but now also experienced a significant surge in frequency of citation, to an even greater extent than Blackstone, following the same edict, which placed Kent with Blackstone on the reading list.[6] After the civil war, Blackstone was still cited several times every year

---

[3] *Parish v Syndics of Phillips*, 1 Mart.(o.s.) 61, 1809 WL 949 (La. Terr. Super. Orleans, 1809).
[4] Ibid.
[5] Rule XIV of the Louisiana Supreme Court, governing applicants for admission to the bar, was adopted on 24 November 1840. Part 3 of that rule specified: 'The Court will not be satisfied with the qualification of a candidate in point of legal learning, unless it shall appear by examination that he is well read in the following courses of studies at least: Vattel's Law of Nations, or Wheaton's Elements of International Law; the History of the Civil Law in Louisiana; the Louisiana Civil Code; the Code of Practice; the Statutes of the State of a General Nature; the Institutes of Justinian; Domat's Civil Law; Pothier's Treatise on Obligations; Blackstone's Commentaries, Fourth Book; Kent's Commentaries; Smith on Mercantile Law; Wood on Insurance; Story of Parsons on Notes; Chitty or Bayley on Bills; Greenleaf, Starkie or Phillips on Evidence; Russell on Crimes; Bishop on Criminal Procedure; and the Jurisprudence of Louisiana, as settled by the decisions of the Supreme Court.' Rule XIV, 36 La. Rep. xi; 43 Law. Rep. Anno xi (1840). W Billings (ed), *The Historic Rules of the Supreme Court of Louisiana 1813–1879* (Lafayette LA, 1985).
[6] There appear to be 67 citations in the Louisiana reports to Kent's works prior to 1840, but there were 145 in the following decade, nearly three times the number of Blackstone citations.

as late as the 1880s. His much-diminished popularity after World War II is apparent, although he experienced something of a revival in the 1970s.

Blackstone was occasionally cited as a source of Louisiana law. According to Cairns's expectations, however, he was much more often cited to illustrate a principle of general law that applied in Louisiana. In other words he was cited as a general legal authority for principles that were presumed to apply in Louisiana as in the rest of the world, regardless of their expression in a text associated with the common law.

In the antebellum years, Blackstone was a reliable indicator of the common law, seen mainly as a legal system distinct from that of Louisiana. Overall, the greatest reliance on Blackstone by the Louisiana bench and bar occurs in the decades before and after the American Civil War.[7] Part of this nineteenth-century rise in Blackstone's influence is surely the effect of the American Blackstones chronicled by Hoeflich.[8] The number of editions reaching Louisiana for easy access increased, as did their apparent utility in the American south. Likewise, part of its decline may be the demise of local editions of Blackstone, the creation of which effectively did not survive World War I. It is not always easy to determine which edition a judge or lawyer cites, any more than to determine which edition of Blackstone was used by Lislett in drafting the Code. When a specific edition is cited, it is likely early on to be either one of Christian or of Tucker. Later, judges and lawyers were probably relying on Sharswood, Cooley or Lewis. After World War II Blackstone is, of course, less commonly cited in most American courts, and he is likewise less authoritative in Louisiana. This was not owing to his Englishness or his infelicity on matters of civil law. Rather, he was just yesterday's news.

To consider a pattern of usage for a given legal source in one jurisdiction invites curiosity about its use in others. Appendix II compares the Blackstone citation rate in Louisiana cases to those in five other state jurisdictions.[9] These are Arkansas—the most proximate common law division from the Louisiana Territory—as well as states with high volumes of case law from distinct regions: Illinois, New York, Massachusetts and Virginia. Louisiana citations of Blackstone seem not dissimilar from the patterns in all these other states, though there are interesting variations in timing. New York is an early and extensive home for Blackstone cites, with a diminished citation rate in the 1830s that is resonant with Louisiana's decline in the 1820s and 1830s. Massachusetts and the still-young Illinois see a similar diminution in use in the same period, with each peaking later in the century.

---

[7] See Appendix I below. For some of the nineteenth-century cases, see R Fonseca, 'Blackstone's Commentaries: Foothold or Footnote in Louisiana's Antebellum Legal History' (MA thesis, University of New Orleans, 2007).
[8] See M Hoeflich, 'American Blackstones' in Prest (ed) Commentaries 171.
[9] The comparison was for rate only, and not for Blackstone-citing cases as a proportion of all reported cases.

Thus New York and Massachusetts reach the highest point in the 1850s, while Illinois, Arkansas and Louisiana peak in the 1880s. But all show a similar slump and then final rise in use through the twentieth century. Some of these variations may be accounted for by varying lengths of statehood, by demographic differences, and by contrasts in both the size of the native lawyer population and modes of legal education. Other relevant factors doubtless include changes in bar admission rules and the local availability of editions of the *Commentaries*.

Without regard to the causes, the effects suggest that Louisiana's judicial reliance on Blackstone was far from unique. Blackstone's influence in Louisiana might have had a somewhat different rationale, but in all states judicial reference to the *Commentaries* gradually diminished during the twentieth century, reaching a nadir in the 1950s and 1960s. Blackstone, for a time, was in near disrepute, before being rehabilitated as both a source of history and of law in the 1970s. In 1956 a judge on the Louisiana Court of Appeals found it appropriate to abuse not only Blackstone but also the lawyer who dared to argue from the *Commentaries* in the interpretation of a precedent, rather than from Louisiana cases:

> [C]ounsels' argument as to the effect of the *Huberwald* case is based, not upon the independent reasoning and opinion of the court, but upon a quotation contained therein, derived from Blackstone's *Commentaries* ... We firmly deny any appropriate relationship between the quoted comment and the point which we have under consideration ... Additionally, we would point out the fact, as above observed, that our codal article, which is the foundation of tort actions, has no relationship with common-law principles ... Furthermore, it should be observed that the antiquated observations of Sir William Blackstone have been long regarded, even in common-law jurisdictions, as bearing little, if any, weight ... The distinguished Barrister-at-Law, Frederick Sherwood, epitomises the low esteem in which both Blackstone as an authority and his commentaries as precepts are held, in the following words: 'Blackstone was by no means a scientific jurist ... He has only the vaguest possible grasp of the elementary concept of law'.[10]

This was not a universal view, however. Even then Blackstone was still occasionally cited to and from the Louisiana bench, mainly as the curator of the museum of the common law, but yet a source of general principles. Indeed that same year, Louisiana Chief Justice Fournet cited 'the great English authority' on the requirements of an indictment.[11]

Despite his diminishing popularity in some quarters by the mid-twentieth century, the bench, quite used to Blackstone, found a new tool for him. In the 1969 case of *Bonfanti Industries v Teke*[12] Judge Ellis was called upon

---

[10] *Hightower v Dr Pepper Bottling Co. of Shreveport, Inc.*, 117 So.2d 642, 654 (La. Ct. App. 2 Cir., 1959), quoting, but not citing Frederick Sherwood. Sherwood wrote the entry for William Blackstone in the mid-century editions of the *Encyclopaedia Britannica*. See, eg, 3 *Encyclopaedia Britannica* 750 (1969).

[11] *Louisiana v Straughan*, 229 La. 1036, 87 So.2d 523) (La. 1959).

[12] *Bonfanti Industries v Teke* 250 La. 141, 194 So.2d 726 (La. Ct. App. 2 Cir., 1969).

to interpret the Louisiana Code's provisions on master and servant. These originated in Article 147 of the 1808 Digest, which allowed recovery by a master for injuries to a servant from the person who committed the injury. Judge Ellis perceived its unacknowledged origin in the first book of Blackstone's *Commentaries*, and, relying on Blackstone to interpret the article, held that it could have applied only to 'indentured servants, apprentices and others who are bound in the service of an individual for a specific period of time' and not to ordinary employees.

By now, even an astute reader might have forgotten how my story began. Remember the jambalaya? It will help if you do, but there are a few useful tangents before it returns.

What puzzles me most is how to reconcile this general picture with the common view of Louisiana law, that Francophile claim for Louisiana exceptionalism, at least in the early, heady days when the City of New Orleans awaited the arrival of a liberated Napoleon Bonaparte. In general, one finds the Francophile argument persistent and unwavering, tempered mostly by acknowledgment of Blackstone's influence on the *Digest* by historians and comparativists, beginning in 1970 with Professor Tucker's work on the law of persons,[13] continued and enlarged by Radolfo Batiza and made much more nuanced by John Cairns. Granted, we now have the benefit of George Dargo's and John Cairns's wonderful accounts of the early struggle between promoters of the common law and the civil law for dominance in New Orleans.[14] Yet there is so little commentary otherwise.

The dominant academic narrative of Louisiana law has long ignored the practical and historical influence of Blackstone and judicial recognition of Blackstone as a general authority. One can read as typical the apparent competition between Blackstone and the civilians in William Wirt Howe's 1903 essay in the *Harvard Law Review*.[15] Standard textbooks of Louisiana law spill pages of ink on Roman, French, and Spanish sources, without a mention of the common law or Blackstone.[16] This is more than academic oversight. It is so profound in the academy and local legal culture that I remember my shock, in New Haven years ago, when I first learned of Batiza's argument from Morris Cohen. It was then not really a part of the academic or the professional story, though known to some of the bench and the bar. Indeed, even the recognition that Blackstone is a source for some parts of the Code was announced first from the bench, in 1969, before being delineated the following year in scholarship. Is this a wilful or a negligent mislabelling of Louisiana's legal-cultural tale?

---

[13] See TW Tucker, 'Sources of Louisiana's Law of Persons: Blackstone, Domat, and the French Codes' (1970) 44 *Tulane Law Review* 264, 267.
[14] See G Dargo, *Jefferson's Louisiana: Politics and the Clash of Legal Traditions* (Clark NJ, 2009).
[15] See WW Howe, 'Roman and Civil Law in America' (1903) 16 *Harvard Law Review*, 342.
[16] See HP Dart, 'The Sources of the Civil Code of Louisiana' in AJ Bonomo (ed), ED Saunders, *Lectures on the Civil Code of Louisiana* (New Orleans LA, 1925).

So, now I return to the jambalaya. Red or brown jambalaya is a debate that raged for decades, though these days it is rarely heard. Most jambalaya is red, to some degree. Commercial jambalaya mixes are more likely to say Cajun, a more recognised and unique regional label, than Creole, a term with several non-Orleans meanings and less understood or popular beyond Lake Pontchartrain. The Creole influence of tomato, meats, and herbs, and the Cajun influences of meats and spice are now all churned into the rice base. Yet its proud 'Cajun' label is defended in New York restaurants and English bistros. The origins are lost, and the label misleads. Or, at least, it overstates its case.

So, it seems, does the French story of Louisiana law. Its Code now more homogeneous with uniform laws, and borne down as never before by the weight of federal regulation, its defenders take refuge in the distinguishing myth of the purity of civilian law. John Cairns nicely foreshadowed this result in contrasting the fears of Governor Claiborne and James Brown that the civilians would pursue their dream of a pure civil law system with the reality of quiet common law integration into the process that loudly brought their dreams to fruition.

APPENDIX I

Citations to Blackstone's *Commentaries* or *Reports* in Louisiana Reported Opinions 1781–1980

Date	1	2	3	4	5	6	7	8	Totals
1781–1790									
1791–1800									
1801–1810		2	2	0		1			5
1811–1820		10	11	3		1		1	26
1821–1830		5	2	1				1	9
1831–1840		1	2	0		1		17	21
1841–1850	1	23	7	0	2	2	2	12	49
1851–1860		19	6	2			2	7	36
1861–1870		2	0	0		1		2	5
1871–1880		11	2	3			2	2	20
1881–1890		26	2		2		1	2	33
1891–1900		9	3		1		1		14
1901–1910		1	0		2		1	3	7
1911–1920	2	11	3		1	2	3	1	23
1921–1930	1	5	3	2		2	1	1	15
1931–1940		3	5				2	0	10

(*Continued*)

Legal Jambalaya

Date	1	2	3	4	5	6	7	8	Totals
1941–1950		0	0					0	0
1951–1960	1	0	0	1			1	1	4
1961–1970		1	0	1			1	1	4
1971–1980		5	1	3			2	0	11
Total	5	134	49	16	8	10	19	51	292

Key (Horizontal axis)

1. Used as a source of Louisiana law
2. Used as a general principle of law
3. As an illustration of the common law
4. As a matter of legal history
5. Miscellaneous
6. Both 2 and 3
7. Both 4 and 2 or 3
8. Both 1 and 2

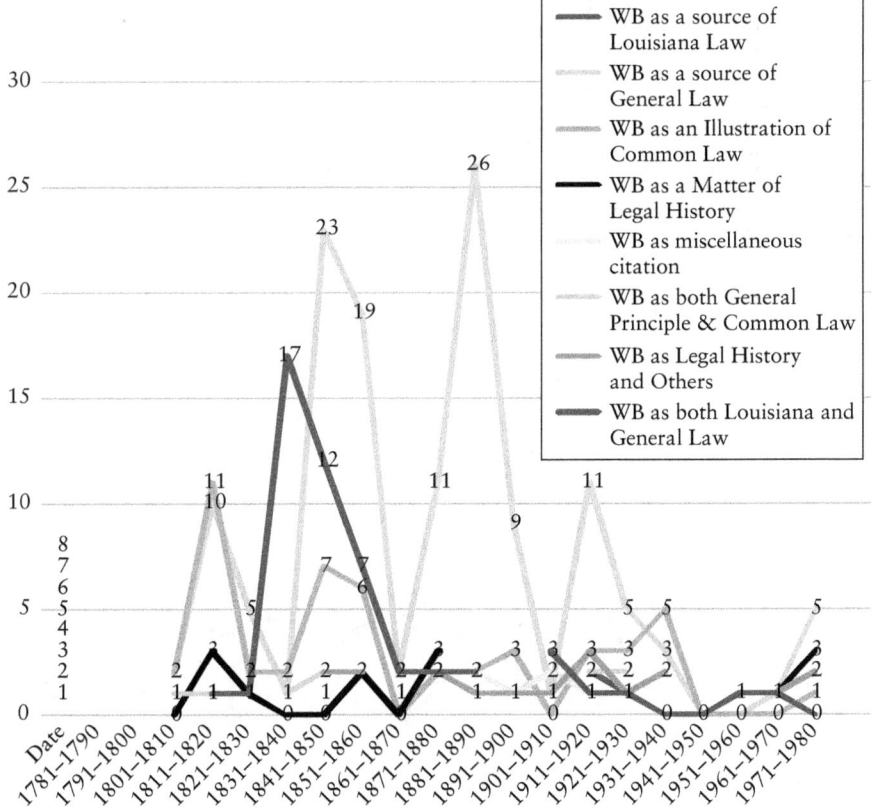

Blackstone Citations In Louisiana Cases

APPENDIX II

Citations to Blackstone's *Commentaries* or *Reports* in Selected US State Courts 1781–1980

Decade	LA	AR	VA	IL	NY	MA
1781–1790	0	0	2	0	0	0
1791–1800	0	0	6	0	2	2
1801–1810	3	0	47	0	55	21
1811–1820	25	0	25	0	100	20
1821–1830	09	0	17	5	153	71
1831–1840	21	8	20	3	54	51
1841–1850	47	11	17	18	149	73
1851–1860	36	19	9	24	181	78
1861–1870	4	8	5	37	131	66
1871–1880	20	24	14	78	145	44
1881–1890	33	25	29	106	109	21
1891–1900	15	8	23	93	53	2
1901–1910	7	15	10	71	60	10
1911–1920	22	22	10	69	74	12
1921–1930	16	13	8	53	53	10
1931–1940	11	7	11	48	56	4
1941–1950	1	10	9	49	41	4
1951–1960	4	5	5	17	34	2
1961–1970	4	2	3	16	27	10
1971–1980	11	4	1	29	40	17

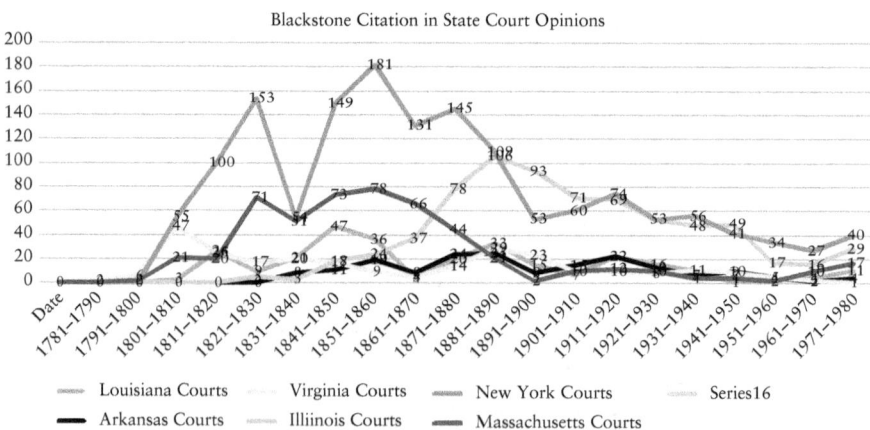

5

Blackstone and the Birth of Quebec's Distinct Legal Culture 1765–1867

MICHEL MORIN*

> But in conquered or ceded countries, that have already laws of their own, the king may indeed alter and change those laws; but, till he does actually change them, the antient laws of the country remain, unless such as are against the law of God, as in the case of an infidel country.
>
> *Commentaries* vol 1, 105.

IN ONE SHORT sentence, Blackstone acknowledged the possibility of preserving the civil law tradition in a British colony, for a time at least. It would probably have been impossible to give an account of the various legal systems of the British Empire in an introductory work on English Laws. Be that as it may, when his celebrated 'general map of the law' appeared, one would not have expected the francophone people of Quebec, who were anxious to preserve their legal culture, to pay much attention. Despite his hostility towards Catholics, Blackstone's synthesis would prove extremely helpful to those inhabitants of the former New France who sought a better understanding of the freedoms and privileges enjoyed by British subjects. To understand why, we must recount the constitutional regimes applicable in Quebec between 1763 and 1867.

In 1760 the French commander-in-chief, Pierre de Rigaud, marquis de Vaudreuil de Cavagnal, proposed articles of capitulation to his British counterpart Jeffery Amherst. Amherst had no problem granting article 37, which guaranteed to Canadians (as the inhabitants of New France were called at

---

* The author gratefully acknowledges funding by SSHRC and the outstanding research assistance of Mr Mathieu Vaugeois, as well as the collaboration of the various research libraries mentioned in this chapter. He is also grateful to Mrs Nathalie Battershill, who has generously checked her research notes to supplement information contained in her Masters thesis, and to his colleagues Jean Leclair and Paul Daly, who read drafts. All translations from French below are by the author.

the time) 'the entire peaceable property and possession of the[ir] goods'.[1] But article 42, which would have kept in force 'the Custom of Paris, and the Laws and usages established for this country', was dismissed curtly: 'They become Subjects of the King'. Three years later, Canada was ceded to Great Britain and a royal proclamation created the province of Quebec.[2] It anticipated the establishment of a provincial assembly and promised all inhabitants of the new province 'the benefit of the laws of ... England', with courts constituted by the governor's council to determine 'all causes, as well criminal as civil, according to law and equity, and as near as may be agreeable to the laws of England'.[3]

In the event, no assembly would be summoned. Confronted with a population of roughly 95 per cent (francophone) Roman Catholics, the two different governors refused to call elections in which only protestants would be eligible to vote.[4] The introduction of English law was also delayed.[5] In 1764 an ordinance established a two-tiered court system for cases in which the amount at issue exceeded 10 pounds.[6] The plaintiff could choose between the King's Bench, where the 'Laws of England' applied, or the Court of Common Pleas, which relied on 'Equity, having regard nevertheless to the laws of England, as far as the circumstances and present situation of things will admit'.

This regime was meant to apply to a population of more than 60,000 'Canadians' and approximately 3,000 British, merchants, tradesmen and soldiers. A few former subjects of the French king now developed a strong interest in the rights of British subjects in general, and in a colonial House of Representatives in particular. However, they were dissuaded from pursuing such claims in order to achieve religious equality for Catholics.[7] Following many years of debate, in 1774 the Quebec Act reinstated the rules relating

---

[1] A Shortt and A Doughty (ed), *Documents relating to the Constitutional History of Canada, 1759–1791* (hereafter CD I), 2nd edn Pt I (Ottawa, 1918) 7.

[2] During the military regime, which ended on 10 August 1764, military courts were said to have applied the private law of New France: J Igartua, 'The Merchants and Negociants of Montreal: A Study in Socio-Economic History' (PhD thesis, Michigan State University, 1974) 174–99; M Trudel, *Histoire de la Nouvelle-France, X, Le régime militaire et la disparition de la Nouvelle-France, 1759–1774* (Montreal, 1999) 137–84.

[3] CD I 97 (treaty of Paris 1763) 163 (Royal Proclamation).

[4] The governor's commission required that all members of the projected assembly swear the oath laid down in the British Test Acts, which no Catholic could do in conscience: ibid 175.

[5] A Decroix, D Gilles and M Morin, *Les tribunaux et l'arbitrage en Nouvelle-France et au Québec, de 1740 à 1784* (Montreal, 2012); D Fyson, 'The Conquered and the Conqueror: The Mutual Adaptation of the Canadiens and the British in Quebec, 1759–1775' in P Buckner and JG Reid (ed), *1759 Revisited: The Conquest in Historical Perspective* (Toronto, 2012) 190–217.

[6] CD I 205; D Fyson, *Magistrates, Police and People: Everyday Criminal Justice in Quebec and Lower Canada, 1764–1837* (Toronto, 2006).

[7] M Morin, 'The Discovery and Assimilation of British Constitutional Law Principles in Quebec, 1764–1774' (2013) 36 *Dalhousie Law Journal* 581 and 'Les revendications des nouveaux sujets, francophones et catholiques, de la Province de Québec, 1764–1774' in

to property and civil rights applied in New France. It also granted civil and religious equality to Catholics, who could henceforth occupy important positions such as judge or member of the governor's council. This accorded with Blackstone's ideas: freedom of belief and worship for Catholics but to preserve the 'King's Supremacy' over spiritual and temporal affairs in his territories, they were required to swear a special oath of allegiance.[8] English criminal law remained, as well as testamentary freedom, but an unelected legislative council was put in place.[9]

After the American war of independence, with the immigration of Loyalists, the Constitutional Act of 1791 granted representative institutions to two new colonies: Upper Canada, in what is now Ontario, and Lower Canada, the new name for the southern part of Quebec.[10] Conflict with the Upper House, whose members were appointed for life, as well as with the Executive Council, which was essentially accountable to London, provoked the Rebellions of 1837–38 and the reunification of the two provinces.[11] After responsible government was granted in 1848, political instability and economic difficulties led to Confederation in 1867.[12] Nonetheless, important reforms between 1848 and 1867 included the creation of a land registry system and abolition of the seigniorial regime. The Civil Code of Lower Canada was adopted in 1865.[13] During that period, and to this day, Quebec has kept its civil law tradition for private law, but adheres to the common law in administrative and criminal law.[14] Its legal culture has

---

B Baker and D Fyson (ed), *Essays in the History of Canadian Law: Old Quebec and the Canadas* (Toronto, 2013) 131.

[8] 'An Act for making more effectual Provision for the Government of the Province of Quebec in North America', 14 Geo III, c 83 (1774) (hereafter Quebec Act), cl 6; *cf* P Lawson, *The Imperial Challenge, Quebec and Britain in the American Revolution* (Montreal, 1989); H Neatby, *The Quebec Act: Protest and Policy* (Scarborough, 1972); K Stanbridge, 'Quebec and the Irish Catholic Relief Act of 1778: An Institutional Approach' (2003) 16 *Journal of Historical Sociology* 375.

[9] Quebec Act, cl 11.

[10] 31 Geo 3 c 31; see H Neatby, *Quebec. The Revolutionary Age, 1760–1791* (Toronto, 1966); KD Milobar, 'The Constitutional Development of Quebec from the Time of the French Regime to the Canada Act of 1791' (PhD thesis, University of London, 1990) 23–28.

[11] Union Act 1840, 3 & 4 Vict, c 35; JMS Careless, *The Union of the Canadas; the Growth of Canadian Institutions, 1841–1857* (Toronto, 1967); M Morin, 'L'évolution du mode de scrutin dans les colonies et les provinces de l'Amérique du nord britannique de 1758 à nos jours' (2008–2009) 39 *Revue De Droit de L'Université de Sherbrooke* 153.

[12] British North America Act, 30–31 Vict c 3; now the Constitution Act, 1867.

[13] Statute of the Province of Canada 1865, sess 1, 29 Vict, c 41; *cf* JEC Brierley, 'Quebec's Civil Law Codification: Viewed and Reviewed' (1968) 14 *McGill Law Journal* 521; JEC Brierley and RA Macdonald (ed), *Quebec Civil Law* (Toronto, 1993); M Morin, 'La perception de l'ancien droit et du nouveau droit français au Bas-Canada, 1774–1866' in HP Glenn (ed), *Droit québécois et droit français: communauté, autonomie, concordance* (Cowansville, 1993) 1; S Normand, 'La codification de 1866: contexte et impact' in ibid 43; B Young, *The Politics of Codification* (Toronto, 1994).

[14] A Morel, 'La réception du droit criminel anglais au Québec (1760–1892)' (1978) 13 *Revue juridique Thémis* 449; D Hay, 'The Meaning of the Criminal Law in Quebec,

become hybrid, in the sense that lawyers and judges in Quebec routinely deal with these two traditions and are influenced by both.[15]

From the Royal Proclamation in 1764 to the beginning of Confederation in 1867, francophone jurists faced a formidable challenge, since they were required to understand many parts of English law. There was no legal literature nor legal education worth mentioning. From the outset governors and colonial law officers were very conscious of this problem. They sought to publicise the basic rules of the criminal law but were not able to accomplish much in this regard. Law books and legal periodicals became more numerous in the nineteenth century but foreign publications remained indispensable. In this context, the *Commentaries* would appear to have been a very useful tool. It has been claimed that francophone lawyers were not familiar with Blackstone's work.[16] But in France as early as the 1780s the *Commentaries* became a standard reference work on the political system of England and its criminal laws. Similarly in Quebec, where Blackstone was even asked to intervene in favour of the restoration of French institutions, following the Quebec Act of 1774, he became a household name for politicians and for lawyers interested in the criminal law or legal reforms. By the second third of the nineteenth century he had achieved an iconic status for the small number of writers who wanted to summarise the public law or the criminal law applicable in the colony, as well as for those interested in legal education.

I BLACKSTONE IN FRANCE PRIOR TO THE REVOLUTION

John Emerson has ably documented the diffusion of the *Commentaries* in France.[17] The first French version, by Auguste-Pierre Damiens de

---

1764–1774' in LA Knafla (ed), *Crime and Criminal Justice in Europe and Canada* (Waterloo, 1981) 77; M Morin, 'Portalis v. Bentham? The Objectives Pursued by the Codification of the Civil and Criminal Law in France, England and Canada' in [Law Commission of Canada], *Perspectives on Legislation* (Ottawa, 2000); translation available at http://hdl.handle.net/1866/1468).

[15] M Dorland and M Charland, *Law, Rhetoric and Irony in the Formation of Canadian Civil Culture* (Toronto, 2002); J-P Garneau, 'Une culture de l'amalgame au prétoire: les avocats de Québec et l'élaboration d'un langage juridique commun (tournant des XVIIIe et XIXe siècles)' (2007) 88 *Canadian Historical Review* 113; S Normand, 'La culture juridique et l'acculturation du droit: le Québec' in JA Sánchez-Cordero (ed), *La culture juridique et l'acculturation du droit—Rapports au XVIIIe Congrès international de droit comparé* (2011) 1 (Special Issue 1) *Isaidat Law Review* (http://isaidat.di.unito.it/index.php/isaidat/); M Morin, 'Dualisme, mixité et métissage juridique: Québec, Hong Kong, Macao, Afrique du Sud et Israël' (2012) 57 *McGill Law Journal* 645; P Girard, *Lawyers and Legal Culture in British North America: Beamish Murdoch of Halifax* (Toronto, 2011) 4–5.

[16] Morel (n 14) 525–33.

[17] 'Did Blackstone get the Gallic Shrug?' in Prest (ed) Commentaries 185.

Gomicourt, appeared in the mid-1770s.[18] Gabriel-François Coyer's translation of the fourth book on criminal law, interspersed with his own comments, was published in 1776.[19] Selected parts of Book four were also translated in 1790, 1792 and 1803; in the latter year a French version of Blackstone's *Analysis of the Laws of England* appeared.[20] Nicholas-Maurice Chompré's more accurate translation of the *Commentaries* was published in 1822–23.[21] Based on the 15th edition, with notes by Edward Christian, this version provided francophone readers with an updated overview of English law.[22]

According to Emerson, Blackstone's work aroused little interest in pre-revolutionary France, except in the case of the comte de Mirabeau, who took copious notes, including quotations in English. Yet Edouard Tillet has shown that only shortly after publication, the *Commentaries* was well known in France among those interested in the British parliamentary system or English criminal law. Among the first francophone readers was the Swiss Jean-Louis de Lolme, who relied extensively on the *Commentaries* to produce what became a standard work on the English constitution.[23]

In 1771 Louis de Bancas, comte de Lauranguais, praised the *Commentaries* in his book on French public law.[24] In 1778 Émilien Petit took it as a point of departure to compare the public law of France and England.[25] From 1781 the volumes of the incomplete dictionary of Prost de Royer made regular and sometimes critical references to the *Commentaries*.[26] By 1789 at the

---

[18] W Blackstone, *Commentaires sur les loix angloises, traduit de l'anglois par M.D.G. sur la 4ième édition d'Oxford* (Brussels, 1774–1776).
[19] *Commentaire sur le code criminel d'Angleterre, traduit de l'anglais de Guillaume Blackstone par l'Abbé Coyer* (Paris, 1776); E Tillet, *La constitution anglaise, un modèle politique et institutionnel dans la France des Lumières* (Aix-en-Provence, 2001) 448.
[20] Ibid 191.
[21] *Commentaires sur les lois anglaises avec des notes de M. Ed. Christian, traduit de l'anglais sur la quinzième édition par N.M. Chompré* (Paris, 1822–1823).
[22] See M Hoeflich, 'American Blackstones' in Prest (ed) Commentaries 172; KM Parker, 'Historicizing Blackstone's *Commentaries on the Laws of England*' in A Fernandez and MD Dubber (ed), *Law Books in Action: Essays on the Anglo-American Legal Treatise* (Oxford, 2012) 22.
[23] *Constitution de l'Angleterre, ou état du gouvernement anglois comparé avec la forme républicaine et avec les autres monarchies de l'Europe* (Amsterdam, 1771). According to Tillet (n 19) 397, 449 n1631, de Lolme relied largely on Blackstone. His work became famous after revision and translation into English as *The Constitution of England, or, An Account of the English Government* (London, 1775). V Monnier, 'Jacques Mallet-Dupan (1749–1800), Entre Genève, France et Angleterre' in [Association française des historiens des idées politiques], *L'influence politique et juridique de l'Angleterre en Europe* (Aix-en-Provence, 2012) 207–26 (hereafter AFHIP).
[24] *Extrait du droit public de la France* (London, 1771) 83, quoted by Tillet (n 19) 446.
[25] *Dissertation sur des parties intéressantes du droit public en France et en Angleterre d'après les Lois des deux nations comparées entre elles* (Geneva, 1778), quoted Tillet (n 19) 459–61 and 495. See also ibid 446, 466–7, 553 and AFHIP.
[26] *Dictionnaire de jurisprudence et des arrêts, ou nouvelle édition du Dictionnaire de Brillon* (Lyon, 1781–1788); see Tillet (n 19) 446, 490–91 and 496.

latest, Condorcet had read Blackstone; so had the obscure jurist Jean-Louis Agier.[27] Though not explicitly linked to Blackstone, it is worth mentioning that 65 *cahiers de doléances* asked for the introduction of habeas corpus, as did some draft Declarations of Rights.[28] Indeed, in year XI of the revolutionary calendar (1802 or 1803), our author was quoted with de Lolme in a factum submitted to the Tribunal of cassation in a criminal appeal, the court of last resort in France.[29] This shows his account of English law remained influential after the many reforms effected during the French Revolution. On the other hand Blackstone's account of English private law aroused very little interest in France.[30]

II BLACKSTONE IN QUEBEC PRIOR TO THE RESTORATION OF FRENCH PRIVATE LAW

When English law was formally introduced to the province of Quebec by the Royal Proclamation, the bilingual *Quebec Gazette* kept its readers informed about the heated debates in Britain and its colonies over taxation by the Imperial Parliament, freedom of the press, the importance of jury trial, etc.[31] Blackstone's *Commentaries* provided the most accessible source of authoritative information on these issues. In 1767 the *Gazette* published an opinion written by three Parisian lawyers concerning the right to be compensated for oak wood taken on some seigneuries in New France. In such a case the wording of the initial grant was crucial. The authors relied on the 'excellent work of Mr Blackstone', who distinguished between colonies 'founded by Englishmen ... first occupying the land; these were from the moment of their creation subject to the laws of England', and 'conquered or ceded countries'. In the latter case, 'the King may, in truth, reform and change their laws, but until he has done so, the ancient laws subsist'. They concluded that the obligation to compensate some seigneurs had been transmitted to the new sovereign.[32] One of the authors was Jean-Baptiste-Jacques Élie de Beaumont, who had visited Blackstone in 1764 and been

---

[27] Tillet (n 19) 496 and 549.
[28] Ibid 483.
[29] Ibid 467.
[30] Ibid 449; D Gilles, 'La common law sous la plume de la doctrine française: Regards "civilistes" sur les institutions juridiques (Angleterre-France-Canada)' in AFHIP (n 23) 368, 373–75; LH Dunoyer, *Blackstone et Pothier* (Paris, 1927); Frank Lessay, 'Blackstone, common law et codification' (1998) 27 *Droits* 3; J Garnier, 'Droit anglais et droit romain: la *consideration* selon sir William Blackstone' in O Vernier, M Bottin and M Ortolani (ed), *Études d'histoire du droit privé en souvenir de Maryse Carlin* (Paris, 2008) 343.
[31] See M Morin, 'La découverte du droit constitutionnel britannique dans une colonie francophone: la Gazette de Québec, 1764–1774' (2013) 47 *Revue juridique Thémis* 319 and Morin, 'Discovery and Assimilation' (n 7). The present section draws on this last paper.
[32] 'Consultations rendues par trois des plus célèbres Avocats de Paris, au sujet des droits et propriétés des Seigneurs du Canada', *Quebec Gazette* (hereafter *QG*), 3 September 1767.

consulted by him the following year in a maritime ransom case.[33] In 1773 the *Commentaries* were being paraphrased in written arguments submitted to the judges of the Common pleas in Quebec.[34]

On 15 July 1773 the *Gazette* reproduced an exchange in the House of Commons earlier that year concerning the legal system of Quebec. Thomas Townshend had referred to the abusive behaviour of Anglophone lawyers and claimed that Canadians had every reason to curse the English and their laws. The influential seigneur Francois-Joseph Cugnet prepared his own annotated translation of this debate, in which he commented that 'reasonable Canadians, after reading the authors who have written on the British Constitution, cannot curse England nor its laws, which they know to be equitable'.[35] Cugnet intended to publish this document but was dissuaded by the lieutenant-governor of the province, who had no wish to encourage a potentially inflammatory discussion.[36]

For Cugnet, the rules relating to property, including those on alienation or successions, were guaranteed by the 1760 Capitulation and could not be affected by the Proclamation of 1763. So he maintained that only English criminal laws or those relating to the enjoyment of personal liberties had been introduced, for which the new subjects 'must be very grateful', an opinion he would repeat on numerous occasions.[37] In order to procure the full benefit of English law to all inhabitants while maintaining French property laws, he believed that testamentary freedom should be expressly guaranteed, which would allow pre-1760 British subjects in Quebec to regulate familial property succession according to their own traditions. At this point, Cugnet buttressed his argument with a reference to Blackstone:

> What the honourable Mister Blackstone says in Book 1 of his Commentaries, page 107, ('that all country conquered or ceded already has its own municipal laws; that the King may in truth alter & change them; but until he has actually changed them, the ancient laws of the countries remain, unless they are opposed to the law of God') destroys the bad construction some want to give (perhaps with evil intent) to this Proclamation.[38]

Cugnet also prepared a draft petition, which met with the disapproval of his francophone allies, who wished to secure a representative assembly to which Catholics would be admitted, but were uncomfortable with more technical issues, such as testamentary freedom. In this draft Cugnet referred to some 'very clear' treatises summarising the laws in force prior to 1760,

---

[33] Prest, *William Blackstone* 185, 212.
[34] Decroix et al (n 5) 249–50.
[35] Reproduced in M Leland, 'François-Joseph Cugnet 1720–1789: XI' (1963) 18 *Revue de l'Université Laval* 339, App G 350.
[36] See Morin, 'Discovery and Assimilation' (n 7).
[37] *Cf* Morel (n 14) 489–90.
[38] Leland (n 35) 356.

without mentioning that he was actually their author and that Governor Carleton had asked other jurists to prepare more accessible abstracts.[39] In 1774 Cugnet sent the documents he had prepared to Blackstone, apparently not realising that since 1770 he had become a puisne justice of the Court of Common Pleas at Westminster, which would make it difficult for him to lobby for the restoration of French private law.

For Cugnet, 'the Laws of England regarding Admiralty and Commerce' were acceptable to Canadians, since they did not concern immovable property. As early as 1771 he expressed the view that restrictions on testamentary freedom were incompatible with a 'free Government' and with English law.[40] In 1774 he argued that Canadians could not reasonably oppose this principle; younger siblings would now fear that fathers might 'dispose of their lands in favour of the eldest son and if they have many, in favour of a few of their children'; they would therefore start working for themselves, pioneering new lands, becoming traders or going to sea, all of which would be to their advantage.[41]

Early next year Blackstone forwarded the documents mentioned above to Attorney General Thurlow.[42] Cugnet's arguments seemed to have carried weight during the preparation of the Quebec Act, which did provide for complete testamentary freedom; it also allowed wills to be made according to either French or English laws.[43] In his treatise on *The Old Laws of Property in Canada* published in 1775, Cugnet added the following reference:[44]

> Les Canadiens qui voudront s'instruire des loix, coutumes et usages Anglais, quant aux testamens, peuvent lire le chapitre 32, page 489. du tome second des commentaires de L'HONORABLE JUGE BLACKSTONE, intitulé *Title by testament and administration*, qui les instruira pleinement sur cette matière, ainsi que ce qu'il dit, quant aux testamens, même tome, pages 10. 12. et 373. Et tome 4. Pages 424 et 430.

> [Canadians who want to learn the English Laws, customs and usages regarding wills, may read chapter 32, page 489. of the second book of the honourable Justice Blackstone's *Commentaries*, entitled, *Title by Testament and administration*,

---

[39] 'Très humbles représentations des habitans de la Province de Québec', Archives of the Université de Montréal, Baby Collection, item L/3, unnumbered page.

[40] FJ Cugnet, 'Loix municipales de Québec, divisées en trois traités', Bibliothèque de l'Assemblée nationale du Québec, Fonds Chauveau, call number 347.14 C965 1771–73, fo 260.

[41] M Leland, 'François-Joseph Cugnet 1720–1789: X' (1963) 17 *Revue de l'Université Laval* 820, App E 839.

[42] Leland (n 35) 339, n 379.

[43] See Quebec Act, cl 8 & 10; A Morel, *Les limites de la liberté testamentaire dans le droit civil de la province de Québec* (Paris, 1960); J-M Brisson, 'Entre le devoir et le sentiment: la liberté testamentaire en droit québécois (1774–1990)' in *Recueils de la Société Jean Bodin*, vol LXII, *Actes à cause de mort—Acts of Last Will* (Brussels, 1994) 277.

[44] F-J Cugnet, *Traité des Anciennes Loix de Propriété en Canada, aujourd'huy Province de Québec* (Québec, 1775) 161.

which will instruct them fully on this subject, also what he says about wills, same Book, pages 10, 12 and 373. And tome 4. Pages 424 and 430.]

Cugnet's list of recommended reading for common-law-trained judges did not include Robert-Joseph Pothier, whose works started to appear in 1761 and who would later eclipse Blackstone as the quintessential reference for practitioners.[45] Indeed, his works are not mentioned in inventories made in the district of Montreal from 1765 to 1790, contrary to Domat, Ferrière and Argou, for instance.[46]

It is clear that, as in France, Blackstone was read in Quebec soon after the appearance of the *Commentaries*, at a time when no translation of his work was available. He was also used as a channel by François-Joseph Cugnet, whose opinions on English criminal law and testamentary freedom did not appear to have been widely known or discussed in Quebec, but may very well have carried the day in London. After the Quebec Act the *Commentaries* retained their usefulness for constitutional and criminal law, as well as the drafting of wills. They were certainly well known by lawyers and politicians, as we shall see presently.

III BLACKSTONE AND POLITICO-LEGAL DEBATE IN QUEBEC, 1774–1867

A number of early editions of Blackstone's works are held by libraries both in Quebec and in Ottawa. When biographical information about the original owners exists (which of course is not always the case) they turn out for the most part to have been lawyers or notaries who practised towards the end of the eighteenth or in the nineteenth centuries. Seven copies of Gomicourt's version, including one incomplete set, are held by as many institutions.[47] In one the following ownership inscription appears: 'Au Séminaire des Missions étrangères de Québec 1785', also called the Seminary of Quebec.[48] While not mentioned in its catalogue two years earlier, this institution evidently owned a copy by 1785.[49] That same year Gomicourt's translation appeared in the inventory of the property of

---

[45] Ibid, unnumbered penultimate page; F Maseres, *Mémoire à la défense d'un Plan d'Acte de Parlement pour l'Établissement des Loix de la Province de Québec* (London, 1773) 148–49.
[46] N Battershill, 'Les bibliothèques privées sur l'île de Montréal, 1765–1790' (MA thesis, Université de Montréal, 1993) 78.
[47] The libraries are located in the following institutions: Université de Montréal; Université Laval; Bibliothèque du Séminaire de Québec, Centre d'histoire de l'Amérique française; Université Sherbrooke; Montreal Courthouse; Ancient Books, Bibliothèques et archives nationales du Québec.
[48] Bibliothèque du Séminaire de Québec, Centre d'histoire de l'Amérique française; N Baillargeon, *Le Séminaire de Québec sous l'épiscopat de Mgr de Laval* (Québec, 1972) 39.
[49] M Laurent, 'Le catalogue de la Bibliothèque du Séminaire de Québec' (Thesis, École des Gradués de l'Université Laval, 1973) 39, 80.

Thérèze Legrand, merchant.[50] Likewise, in 1788 the inventory of Benjamin Frobisher, merchant, included the *Commentaries*.[51] Among other early owners were René Boileau (1754–1831) commissioner for the Court of Requests, politician and justice of the peace;[52] Pierre-Amable De Bonne (1758–1816), lawyer, politician and judge (from 1794);[53] and one 'Plante', possibly Joseph-Bernard Planté (1768–1826), notary and politician.[54]

In Quebec City there are two copies of Coyer's translation of Book IV and two copies of the translation of the *Analysis of the laws of England*.[55] As for Chompré's translation of 1822–23, there are six full sets, comprising six volumes each, a five-volume incomplete set and a three-volume one.[56] Six full sets of the first English editions have been found, plus a dozen or so individual volumes.[57] Finally, two copies of the first edition of de Lolme's work (in French) are extant, which may confirm the relatively limited impact of this book in the 1770s.[58] It should be noted that not all copies of Blackstone's works in Quebec have been retraced; others are certainly in private hands or have left the province. Many seem to have arrived in the province during the nineteenth century.

In 1781 the *Commentaries* were referred to in a King's Bench judgment.[59] This is doubtless but one example of a regular practice. Likewise in 1791 a heated debate canvassed the possibility of allowing in a given seigneury, upon the request of its owner, the substitution of the free and common socage tenure for the feudal rules inherited from France. Thomas[-Laurent] Bédard, a priest and bursar of the Seminary of Quebec, published in the *Gazette* his 'Observations on the Report Respecting a change in the Tenures

---

[50] Battershill (n 46) 102.

[51] Ibid 107–08 and private communication.

[52] Library of the Montreal Courthouse; www.assnat.qc.ca/fr/deputes/boileau-rene-2153/biographie.html.

[53] Library of the Supreme Court of Canada; P Tousignant and J-P Wallot, 'De Bonne, Pierre-Amable' in *Dictionary of Canadian Biography* (Quebec, 1966–2003) vol 5, 230.

[54] Université de Sherbrooke (Droit).

[55] Université Laval and the Quebec Courthouse each have one copy of Coyer's work; Université Laval holds two copies of *Analyse des lois anglaises* AM Joguet (tr) (Paris, 1803). Dates of acquisition or initial ownership are unknown, but they were probably imported during the nineteenth century.

[56] Libraries with full sets are those of Université de Montréal (two copies); Université Laval; Université Sherbrooke (Droit); Montreal Courthouse; National Assembly of Quebec.

[57] I have focused on editions published before 1785 and excluded missing volumes mentioned in library catalogues. Full sets are held by the Nahum Gelber Law Library, McGill University (3 copies); Université Laval, Supreme Court of Canada and University of Ottawa; there are individual volumes at Centre d'histoire de l'Amérique française; Université de Sherbrooke (Droit) and Library and Archives Canada.

[58] These are held by the libraries of the Université Laval and the Université de Montréal; at least 25 editions published after 1783 have been found.

[59] 'Petition of Mary Hay, Court of King's Bench, Province of Quebec, 1 May 1781' in FM Greenwood and B Wright (ed), *Canadian State Trials. Law, Politics, and Security Measures, 1608–1837* (Toronto, 1996) App E, 627.

of this Province'.⁶⁰ Bédard was clearly learned in the law of New France and appreciated the poor quality of available translations of English law books.⁶¹ So in his discussion of tenures it is not surprising to see him quoting from the 8th edition of the *Commentaries*.⁶² In 1821 a quotation from the English version was also found in a paper written in French, which discussed the usefulness of a public registration system for immovable rights.⁶³

As for the French version, in 1784 Colonel Hope had offered this work to the merchant Jacques-Nicolas Perrault, who was active in the movement for an elected assembly.⁶⁴ Shortly thereafter, prior to the adoption in 1791 of a new constitution providing for representative institutions, the *Commentaries* became a veritable bestseller.⁶⁵ Blackstone was quoted by many francophone writers in political and legal contexts.⁶⁶ By 1792 subscribers of the Quebec library could borrow de Lolme's 1777 edition (in French), as well as two editions of the *Commentaries* (1778 and 1783); in 1830 a French translation of the latter was added to the collection.⁶⁷

One finds numerous references to Blackstone's work in Quebec's newspapers, both before and after the creation of a representative assembly. In 1791, in a sardonic address, fictitious and arrogant seigniors were made to reject out of hand the idea that government was a civil pact and not a divine institution, even if the former principle was defended by 'Pufendorf, Locke, Montesquieu, Helevétius, Blackstone and all the good authors' whom these aristocrats prided themselves on never having read.⁶⁸ They did acknowledge, however, that the 'spirit of the English Constitution' consisted in tying the hands of clergymen as tightly as possible, in order to prevent them from doing harm. In 1792, discussing Quebec's new constitution, 'Solon' stressed the 'weight and consequence of the people in the scale of Government'; on the other hand, he relied upon Montesquieu, Blackstone and de Lolme to underline 'the high importance and advantage of a Senate or Legislative

---

⁶⁰ *QG*, 24 March 1791 (supp), 31 March 1791 (supp) and 07 April 1791 (supp); see N Baillargeon, 'Bédard, Thomas-Laurent', in *Dictionary of Canadian Biography* (Quebec & Toronto, 1966–2003) vol 4, 49 and E Kolish, *Nationalismes et Conflits de Droits: Le débat du droit privé au Québec, 1760–1840* (Ville La Salle, 1994) 224–26.

⁶¹ See *QG*, 24 March 1791 (supp).

⁶² Ibid.

⁶³ Kolish (n 60) 276–77.

⁶⁴ Neatby (n 8) 240; P Matteau, 'Perrault, Jacques-Nicolas' in *Dictionary of Canadian Biography* (Quebec & Toronto, 1966–2003) vol 4, 667.

⁶⁵ J-P Wallot, *Un Québec qui bougeait, trame socio-politique au tournant du XIXe siècle* (Montreal, 1973) 299.

⁶⁶ Ibid.

⁶⁷ G Gallichan, *Livre et politique au Bas-Canada, 1791–1849* (Sillery, 1991) 396, 400, 416.

⁶⁸ 'Horrificus de Maledissimus', 'Sous-familier du Divan Aristocratique et seigneurial, à la Nations Canadienne—Salut', *QG* 30 June1791, quoted in Wallot (n 65) 263.

Council, and of a class of men distinguished by Titles or Dignities for their Talents and Wealth'.[69]

From 1797 to 1837, in their criticisms of the colonial executive and claims to enjoy the privileges of the House of Commons, francophone members of the provincial Assembly quoted regularly Burke, Fox, Montesquieu, Voltaire, Blackstone, de Lolme and Locke.[70] The *Commentaries* were even termed the 'catechism' of the British constitution, whose 'sublime doctrine' was worthy of imitation, especially the rule that persons receiving a pension from the Crown should be ineligible for elective office.[71] In 1801 a committee of the Assembly, composed mostly of francophone members, prepared a list of essential books for a future library, which included the *Commentaries* (in English) and de Lolme's work (in French).[72] The Legislative Council included Blackstone in the similar list it prepared the following year.[73] In Upper Canada as well, many of the authors just mentioned were read and admired,[74] though Blackstone's success there may have been due to his conservative vision, which was certainly very appealing to the local oligarchy.[75]

IV BLACKSTONE AND QUEBEC'S LEGAL CULTURE 1774–1867

In 1789 François-Joseph Perrault offered the following assessment:

> L'introduction des loix criminelles d'Angleterre dans cette Province, où la langue Angloise n'est connue que d'un très petit-nombre de ses habitants, exigeoit fortement que quelqu'un voulût bien prendre la peine d'extraire & de traduire de quelque bon Auteur, tout ce qui pouvoit concerner la pratique de ses loix, afin d'en rendre la connoissance plus générale. Le Traité de Burn sur l'Office des Juges à paix a paru le plus propre à remplir cet objet.

> [The introduction of the Criminal Laws of England to this Province, where only a very small number of inhabitants know the English language, necessitated that someone would take pains to excerpt and translate from some good author, everything about the practice of these laws, in order to make them more generally known. Burn's treatise on the office of Justices of the Peace seemed the most appropriate to achieve this end.][76]

---

[69] Montreal Gazette, 22 March 1792, quoted in M Ducharme, *Le concept de liberté au Canada à l'époque des Révolutions atlantiques 1776–1838* (Montreal, 2010) 62.

[70] Wallot (n 65) 277; for references to Blackstone, see ibid, 312, n 211; Gallichan (n 67) 185–86, 260; Ducharme (n 69) 69–71, 79, 89.

[71] *Le Canadien*, 7 May 1808, quoted in Ducharme (n 69) 71.

[72] Gallichan (n 67) 224–25.

[73] Ibid 229.

[74] Ibid 108, 165.

[75] GB Baker, 'The Reconstitution of Upper Canadian Legal Thought in the Late-Victorian Empire' (1985) 3 *Law and History Review* 219, 255–58.

[76] *Le juge à paix et officier de paroisse, pour la province de Québec: extrait de Richard Burn, chancellier du diocèse de Charlisle, & un des juges à paix de Sa Majesté, pour les comtés de Westmorland & Cumberland* (Montreal, 1789) v.

François-Joseph Perrault was the cousin of Jacques-Nicolas Perrault, who had been offered a copy of Gomicourt's translation in 1784. He was not legally trained in 1789, although he later began articles; before being admitted to the bar, he was appointed a clerk of the Court of King's Bench.[77] His 1789 preface did not mention Blackstone, perhaps out of ignorance, or else because he considered that the availability of two French versions of the final book of the *Commentaries* was well known. As a former merchant, he may have been more concerned with the role played by Justices of the Peace than with lawyers, who were not allowed to represent accused persons in felony cases until 1836.[78] Nor do his various subsequent legal and political publications refer to our author, probably because he intended only to provide elementary outlines of the law to students and lay persons.

But 20 years later, the importance of Blackstone's work could be taken for granted. A certain Jean Mackay, living in Montreal, who claimed to be a member of the bar in the neighbouring province of Upper Canada and to have studied law professionally for 16 years, announced his intention of translating the 'criminal laws of England', more specifically Book four of the 11th edition of the *Commentaries* and a few other parts, followed by excerpts from or discussion of 160 statutes, 50 to 60 different authors and an unknown number of cases.[79] Indeed he proposed to produce 'a complete course on the criminal laws of England which govern us in this province'. No more was heard of this project, which is hardly surprising given that law publishing was generally not profitable in Lower Canada at this time.[80] But it demonstrates that the *Commentaries* remained the essential starting point for anyone wishing to write on the criminal law of Lower Canada.

In 1827 Jacques Labrie published a book on the British constitution 'intended for the instruction of Canadian youth'.[81] He claimed that few works existed on the new parliamentary system established by the Constitution Act of 1791, and those few were written in a language most

---

[77] C Galarneau, 'Perrault, Joseph-François' in *Dictionary of Canadian Biography* (Quebec, 1966–2003) vol 7, 687.

[78] 'An Act to authorise Counsel to address Jurors in behalf of Prisoners in Capital Cases', SLC 1836, 5 Gul IV, c 1.

[79] J Mackay, 'Nouvelle Publication', *Le Canadien*, 11 February 1809, 1.

[80] S Normand, 'L'histoire de l'imprimé juridique au Québec, Un champs de recherche inexploré' (1993) 38 *McGill Law Journal* 130–46 at 140; S Normand, 'La littérature du droit comme élément structurant du champ juridique québécois: une perspective historique' in Y Gendreau (ed), *La doctrine et développement du droit* (Montreal, 2005) 5; Y Gendreau, 'L'imprimé juridique au Québec' in Y Lamonde and F Black (ed), *Histoire du livre et de l'imprimé au Canada, volume II (1840–1918)* (Montreal, 2005) 436–39; R Crête, S Normand and T Copeland, 'Law Reporting in Nineteenth-Century Quebec' (1995) 16 *Journal of Legal History* 147.

[81] *Les premiers rudimens de la constitution britannique; traduits de l'anglais de M. Brooke* (Montreal, 1827).

of the population did not understand.[82] Labrie further explained that he had relied on Blackstone and de Lolme, 'les auteurs qui nous sont les plus connus au Canada', but are 'trop chers pour le commun de ceux qui en ont besoin' [the authors who are the best known to us in Canada' but are 'too expensive for the majority who need them']; furthermore, de Lolme was said to be 'more a skillful publicist than a judicious commentator'.[83] Also written with a 'view of assisting law students in their studies', although in the English language, the overview of Canadian law by Nicolas Benjamin Doucet referred regularly to Blackstone in discussing legal education and the origins and contents of English law.[84]

In 1842 Jacques Crémazie completed a book on English criminal law, translated and compiled from Blackstone, Chitty, Russell and other authors.[85] Holding that it was generally impossible to find exact French equivalents for technical English terms, he stuck to the original wording, although he acknowledged having occasionally used the 'excellent' translation of Chompré.[86] In the same year Louis-Hippolyte La Fontaine, a future Attorney General, co-prime minister and chief justice of Lower Canada, wrote a scathing criticism of the ordinance for the registration of titles to lands. This law had been adopted by the unelected Special Council (1838–1841) one day before the Union Act, which provided for the reinstatement of a bicameral legislature, came into force.[87] On the cover of his tract, the following quotation from Blackstone appeared: 'On ne peut prévoir ni prévenir toutes les conséquences des innovations' ['how impossible is it to foresee, and provide against, all the consequences of innovations'].[88] The ordinance itself was an indigestible mixture of the French Civil Code and British or Upper Canadian statutes.[89] La Fontaine corrected the translations of specific words, both in the English and the French version. For English terms of art, he relied on Chompré's translation.[90] Another prominent contemporary lawyer who had a French version of Blackstone in his library

---

[82] Ibid iii. Labrie quotes Blackstone only once (vii), while de Lolme is quoted more frequently (eg viii, 15, 18).

[83] QG 1 October 1827, quoted in Gallichan (n 67) 87.

[84] *Fundamental Principles of the Laws of Canada ... Prefaced by an Historical Sketch Compiled with a View of Assisting Law Students in their Studies* (Montreal, 1840) passim.

[85] *Les lois criminelles anglaises: traduites et compilées de Blackstone, Chitty, Russell et autres criminalistes anglais et telles que suivies en Canada* (Quebec, 1842).

[86] Ibid v, vi. The book does indeed contain numerous excerpts from, or reference to, Blackstone's *Commentaries*, although the latter may come from more recent works translated by Crémazie, who cites no authors in his introduction to the legal system for lay persons: J Crémazie, *Manuel des notions utiles sur les droits politiques, le droit civil, la loi criminelle, et municipale, les lois rurales, etc.* (Quebec, 1852).

[87] LH Lafontaine, *Analyse de l'ordonnance du Conseil spécial sur les bureaux d'hypothèques* (Montreal, 1842).

[88] Ibid i. *Commentaries* vol 2, 338–39.

[89] Lafontaine (n 87) iv–v.

[90] Ibid 25, 41, 108–11.

was George-Étienne Cartier, who in 1857 would spearhead adoption of the Civil Code as Attorney General for Lower Canada.[91]

Blackstone was also considered essential reading for students. At this time legal training in Lower Canada consisted of articles for five years followed by an examination before the judges. A similar system existed in most British colonies. After the creation of Upper Canada, Blackstone became the main source of legal information.[92] From 1832 to 1883 candidates for admission to the bar were asked questions on his work.[93] Adaptations of selected parts of the *Commentaries* for readers in Ontario appeared from 1864 onwards.[94] The work was also considered essential reading in 1820s' Nova Scotia.[95] In 1832 Beamish Murdoch declared that his *Epitome of the Laws of Nova Scotia* was composed 'in humble imitation of the Commentaries of Blackstone'; as Philip Girard has observed, a 'considerable amount is cribbed directly from Blackstone and other authors, often without attribution'.[96] Murdoch recommended reading through the *Commentaries* three times during a student's preparation for the bar.[97]

In Lower Canada, the supervising lawyer typically told his articling student 'lisez Domat, ou le traité des obligations, ou "le parfait notaire"' ('read Domat, or [Pothier's] treatise on obligations, or the 'perfect notary [by Ferrière]').[98] Law schools appeared only in 1848 at McGill University and in 1851 at the College Sainte-Marie, both in Montreal; in Quebec City, the Université Laval followed in 1854. From 1853 university law school graduates needed to serve only three years in articles; those who held only a generic university degree were required to complete four years.[99]

---

[91] Young (n 13) 62.

[92] WNT Wylie, '"Instruments of Commerce and Authority": The Civil Courts of Upper Canada 1789–1812' in DH Flaherty (ed), *Essays in the History of Canadian Law*, vol 2 (Toronto, 1983) 7.

[93] GB Baker, 'Legal Education in Upper Canada 1785–1889' in Flaherty (n 92) 94, 112, 116; Baker (n 75) 238.

[94] P Girard, '"Of Institutes and Treaties": Blackstone's *Commentaries*, Kent's *Commentaries* and Murdoch's *Epitome of the Laws of Nova Scotia*' in Fernandez and Dubber (n 22) 43.

[95] Girard (n 15) 39–40.

[96] P Girard, 'Themes and Variations in Early Canadian Legal Culture: Beamish Murdoch and his *Epitome of the Laws of Nova-Scotia*' (1993) 11 *Law and History Review* 101, 105, 144.

[97] Girard (n 15) 39.

[98] J Huston, '1847. Essai Lu Devant l'Institut Canadien de Montréal. De la position et des besoins de la jeunesse Canadienne-Français' in J Huston (ed), *Le répertoire national ou Recueil de la littérature canadienne*, vol 4 (Montreal, 1982 [1850]) 141–42; S Normand, *Le droit comme discipline universitaire, une histoire de la Faculté de droit de l'Université Laval* (Quebec, 2005) 2–3.

[99] IC Pilarczyk, *A Noble Roster: One Hundred and Fifty Years of Law at McGill* (Montreal, 1999); RA Macdonald, 'The National Programme at McGill: Origins, Establishment, Prospects' (1990) 13 *Dalhousie Law Journal* 211; D Howes, 'The Origin and Demise of Legal Education in Quebec (or Hercules Bound)' (1989) 38 *University of New Brunswick Law Journal* 127; RStJ Macdonald, 'Maximilien Bibaud, 1823–1887: The Pioneer Law Teacher of International Law in Canada' (1987–88) 11 *Dalhousie Law Journal* 721.

In 1836 an anonymous writer complained that examinations for admission to the bar were too easy, since students began practising 'sans qu'ils aient lu même les *Commentaires* de Blackstone' ('without even having read the *Commentaries* of Blackstone').[100] When law lecturing started on a regular basis at McGill in 1853, Maximilien Bibaud, who taught law courses in French at the Collège Sainte-Marie, asserted that 'A en juger par les programmes, leurs cours sont plutôt calqués sur Blackstone que sur les lois françaises en force au Canada' and 'la terminologie de Blackstone est greffée sur notre système de droit' [judging from the syllabus, courses there are rather patterned after Blackstone than on the French laws in force in (Lower) Canada] and [the terminology of Blackstone is grafted upon our system of law].[101] In fact the first proposed McGill curriculum included Justinian's Institutes, the first and second titles of the 1580 Custom of Paris (which still applied in Lower Canada) as explained by Ferrière, Pothier on Obligations—and Book four of the *Commentaries*.[102]

William Torrance, foundation professor of Roman law, maintained that before the local courts, for issues of French law, the 'author of greatest renown' was 'unquestionably Robert-Joseph Pothier, born in 1699, the most distinguished jurisconsult of France in the last century, and eminent both as a Commentator on the Customary Law and on the Roman Law in France'. Pothier was 'emphatically to the French and Lower Canada lawyer, what Blackstone in the popular mind' was 'to the English lawyer, though in intellectual power and accomplishments, immeasurably the superior'.[103]

During his own time in articles, Bibaud had prepared for the judges' examination by writing an abridged version of the *Commentaries*.[104] Much later, to justify the fact that he was the sole teacher in his institution, he reminded readers that Blackstone had also offered a complete course of law at Oxford.[105] His own publication was entitled *Commentaries on the Laws of Lower Canada*.[106] He may have chosen that title for commercial reasons, in imitation of Kent's *Commentaries*, for in Nova Scotia, this author ranked almost equally with Blackstone.[107] But it seems more likely that

---

[100] *QG* 4 Feb1836 quoted in G Gallichan, 'La Bibliothèque du Barreau de Québec: l'émergence d'une institution'(1993) 34 *Cahiers de Droit* 131.

[101] M Bibaud, *Notice historique sur l'enseignement du droit en Canada* (Montreal, 1862) vii, lxxxvi.

[102] Pilarczyck (n 99) 6.

[103] FW Torrance, *The Roman Law* (Montreal, 1854) 25; Young (n 13) 167; see also Macdonald (n 99) 216–29.

[104] A Morel and Y Lamonde, 'Bibaud, François-Maximilien' *Dictionary of Canadian Biography* (Quebec, 1966–2003) vol 11, 70.

[105] Bibaud (n 101), xliv, n*. Bibaud adds this footnote to a letter initially published in a newspaper and signed 'le doyen' ('the dean') Bibaud's self-assumed title.

[106] *Commentaires sur les lois du Bas-Canada, ou, Conférences de l'Ecole de droit liée au Collège des RR. PP. Jésuites: suivis d'une notice historique* (Montreal, 1859, 1861).

[107] J Kent, *Commentaries on American Law* (New York NY, 1826); *cf* Girard (n 94).

Bibaud held a positive opinion of Blackstone. When discussing the rules of English law, Bibaud often referred to him, although at times disagreeing with his opinions.[108] Occasionally even Blackstone's more debatable assertions came in handy, as with the claim that feudalism began under the Roman Emperor Alexander Severus, for he was a 'jurisconsulte érudit par excellence'.[109]

It should also be pointed out that in Lower Canada, besides constitutional, administrative and criminal law, a small element of English private law had been introduced by statute, for example the formalities required for making a will, the rules of evidence in commercial matters, and trial by jury between merchants or for personal injuries. In addition, because it had not been registered prior to 1760 by the *Conseil souverain*, the *Ordonnance sur le commerce* of 1673 had been held not to be in force. The resultant gap had been filled by legislation based on English models and by a mixture of French, English, Scottish and American legal doctrines.[110]

The commissioners charged with the preparation of the Civil Code of Lower Canada paid careful attention to this hybrid legal culture, since they were required to draft provisions embodying rules 'then actually in force', and to provide supporting 'authorities'; any amendment to the law in force had to be presented 'separately and distinctly'.[111] Unsurprisingly, they quoted Blackstone in their reports to the legislature, generally in the field of public law or commercial law, as on the applicability of Imperial statutes to colonies, rules governing civil death following a conviction or entrance into religious orders, coroners' inquests, corporations, the Crown's domain and lands reclaimed from the sea.[112]

---

[108] Bibaud (n 101) 6, n*, 44, 56, 108, 115, 181, 292, 382, 480, 586, 588.

[109] Ibid 243, quoted in S Normand and M Dumais, 'Le droit romain dans le droit coutumier du Bas-Canada selon François-Maximilien Bibaud' in E Hermon (ed), *La question agraire à Rome: droit romain et société. Perceptions historiques et historiographiques* (Côme, 1999) 171–72.

[110] For a detailed description, see Brierley and Macdonald (n 13); Morin (n 13).

[111] 'An Act to provide for the Codification of the Laws of Lower Canada relative to Civil matters and Procedure' (1857), 20 Vict c 43 s 6.

[112] For the excerpts quoted by the commissioners, see under arts 1, 32, 33–35 and 69, CC De Lorimier and CA Vilbon, *La Bibliothèque du code civil de la province de Québec* (Montreal, 1871) 35–38, 301–03, 307, 321, 322–24, 466; under arts 352, 354–58, 361–65, 368, 421 CC De Lorimier and CA Vilbon, *La Bibliothèque du code civil de la province de Québec* (Montreal, 1874) 155–57, 168–69, 172–73, 179, 181, 186–87, 195, 205, 206, 207, 209–10, 228–29, 500–01; under art 766, CC De Lorimier, *La Bibliothèque du code civil de la province de Québec* (Montreal, 1881) 350; the reference to Blackstone under art 400 seems to have escaped De Lorimier and Vilbon (E Lefebvre de Bellefeuille, *Le Code civil annoté: étant le Code civil du Bas-Canada* (Montreal, 1866) 89; *cf* S Normand and M Saint-Hilaire, 'La Bibliothèque du Code civil: un ouvrage au confluent de la tradition et de la modernité' (2002) 32 Revue générale de droit 305.

The commissioners also quoted from Stephen's edition of the *Commentaries*[113] on British subjecthood,[114] and the appropriation of things found floating or ashore.[115] In all, some edition of his work appears among the references appended to 26 articles, roughly 1 per cent of the total number. This is a small proportion compared to Jean Domat, who appears under 275 articles (11 per cent), or to Pothier, who is present under 87 per cent of the articles relating to obligations and under 1,349 (52 per cent) of the total.[116] Similarly, references to Roman law represent 31 per cent in the initial draft.[117]

Overall these variations reflect the limited role played by English law in the private law of Quebec, except in commercial law. The *Commentaries* evidently remained a work of reference in Quebec, albeit a fading one. There is some debate on the extent to which a 'dialogical literature' emerged in domains where English law had not been formally introduced, both before codification and in subsequent decades.[118] But during the second half of the nineteenth century there can be no doubt that regular reference was made to English legal literature in general, and to Blackstone in particular.[119] Local lawyers had first-hand knowledge of his writings, unlike, for example, German legal literature.[120] On the other hand, in the last quarter

---

[113] HJ Stephen, *New Commentaries on the Laws of England (Partly Founded on Blackstone)* 4 vols (London, 1841). Parker (n 22) 32.

[114] Arts 20–21 and 30, De Lorimier and Vilbon (n 112) (1871), 262–63, 268, 291–94.

[115] Arts 588–89, CC De Lorimier, *La Bibliothèque du code civil de la province de Québec* (Montreal, 1880) 171–75; Lefebvre de Bellefeuille (n 112) 136.

[116] D Gilles, 'Les Lois civiles de Jean Domat, prémices à la Codification. Du Code Napoléon au Code civil du Bas Canada' (2009) 43 *Revue juridique Thémis* 35–36 and 43.

[117] S Normand and D Fyson, 'Le droit romain comme source du Code civil du Bas Canada' (2001) 103 *Revue du Notariat* 87, 90.

[118] D Howes, 'From Polyjurality to Monojurality: The Transformation of Quebec Law, 1875–1929' (1986–87) 32 *McGill Law Journal* 523; D Howes, 'Dialogical jurisprudence' in WW Pue and B Wright (ed), *Canadian Perspectives on Law & Society: Issues in Legal History* (Ottawa, 1988) 71; D Howes, 'La domestication de la pensée juridique québécoise' (1989) 13 *Anthropologie et Sociétés* 103; D Howes, 'Nomadic Jurisprudence: Changing Conceptions of the "Sources of Law" in Quebec from Codification to the Present' in [Canadian Association of Comparative Law, Association québécoise de droit comparé and McGill Institute of Comparative Law], *Contemporary Law: Canadian Reports to the 1990 International Congress of Comparative Law* (Montreal, 1992) 1; Morin (n 11); S Normand, 'Une culture en redéfinition: la culture juridique québécoise durant la seconde moitié du XIXe siècle' in B Melkevik (ed), *Transformation de la culture juridique québécoise* (Quebec, 1998) 221; M Morin, 'Des juristes sédentaires? L'influence du droit anglais et du droit français sur l'interprétation du Code civil du Bas Canada' (2000) 60 *Revue du Barreau* 247; see also GB Baker, 'Law Practice and Statecraft in Mid-Nineteenth-Century Montreal: The Torrance-Morris Firm, 1848 to 1868' in C Wilton (ed), *Beyond the Law: Lawyers and Business in Canada 1830 to 1930* (Toronto, 1990) 45.

[119] During the last quarter of the 19th century, judges do not appear to have quoted Blackstone regularly on commercial law issues, which he barely discussed in any case: R Crête, 'Aspects méthodologiques de la jurisprudence en droit commercial à la fin du XIXe siècle' (1993) 34 *Cahiers de Droit* 253.

[120] E Reiter, 'Imported Books, Imported Ideas: Reading European Jurisprudence in Mid-Nineteenth-Century Quebec' (2004) 22 *Law & History Review* 445–92.

of the nineteenth century those who could not easily read English still found difficulty in mastering the intricacies of Canadian criminal law.[121]

V CONCLUSION

The very fact that the *Commentaries* had been translated into French less than a decade after publication attests to the work's importance before the French Revolution. Though hardly a household name like Montesquieu or Beccaria, Blackstone quickly became the first point of reference for basic principles of the British constitution and of the criminal laws of England. In Quebec, the recently conquered francophone subjects learned of his work in 1767. They found his *Commentaries* an invaluable source for building arguments supporting the preservation of their civil laws. François-Joseph Cugnet even sought his personal help. Blackstone duly forwarded Cugnet's case for recognition of testamentary freedom and the retention of English criminal laws to the ministry, where they may well have influenced the final drafting of the Quebec Act.

Library holdings indicate that translations of the *Commentaries* were available in Quebec City by 1784 or soon after. Following the 1791 Constitution Act, opposition politicians who wanted to assimilate the provincial Assembly to the British House of Commons regularly quoted Blackstone. From 1809 attempts to summarise and translate the rules of English constitutional and criminal law all took him as their starting point. Indeed, a substantial part of the first thorough work on criminal law published in French was drawn from Book four of the *Commentaries*. Even authors focusing on the civil law of Lower Canada, such as Maximilien Bibaud, were spellbound by him.

No doubt many more references to Blackstone by lawyers or politicians could be found, especially in court reports, which we have not examined. Although the reports of the commissioners who drafted the Civil Code of Lower Canada contain few references to his work, they illustrate the bewildering array of sources that coexisted in the legal culture of the time: French ancient law, the Napoleonic codes and their commentators, English, American and Scottish authors, Imperial and Canadian legislation, and more.

Blackstone had a considerable influence on Quebec's legal culture. If unilingual French jurists may have had some difficulties in locating Gomicourt's translation of 1774–76, Chompré's version (1822–23) seems to have been more accessible. It had the advantage of reproducing the 15th edition, updated by Edward Christian in 1809. It was one of the few available

---

[121] Morel (n 14) 529–41.

works in French on the technical rules of English law, if not the only one. Furthermore, a few decades after the Conquest, one would expect many lawyers to have been able to read him in English. In the nineteenth century, the parliamentary system and the criminal justice of the *loix angloises* had clearly become a feature of Quebec's identity.[122] They have remained so until this very day. Blackstone's pedagogical talent eased the way for this acculturation process, but this aspect of his contribution has generally gone unnoticed.

It is ironic that his importance has been underscored in a very different way. In 1797 his son Henry was appointed comptroller of customs at Saint-Johns in Lower Canada. In 1799 Henry was removed from this position after constant complaints from his colleagues about his insolent and neglectful conduct.[123] He became sheriff of the district of Three Rivers that same year, but he was replaced in 1805, after having been severely criticised for mishandling of funds in a report prepared by the Executive Council. Henry was then appointed coroner in the City of Quebec, a position which he held until his death in 1825. To add injury to insult, it is reported that he regularly beat his wife, and was an alcoholic. Obviously, the sins of the son should not be visited on the father, whose legacy must be distinguished from his progeny. The former consists of a hybrid political and legal identity that coalesced in the eighteenth century, when a translated English public law was grafted on to the French private law of New France. This fragile plant has evolved and survived in a difficult environment, nurtured by an unexpected and strategic use of the *Commentaries* and their luminous prose.

---

[122] Morel (n 14) 509–14.
[123] WR Riddell, 'The Blackstones in Canada' (1921–22) 16 *Illinois Law Review* 255–67.

6

Blackstone's Ghost: Law and Legal Education in North Carolina

JOHN V ORTH*

On 31 July 1771 an ambitious teenager reading law in the Crown colony of North Carolina wrote to his father in England:

> I am too often troubling you, but I will hope for your excuse of this last request, as it will be of particular, perhaps necessary, service to me. It is that you will be so obliging as to procure Dr. Blackstone's *Commentaries on the Laws of England* for me, and send them by the first opportunity. I have, indeed, read them by the favor of Mr. [Samuel] Johnston who lent them to me; but it is proper I should read them frequently, and with great attention.[1]

The young man was true to his word. As appears from his journal entries for the following year, he spent many hours poring over his Blackstone.[2] 'No one can possibly read him,' he wrote, 'without infinite pleasure and improvement'.[3] But however great their admiration of the Tory Blackstone, Johnston and his young apprentice (and future brother-in-law) James Iredell soon enthusiastically enlisted in the cause of American Independence.[4] Later a determined advocate for North Carolina's ratification of the US

---

* The author is specially indebted to Thomas P Davis, Librarian of the Supreme Court of North Carolina, for locating the Court's reading assignments for bar applicants and to Joseph L Hyde, Assistant Attorney General, State of North Carolina, for material on Blackstone's influence on North Carolina criminal law.

[1] James Iredell to his father, 31 July 1771, in GJ McRee, *Life and Correspondence of James Iredell* (New York NY, 1857–58) vol 1, 91.

[2] Ibid 134–63 (entries for 21 November 1772 to 27 January 1773).

[3] Ibid 140 (12 December 1772). The occasion of this remark was a conversation with a local attorney. Iredell added: 'I was more pleased with the manner Mr [Jasper] Charlton spoke of [Blackstone], as upon a superficial view he had formerly mentioned him with indifference'.

[4] WW Whichard, *Justice James Iredell* (Durham NC, 2000) 25–41. Samuel Johnston (1733–1816), 'Revolutionary War leader', was successively North Carolina governor, US senator, and state judge: WS Powell (ed), *Dictionary of North Carolina Biography* (Chapel Hill NC, 1979–96) vol 3, 306–08 (hereafter *DNCB*).

Constitution,[5] Iredell ended his days as a justice of the US Supreme Court, but until his dying day he referred to Blackstone as the authoritative source on the common law.[6]

Iredell was not alone among colonial lawyers. In an oft-quoted passage, Edmund Burke reported that American printers had sold 'nearly as many of Blackstone's *Commentaries* in America as in England'—and this figure did not include copies purchased in England and shipped to America by individuals like Iredell's father.[7] After the Revolution, North Carolinians continued to learn their law from Blackstone. From 1813 to 1816 John Louis Taylor, law reporter and judge, published the semi-annual *Carolina Law Repository*, a collection of 'biographical sketches of eminent judges, opinions of American and foreign jurists, and reports of cases adjudged in the Supreme Court of North Carolina'.[8] Among the miscellany was 'Mr [John] Dunning's Letter to a Law Student', written at Lincoln's Inn, 3 March 1779, including 'a list of books necessary for your personal instruction'.[9] Prominent among them was 'Blackstone', with the admonition: 'on the second reading turn to the references'.[10] George Badger, later a prominent North Carolina lawyer,[11] reported that he began to prepare for his examination in 1814 by Judge Taylor with a diligent reading of the *Commentaries*.[12] Unlike Iredell, Badger found the pleasure distinctly finite.

---

[5] Whichard (n 4) 43–86. See also WF Pratt Jr, 'Law and the Experience of Politics in Late Eighteenth-Century North Carolina: North Carolina Considers the Constitution' (1987) 22 *Wake Forest Law Review* 577.

[6] Iredell quoted Blackstone in his most important opinions while a US Supreme Court justice: *Chisholm v Georgia*, 2 US (2 Dall) 419, 429 (1793) (Iredell J dissenting); *Calder v Bull*, 3 US (3 Dall) 386 (1798) (Iredell J concurring). On *Chisholm*, see JV Orth, 'The Truth about Justice Iredell's Dissent in Chisholm v Georgia' (1994) 73 *North Carolina Law Review* 255.

[7] E Burke, 'Speech on Moving his Resolutions for Conciliation with the Colonies, 22 March 1775' in PJ Stanlis (ed), *Edmund Burke Selected Writing and Speeches* (Chicago IL, 1963) 147, 161.

[8] When the nominative reports were organised in the North Carolina Reports, the North Carolina cases in the *Carolina Law Repository* for 1811–16 were incorporated in 4 NC. Taylor (1769–1829) was successively judge of the superior court, chief justice of the informal 'court of conference', and after 1818 the first chief justice of the newly created North Carolina Supreme Court. In 1822 he opened 'the first place for legal education in North Carolina which might be called a law school': *DNCB* vol 6, 11.

[9] *Carolina Law Repository* (Raleigh NC, 1816) vol 2, 223. Dunning's 'Letter to a Law Student' first appeared in the number of the *Carolina Law Repository* published in September 1815. 'In Parliament [Dunning] was a consistent opponent of the coercion of America', WS Holdsworth, *History of English Law* (London, 1936–72) vol 12, 562–63, a fact that would have made him an acceptable mentor for post-Revolutionary North Carolina law students.

[10] *Carolina Law Repository* (n 9) 225.

[11] Badger (1795–1866) became a superior court judge and later a US senator. His nomination to the US Supreme Court in 1853 was narrowly rejected by the Senate: *DNCB*, vol 1, 79–80.

[12] T Hunter, 'The Institutionalization of Legal Education in North Carolina, 1790–1920' in S Sheppard (ed), *The History of Legal Education in the United States: Commentaries and Primary Sources* (Pasadena CA, 1999) vol 1, 406, 408. Badger began reading law before Judge

He confided in his commonplace book that when he finished volume two, he prayed he was 'done with it forever!!!'.[13]

To aid students like Badger, the Raleigh booksellers Turner and Hughes advertised for sale in 1838 an elaborate and expensive chart, 'in the form of a large Map', called *The Tree of Legal Knowledge*, prepared by an unnamed North Carolina lawyer:

> The great object of the work is to impress upon the mind the methodical divisions and subdivisions of Blackstone's Commentaries, and thus enable the student effectually to master the work and preserve the arrangement as the general guide of his future studies.[14]

Thomas Ruffin Jr, son of North Carolina's famous Chief Justice Thomas Ruffin, might have found *The Tree* useful. In 1846 he wrote to his father with perhaps pardonable exaggeration that he had read the second volume of the *Commentaries* no fewer than 10 times and was beginning the third volume.[15] In 1849 Kemp Plummer Battle, later President of the University of North Carolina began the study of law under his father's tuition. Referring to the second volume of the *Commentaries* familiarly as 'second Blackstone', Battle claimed that he knew it 'by heart' and 'could give every principle laid down in that volume in the order in which it occurs'.[16]

As the state's legal institutions assumed their modern form in the early decades of the nineteenth century,[17] the state supreme court began to publish the reading required for applicants to the bar.[18] Blackstone's

---

Taylor published Dunning's letter in the *Carolina Law Repository*, but he already knew what the judge expected.

[13] Ibid 408.

[14] *Raleigh Register & North Carolina Gazette*, 21 May 1838. 'For a copy mounted on rollers in the form of a large Map, EIGHT DOLLARS—bound as Atlas, SIX DOLLARS—or in sheets, consisting of seven plates, FIVE DOLLARS'. An earlier notice reported that *The Tree of Legal Knowledge*, which was dedicated to William Gaston, a prominent justice of the North Carolina Supreme Court, was 'highly spoken of in New York': *Raleigh Register & North Carolina Gazette* 14 May 1838; see below, pp 132, 136.

[15] Thomas Ruffin Jr to his father, 17 February 1846, in JGdeR Hamilton (ed), *The Papers of Thomas Ruffin* (Raleigh NC, 1918–20) vol 2, 239–40. Thomas Ruffin Jr (1824–89) was himself later chief justice of the North Carolina Supreme Court: *DNCB* vol 5, 266.

[16] WJ Battle (ed), KP Battle, *Memories of an Old-Time Tar Heel* (Chapel Hill NC, 1945) 81. The son of William Horn Battle, law professor and justice of the state supreme court, Kemp Plummer Battle was president of the University of North Carolina from 1876 to 1891: *DNCB*, vol 1, 114–15.

[17] The North Carolina Supreme Court was first created by statute in 1818. Since 1868, it has owed its existence to a provision in the state constitution. See JV Orth and PM Newby, *The North Carolina State Constitution*, 2nd edn (New York NY, 2013) 130–31.

[18] For citations to all published court lists, see Appendix I. It is probably not coincidental that the first list appeared shortly after Richmond Pearson joined Frederick Nash on the three-judge court. Nash, in collaboration with John L Bailey, conducted a law school in Hillsborough NC, and Pearson operated a law school at his Richmond Hill plantation in western North Carolina. See FM Farmer, 'Legal Education in North Carolina, 1820–1860' (1951) 28 *North Carolina Historical Review* 271, 280–81.

Figure 1. Title Page: **The Tree of Legal Knowledge (1838)**
Reproduced by permission of the Boston Athenaeum.

Commentaries topped the first list in 1849. Reflecting the differing jurisdictions of the state's two trial courts, the supreme court assigned all four volumes—'2d volume *particularly*'—for practice in the county courts, while only the fourth volume on 'public wrongs' (crimes) was required for practice in the superior courts.[19] After the Civil War, the restored court continued the practice, and continued to assign Blackstone pride of place subject only—perhaps in recognition of the outcome of the war—to the state and federal constitutions.[20] Joseph Blount Cheshire, who read law in 1871 under William Kirkland Ruffin, another son of Chief Justice Thomas

---

[19] 32 NC (10 Ired) 607 (1849).
[20] 61 NC (Phil) 249 (1867). For practice in the county court, 'the first, second and fourth books of Blackstone's Commentaries' were required, while the third book on 'private wrongs' (torts and civil procedure) was alone required for practice in the superior court.

Ruffin, reported spending 'two or three months' on 'Second Blackstone and Cruise on Real Property' in preparation for his bar examination.[21] In 1879 the supreme court assigned 'Blackstone's Commentaries (2nd book diligently)'.[22] The 1889 list repeated the assignment of 'Blackstone's Commentaries (the second book with care)', but in a sign of open-mindedness and of the increasing availability of law books, the court concluded with the helpful note: 'It is not intended to confine the student to the special treatises above mentioned'—with the significant qualification 'other than Blackstone'.[23]

Although the *Commentaries* as such disappeared from the court list in 1895,[24] it was replaced by 'Ewell's Essentials', that is, Marshall Davis Ewell's three-volume *Essentials of the Law: For the Use of Students at Law*, which had first appeared under that title in 1889.[25] Previously Ewell had published *Blackstone's Commentaries for the Use of Students and the General Reader, Obsolete and Unimportant Matter Being Eliminated*,[26] which subsequently became volume one of his *Essentials*.[27] Ewell's three volumes held their place in later court lists,[28] until in 1923 the justices deleted the assignment of the second and third volumes but retained 'Blackstone's Commentaries as Contained in vol. 1 of Ewell's Essentials of the Law', an assignment thereafter regularly repeated until 1931, when the last list appeared.[29]

As Blackstone faded from the court lists, the state's law schools kept his memory green.[30] Professor John Manning began teaching law at the University of North Carolina in 1881 and developed 'commentaries on

---

[21] JB Cheshire, *Nonnulla: Memories, Stories, Traditions, More or Less Authentic* (Chapel Hill NC, 1930) 132. 'Second Blackstone' (*Commentaries*, vol 2) is devoted to 'the rights of things', ie property law. 'Cruise on Real Property' refers to W Cruise, *A Digest of the Laws of England Respecting Real Property* (London, 1804–1807 and many subsequent editions).
[22] 80 NC 488 (1879).
[23] 89 NC 595 (1884).
[24] 115 NC 833 (1895).
[25] MD Ewell, *Essentials of the Law* (Boston MA, 1889).
[26] MD Ewell, *Blackstone's Commentaries for the Use of Students and the General Reader* (Boston MA, 1882).
[27] Volume 2 of Ewell's *Essentials of the Law* included 'essentials' from *Stephen on Pleading*, *Smith on Contracts* and *Adams on Equity*. Volume 3 included 'essentials' from *Pollock on Torts*, *Williams on Real Property* and *Best on Evidence*.
[28] 119 NC 929 (1897); 125 NC xi (1899); 128 NC 633 (1901); 135 NC 747 (1904); 140 NC 653 (1906); 164 NC 539 (1913); 174 NC 827 (1917).
[29] 185 NC 787 (1923); 188 NC 837 (1924); 192 NC 839 (1926); 200 NC 813 (1931). The organisation of the Board of Bar Examiners in 1933 led to the end of the court lists: 1933 NC Sess Laws 313, 319 ('An Act ... for the Organization as an Agency of the State of North Carolina of the North Carolina State Bar').
[30] Blackstone had been part of the curriculum since the founding of the University of the North Carolina School of Law in 1845: A Coates, 'The Task of Legal Education in the South' (1930) 16 *American Bar Association Journal* 464.

Blackstone' for classroom use.[31] As reported by his son, the elder Manning 'regarded the study of Blackstone as necessary to the completeness of a legal education ... providing a basis upon which modern law ... could be elaborated and built'.[32] Manning's death in 1899 may have prevented him from publishing more than his *Commentaries on the First Book of Blackstone* (1899), but Samuel Mordecai, who began teaching law the following year, first at Wake Forest College then at Trinity (later Duke) Law School where he became dean, took up the cause. In 1907 Mordecai published his *Law Lectures: A Treatise from a North Carolina Standpoint on Those Portions of the First and Second Books of the Commentaries of Sir William Blackstone Which Have Not Become Obsolete in the United States*. An expanded second edition in two volumes appeared in 1916.[33]

Manning's title, promising 'commentaries on Blackstone', is misleading. Unlike Sir Edward Coke's *Commentary on Littleton*, Manning's Blackstone does not offer commentaries in the sense of reprinting an original text with extensive glosses. Neither does it annotate Blackstone's text with 'copious notes' in the manner of William Hammond's contemporary 1890 edition of the *Commentaries*.[34] Nor is it a reduced Blackstone like Ewell's *Essentials* or, later, *Ehrlich's Blackstone*.[35] Instead, Manning's book more closely resembles Blackstone's original, in the sense that it is a textbook of current law.

Blackstone's 'First Book', after an introduction on jurisprudence and legal education, is devoted to an array of topics that today are distributed among constitutional law (civil rights), labour law (master and servant), domestic relations (husband and wife, parent and child), decedents' estates (guardian and ward), and local government and business associations (corporations). Manning's *Commentaries*, about half the length of 'First Blackstone' (to use the local terminology), begins with a brief discussion of jurisprudence and civil rights, but then skips the topics specific to English government to concentrate on relational rights.[36] In fact more than half of Manning's book (151 out of 258 pages) is devoted to the law of husband and wife, a topic

---

[31] Typescripts of drafts used for classroom instruction are in Series 4, John Manning Papers #1970, Southern Historical Collection, The Wilson Library, University of North Carolina at Chapel Hill.

[32] J Manning, *Commentaries on the First Book of Blackstone* (Chapel Hill NC, 1899) iii (preface by JS Manning). The younger Manning (1859–1938) was later a justice of the North Carolina Supreme Court and state Attorney General: *DNCB* vol 4, 213.

[33] SF Mordecai, *Law Lectures* (Raleigh NC, 1916). On the family name, see *DNCB* vol 4, 312.

[34] W Blackstone, *Commentaries on the Laws of England* (ed) WG Hammond (San Francisco CA, 1890).

[35] JW Ehrlich, *Ehrlich's Blackstone* (San Carlos CA, 1950) v: 'I have taken Blackstone's original editions, excised the unnecessary and confusing passages and digressions which are not of interest to the law today, translated any necessary Latin, and deleted all footnotes'.

[36] For a tabular comparison of Blackstone's chapters with Manning's sections, see App II below. Death may have prevented Manning from completing his commentary on corporations, the final topic in Blackstone's vol 1.

that occupies less than 3 per cent of Blackstone's *Commentaries* (13 pages). A further 59 pages cover master and servant, as compared to Blackstone's 11. In Manning's *Commentaries* labour law and domestic relations together account for over 80 per cent of the total. In fact, the volume could have been descriptively subtitled 'The Law of Master and Servant and Husband and Wife in North Carolina'.[37]

Manning uses Blackstone as a convenient source of common law rules, such as the master's liability for injuries caused by a servant's negligence.[38] But he necessarily addresses issues the Commentator had not confronted, such as the increasing incidence of injuries to a servant caused by the hazardous new technologies introduced by the Industrial Revolution. In this respect Manning states the 'fellow servant rule' that developed in England and America after Blackstone's death, although he notes the exception recently made by statute in North Carolina in favour of railroad workers, and predicts that 'if it works well it will be extended by the General Assembly to other workers as well'.[39] Some topics of the law of husband and wife, unfamiliar to Blackstone, were peculiarly relevant in North Carolina, such as the 'marriage of persons who were slaves'[40] and the inheritance rights of 'children of colored parents born at any time prior to January 1, 1866'.[41]

Dean Mordecai, commenting on the first and second books of the *Commentaries* 'from a North Carolina standpoint', yields nothing to Manning in his regard for Blackstone, although he expresses it with characteristic flair:

> I would like to say a word to express my love and admiration for Blackstone; but the following incident reminds me that it would be well for me to abandon that idea ... when it was related that Mrs Montague, in an excess of compliment to the author of a modern tragedy, had exclaimed, 'I tremble for Shakespeare', Johnson said, 'When Shakespeare has got—for his rival and Mrs Montague for his defender, he is in a poor state indeed'.[42]

Mordecai covers the same topics from First Blackstone at about twice the length as Manning (460 pages), but devotes two-thirds of his 1,300 pages to 'Second Blackstone' on 'the rights of things', that is, property law.[43] Like Manning, Mordecai does not reprint Blackstone's text with notes but restates the law for contemporary North Carolina law students. Reflecting the realities of practice, Mordecai devotes six times as many pages to deeds

---

[37] It should be recalled that Manning planned to comment on each volume of Blackstone's *Commentaries*. The amount of material from the original might well have been much greater in later volumes, particularly in his commentary on vol 2.
[38] *Cf Commentaries* vol 1, 418–19 with Manning (n 32) § 91, 70–74.
[39] Manning (n 32) § 92, 74.
[40] Ibid § 126, 123–24.
[41] Ibid § 127, 124–25.
[42] Mordecai (n 33) vol 1, xi quoting J Boswell, *Life of Samuel Johnson*.
[43] For a tabular comparison of Blackstone's chapters with Mordecai's, see App III below.

Figure 2. 'Rights of Things'
Reproduced by permission of the Boston Athenaeum.
Following Blackstone's division of the law into Rights and Wrongs, the Tree of Legal Knowledge has two principal branches. The branch of Rights divides into two further branches, the Rights of Things and the Rights of Persons. Blackstone's second volume on the Rights of Things, that is, property law, exercised a profound and continuing influence on the law of North Carolina.

and wills as Blackstone does. In some cases, in addition to his own extensive lectures on North Carolina law, Mordecai assigns Blackstone as well: 'The student should carefully read and digest what Blackstone has to say on the subject [of the English law of title by descent], as such a course is essential to a clear comprehension of our present North Carolina law governing inheritances'.[44] On other topics copious citations to North Carolina cases and statutes are accompanied in the footnotes by hundreds of citations to Blackstone's *Commentaries*.[45]

The air of the classroom still lingers about Mordecai's *Law Lectures*, but unlike Blackstone's formal Oxford lectures, Mordecai's North Carolina lectures are laced with digressions and editorial comments, enlivened occasionally by pungent asides, including comic anecdotes from English literature.[46] Gilbert À Beckett's *Comic Blackstone* is quoted on the question of whether there is such a thing as judge-made law: judges 'in fact, make the law by saying what it means, which, as it scarcely ever means what it says, opens the door to much variety'.[47] Illustrating the lesson that the Rule in *Shelley's Case* is not a mere rule of construction but a peremptory rule of law, Mordecai comments that the grantor's intentions, 'like "The flowers that bloom in the spring! Tra-la!! Have nothing to do with the case"'.[48] Mordecai concedes that at first sight the 'doctrine of interesse termini may have an air of tweedledum and tweedledee about it'.[49] And he memorably describes the outmoded estate of fee simple conditional as 'the tadpole state of estates tail; the metamorphosis being brought about by the statute *de donis conditionalibus*'.[50]

---

[44] Mordecai (n 33) vol 1, 641. Mordecai summarises Acts of 1784, 1795, 1801, 1808, 1823, 1836, 1856 and 1905, useful for title searchers, but undoubtedly boring and more than a little confusing for students.

[45] There are 442 separate citations to Blackstone's *Commentaries* in Mordecai's footnotes.

[46] Mordecai was 'perhaps as famous for his wit and erudition as for his legal ability ... He delighted in writing clever prose and mediocre poetry, the best of which he collected and published in *Mordecai's Miscellanies* (1927)': DNCB vol 4, 318–19. The *Miscellanies* (privately printed) open with a spirited defence of Blackstone against the charge of North Carolina Chief Justice Walter Clark that 'the influence of Blackstone and Coke has had a very narrowing effect upon our Profession'. Mordecai replied that Blackstone and Coke had conferred 'inestimable benefits upon mankind in making and elucidating laws for its government', but characteristically concluded 'in re Blackstone I stand by my prejudices, and if the facts be against me, so much the worse for the facts. I won't read 'em' (3–5).

[47] Eg Mordecai (n 33) vol 1, 26 quoting GA À Beckett, *The Comic Blackstone* (London, 1857) 10.

[48] Mordecai (n 33) vol 1, 654. The reference is to Gilbert and Sullivan's comic opera *The Mikado*. See also JV Orth, 'Requiem for the Rule in Shelley's Case' (1988) 67 *North Carolina Law Review* 681.

[49] Mordecai (n 33) vol 1, 530. *Interesse termini* or interest in a term describes the interest a lessee has prior to entry and commencement of a lease.

[50] Ibid vol 1, 500. The statute *de donis*, 13 Edw 1, c 1 (1285) began the history of entailment. See JV Orth, 'Does the Fee Tail Exist in North Carolina?' (1988) 23 *Wake Forest Law Review* 767.

The contents of Manning's and Mordecai's Blackstones inevitably depart from the English original. Not only had more than an eventful century intervened since the separation of the Crown colony from the British Empire, but the intended readership of North Carolina's Blackstones was far narrower. Whereas Blackstone's original Oxford lectures offered a 'general and comprehensive plan of the laws of England' for gentlemen 'desirous to be in some Degree acquainted with the Constitution and Polity of their own country', not just those 'more immediately designed for the Profession of the Common Law', the North Carolina Blackstones were textbooks for law students. And whereas Blackstone could exclude the 'practical niceties' and 'minute distinctions of particular cases', the North Carolina versions were intended for students preparing for examination in just such minutiae.[51]

Details of state statutes that rubbished common law landmarks such as the fee tail[52] and the right of survivorship in joint tenancy[53] or that recognised the homestead as a new form of property interest[54] could not be avoided. Judicial innovations, such as Chief Justice Ruffin's rejection of the equitable doctrine of part performance,[55] obviously demanded attention. The need for such detail goes far to explain the lessened readability of North Carolina's Blackstones, just as modern economics textbooks fail to meet the literary standards of Adam Smith's *Wealth of Nations*.

While much was lost, much was retained. The long shelf life of 'Second Blackstone' in North Carolina is attributable to the remarkable stability of the law of real property in the state, but it also suited a largely rural and traditionalist society. The North Carolina Blackstones shared the general complacency about the way things were with their English model—what AV Dicey called Blackstonian optimism shading into Tory reaction.[56] 'No North Carolinian need be in haste to exchange his laws for those of others', Mordecai roundly declared, 'and in our laws we preserve in its integrity more than does any other state and, in some particulars, more than does England herself, the best principles of the common law'. 'Our population is but little mixed with other than that of the mother country',[57] the lecturer explained, overlooking nearly three-quarters of a million of his

---

[51] Holdsworth (n 9) 745–46.

[52] NC Gen Stat § 41-1. See North Carolina Constitution of 1776, § 43: '[T]he future legislature of this State shall regulate entails, in such a manner as to prevent perpetuities'; *cf* JV Orth, 'Allowing Perpetuities in North Carolina' (2009) 31 *Campbell Law Review* 399.

[53] NC Gen Stat § 41-2. See JV Orth, 'The Joint Tenancy Makes a Comeback in North Carolina' (1991) 69 *North Carolina Law Review* 491.

[54] Originating with the North Carolina Constitution of 1868, the homestead exemption is now in NC Const art X § 2. See Orth and Newby (n 17) 187–89.

[55] See *Baker v Carson*, 21 NC 381 (1836) (Ruffin CJ). See also D Malone (ed), *Dictionary of American Biography* (New York NY, 1928–58) vol 8, 217.

[56] AV Dicey, *Lectures on the Relation Between Law and Public Opinion in England During the Nineteenth Century* (London, 1914) 45.

[57] Mordecai (n 33) vol 1, x.

fellow citizens who traced their ancestry to a different 'mother country'. In the 1910 census African-Americans accounted for almost one out of three North Carolinians.[58]

If Manning and Mordecai did not repeat much of Blackstone's text, what did they derive from the original *Commentaries*? And why did they claim the mantle of the Commentator? Most obviously, they adopted Blackstone's organisation. If *The Tree of Legal Knowledge* from 1838 charted the general 'divisions and subdivisions of Blackstone's *Commentaries*', Manning and Mordecai, 60 years later, filled in the blank spaces on the map. Into the handy outline provided by First and Second Blackstone they inserted all the relevant North Carolina law that had accumulated since Independence. It is testimony to the practical organisation of the original that this worked remarkably well. More than structure, Blackstone also supplied the common law baseline from which all subsequent North Carolina developments departed.[59] But Blackstone's greatest contribution to Manning's and Mordecai's books was the enormous prestige of his name. Knowing Blackstone meant knowing the law. Connecting their books to the master enhanced their credibility—and saleability.

After Manning and Mordecai no later North Carolinian essayed a similar task. There were to be no more commentaries on the *Commentaries*. Modern legal treatises had by then begun to proliferate.[60] Blackstone's presence in North Carolina classrooms, which persisted well into the twentieth century, finally began to recede. In 1971, when a modern text on North Carolina property law supplanted Mordecai's *Law Lectures*, Blackstone's name largely disappeared, along with Mordecai's jokiness. But in Professor James Webster's treatise, regularly updated, Mordecai channels Blackstone.[61] The original *Commentaries* merits fewer than 10 footnote

---

[58] Out of a total population of 2,207,287 counted in the 1910 census, African-Americans numbered 697,843 or 31.62%: Historical Census Browser (University of Virginia, Geospatial and Statistical Data Center, 2004) www.mapserver.lib.virginia.edu. Mordecai also overlooked the fact that, as a descendant of a Jewish immigrant from Germany, he too had a different 'mother country': *DNCB* vol 4, 316 (entry on Jacob Mordecai, the oldest son of the immigrant Moses Mordecai, whose grandson was Samuel's grandfather and the dedicatee of his *Law Lectures*).

[59] The practice continues into the twenty-first century: JV Orth in vol 4, D Thomas (ed), *Thompson on Real Property* (LexisNexis, 2004; annual supplements) § 31-01, 2, n 1: 'The "common law" referred to [in this chapter] is the common law of England as it was at the time of American independence, for which the best and most convenient source is Sir William Blackstone's four-volume Commentaries on the Laws of England, first published in 1765 to 1768'.

[60] See AWB Simpson, 'The Rise and Fall of the Legal Treatise: Legal Principles and the Forms of Legal Literature' (1981) 48 *University of Chicago Law Review* 632; A Fernandez and MD Dubber (ed), *Law Books in Action: Essays on the Anglo-American Legal Treatise* (Oxford, 2012).

[61] J Webster, *North Carolina Real Property* (Charlottesville VA, 1971), now in a sixth edition and canonised as *Webster on North Carolina Real Property*.

Figure 3. '*Public Wrongs*' (Detail)
Reproduced by permission of the Boston Athenaeum.
Just as the branch of Rights on the Tree of Legal Knowledge divides into two branches, so the branch of Wrongs divides into two branches, Private Wrongs and Public Wrongs, complete with birds bearing the writs by which they are remedied. Blackstone's analysis of the common law of crimes, 'Public Wrongs', remains an important source for criminal jurisprudence in modern North Carolina.

citations, but Mordecai's restatement of the *Commentaries* 'from a North Carolina standpoint' is cited over 100 times.

Even as Blackstone faded from North Carolina classrooms, he continued to put in occasional appearances in North Carolina courtrooms. Much of the state's criminal law has never been codified. Arson and burglary remain by statute 'as defined at the common law',[62] while robbery is prosecuted to this day without any statutory authority whatsoever.[63] Even the definition of murder is left by statute 'as it was at common law'.[64] For the common law of crimes, the fourth volume of Blackstone's *Commentaries* remains authoritative. Indeed, if one takes OW Holmes's advice and looks at the *Commentaries* from the standpoint of 'a bad man' who cares only about what the law will do to him, it is Fourth Blackstone that matters most of all.[65]

When in the twenty-first century a criminal defendant appealed his conviction for burglary, the North Carolina Court of Appeals quoted Blackstone on the 'entry' required as an element of the crime:

> As for the entry, any the least degree of it, with any part of the body, or with an instrument held in the hand, is sufficient: as, to step over the threshold, to put a hand or a hook in at a window to draw out goods, or a pistol to demand one's money, are all of them burglarious entries.[66]

Because the state had not proved all the necessary elements, the court reversed the conviction on that charge.[67]

---

[62] NC Gen Stat § 14-58 (dividing arson into first and second degree arson); NC Gen Stat § 14-51 (dividing burglary into first and second degree burglary). Similarly, there are no statutes defining the crimes of conspiracy, attempt, and solicitation, although there are statutes prescribing the punishment for these offences.

[63] See *State v Black*, 209 SE2d 458, 460 (NC 1974): 'Robbery at common law is the felonious taking of money or goods of any value from the person of another, or in his presence, against his will, by violence or putting him in fear … G.S. s 14-87 creates no new offense, but provides that when firearms or other dangerous weapons are used, more severe punishment may be imposed'; *cf* Blackstone: 'the felonious and forcible taking, from the person of another, of goods or money to any value, by putting him in fear': *Commentaries*, vol 4, 241. See also NC Gen Stat § 14-87.1 (prescribing punishment for 'common law robbery').

[64] See *State v Streeton*, 56 SE2d 649, 652 (NC 1945): 'This statute [NC Gen Stat § 14-17 dividing murder into first and second degree murder] does not give any new definition of murder, but permits that to remain as it was at common law'.

[65] OW Holmes, 'The Path of the Law' (1897) 10 *Harvard Law Review* 457, 459: 'If you want to know the law and nothing else, you must look at it as a bad man, who cares only for the material consequences which such knowledge enables him to predict.'

[66] *State v Watkins*, 720 SE2d 844, 848 (NC App 2012) (quoting *State v Sneed*, 247 SE2d 658, 659 (NC App 1978) quoting *Commentaries*, vol 4, 226–27).

[67] Although Watkins had broken a house window before he fled, no part of his body or any instrument used to commit robbery 'entered' the dwelling. The court therefore reduced the offence from first degree burglary to felonious breaking and entering, a violation of NC Gen Stat § 14-54(a).

While Fourth Blackstone is still occasionally quoted in court, more often the influence of the *Commentaries* is mediated through a daisy chain of prior cases. One 'bad man' was sentenced to death in 2006 for two murders committed in the course of a burglary.[68] On appeal, he argued (among other things) that the state had failed to present sufficient evidence of the burglary. Rejecting that argument, the North Carolina Supreme Court cited *State v Maness* (1988) on the elements of the crime.[69] For authority, *Maness* cited *State v Ledford* (1986), which cited *State v Harold* (1985), which cited *State v Allen* (1923), which cited the pre-Civil War case of *State v Willis* (1859).[70] The latter cited no prior cases, only Fourth Blackstone, along with *Archbold on Criminal Pleading* and Coke's Third Institute.[71] A similar exercise could be performed for other common law crimes still basically defined as they were when Blackstone published the *Commentaries* more than two centuries ago.

Starting in colonial days, generations of North Carolina lawyers read Blackstone diligently, if not always with 'infinite pleasure'. For almost a hundred years, every applicant for admission to the state bar was expected to be familiar with the *Commentaries*—'2d volume *particularly*'. Supreme Court justices quizzed bar applicants on it, and law professors tested their students on it. Little wonder that Blackstone sank deep into North Carolina law, particularly the state's property law. Scholars like Mordecai who admired—even loved—the Commentator kept his volumes up to date. Yet even as he transmitted Blackstone to a new generation, Mordecai made the work his own, so that Second Blackstone now comes through Webster's citations to Mordecai. Similarly North Carolina judges long ago turned citations to Fourth Blackstone into precedents, obscuring the contribution of the English original. Today Blackstone may have faded into the background, but his ghostly influence on North Carolina law and legal education continues.

---

[68] *State v Wilkerson*, 683 SE2d 174 (NC 2009). Wilkerson was convicted of two counts of first degree murder under theories both of premeditation and of felony murder, as well as one count of first degree burglary. Felony murder, known as constructive murder in England, is murder that is committed during the commission of arson, rape, robbery, burglary, or other felony: NC Gen Stat § 14-17.

[69] 364 SE2d 349, 352 (NC 1988): 'The essential elements of first degree burglary are: (1) the breaking, (2) and entering, (3) in the nighttime, (4) into a dwelling house or a room used as a sleeping apartment, (5) of another, (6) which is actually occupied at the time of the offense, and (7) with the intent to commit a felony therein.'

[70] 340 SE2d 309 (NC 1986); 325 SE2d 219 (NC 1985); 119 SE 504 (NC 1923); 52 NC 190 (1859), where the caption describes Willis as 'a slave'.

[71] *Commentaries* vol 4, 223–28. *Archbold's Summary of the Law Relative to Pleading and Evidence in Criminal Cases* (New York NY, 1835) 251.

APPENDIX I

Blackstone's *Commentaries* in Court Lists of Reading Required for North Carolina Bar Applicants

Note. The reading lists promulgated by the Supreme Court of North Carolina are not reproduced by WestLaw and must be examined in the original volumes of the North Carolina Reports.

1849 32 NC (10 Ired) 607; same in 41 NC (6 Ired Eq) 505: requiring all four volumes of the Commentaries—'2d volume *particularly*'—for practice in the county courts, the fourth volume alone for practice in the superior courts

1850 33 NC (11 Ired) 658 (making substitution not affecting Blackstone); same in 42 NC (7 Ired Eq) 174

1854 47 NC (2 Jones) 607 (making substitution not affecting Blackstone); same in 55 NC (2 Jones Eq) 505

1867 61 NC (Phil) 249: requiring for the county court 'first, second, and fourth books of Blackstone's Commentaries' and for the superior court 'third book of Blackstone's Commentaries'

1879 80 NC 488: requiring of all applicants 'Blackstone's Commentaries (2nd book diligently)'

1884 89 NC 595: requiring 'Blackstone's Commentaries (the second book with care)' and noting 'It is not intended to confine the student to the special treatises above mentioned, other than Blackstone'

1885 92 NC 837: requiring 'Blackstone's Commentaries (the second book with care)' and including a note as above

1889 104 NC 915–16: requiring 'Ewell's Essentials (Vol 1)', condensing Blackstone's Commentaries

1897 119 NC 929: requiring 'Ewell's Essentials, 3 volumes'

1899 125 NC xi: as above

1901 128 NC 633: as above

1904 135 NC 747: as above

1906 140 NC 653–54: as above

1913 164 NC 539–40: as above

1917 174 NC 827: as above

1923 185 NC 787: requiring 'Blackstone's Commentaries, as contained in vol 1 of Ewell's Essentials of the Law'

1924 188 NC 837–38: as above

1926 192 NC 839–40: as above

1931 200 NC 813–14: as above

1935 208 NC 813 (continuing the course of study prescribed in 1931 until Summer 1936 bar examination)

APPENDIX II

Blackstone's *Commentaries* Correlated with Manning's *Commentaries*

The column on the left lists the chapter titles and pages in the first volume of Blackstone's *Commentaries on the Laws of England* (1765). The columns on the right list the corresponding sections and pages in Manning's *Commentaries on the First Book of Blackstone* (1899). Where there is no section in Manning corresponding to a chapter in Blackstone, the fact is indicated with —.

Commentaries vol 1 ch	pages	Manning sections	pages
The Study, Nature, and Extent of the Law	1–115	1–28	1–21
I Of the absolute Rights of Individuals	117–141	29–57	21–34
II Of the Parliament	142–182	—	
III Of the King, and his Title	183–211	—	
IV Of the King's Royal Family	212–219	—	
V Of the councils belonging to the King	220–225	—	
VI Of the King's Duties	226–229	—	
VII Of the King's Prerogative	230–270	—	
VIII Of the King's Revenue	271–326	—	
IX Of subordinate Magistrates	327–353	—	
X Of the People, whether Aliens, Denizens, or Natives	354–63	58–67	34–37
XI Of the Clergy	364–383	—	
XII Of the Civil State	384–394	—	
XIII Of the Military and Maritime States	395–409	—	
XIV Of Master and Servant	410–420	68–112	37–96
XV Of Husband and Wife	421–433	113–68	96–247
XVI Of Parent and Child	434–447	169–71	247–52
XVII Of Guardian and Ward	449–454	172–74	252–58
XVIII Of Corporations	455–473	—	

APPENDIX III

Blackstone's *Commentaries* Correlated with Mordecai's *Law Lectures*

The column on the left lists the chapter titles and pages in the first and second volumes of Blackstone's *Commentaries on the Laws of England*. The columns on the right list the chapters and pages in Mordecai's *Law Lectures: A Treatise From a North Carolina Standpoint on Those Portions of the First and Second Books of the Commentaries of Sir William Blackstone Which Have Not Become Obsolete in the United States* (2nd ed 1916). Mordecai actually uses Roman numerals for numbering chapters. To avoid confusion with Blackstone's Roman numerals (and in the interest of consistency with Appendix II), I have substituted Arabic numbers. Where there is no chapter in Mordecai corresponding to a chapter in Blackstone, the fact is indicated with —. Where one chapter in Mordecai correlates with more than one chapter in Blackstone, that is indicated in brackets.

Commentaries vol 1 ch	pages	Mordecai ch	pages
The Study, Nature, and Extent of the Law	1–115	1–2	1–32
I Of the absolute Rights of Individuals	117–41	3	32–50
II Of the Parliament	142–82	—	
III Of the King, and his Title	183–211	—	
IV Of the King's Royal Family	212–219	—	
V Of the councils belonging to the King	220–225	—	
VI Of the King's Duties	226–229	—	
VII Of the King's Prerogative	230–270	—	
VIII Of the King's Revenue	211–326	—	
IX Of subordinate Magistrates	327–353	—	
X Of the People, whether Aliens, Denizens, or Natives	354–363	4	51–59
XI Of the Clergy	364–383	—	
XII Of the Civil State	384–394	—	
XIII Of the Military and Maritime States	395–409	—	
XIV Of Master and Servant	410–420	5	60–186
XV Of Husband and Wife	421–433	6	187–394

(*Continued*)

Commentaries vol 1 ch	pages	Mordecai ch	pages
XVI Of Parent and Child	434–447	7	395–412
XVII Of Guardian and Ward	449–454	8	413–35
XVIII Of Corporations	455–473	9	436–59
Commentaries vol 2 ch	pages	Mordecai ch	pages
I Of Property, in general	1–15	—	—
II Of Real Property; and first of Corporeal Hereditaments	16–19	10 [II–III]	460–84
III Of Incorporeal Hereditaments	20–43		
IV Of the Feodal System	44–58	11 [IV–VI]	485–88
V Of the antient English Tenures	59–77		
VI Of the modern English Tenures	78–102		
VII Of Freehold Estates, of Inheritance	103–119	12	489–501
VIII Of Freeholds not of Inheritance	120–139	13	502–21
IX Of Estates, less than Freehold	140–151	14	522–47
X Of Estates upon Condition	152–162	15	548–87
XI Of Estates in Possession, Remainder, and Reversion	163–798	16	588–600
XII Of Estates in Severalty, Joint-tenancy, Co-parcenary, and Common	179–94	17	601–35
XIII Of the Title to Things Real, in general	195–199	18 [XIII–XIV]	636–47
XIV Of Title by Descent	200–240		
XV Of Title by Purchase; and, first, by Escheat	241–257	19	648–66
XVI Of Title by Occupancy	258–262	20	667–79
XVII Of Title by Prescription	263–266	21	680–93
XVIII Of Title by Forfeiture	267–286	22	694–715
XIX Of Title by Alienation	287–294	23	716–764
XX Of Alienation by Deed	295–343	24	765–1075
XXI Of Alienation by Matter of Record	344–364	25	1076–1086

(*Continued*)

Commentaries vol 2 ch	pages	Mordecai ch	pages
XXII. Of Alienation by Special Custom	365–372	26	1087–88
XXIII. Of Alienation by Devise	373–383	33	1132–1286
XXIV Of Things Personal	384–388	27 [XXIV–XXVIII]	1089–98
XXV Of Property in Things Personal	389–399		
XXVI Of Title to Things Personal, by Occupancy	400–407		
XXVII Of Title by Prerogative, and Forfeiture	408–421		
XXVIII. Of Title by Custom	422–429		
XXIX. Of Title by Succession, Marriage, and Judgment	430–439	28	1099–1102
XXX. Of Title by Gift, Grant, and Contract	440–470	29–31	1103–30
XXXI. Of Title by Bankruptcy	471–488	32 [see 22]	1131
XXXII. Of Title by Testament, and Administration	489–520	34	1287–1371

7

Antipodean Blackstone

WILFRID PREST*

A SUBSTANTIAL LITERATURE surveys the dissemination, reception and influence of the *Commentaries* in England and North America. But the role of Blackstone's book in other common law jurisdictions, including Britain's former white settler colonies in the South Pacific, has hitherto attracted little attention. From some perspectives Australia and New Zealand share a similar history of European encroachment and indigenous dispossession after 1769–70, when Captain James Cook first raised the Union Jack on these shores. Yet both the colonial and the postcolonial experiences of the two lands have diverged in many respects. The once confident expectation that New Zealand must eventually join a federated commonwealth of Australasia now seems quite implausible, as the two nations have each developed a distinctive cultural, demographic, economic, political and social identity.

Hence it should not be entirely surprising to find that Blackstone's *Commentaries* had a slightly different history on either side of the Tasman Sea. For chronological reasons alone, we might well expect that New Zealand is likely to have been less receptive to Blackstone's text—which first appeared some 70 years before those islands were formally absorbed into the British Empire in 1840—than the Australian colonies, where rudimentary British governmental and legal institutions were in place from the arrival of the First Fleet to establish a penal colony at Botany Bay in 1788. While this does in fact seem to be the case, the main importance of the *Commentaries* in both societies has been as a source of general constitutional principles as well as a formal legal authority.

---

* This chapter draws heavily on my Alex Castles Legal History Lecture of 2002, published in the *Flinders Journal of Law Reform* 6 (2003) 151–67. Besides those whose help is acknowledged there and in footnotes below, I wish to thank Richard Boast, Cheryl Hoskin, Stefan Petrow, David Williams and the staff of the University of Adelaide Archives for various kind offices.

I BLACKSTONE IN AUSTRALIA

Blackstone's visible public presence in Australia seems to be entirely lacking a New Zealand equivalent. There are two such manifestations, each associated with an educational institution. The earliest was commissioned for the first university established on the continent, shortly after the granting of responsible government to the colony of New South Wales. A stained glass image of the commentator clad in judicial robes, flanked to the left by Captain Cook and to the right by the Scottish chemist Joseph Black, is one of 36 windows depicting British philosophers, scientists and men of letters made by the London firm of Clayton and Bell for the neo-Gothic Great Hall at Sydney University, opened in 1859 (see Figure 1). Blackstone's central placing in this triptych is certainly not by mere chance or alphabetical arrangement. On the contrary, it reflects the determination of those colonial leaders who founded the university to downplay their polity's convict origins, while celebrating its flourishing state under the rule of English law and government, as epitomised by Blackstone's *Commentaries*.[1]

The second and more overtly public acknowledgement of book and author appeared almost a century later, on the University of Queensland's Forgan Smith Building (constructed *c* 1940), where above the entrance to the Law School the name 'Blackstone' is carved in large bas-relief capital letters, together with those of Aristotle, Socrates, Bacon, Coke and Hobbes (see Figure 2). How, why and by whom the author of the *Commentaries* was selected for immortalisation in this company and manner seems now to be unknown. Such graphic appropriation of and homage to past greatness is a familiar feature of North American campus architecture, from which the Queensland building may well have derived some inspiration.[2]

The long-term significance of these visual markers of Blackstone in Australia may be open to debate. Yet legal historians seem agreed in their assessment of his work's immediate post-1788 impact. According to Alex Castles, 'In the early years of the British occupation of New South Wales, [the *Commentaries*] was one of the few law books available'.[3] Bruce Kercher adds that

> Blackstone's multi-volume *Commentaries* were the most important law books carried on the First Fleet in 1788 ... they soon acquired such authority that they

---

[1] JH Baker and W Prest, 'Iconography' in Prest (ed) Commentaries 242.
[2] F Robinson, *The University of Queensland, St. Lucia, Brisbane* (Brisbane, 1957) 9; B Pascoe, *A Guide to the Great Court* (St Lucia, 1992) 88–93; I owe these references and help in contextualising them to Warren Swain.
[3] AC Castles, *Annotated Bibliography of Printed Materials on Australian Law 1788–1900* (North Ryde, 1994) 60.

Figure 1. Stained Glass Window (Detail), Clayton and Bell (1857–58), Great Hall, University of Sydney
Stained Glass Window from The Great Hall, University of Sydney—The Eighteenth Century, with William Blackstone, centre. Copy provided by the University of Sydney Archives from B McKenzie, *Stained Glass and Stone* (1989), University of Sydney Monographs, No 5; photographer Raymond de Berquelle.

Figure 2. Law School Entrance, Forgan Smith Building (1940), University of Queensland Photograph by Wilfrid Prest.

were treated as reverently as any superior court judgment. In the frontier period at Sydney Cove, when the only lawyers in the colony were convicts, the possession of the latest edition of Blackstone was almost as good as a qualification in law.[4]

We might well assume the presence on the First Fleet of at least one copy of Blackstone's *Commentaries*, from the request which Judge-Advocate David Collins sent back to London from Sydney in November 1788, for 'a fresh supply of paper' and Blackstone's *Reports*, as well as 'any law publication of note that has appeared since my departure'.[5] But conclusive evidence is provided by a letter from Deputy Judge-Advocate Thomas Hibbins to Governor Hunter in 1795, requesting that he be furnished with the same law books that Collins was 'supplied by Government when he first came out as Judge-Advocate of New South Wales'. Although these are mostly and perhaps unsurprisingly works dealing with criminal law, Hibbins's list does also specifically mention Blackstone's *Commentaries*.[6]

---

[4] B Kercher, *An Unruly Child: a History of Law in Australia* (Sydney, 1995) xii.
[5] A Britton (ed), *Historical Records of New South Wales*, vol 1, pt 2 (Sydney, 1892, 1978) 210.
[6] FM Bladen (ed), *Historical Records of New South Wales* (Sydney, 1893, 1978) 359–40. Phillip Lisle and Bruce Kercher both kindly drew my attention to this reference.

In 1808 Judge-Advocate Richard Atkins, drawing up the criminal charges against John Macarthur which precipitated the 'Rum Rebellion' against Governor Bligh, relied in part upon one of Pitt's 1795 Treason Acts. Because no copy of that statute was available in the colony, the convict attorney George Crossley advised Atkins to borrow the ex-convict merchant Simeon Lord's copy of the latest edition of Blackstone's *Commentaries*, in which an editorial note quoted the relevant portion of the Act. Ironically enough, 'Mr Christian, the Editor of that last Edition' was Edward Christian, first Downing Professor of the Laws of England at Cambridge University, whose brother Fletcher Christian had led the Bounty mutiny against Bligh nearly 20 years before.[7] Atkins may have inherited Collins's small legal library; when John Graunt paid him a call the previous year, he was received by Atkins in his office, 'where I found myself surrounded by Blackstone's Commentaries and a few other Law Books'.[8]

Advertisements and announcements in the *Sydney Gazette* during the first decade of the nineteenth century show copies of the *Commentaries* being bought and sold by colonists, along with more down-to-earth practice books, like Richard Burn's multivolume *Justice of the Peace and Parish Officer* and a work described as 'The Attorney's Pocket Book Companion', which might have been one of several titles, including *The Attorneys Compleat Pocket-Book* (London, 1741 and five further editions).[9] It was his lack of such workaday manuals that Deputy Judge-Advocate Dore lamented in 1798:

> [P]ractical law books ... for my Information in general matters of Business, particularly such as relate to the official duties of a Proctor, Attorney, Notary Publick etc., Civil Magistracy, and a general system of Professional Instructions, in which the practical points are more my object than any theoretical Essays ...[10]

Could Dore's disdain for impractical theorising have been made with the *Commentaries* in mind?

From this scattered evidence for the early presence of the *Commentaries* in Australia we turn to consider their use in legal process. The first Supreme Court of New South Wales exercised jurisdiction in civil matters only; Barron Field, author of a popular *Analysis of Blackstone's Commentaries on the Laws of England* (1811 and two further editions) served as judge from 1817 until the establishment of permanent and virtually omnicompetent supreme courts in New South Wales and Tasmania (or Van Diemen's

---

[7] F Watson (ed) *Historical Records of Australia*, ser I vol 6 (Sydney, 1916) 306; HV Evatt, *Rum Rebellion* (Sydney, 1944) 135.
[8] Y Cramer, *This Beauteous Wicked Place: Letters and Journals of John Graunt, Gentleman Convict* (Canberra, 2000) 34; thanks to Alan Frost for this reference.
[9] *Sydney Gazette*, 21, 28 August 1803, 20 January 1805, 1, 15 September 1805, 30 August 1807, 19 October 1811.
[10] F Watson (ed), *Historical Records of Australia*, ser IV vol 1 (Sydney, 1922) 31.

Land) in 1824. Intermittent publication of case reports based on decisions in these courts did not begin until the 1840s. However, notes on about 1,400 cases tried before the New South Wales Supreme Court during the period 1824–39, based mainly on newspaper accounts, have been brought together by Prof Kercher and a team from Macquarie University, while Dr Stefan Petrow and Kercher have edited similar reports on early litigation before the Supreme Court of Van Diemen's Land.[11] In both these early Australian jurisdictions the *Commentaries* figured prominently.

The *Hobart Town Gazette's* report of *R v Tibbs*, the opening case heard before Chief Justice John Pedder in the Supreme Court of Tasmania on 24 May 1824, a fortnight before the first trial in the Supreme Court of New South Wales, includes extensive extracts from the speech of the prosecutor, Attorney General Gellibrand, extolling the benefits of trial by jury as

> one of the greatest boons conferred by the Legislature upon this colony: I trust the Court will pardon me, if instead of stating my own opinion, I give the opinions of some of those who have written upon this important subject. Mr Justice Blackstone's encomium is so just, striking and beautiful, that I shall read it to the Court at Length.

This he proceeded to do, quoting from Book 3, chapter 23 of the *Commentaries* an entire 17-line paragraph, complete with its concluding patriotic reflection that, whereas Montesquieu had predicted British liberties would eventually go the same way as those of previous great powers, he 'should have recollected, that Rome, Sparta and Carthage were strangers to the trial by jury'.[12]

However appropriate to its particular occasion, this seems to have been a somewhat exceptional instance of Blackstone's words invoked for merely expressive or rhetorical purposes, even if a similar end was served by Chief Justice of New South Wales Francis Forbes's long quotation of Blackstone on the freedom of the press as a basic constitutional right, in withholding his approval of Governor Darling's attempted political censorship measure, the 1827 Act for Regulating the Publication of Newspapers.[13] The more typical forensic use of Blackstone was entirely instrumental, to provide authority for a particular legal argument or proposition, whether procedural or substantive. Thus in *R v Lee* (1830) the NSW Supreme Court was urged, unsuccessfully, to reject an indictment for the theft of two caged emus on the grounds that 'Blackstone 4.336 laid it down, that stealing of animals, kept for whim or pleasure, was not indictable at common law', while in *R v Claig* (1825) Solicitor General Stephen 'argued that in all cases

---

[11] The results are now available via the Australasian Colonial Legal History Library of the Australian Legal Information Institute: www.austlii.edu.au/au/special/legalhistory.

[12] www.austlii.edu.au/au/cases/tas/TASSupC/1824/1.html; *Commentaries* vol 3, 379.

[13] F Watson (ed), *Historical Records of Australia*, ser I, vol 13 (Sydney, 1920) 290; *cf R v Sheriff of New South Wales* (1825), www.austlii.edu.au/au/cases/nsw/NSWSupC/1825/2.html.

of murder the law assumes malicious intent, and according to Blackstone, the defendant had to prove otherwise'. Another murder trial (*R v Johnson, Smith and Gilroy*) saw the jury informed by Justice Dowling 'on the authority of Lord Hale and Mr Justice Blackstone, whose dictum he quoted, that no degree of provocation could justify a homicide, the utmost it could do would be to mitigate it to manslaughter'.[14]

As these scattered examples sufficiently indicate, Blackstone was sometimes cited alone, and sometimes invoked together with other authorities, both ancient and modern. On one occasion Forbes accepted the Crown's contention that 'The authority of Blackstone might be very good but it was too general in its application' to the specific issue of whether a new commission to magistrates impugned the validity of previous commissions, while in 1836 Mr Justice Burton referred to 'Sir William Blackstone and other elementary writers'.[15] Otherwise there is no suggestion that the persuasive authority of the *Commentaries* was regarded as in any sense compromised or diminished by its character as an introductory text.

The fundamental question of the colony's legal status, and hence the applicability or otherwise of specific aspects of English law, was the issue on which Blackstone seems most often to have been invoked before the New South Wales Supreme Court in the 1820s and 1830s. In his introductory section from Book I, 'Of the Countries Subject to the Laws of England', Blackstone had famously written in 1765 that 'as the law is the birthright of every subject, so wherever they go they carry their laws with them'.[16] However, the second edition of 1766 introduced significant qualifications, noting that the general statement must be understood 'with very many and very great restrictions'. In its careful phrasing—'Such colonists carry with them only so much of the English law, as is applicable to their own situation and the condition of an infant colony', with explicit exclusion of 'laws of police and revenue' and reservation of a 'general superintending power of the legislature in the mother country'—this rider reflected Blackstone's immediate reaction to the constitutionalist protests and trade boycotts of the North American colonists during the Stamp Act crisis of 1765.[17]

Yet long afterwards, and in another hemisphere, we find his words being used by Australian courts to support a restrictive, colonial-centred approach to the reception of English law. Take, for example, the civil case of *Macdonald v Levy* (1833) before the NSW Supreme Court, where Chief Justice Forbes upheld the validity of colonial practice, which permitted the

---

[14] www.austlii.edu.au/au/cases/nsw//NSWSupC/: *R v Lee* (1830) NSWSupC 3; (1830) NSW Sel Cas (Dowling) 19 (6 March 1830); *R v Claig* [1825] NSWSupC 18; *R v Johnson, Smith and Gilroy* [1828] NSWSupC 21 (23 March 1828); *Sydney Gazette*, 24 March 1828.

[15] www.austlii.edu.au/au/cases/nsw//NSWSupC/: *R. v Dargan and Wildred* (1824); *R. v Schofield* (1838).

[16] *Commentaries* vol 1, 105.

[17] *Commentaries*, 2nd edn (Oxford, 1766) vol 1, 107–09.

charging of interest at a rate 3 per cent higher than that allowed under the relevant English statute dating back to Queen Anne's reign. According to Forbes, Blackstone's exposition was 'clear and comprehensive'. This passage in the *Commentaries* is considered to be a sound exposition of the law by all the writers on colonial law, and is received as an authority in our courts'. If the role of judges was merely to determine whether English laws could possibly be applied to New South Wales,

> what is there to prevent the application of a 'multitude' of provisions, as Blackstone expresses it, which hitherto no-one has dreamed of extending to this colony—the law of marriage—the law of tithes, with their particular exemptions—the poor laws—the excise laws[?][18]

Finally, of course, Blackstone had famously pronounced that the nature of colonial legal regimes was determined by the law of nature or nations according to the manner in which the 'distant plantations' had been acquired, whether by 'right of occupancy' of 'desart and uncultivated' lands, or by conquest. As early as 1836, in the case of *R v Murrell and Bummaree*, Sidney Stephen, assigned as counsel for an Aboriginal defendant arraigned on the charge of murdering another Aborigine, argued that

> [i]t was laid down in First Blackstone, 102, and in fact in every other work upon the subject, that land obtained like the present were not desart [*sic*] or uncultivated, or peopled from the mother country, they having a population of [their] own more numerous than those who have since arrived from the other country ... therefore in point of strictness and analogy to our law, we were bound to obey their laws, not they to obey ours.[19]

The bench unanimously rejected this plea to its jurisdiction, relying on Vattel and other passages of Blackstone which were held to support the doctrine of undivided Crown sovereignty. But at trial the jury acquitted the accused Jack Congo Murrell, despite no witnesses being produced in his defence.[20] The jurisdictional issues raised in this case have continued to come before Australian courts down to the present day.[21]

It is easy to understand how the *Commentaries* acquired oracular status in the earliest days after European occupation of Australia, when law books of any kind were evidently in very short supply. They continued to play a similar role as the British frontier expanded, both overland from Sydney Cove and Hobart Town, and by the establishment of new settlements on Moreton Bay, Port Phillip Bay and the Swan River. Sir John Hindmarsh, first governor of the 'free province' (as distinct from

---

[18] *Commentaries* vol 1, 105.
[19] www.austlii.edu.au/au/cases/nsw//NSWSupC/: *R v Murrell and Bummaree* (1836).
[20] *Commentaries* vol 1, 104–05; AC Castles, *An Australian Legal History* (Sydney, 1982) 526–31.
[21] *Cf* S Cooke, 'Arguments for the Survival of Aboriginal Customary Law in Victoria: A Case Note on R v Peter (1860) and R v Jemmy (1860)' (1999) 5 *Australian Journal of Legal History* 200–41.

convict colony) of South Australia, requested a copy of the *Commentaries* to bring out with him on the HMS *Buffalo* in 1836. Doubtless seeking to anticipate all possible contingencies, Hindmarsh also ordered a copy of the *Code Napoleon*.[22] Because the local market was too small to support a local printing, let alone versions of Blackstone specifically adapted to Antipodean needs, Australasian lawyers, readers and students continued to rely upon imported English, Irish or indeed American editions. In this respect the history of Blackstone in Australia and New Zealand diverges from the history of Blackstone in Canada and the USA, where specialised North American versions continued to appear throughout the nineteenth and into the twentieth centuries.[23]

But whatever their geographical location, all Blackstone's editors (not to mention his abridgers and adapters) increasingly faced the problem of chronological obsolescence. By the 1830s Blackstone's text was more than 60 years old. Its standing as the classical introduction to and overview of English law was firmly established. But, according to the barrister James Stewart, in a prefatory note to his *The Rights of Persons According to the Text of Blackstone, Incorporating the Alterations Down to the Present Time* (London, 1839), as 'an authentic account of the law' the *Commentaries* had 'lost much of their original value. They can no longer be referred to for the existing law, and their practical advantages are thus unavoidably diminished'. Posthumous editions appearing after 1780 continued to be updated with additional footnotes and references to later cases and statutes, as with Edward Christian's 12th edition of 1793–94.[24] But the sweeping legislative changes wrought by Parliament from 1830 onwards called for radical reconstructive surgery if Blackstone's *Commentaries* was still to retain its place as the most authoritative comprehensive overview of current English law. The redrafting was undertaken by Henry John Stephen in his *New Commentaries on the Laws of England (partly founded on Blackstone)*, which first appeared under Butterworth's imprint in 1841, with successive editions down to the 21st in 1950. Stephen endeavoured to 'interweave my own composition' with Blackstone's text 'as freely as the purpose of general improvement might require'. Hence 'deviations from the original work' were admittedly 'frequent and extensive', although the basic structure of Blackstone's four volumes was maintained.[25]

---

[22] RM Hague, *Hague's History of the Law in South Australia 1837–1867* (Adelaide, 2005) vol 2, 589. In 1829 James Stirling, first governor of Western Australia, also brought a copy of Blackstone to his new post: CT Stannage, *The People of Perth: A Social History of Western Australia's Capital City* (Perth, 1979) 11–12.

[23] LM Friedman, *A History of American Law* (New York NY, 1973) 285–86, 290–91; M Hoeflich, 'American Blackstones' in Prest (ed), Commentaries 171–84.

[24] MH Hoffheimer, 'The Common Law of Edward Christian' (1994) 53 *Cambridge Law Journal* 146.

[25] HJ Stephen, *New Commentaries on the Laws of England* (London, 1841) v–vii. AV Dicey, 'Blackstone's Commentaries' (1932) 4 *Cambridge Law Journal* 288–90 [first published 1909].

Both in England and throughout the British Empire, Stephen's *Commentaries* became the standard examination text for admission to legal practice. Its ever-swelling bulk and complexity spawned a flotilla of pilotfish-like guides and abridgements: for example, Albert Gibson's *Intermediate Law Examinations Made Easy: A Complete Guide to Self-Preparation in Mr Serjeant Stephen's New Commentaries on the Laws of England* (3rd edition, London, 1882) and Edward Henslowe Bedford's *Student's Guide to Stephen's New Commentaries on the Laws of England* (9th edition, London, 1884).[26] It was largely in this form, as crib or key to Stephen's text, or in Stephen's increasingly heavily annotated volumes in which Blackstone's original words played an ever-diminishing part, that most Australian legal practitioners encountered Blackstone from the mid-nineteenth century onwards. Yet some were still encouraged to read Blackstone in the original as a general introduction to legal studies. The Adelaide stipendiary magistrate Thomas Bright recalled that as an articled clerk in the late 1860s he was urged by his English-educated master to 'read, mark, learn and inwardly digest' all four volumes of Blackstone's work.[27]

The apprenticeship model of legal education survived well into the twentieth century, in Australia as in England. In New South Wales it may not have been until the late 1970s that university-qualified lawyers with an LLB outnumbered those who had gained professional admission via service as articled clerks in a solicitor's office or pupils in bar chambers, and an examination administered by the Supreme Court's judges.[28] Regulations governing the admission of practitioners varied significantly across both the six original Australian colonies and the states which succeeded them in the federated Commonwealth of Australia. From 1883 the South Australian Supreme Court required from local aspirants to legal practice either certified passes in five 'practical' university law subjects or an LLB degree, whereas no universities existed in the outlying colonies of Queensland and Western Australia until well after Federation.[29] But the four colonial universities in New South Wales, South Australia, Tasmania and Victoria all provided some law teaching.

---

[26] Copies of these two books are held by the Sir John Salmond Law Library, University of Adelaide; Gibson's *Intermediate Law Examinations* bears a flyleaf ownership inscription, 'Thomas A Halloran| Articled Clerk| Mt Barker', with a title-page signature dated 'March 1882'; the copy of Bedford's *Student Guide* presented to the library in 1965 by a Mrs J Woolridge has had an ownership signature cut from the title page.

[27] TR Bright, 'First 25 Years of the Law' *Register* (South Australia) 22 June 1922; thanks to Peter Moore for this reference and further biographical information.

[28] D Weisbrot, *Australian Lawyers* (Sydney, 1990) 171.

[29] *Calendar of the Adelaide University ... 1883* (Adelaide, 1883) 84; VA Edgeloe, *Annals of the University of Adelaide* (Adelaide, 2003) 78–79.

Lectures in law commenced at the University of Melbourne as early as 1857, when Richard Sewell, the first law 'Reader', announced that Blackstone's *Commentaries* would be his main text. Although Sewell abandoned his post after the first year, four volumes of the *Commentaries* head the table of 'Works to be read' appended to the ambitious 'Course of Reading for Law Students', the first surviving Australian academic law reading list, printed in the university's calendar for 1859–60.[30] But thereafter the *Commentaries* prescribed by the practitioners who doubled as part-time law lecturers were those of Stephen, not Blackstone. Melbourne's most important early teacher of law (and much else) was the Irish-born polymath William Edward Hearn, who from 1873 added the duties of Dean of Law to his existing responsibilities as Professor of Modern History and Literature, Political Economy and Logic, besides filling a gap following the resignation of one professor of Classics and the arrival of his replacement. Surviving examination papers suggest that Hearn did at least refer to Blackstone in courses on constitutional and legal history, as also perhaps did Henry Samuel Chapman in his 1864 Law Part I lectures. Like Chapman, however, Hearn was a committed utilitarian. His ultimately unsuccessful attempts to codify the laws of Victoria owed a large debt to Jeremy Bentham and Bentham's jurisprudential disciple John Austin. Indeed, Hearn's disdain for Blackstone is succinctly conveyed by a question from the examination on the 'Laws of England' set for the degree of LLD in February term 1868: 'Define a crime. What is the defect in Blackstone's definition of this word?'[31] It is scarcely surprising that early Melbourne University book lists for 'Jurisprudence' are dominated by the works of Bentham and Austin.

Not until after Hearn's death and the arrival in 1889 of the brilliant young Cambridge-educated Edward Jenks as first Professor of Law was Blackstone restored to the reading lists, and then only for the general or 'non-professional' subjects of 'Jurisprudence' and 'Constitutional and Legal History'.[32] When Jenks departed in 1892 Blackstone disappeared again, except for Honours work in 'Jurisprudence'. Immediately after Federation the calendars for 1902 and 1903 abandon his name altogether. Yet from 1904 to 1914, under Jenks's able successor William Harrison Moore,

---

[30] J Waugh, *First Principles. The Melbourne Law School 1857–2007* (Melbourne, 2007) 9, 11, 14; *The University of Melbourne Calendar for the Academic Year 1859–60* (Melbourne [1859]) 76.

[31] JA LaNauze, 'William Edward Hearn (1826–1888)', *Australian Dictionary of Biography*, vol 4 (Melbourne, 1972) 370–72; E Scott, *A History of the University of Melbourne* (Melbourne, 1936) 24–33; R Selleck, *The Shop: the University of Melbourne 1850–1939* (Melbourne, 2003) 58–64, 126–28; *The University of Melbourne Calendar for the Academic year 1864–65* (Melbourne, 1864) app (Constitutional and Legal History and Law Part I examination papers); *The University of Melbourne Calendar ... 1867–68* (Melbourne, 1867) ccxxxii–ccxxxiv.

[32] *University of Melbourne Calendar for the Academic Year 1891* (Melbourne, 1890) 264; Scott (n 31) 160–62; Selleck (n 31) 300–11, 330–52.

Melbourne law students were once more recommended to acquire some slight acquaintance with the writings of the first Vinerian Professor by referring to the introductory section of the *Commentaries* (on the grounds or contents of the laws of England), as part of their reading for 'Constitutional History' and 'Law Part II'. While this subject actually dealt with the history of Federation and the Commonwealth of Australia Constitution Act, the intention was doubtless to highlight the contrast between Australia's written constitution and the unwritten or customary sources of (English) common law.[33]

At the University of Adelaide, founded nearly a quarter-century after its eastern counterparts, a Faculty of Laws was established in 1882. This followed close upon the Supreme Court's announcement that henceforth all local applicants for entry to the South Australian legal profession must undertake some university law studies, a decision doubtless facilitated by Samuel Way in his twin capacities of chief justice and vice-chancellor. The three-year course for the LLB and the five sub-degree certificate subjects were taught by part-time practitioner lecturers from 1883 until the appointment of one of their number, FW Pennefather LLM, as Professor of Law in 1891.[34] According to the reading lists in successive volumes of the University calendar, Stephen's *Commentaries* 'as far as relates to personal property' was regularly prescribed for the subject 'Property', as also occasionally for 'Constitutional Law' and 'The Law of Wrongs'. But Blackstone's name does not appear in the examination papers set for 'Jurisprudence' or any other subject until Pennefather's first appointment as lecturer in 1888, when students were invited to discuss his statement that 'no human laws are of any validity' if contrary to the law of nature. As 'Campbell's Students Austin', together with 'Maine's Ancient Law', 'Holland's Jurisprudence' and Hearn's 'Legal Rights and Duties' were the set texts, students were hardly encouraged to endorse Blackstone's assertion. By the same token, the 1896 jurisprudence paper asked 'How do Austin and Bentham differ in distinguishing crimes and civil injuries?'.[35]

The authors of Sydney University Law School's centenary history note that there the Faculty of Law led 'a somewhat shadowy existence' before the appointment of Pitt Cobbett as first incumbent of the Challis law chair

---

[33] *The University of Melbourne Calendar*: 1892, 264; 1899, 259; 1904, 56; 1914, 490. Selleck (n 31) 621–23.

[34] Edgeloe notes that Charles Henry Pearson was approached by the University to offer a course of public lectures on constitutional law in 1877 (Edgeloe (n 29) 75–76); *cf* J Tregenza, *Professor of Democracy* (Melbourne, 1968) 59, 64, 108. AC Castles, A Ligertwood and P Kelly (ed), *Law on North Terrace: the Adelaide University Law School 1883–1938* (Adelaide, 1983) 5, 10–17.

[35] *The Adelaide University* Calendar: 1883, 45, app cxlii; 1884, 102–03; 1889, lxxvi; 1891, 127–29, lxxxi; 1892, lxxii; 1895, App B7–B9; 1897, App B17.

in 1890.[36] Occasional lecture courses were previously offered by practising lawyers, among them John Fletcher Hargrave, a future Supreme Court judge who reached Sydney in 1857 after preparing the first volume for the 21st edition of Blackstone's *Commentaries*. As 'Reader in Jurisprudence of the University of Sydney' Hargrave told a parliamentary committee of enquiry into the university that when discussing Blackstone's *Commentaries* with his small class of students he omitted mere 'professional details'.[37] The university's calendars do not include law reading lists and only occasional examination papers; indeed lectures seem to have ceased altogether within 10 years of their inception in 1859.[38] Only from 1890, when its historians tell us that the 'Law School came into being', do reading lists and syllabi survive. From these Blackstone is conspicuously absent, except for one examination question from a constitutional law examination paper of 1907.[39] As at Melbourne and Adelaide, Stephen's *Commentaries* remained well to the fore, although Pitt Cobbett, the first professor of law, evidently made it his mission to shift the educational 'centre of gravity away from Blackstone and Stephen and towards the law as it was then practised in Australia from day to day'.[40] That pragmatic ambition was fully shared by W Jethro Brown, who had succeeded the redoubtable JW Salmond as Adelaide's law professor in 1906, following a stint as inaugural 'Lecturer in Law and History' at the University of Tasmania from 1893.[41] Sydney jurisprudence long retained a strikingly positivistic character, with Austin's writings and Bentham's *Theory of Legislation* still recommended texts as late as 1927; Austin, indeed, persisted into the 1940s.[42] Yet the barrister and later High Court judge WJ Windeyer, who taught legal history at his alma mater from 1929 to 1936, held Blackstone in sufficiently high regard to give him

---

[36] J and J Mackinolty, *A Century Down Town: Sydney University's Law School's First Hundred Years* (Sydney, 1991) 19.

[37] JM Bennett, 'John Fletcher Hargrave (1815–1885)' *Australian Dictionary of Biography* vol 4 (Melbourne, 1972) 345–46; Eller 21; cf [JF Hargrave], *Syllabus of the Two Courses of Lectures on General Jurisprudence Delivered at the University of Sydney During the Years 1859, 1860 and 1861* (Sydney, 1861). The Mitchell Library copy tp is annotated with the additional dates '1862 & 1863'; L Martin, 'From Apprenticeship to Law School: A Social History of Legal Education in Nineteenth Century New South Wales' (1986) 9 *University of New South Wales Law Journal* 127.

[38] Martin (n 37) 128.

[39] *The Sydney University Calendar 1852–53* (Sydney, nd) 58, prints Sir Charles Nicholson's inaugural address, which expressed the wish that 'From these walls ... will go forth ... lawyers, not merely indexes of a statutory code'; see also *Sydney University Calendar*: 1859, 84; 1861, 103; 1866, vii; 1887, 224–38, 263–67; 1890, 186 ff; 1891, 196–97; 1908, ccxvi.

[40] Mackinolty (n 36) 19–20, 34. T Bavin (ed), *The Jubilee Book of the Law School of the University of Sydney 1890–1940* (Sydney, 1940) 5–6.

[41] A Frame, *Salmond Southern Jurist* (Wellington, 1995); M Roe, *William Jethro Brown: an Australian Progressive 1868–1930* (Hobart, 1977) 15; WJ Brown, 'Law Schools and the Legal Profession' (1908) 6 *Commonwealth Law Review* 3–15; R Davis, *100 Years: A Centenary History of the Faculty of Law, University of Tasmania 1893–1993* (Hobart, 1993) 3–11.

[42] *University of Sydney Calendar*: 1927, 241; 1941, 410.

and the *Commentaries* a separate chapter in the published version of his lectures, which became a standard student text.[43]

II BLACKSTONE IN NEW ZEALAND

The University of Otago at Dunedin and the Canterbury University College in New Zealand's South Island both began law lectures during the 1870s; their northern counterparts at Auckland and Wellington followed suit from 1883 and 1899 respectively. Teaching, mostly provided as in Australia by part-time practitioners, was similarly geared to the needs of articled clerk students, and practical private-law subjects dominated. Charles Foster, formerly professor of jurisprudence at University College London, was reckoned a failure as Canterbury's first law lecturer because of his excessively academic approach; the text of Foster's first lecture, as printed in the local newspaper, tends to vindicate that judgment. (Foster, incidentally, compared Blackstone's *Commentaries* unfavourably to 'Kent's (American) Commentaries'.)[44]

The inaugural lectures given at Otago in 1877 by Henry Chapman's son Frederick were on 'The Law of Contracts' and 'The Law of Property'. By 1879 the syllabus had extended to 'General Jurisprudence' and 'The Laws of England', for which the respective texts (Austin's *Jurisprudence* and Stephen's *Commentaries*) continued to be prescribed over the next decade. A course on constitutional history was added in 1882, and from 1887 the general course was retitled 'The Laws of New Zealand'. At Auckland District Judge Seth Smith's lectures on equity and property in 1883–84 were followed by a long hiatus until the turn of the century, when a Dr McArthur began teaching jurisprudence and constitutional history, listing Austin as one of his texts. What from 1914 was termed the 'School of Law' gradually introduced a broader range of subjects, taught by academic lecturers as well as practitioners. But the overall orientation remained pragmatic and technical, as exemplified by a 1920s course on 'the practical work of a legal office'.[45]

So there was seemingly no more and perhaps even less room for Blackstone in the training of New Zealand lawyers during the later

---

[43] WJV Windeyer, *Lectures on Legal History* (Sydney, 1938) ch 31.

[44] P Spiller, J Finn and R Boast (ed), *A New Zealand Legal History* (Wellington, 2001) 291–94; J Farrar, 'Dr Charles Foster' (1980) *Canterbury Law Review* 1, 5–14. *The Press* (Canterbury), 7 April 1876, 3l; I owe this last reference and much other valuable assistance with New Zealand sources to Ms Tracey Thomas.

[45] *University of Otago Calendar*: 1877, 32; 1879, 36; 1880, 51; 1882, 86; 1887, 63–64; *Auckland University College Regulations Second Term 1883*; *Auckland University College Calendar*: 1884, 41; 1899, 51; 1904, 44; 1912, 47; 1913, 51; 1914, 51; 1923, 82; 1927, 97. KW Sinclair, *A History of the University of Auckland 1883–1983* (Auckland, 1983) 43, notes the 'deplorably low' standard of legal education before World War II.

nineteenth and early twentieth centuries than in Australia over the same period. This would scarcely have perturbed Henry Chapman, first puisne judge of New Zealand from 1843 to 1852, who sat again on the Supreme Court bench in Dunedin between 1864 and his death in 1881. Before leaving London, Chapman had assisted in preparing the works of Jeremy Bentham for publication, and after his arrival rejoiced that Bentham's 'spirit animates the procedure of the tribunals of a country unknown to him'.[46] Yet in fairness to Chapman it should also be noted that his opening address to the grand jury at the first sitting of the Supreme Court in Wellington in 1844 quoted Blackstone as 'a great authority'. Counsel appearing before Chapman and his fellow justices in Supreme Court and Court of Appeals cases between the 1840s and 1870s also occasionally cited Blackstone, whether in the original or the updated editions by Kerr and Stephen. So too did Acting Chief Justice Sidney Stephen, who in 1852 asserted that 'there was no other legal authority higher than Blackstone', a claim to which counsel took exception, answering that 'Blackstone is all very well as a textbook, or for the law student; but it would never do in these days to quote Blackstone in opposition to the recognised reports of the Superior Courts at Westminster'. In 1868 before the Wanganui magistrates' court, counsel for the plaintiff, who relied on Blackstone in a master and servant case, was met by the opposing lawyer's response that 'Blackstone was no authority now', to which Mr Caffry reportedly replied that 'Sir Wm Blackstone will be an authority as long as there is a stone in the temple'.[47]

Like their Australian and North American counterparts, country lawyers in New Zealand who lacked easy access to any legal library but their own doubtless found the *Commentaries* a useful resource. The University of Auckland Law School Library holds a single volume of the 1857 'New Edition Adapted to the Present State of the Law by Robert Malcolm Kerr', which bears the ownership stamps of both 'W. Douglas Lysnar, Solicitor, Gisborne' (admitted to the bar in 1891, Lysnar thereafter followed an energetic local and national political career) and the Gisborne legal firm of Wauchop, Kohn, McIntyre.[48] Yet remarkably few copies of Blackstone's *Commentaries* seem to survive in New Zealand. Whereas multiple copies of most of the eight editions published during the author's lifetime appear

---

[46] P Spiller, *The Chapman Legal Family* (Wellington, 1992) 30, 37–38.
[47] www.victoria.ac.nz/law/nzlostcases: *R v Reynolds* (1844); cf *White v Richards* (1848); *R v Robinson and McKenzie* (1852); *Welsh v Andrew* (1858); *White v Busby* (1859); *Reynolds v Tuangau* (1866); *Kawatine v Parker & Parker* (1869). *Wellington Independent*, 28 July 1852; *Wanganui Herald*, 28 February 1868. Many thanks to David Williams, who notes Blackstone's transmission via Charles Clark's much-cited *A Summary of Colonial Law* (London, 1834): cf D V Williams, 'The Pre-history of the English Laws Act 1858: *McIver v Macky* (1856)', (2010) 41 *Victoria University of Wellington Law Review* 361–80.
[48] Davis Law Library, Marilyn Mayo Rare Book Room, University of Auckland, item KL401.7 BLA 1857; M Chrisp, 'Lysnar, William Douglas 1867–1942', *The Dictionary of New Zealand Biography Volume Three 1901–1920* (Auckland, 1996) 285–86.

in the national union list of Australian library holdings, its New Zealand equivalent records only one copy of the first edition. The online 'New Zealand Libraries Catalogue' may be less comprehensive in coverage than its Australian counterpart (for example, it appears not to include the New Zealand Law Society's collections), but such a large disparity can hardly be explained on this basis alone.

III CONCLUSION

We lack a systematic conspectus of library holdings, public and private, booksellers' listings and book auction advertisements in Australia and New Zealand, with which to map the geographical and social distribution of the *Commentaries* in these two countries. Some lawyer bibliophiles are known to have possessed more than one edition; Samuel Way, South Australia's long-serving chief justice and university chancellor, whose 'large-minded cultivation' much impressed Beatrice and Sidney Webb, possessed among his personal library of 15,000 volumes not only the 16th (1825) and 18th (1829) London editions, but also the now rare San Francisco variorum edition (1890) of William L Hammond.[49] Yet notwithstanding a strong early showing at Melbourne, it seems that neither Australian nor New Zealand legal education gave much attention to Blackstone, except in the considerably modified form of Stephen's *Commentaries*. The contrast with North America is striking. According to David Lockmiller, writing in 1938, 'it may be safely assumed that practically all lawyers in the United States, prior to 1900, at one time or another read all or part of [Blackstone's] *Commentaries*'.[50] How are we to explain this difference?

Part of the answer is that 'By accident, circumstance, intention and development, American law put more emphasis on substantive law than adjective law, less emphasis on the forms of action and more on the rights extended and the rules governing those rights'.[51] While Australasian judges, lawyers and legal academics may not have been mere passive recipients of English law, until at least the middle of the twentieth century they were more influenced by British than American modes of legal education and theory. They may also have been more strongly affected by Austinian positivism than their American counterparts. Last, and far from least, unabridged editions of Blackstone's *Commentaries* were relatively expensive imports, with no locally printed adaptations or versions available. A two-volume

---

[49] [SJ Way], 'Catalogue of the Library: Law'; Special Collections, Barr Smith Library, University of Adelaide; JJ Bray, 'Way, Sir Samuel James (1836–1916)', *Australian Dictionary of Biography* vol 12 (Melbourne, 1990) 417–20.
[50] Lockmiller, 172.
[51] TG Barnes, *Hastings College of the Law The First Century* (San Francisco CA, 1978) 41.

edition bought new in 1894 would have cost a Melbourne law student £2/10/-, substantially more than Holland's *Elements of Jurisprudence* (10/6d), Jenks's *Government of Victoria* (14/-) and Broom's *Legal Maxims* (£1/11/6). Indeed the only more expensive law texts listed in the university bookseller's advertisement for that year were Tudor's *Leading Cases in Real Property*, and *Cases in Mercantile Law*, which each retailed for £2/12/6d.[52] On the other hand, booksellers in both Adelaide and Auckland advertised copies of Kerr's abridgement, *The Student's Blackstone* (which went through at least 12 editions between 1858 and 1896), for less than 10 shillings.[53]

While they evidently survived the disdain of Bentham and his disciples, as conveyed well into the twentieth century via law school jurisprudence, Blackstone and his *Commentaries* might have sunk without trace beneath the rising nationalist tide, which from the 1960s onwards led Australian (and to a lesser extent New Zealand) lawyers to reject what Bruce Kercher terms 'the symbols of deference' to English mores and models.[54] Yet we still await Blackstone's antipodean demise. A perceptive analysis of the continued staying power of the *Commentaries* has observed that although

> written as a mere textbook, containing no more than 'rudiments' (4:399), it has been ushered, with virtually the authority and symbolic status of a legal code, into the canonical realms of legal authority, and to the heart of the Anglo-America lex non scripta, with citations in the High Court of Australia alone running well into triple figures ...[55]

The online database Austlii currently lists 145 cases where Blackstone's *Commentaries* were cited in High Court of Australia judgments from 1973 to 2012 inclusive, with a maximum of 11 citations in 1992 and at least one citation every year. Over the immediate past decade 2003–2012 Blackstone was cited in 37 judgments, a decrease from the 48 citations of the previous 10 years, but on a par with the decade 1983–1992, which itself saw a significant increase after the 24 Blackstone citations reported between 1973 and 1982. A recent study of the use of secondary sources (in the lawyer's rather than the historian's sense) in Australian High Court judgments shows that in five sampled years between 1960 and 1996 the *Commentaries* gained a

---

[52] *University of Melbourne Calendar, 1893–94*: [advertisement] 'Price List of University Text Books for Examination Term 1893 and First Term 1894 to be obtained from Melville, Mullen and Slade, Booksellers to Melbourne University by Special Appointment'.
[53] Cf *New Zealand Herald*, 26 April 1889; *Register* (South Australia) 24 May 1913; Eller, 29–31.
[54] Kercher (n 4) 202.
[55] M Meehan, 'Authorship and Imagination in Blackstone's *Commentaries on the Laws of England*' (1992) 16 *Eighteenth-Century Life* 114. See also KM Parker, 'Historicising Blackstone's *Commentaries on the Laws of England*: Difference and Sameness in Historical Time' in A Fernandez and MD Dubber (ed), *Law Books in Action: Essays on the Anglo-American Historical Treatise* (Oxford, 2012) 23–42.

total of 24 citations, making it the runner-up only to Quick and Garran's indispensable *Annotated Constitution of the Australian Commonwealth* (with 30 citations).[56]

This intriguing result comes from a series of articles in which Professor Russell Smyth analyses citation practices of appellate courts in Australia and New Zealand. His more chronologically limited survey of works cited in judgments of the New Zealand Court of Appeals, based on 300 reported decisions from 1995 to 1999, shows that among the 8–9 per cent of secondary source citations, the *Commentaries* attracted a total of 7, as against 23 for Todd's *Law of Torts in New Zealand* and 16 for *Archbold's Criminal Pleading*.[57] Smyth has also looked at citation practices in subordinate Australian jurisdictions. From all 369 Federal Court cases reported from 1996 to 1998, it seems that judges there cited far fewer secondary authorities than their High Court colleagues, nor does Blackstone's *Commentaries* appear among the 'Legal Books cited on Three or More Occasions'.[58] Among a total of 300 cases, made up of 'the 50 most recent court of appeal or full court decisions of each state supreme court reported in the authorised reports as of June 1999', secondary authorities constituted only 6–7 per cent of the total number of citations; here Blackstone made a fleeting appearance on three occasions, once in the South Australian and twice in the Tasmanian Supreme Courts. Viewing the latter jurisdiction from a longer chronological perspective, the *Commentaries* was among texts cited in two or more decennial sample years between 1905 and 2005, along with Austin's *Jurisprudence*. A nationwide decennial sample of cases drawn from the same century-long period reveals that the *Commentaries* was treated as a 'de facto primary authority' by Australian state supreme courts, although its 12 recorded citations are only a quarter as many as those of the most referred-to text, *Cross on Evidence*.[59]

Apart from Blackstone's evident survival as an authority, it is hard to know what to make of these figures and findings. The samples analysed are quite small and since textbooks and treatises comprise only a fraction of all cited authorities, another sample set might yield at least slightly different

---

[56] R Smyth, '"Other than 'Accepted Sources of Law'": A Quantitative Study of Secondary Source Citations in the High Court' (1999) 22 *University of New South Wales Law Journal* 35, 45.

[57] R Smyth, 'Judicial Citations: An Empirical Study of Citation Practice in the New Zealand Court of Appeals' (2000) 31 *Victoria University of Wellington Law Review* 847–95.

[58] R Smyth, 'The Authority of Secondary Authority: A Quantitative Study of Secondary Source Citation in the Federal Court' (2000) 9 *Griffith Law Review* 40.

[59] R Smyth, 'What do Intermediate Appellate Courts Cite? A Quantitative Study of the Citation Practice of Australian State Supreme Courts' (1990) 21 *Adelaide Law Review* 78–79; R Smyth, 'Citation Practices in the Supreme Court of Tasmania 1905–2005' (2007) 59 *University of Tasmania Law Review* 59; R Smyth, 'Citing Outside the Law Reports: Citations of Secondary Authorities in the Australian State Supreme Courts over the Twentieth Century' (2009) 18 *Griffith Law Review* 714, 717.

results. Citations of Blackstone in Australian High Court judgments fluctuate widely from year to year. Thus between 2005 and 2010 inclusive the annual totals run as follow: 1, 2, 9, 1, 8, 4. But in any case the meaning and purpose of citations in general and those of Blackstone in particular remain problematical, especially when the evidence is quantitative rather than qualitative in nature. According to Meehan, Blackstone serves 'on many points, as the "last port of call" in legal retrospection, the very "headwaters" of those "streams of authority" that our judges still habitually chart as flowing from the imperial source'.[60] Yet it does not follow that appealing to Blackstone is an inherently conservative move, particularly where indigenous rights are concerned.

The first chapter of Castles's 1982 *Australian Legal History* drew attention to the fundamental importance of Blackstone's 'statement on the constitutional position of settled colonies'.[61] Five years later the historian Henry Reynolds proposed an interpretation openly at odds with then prevailing judicial orthodoxy and also representing a shift in his own previous understanding of Blackstone:

> The balance of evidence suggests that when he referred to desert and uncultivated land Blackstone meant uninhabited land ... Given Blackstone's views on the colonization of already inhabited lands, and his comments on the rights acquired by original occupation, it is clear that it is only by a very selective reading that he can be presented as the de facto apologist for the expropriation of Aboriginal land.[62]

Reynolds' radical critique of the legal rationale for European occupation of Australia was notoriously instrumental to, as well as explicitly embodied in, the High Court decisions which overturned the previous classification of Australia as 'terra nullius', again with specific invocation of Blackstone.[63] On the basis of the *Mabo* and *Wik* judgments, particularly those of Justices Brennan, Dean and Gaudron, a recent dissenting opinion by Justice Merkel in the Federal Court of Appeals actually refers to 'the Blackstone approach to a native title right', where, by invoking 'Blackstone's theory of the adaptation of the common law to the circumstances of a new colony ... the Crown's radical title under the common law is burdened by pre-existing native title'.[64]

---

[60] Meehan (n 55) 114.
[61] Castles (n 20) 11.
[62] H Reynolds, *The Law of the Land* (Ringwood, 1987) 34–35. The radical nature of Reynolds's analysis is brought out in the notice of his book by a former chief justice of South Australia: see (1998 Feb) 47 *The Adelaide Review* 11. See also Reynolds's 1986 Harold White lecture, *Aboriginal Land Rights in Colonial Australia* (Canberra, 1988) 17–18.
[63] *Cf* G Davison, *The Use and Abuse of Australian History* (St Leonards, 2000) 15.
[64] *Commonwealth of Australia v Yarmirr* [1999] FCA 1668 (3 December 1999). Of course Blackstone can also be cited against native title claimants, as in *Kartinyeri v Commonwealth* (1998) HCA 22, where the defendants relied in part on *Commentaries*, vol 1, 160, re Parliament's transcendent jurisdiction.

The fertility of Blackstone's constitutionalist, humanist, rights-based, outcome-oriented jurisprudence has hitherto been notably more apparent in North America than either his native England or her former Commonwealth colonies. But an increasingly sceptical attitude towards legal positivism which began to emerge even in 'Benthamite' Australia from the middle years of the twentieth century doubtless created a more receptive climate for the *Commentaries*.[65] Whatever the reason, it was not at all inappropriate for the widely respected activist Michael Dodson to end the introduction to his first (1993) report as Aboriginal and Torres Strait Islander Social Justice Commissioner with an iconic quotation from the opening chapter of Book II of the *Commentaries*.[66]

> There is nothing which so generally engages the affections of mankind, as the right of property; or that sole and despotic dominion which one man claims and exercises over the external things of the world, in total exclusion of the rights of any other individual in the universe. And yet there are very few, that will give themselves the trouble to consider the original and foundation of this right. Pleased as we are with the possession, we seem afraid to look back to the means by which it was acquired, as if fearful of some defect in our title; or at best we rest satisfied with the decision of the laws in our favour, without examining the reason or authority upon which those laws have been built.

The following year Blackstone's assertion, from the second edition of the *Commentaries* onwards, that colonists only imported as much English law as the circumstances of a new colony required, was invoked to support the claim that Aboriginal customary criminal law retained its validity, on an analogous basis to native land title. This proposition was firmly rejected by the High Court, on the grounds that a penal code must have universal application. So if Aboriginal criminal law had indeed survived the advent of British settlement, it was subsequently extinguished by the passing of general statutes.[67]

Even after that ruling, the absence of a foundational document expressing the rights and obligations of Australia's aboriginal inhabitants vis-à-vis the British Crown might still encourage hopes that Blackstone's canonical text could offer some form of partial equivalent. By contrast New Zealand's 1840 treaty of Waitangi provides a statement of the respective duties and expectations of Maori and government beyond which it is not necessary to go. Although controversy may continue about the precise meaning of that agreement, the fact of its existence renders Blackstone's *dicta* on settled and

---

[65] *Cf* H Collins, 'Political Ideology in Australia: the Distinctiveness of a Benthamite Society' in SR Grabaud (ed), *Australia: the Daedalus Symposium* (North Ryde, 1985) 147–70. As noted by Jessie Allen below (pp. 215–20), Blackstone's jurisprudential standing in the United States has also risen during the past century.
[66] www.austlii.edu.au/au/special/rsjproject/rsjlibrary/hreoc/atsisjc_1993/.
[67] *Walker v NSW* (1994) 182 CLR 45. *Cf* Cooke (n 21).

conquered colonies irrelevant. This is perhaps a further reason beyond mere chronology for Blackstone's relatively low profile in New Zealand.

Yet outside the legal profession and irrespective of his work's standing within the law courts, Blackstone's role and status as the standard authority on the institutions and practices of government in the Westminster tradition has probably differed relatively little between Australia and New Zealand, or indeed Great Britain, over the past two centuries and more. If the common law occupied a central place in the cultural baggage imported to Botany Bay with the First Fleet, the political ideology of New Zealand similarly depended upon notions of 'rights guaranteed by Magna Carta, Habeas Corpus, the Bill of Rights, the Act of Settlement, and the great synthesis of that inheritance, Blackstone's *Commentaries*'.[68] From the middle of the nineteenth century until the eve of World War II, articles, leaders and letters to the editor in both Australian and New Zealand newspapers typically characterised the *Commentaries* as 'a legal work of undisputed authority', 'the greatest and simplest digest of English fundamental law', 'this eminent authority', 'so great an authority', 'that great legal and constitutional classic'.[69] (The odd dismissive reference to 'that antique legal primer' is a rare questioning of conventional wisdom.)[70] Blackstone was accordingly invoked and cited in relation to almost every conceivable cause and position, from squatters' rights to single-tax land reform, from Irish Home Rule to prohibition and the regulation of prostitution.[71] For the most pervasive and enduring influence of the *Commentaries* on both sides of the Tasman has been as an authoritative source of constitutional and legal assumptions, conventions, definitions and principles, scarcely less accessible to the general public than to practising lawyers.

---

[68] D Neal, *The Rule of Law in a Penal Colony: Law and Power in Early New South Wales* (Cambridge, 1991) 23.
[69] Cf *Wairarapa Daily Times*, 8 February 1901; *Richmond River Herald and Northern Districts Advertiser* [NSW] 31 October 1924; *Windsor and Richmond Gazette* [NSW] 11 May 1895; *Clarence River Advocate* [NSW] 1 November 1901; *Evening News* [Sydney] 28 December 1901; *Dominion* [Wellington] 9 September 1911; *Feilding Star*, 10 July 1915.
[70] *New Zealand Herald*, 23 June 1888.
[71] Cf *Sydney Morning Herald*, 4 May 1866; *South Australian Register*, 2 March 1892; *Goulburn Evening Penny Post*, 2 July 1912; *Freeman's Journal* (Sydney), 23 August 1902; *Gippsland Times*, 27 September 1920; *Argus* (Melbourne) 7 April 1859.

III

Law and Politics

Each of the four final essays in this collection is largely focused on the *Commentaries* in trans-Atlantic perspective. Paul Halliday's concern with the uses of Blackstone in the early twenty-first century is brought into sharp relief by his reference to analogies between the 'supreme executive power' Blackstone attributed to the King of England and those extensive prerogatives claimed in recent (post-9/11) times for the American president. As Halliday's sensitive textual exegesis makes clear, Blackstone's king was a far more complex and ambiguous figure than such parallels might suggest. While sharing Halliday's misgivings about simplistic readings of the *Commentaries* for present political purposes, Ruth Paley turns a pragmatic and sceptical gaze on Blackstone as well as those who would harness him to their own ends. That a professedly elementary text originally compiled for English undergraduates 250 years ago should today be scoured for guidance on the constitutional position of the president of the United States may indeed strike the outsider as somewhat extraordinary, even as it also reminds us that the modern American polity remains an essentially unreconstructed product of eighteenth-century constitution making.

Blackstone's significant influence on that process is the theme taken up by Horst Dippel, who points to the general familiarity with the *Commentaries* on the part of those charged with drafting not only the Federal Constitution, but those of the Union's constituent states. From the 1760s to the 1790s, Blackstone's text was continually referred to as an authority in debates on constitutional issues. Even where not specifically invoked or mentioned by name, its pervasive influence is apparent in various principles and provisions, including the absolute nature of human rights and separation of powers ensured by checks and balances, which have become 'essentials of modern constitutionalism'.

Jessie Allen rounds off the collection by further considering Blackstone's relevance to our contemporary condition, with special but not exclusive reference to the United States. In a close analysis of the remarkable revival of Blackstone's authority manifested in recent judgments of the US Supreme Court, she suggests that the *Commentaries* has been caught up in varieties of judicial myth making, which pay insufficient attention to the historical context in which the work was first read by Americans of the founding generation. At the same time she draws on her own reading of the *Commentaries* to point out that while Blackstone was no mean myth maker himself, the ordered eighteenth-century hierarchy of ranks and status depicted in his text is not so far removed from our present social world as casual first impressions might suggest.

8

Blackstone's King

PAUL D HALLIDAY

FOR MORE THAN two centuries we have stared at Blackstone's *Commentaries* as if they provide some kind of jurisprudential inkblot test. He has been *the* theorist of Anglophone law because there seem to be no needs or norms he cannot serve. He was a reformist and a reactionary, tolerant and intolerant, an Anglican apologist and an exemplar of liberal enlightenment, a Tory in his politics and a Whig in his historical sensibility.[1]

For all these competing possibilities, surely we know what he thought about the king. Tories liked their kings, and they liked them strong. That strength came from the prerogative.

> By the word prerogative we usually understand that special pre-eminence, which the king hath, over and above all other persons, and out of the ordinary course of the common law, in right of his regal dignity ... it can only be applied to those rights and capacities which the king enjoys alone, in contradistinction to others.[2]

It is hardly surprising then that Blackstone's king has provided the basis for some of the more lavish claims made about the powers of American presidents. Didn't Blackstone open his chapter, 'Of the King and his Title', by declaring that 'The supreme executive power of these kingdoms is vested by our laws in a single person, the king or queen'?[3] His meaning in discussing

---

[1] Even one of the 'icons of regime Whiggism', in the words of JGA Pocock, *Virtue, Commerce, and History: Essays on Political Thought and History, Chiefly in the Eighteenth Century* (Cambridge, 1985) 276. JCD Clark calls him an 'ex-Tory': *English Society, 1688–1832* (Cambridge, 1985) 180.

[2] *Commentaries* vol 1, 232.

[3] Ibid, 183. For recent appropriations of passages like this one, by which our own uses of the word 'executive' are read backwards onto Blackstone, see: JC Yoo, 'Clio at War: The Misuse of History in the War Powers Debate' (1999) 70 *University of Colorado Law Review* 1169; JC Yoo, 'War and the Constitutional Text' (2002) 69 *University of Chicago Law Review* 1639; and MD Ramsey, 'Text and History in the War Powers Debate: A Reply to Professor Yoo' (2002) 69 *University of Chicago Law Review* 1685. Discussions like these rely on an imposition of modern 'separation of powers' ideas on Blackstone's discussion of 'executive' and 'legislative' functions, as if these words map neatly onto king and parliament, which in turn might be mapped forward onto president and congress. A brief essay does not allow

the prerogative seems equally clear: 'in the exertion of lawful prerogative, the king is and ought to be absolute'.[4] It looks as if Blackstone's king is drawn as clearly as one might desire, especially if one is a modern American lawyer who must fold the king into the tripartite constitutional structures of the United States for purposes of contemporary legal-political argument. But what if Blackstone's ideas defy such easy appropriation?[5] Perhaps Blackstone's king has seen more use than understanding.

Blackstone's king is as complex a figure as Blackstone himself, a figure who might, at first encounter, seem legible in contradictory ways. This results from Blackstone's poetics. If, as Hayden White has put it, the historian 'performs an essentially *poetic* act', certainly we may say the same of the legal commentator.[6] Legal theorist Steven Winter makes much the same point about the poetic imagination in legal reasoning. Law, he argues, is 'but one consequence of more pervasive cultural processes of meaning-making'.[7] Blackstone appreciated that we make meanings through metaphor; he exploited the figurative capacity of language as well as anyone.[8] Whatever criticisms one might make of Blackstone—his attempt at systematic thinking was often defeated by apparent self-contradiction, he could wax too lyrical on favourite themes—he was ever the poet, attentive to the plasticity

---

for a full response to this problem, though for discussion of the ways 'the Crown' signalled Blackstone's identification of what we might call 'unity of powers' and the dangers to liberty this might portend, see below.

[4] *Commentaries* vol 1, 243. For the use of this or similar passages to discuss the 'unitary theory' of executive power, see L Fisher, 'The Unitary Executive and Inherent Executive Power' (2010) 12 *University of Pennsylvania Journal of Constitutional Law* 569, 570; L Fisher, 'Basic Principles of the War Power' (2012) 5 *Journal of National Security Law and Policy* 319; and L Fisher, 'John Yoo and the Republic' (2011) 41 *Presidential Studies Quarterly* 177.

[5] For a succinct recent review of Blackstone's influence in early America and a critique of latter-day appropriations of him in American law, see S Cornell, 'The Original Meaning of Original Understanding: A Neo-Blackstonian Critique' (2007) 67 *Maryland Law Review* 150. See also Nolan 731–59.

[6] H White, *Metahistory: The Historical Imagination in Nineteenth-Century Europe* (Baltimore MD, 1973) x. White has developed this point further, noting how '"poetizing" is not an activity that hovers over, transcends, or otherwise remains alienated from life or reality, but represents a mode of praxis which serves as the immediate base of all cultural activity'. H White, 'Fictions of Factual Representation' in *Tropics of Discourse: Essays in Cultural Criticism* (Baltimore MD, 1978) 126.

[7] S Winter, *A Clearing in the Forest: Law, Life, and Mind* (Chicago IL, 2001) xiv. Winter continues: 'Most of us were brought up to believe that we spoke prose and that poetry, creativity, metaphor, and the like were special gifts. One of the truly wonderful aspects of the recent developments in cognitive theory is the democratization of imagination, the discovery—in Alasdair MacIntyre's words—of "that part of the ability of every language-user which is poetic"'(ibid 21).

[8] Blackstone 'delighted in and took some care with the use of language to suit his purpose, whether breezy, humorous, intimate, laconic, sardonic, ornate, ponderous, affectionate, angry, grim, or tender': *Letters*, xx.

of words, long after his career as a published poet ended.⁹ Much seeming contradiction begins to fade if we read Blackstone with this in mind.

My approach here is to focus less on Blackstone's contexts than on his text. That said, this brief textualist essay must be considered as a prologue to a proper consideration of Blackstone's king as illuminated by the contexts in which he wrote, lectured and published. Those contexts included the political and professional circles in which he moved, as well as the political ideas of others that motivated his legal thought, especially those associated with the so-called patriot king.¹⁰ After all, Blackstone did not just write a legal treatise. He was 'doing something as well as saying something', to use Quentin Skinner's formulation.¹¹ While ultimately we must understand just what he was *doing* when he wrote about the king in the ways he did, for now we can sketch his king's basic features.

Blackstone's king was an ironic figure. This may seem like a strange claim. He liked George III, 'the most amiable Prince that ever yet filled the British Throne', a prince who 'manifested the highest veneration for the free constitution of Britain'.¹² Few writers seem so deferential and earnest. Irony would not seem to be one of Blackstone's moods. But respect for the king's person and earnestness—unsurprising qualities to find in texts written for public performance—are not at odds with a detached, ironic and thus critical mode of engagement with the idea of the king. Here, I follow White's account of irony:

> The basic figurative tactic of Irony is catachresis (literally 'misuse'), the manifestly absurd Metaphor designed to inspire Ironic second thoughts about the nature of the thing characterized or the inadequacy of the characterization itself ... It presupposes that the reader or auditor already knows, or is capable of recognizing, the absurdity of the characterization.¹³

Blackstone expounded a traditional, 'sacred' king as a rhetorical device of just this kind: as a foil everyone knew operated as such. That device would

---

⁹ As Prest notes, Blackstone was still writing poetry in the same years that he began lecturing in Oxford on the law: *William Blackstone* 41.

¹⁰ In saying this, I do not want to rely on any simple distinction between texts and contexts. As Quentin Skinner notes, contexts help elucidate texts by illuminating what authors may have been *doing* in making a given text or utterance. Skinner in essence endorses the notion that we might first explore texts, then move beyond them, when he suggests that 'we should start by elucidating the meaning, and hence the subject matter, of the utterances in which we are interested and then turn to the argumentative context of their occurrence to determine how exactly they connect with, or relate to, other utterances concerned with the same subject matter'. Q Skinner, 'Interpretation and the Understanding of Speech Acts' in *Regarding Method*, vol 1 of *Visions of Politics* (Cambridge, 2002) 116.

¹¹ Ibid 2.

¹² *Letters* 103; *Commentaries* vol 1, 326. For evidence that Blackstone's praise was not misplaced, and that George had imbibed ideas about the need to limit the power of the crown, see PDG Thomas, '"Thoughts on the British Constitution" by George III in 1760' (1987) 60 *Bulletin of the Institute of Historical Research* 361.

¹³ White, *Metahistory* (n 6) 37.

have been identifiable by his audiences in the lecture hall and on the page. Those audiences knew as well as he did that sacredness was a trope: not a description of the centre of their legal-political world, but a figuration through which claims about that centre might be critiqued and its realities—transformed by history—fully apprehended. Blackstone presented a sacred king only to disembody him, reducing him to acting through a metonym of himself: through a 'crown' that had entirely absorbed those attributes once associated with the 'king'.[14] As he reduced the king, Blackstone comforted himself by believing that what he did was simply to explicate the operation of laudable historical processes. But projecting into the future those same processes by which the crown consumed the king left him nervous.[15] After all, the crown, as the place where the various powers of governance converged, had consumed the whole of 'the state', and the king along with it. This endangered the monarchical republic and attendant British freedoms Blackstone believed had been achieved since the 1660s. To see how Blackstone's king became but a crown, and to see what this meant, we must begin with the person of the king as Blackstone received him from his forebears.

I THE PREROGATIVE AND THE KING'S PERSON

Accounts of the royal prerogative in the two centuries before Blackstone wrote emphasised two mutually reinforcing attributes: its inherently spiritual aspect and its embodiment in and activation through a living, physical being. Sir John Doddridge put this in the language of the Psalmist: 'The heavens in height, the earth in deepness, and the king's heart none can search. The royal prerogative[s] of princes are sacred mysteries not to be touched.'[16] By this view, law, like nature, normally operates according to rules. If so, the king, like God, might step outside the rules to serve the public welfare. Sir John Davies, like others, thus analogised the king's prerogative 'to the government of God himself, who suffers things generally

---

[14] I thus take issue with claims that Blackstone's king should be understood as 'despotic', though, as we shall see below, Blackstone worried that the 'Crown'—a distinct force subsuming the king—offered the possibility of corruption and thus of tyranny. For a reading of Blackstone's king as 'despotic', based on an anachronistic emphasis on a supposed 'separation of powers' and 'independent' executive and judicial functions, see HL Lubert, 'Sovereignty and Liberty in William Blackstone's *Commentaries on the Laws of England*' (2010) 72 *Review of Politics* 271.

[15] I thus reject John Yoo's conclusion that 'Blackstone's description of the English king's powers ... failed to describe the manner in which that power was evolving'. Yoo, 'Clio at War' (n 3) 1188.

[16] BL, MS Harleian 5220, fo 3.

to go in their usual course, but reserves to himself to go out of that by a miracle when he pleases'.[17]

The king performed miracles with a mortal body. He also had an immortal body. Sir Edward Coke explained the traditional theory of the king's two bodies in his report of *Calvin's Case* (1608). One was 'a natural body, being descended of the blood royal of the Realm; and this body is of the creation of Almighty God, and is subject to death'. The other was 'a politic body ... framed by the policy of man ... and in this capacity the King is esteemed to be immortal, invisible, not subject to death'.[18]

To which body did the subject owe his allegiance? Coke's answer was unequivocal. Allegiance is 'due to the natural person of the King ... and it is not due to the politique capacity only, that is, to his crown or kingdom distinct from his natural capacity'.[19] Sir Thomas Fleming, who sat with Coke and the other justices on *Calvin's Case*, explained: 'They will make fearful conclusions if they lay the allegiance upon the kingdom, upon the crown, or upon the laws'.[20] England's history demonstrated how claiming allegiance to an abstraction of the king—for instance, to his crown—might justify treason against the physical person of the king. Coke gave the example of those who rebelled against Edward II when they

> invented this damnable and damned opinion, that homage and oath of ligeance was more by reason of the King's Crown (that is, of his politic capacity) than by reason of the person of the King, upon which opinion they inferred execrable and detestable consequences.

The crown could never be the locus of true obedience. It is but 'an Hieroglyphick of the Laws': a marker of royal capacities, but not the king himself, who could only do justice by and through his physical self.[21]

The politic body might be immortal, but the king's immortal soul could only reside in his natural body, just as souls reside in the bodies of his subjects. This made possible the 'ligamen' of allegiance between king and subject. Only the possession of a soul by each made it possible to swear the oaths that expressed this tie: reciprocal oaths, real or implied, by which the king offered protection in return for the subject's obedience.

We shall see shortly how important was the impact of Blackstone's transposition of the language of bonds constituting the relationship of king and subject into bounds around the king. But first, we must examine

---

[17] BL, MS Stowe 1011, fo 88. For more on these aspects of the prerogative, see PD Halliday, *Habeas Corpus: From England to Empire* (Cambridge MA, 2010) 65–69.
[18] E Coke, *La Sept Part des Reports Sr. Edw. Coke chivalier* (London, 1608) 10a [hereafter 7 Co Rep].
[19] Ibid.
[20] WP Baildon (ed), *Les Reportes del Cases in Camera Stellata, 1593 to 1609* (np, 1894) 362.
[21] 7 Co Rep 11a–11b.

Blackstone's account of the prerogative in light of what we have seen of these traditional views.

The discussion of rights in Book I of the *Commentaries* has been the subject of much comment. But for all the efforts to read this part of Blackstone as a natural law or proto-liberal account of the purposes of law relative to what are often taken to be natural rights, a difficult question arises. Why does Blackstone use more words in Book I to discuss the 'rights of the king' than the rights of anyone else?[22]

At first blush, chapters 3 (Of the King and his Title), 6 (Of the King's Duties), and 7 (Of the King's Prerogative) of Book I look like standard fare, easily read in terms familiar for centuries. Blackstone opens chapter 3 with confidence: 'The supreme executive power of these kingdoms is vested by our laws in a single person, the king or queen ... [who] is immediately invested with all the ensigns, rights, and prerogatives of sovereign power'. The monarch has '(in subservience to the law of the land) the care and protection of the community'; to the king 'in return, the duty and allegiance of every individual are due'.[23] In chapter 6—and again in chapter 10, on aliens and natives—Blackstone develops this point, drawing straight from *Calvin's Case*: 'protection and subjection are reciprocal'.[24] Blackstone offers further definition of the prerogative in chapter 7. 'By the word prerogative we usually understand that special pre-eminence, which the king hath, over and above all other persons, and out of the ordinary course of the common law, in right of his regal dignity.'[25] There is nothing here of the mystical being that one encounters in discussions of the prerogative two centuries earlier. But Blackstone obliges soon enough, noting how 'The law therefore ascribes to the king ... certain attributes of a great and transcendent nature ... by law the person of the king is sacred'.[26]

The key in this last passage, as in all those quoted above, is not the king's sacredness, but the fact that law ascribes that quality to him. The king is 'vested by our laws'; he performs the protection of the community 'in subservience to the law'. Here we see how Blackstone transposed the language of binding, shifting the locus of bonds from those tying the king to his subjects in a mystical union to bounds around the king's mystical body. As bonds became bounds, Blackstone disembodied and thereby contained his king.

---

[22] As Michael Lobban has pointed out, in Book I, 'the absolute rights of natural persons were given only one chapter, while the relative rights were given sixteen ... [T]he structure ... was largely hierarchical in principle, describing a series of relations'. Blackstone's account of rights is thus positivist rather than natural. M Lobban, 'Blackstone and the Science of Law' (1987) 30 *Historical Journal* 311, 328–29.

[23] *Commentaries* vol 1, 183.

[24] Ibid 226.

[25] Ibid 232.

[26] Ibid 234–35.

II THE FOUNTAIN REDUCED TO A RESERVOIR

It had been a common rhetorical conceit for centuries. Little wonder that Blackstone's king was a fountain: of honour, of office and of justice. As a fountain, the king acts without restraint. He confers nobility 'on which of them he pleases'.[27] 'The course of justice' flows from the king 'in large streams'. As those streams run through his courts, justice is 'subdivided into smaller channels'. Through these, the king bestows his bounty, 'till the whole and every part of the kingdom were plentifully watered and refreshed'.[28] The king acts, the fountain pours forth, justice flows along its courses, as the king wills.

But does the fountain pour without limits; does the king will and act so simply, with such abundance? Blackstone's king, 'as the fountain of justice', is 'bound' to redress wrongs between subjects through 'the ordinary forms of law'.[29] But Blackstone's king soon disappears into a crown that is no longer his: 'the crown' becomes 'the fountain of all justice' as Blackstone discusses the provision of the original writs by which subjects proceed in the courts.[30] That Blackstone intended the king, as fountain of justice, to be limited is plain in his handling of the king's capacities as the fountain of honour, office and privilege. These capacities, Blackstone explained, should be taken 'in a different sense from that wherein he is styled the fountain of justice', for in the case of honours and offices, 'he is *really* the parent of them'.[31] The *reality* of the king's independent capacity for action as the progenitor of honour and office highlights the *unreality* Blackstone ascribed to the king's capacity as the source of justice.

Blackstone's king turns out to be no source at all. Tellingly, it is in his chapter on the prerogative, not in his later discussions of the origin of courts, that Blackstone is most explicit about the bounds around the king. There he qualifies what it means to be 'the fountain of justice':

> By the fountain of justice the law does not mean the *author* or *original*, but only the *distributor*. Justice is not derived from the king, as from his *free gift*; but he is the steward of the public, to dispense it to whom it is *due*. He is not the spring, but the reservoir; from whence right and equity are conducted, by a thousand channels, to every individual.[32]

---

[27] Ibid vol 2, 216.
[28] Ibid vol 3, 30–31.
[29] Ibid 115–16.
[30] Ibid 273.
[31] Ibid vol 1, 261 (emphasis added).
[32] Ibid 257 (emphasis in original). Blackstone repeats the reservoir image in the final, historical chapter at the end of Book IV. There he explains how King Alfred's legal reforms put all under 'one supreme magistrate, the king; in whom, as in a general reservoir, all the executive authority of the law was lodged, and from whom justice was dispersed to every part of the nation by distinct, yet communicating, ducts and channels': ibid vol 4, 404.

Justice is distributed by the king; it does not originate in him. No longer a source, he is but a bounded and artificial 'reservoir', subject to law's 'meaning': a vessel made by others to contain something they desire, something they receive not because he decides, but because it is owed them. This is because 'the original power of judicature, by the fundamental principles of society, is lodged in the society at large'.[33]

If the first binding of the king occurred because the original power of judicature lay with his people, then the capacity to continue to bind the king was now exercised through Parliament, whose statutes 'bind every subject in the land ... nay, even the king himself'.[34] We have come a long way from the original conception of the prerogative. But perhaps we should not be surprised to see how Blackstone bound his king. Though God made 'the eternal, immutable laws of good and evil', Blackstone's God was bound, too: 'the creator himself in all his dispensations conforms' to the laws of nature that he authored.[35] Blackstone runs the ancient analogy of gods to kings through an unexpected implied syllogism: if kings are like gods, and kings have now been bounded by law, then gods, too, are bounded. This might surprise us given our tendency to emphasise Blackstone's traditional piety. And Blackstone placed great emphasis on scripture as the means by which God revealed law to humanity.[36] But though scripture included accounts of miraculous interventions in human affairs, those miracles had occurred in another epoch. Blackstone's age was not one of miracles, whether those wrought by God or by the king. Blackstone had bounded both. He did so with words.

III SPEECH AND PEN: CONTAINING THE PREROGATIVE

Blackstone celebrated the fact that there was no 'stronger proof of that genuine freedom' that Britons enjoyed 'than the power of discussing and examining, with decency and respect, the limits of the king's prerogative'.[37] They had not always possessed this freedom. Queen Elizabeth had commanded her parliaments 'to abstain from discoursing of matters of state'. James I declared it a 'presumption and sedition in a subject to dispute what a king may do in the height of his power'.[38] In that earlier era, in which notions of the prerogative inclined towards mystical grandeur, the prerogative was 'too delicate and sacred to be profaned by the pen'.[39]

---

[33] Ibid vol 1, 257.
[34] Ibid 178.
[35] Ibid 40.
[36] Ibid 41–42.
[37] Ibid 230.
[38] Ibid 231.
[39] Ibid 230. Blackstone's words echo those of Sir John Doddridge, quoted above, that the prerogatives 'are sacred mysteries not to be touched'. BL, MS Harleian 5220, fo 3.

Here we encounter what might be the clearest demonstration of Blackstone's awareness of the force of language, a force shaping and shaped by historical processes. His point was not simply that the prerogative, in his own age, had 'limits' and that those might be discussed. Rather, he understood that acts of discussion, including his own, constituted those limits. His pen drew the bounds around the king. Blackstone was sometimes ambivalent about this power, even as he wielded it. His anxiety is especially apparent when he addresses whether the events of 1688–89 demonstrated a power in subjects to answer 'constitutional oppressions' by removing the king. Blackstone answered in conditional form: 'If' any future prince performed virtually all the same acts that James II had performed—'If' precisely the same 'conjunction of circumstances' occurred—that would produce an abdication. But how many of the specific circumstances enumerated would make such a conjunction? '[I]t is not for us to say ... [S]ince both law and history are silent' on this point, 'it becomes us to be silent, too'.[40] Silence opens the bounds around the king, speech closes them. Blackstone's words brought him to a line that he would not cross. Nonetheless, by declaring the need for silence, he reminded his listeners and readers that there was indeed a line and that words mark it. Even as he stopped his pen, his words constituted the bounds around the king. These were bounds of law, which denatured the once great king who acted through his body natural.

IV DISEMBODIED KING, EMBODIED LAW

Traditional accounts of the prerogative and of the relationship between king and subject emphasised the significance of the king's natural body. It was no paradox to stress the physical, mortal body as the lodging place of the soul. Thus it is remarkable to discover just how thoroughly Blackstone disembodied his king.

Blackstone's main discussion of the issue appears to repeat older verities. His account of subjecthood, most fully developed in Book I, Chapter 10—'Of the People, whether Aliens, Denizens, or Natives'—relies heavily on Coke's report of *Calvin's Case*. Blackstone makes the same claims about how the king–subject relationship arises by the operation of natural law; each is born into this relationship with the other. This constitutes allegiance, 'the tie, or *ligamen*, which binds the subject to the king, in return for that protection which the king affords the subject'.[41] But Blackstone largely sidesteps the point on which Coke had been so insistent: that the subject's allegiance was owed to the king's natural body, not his political one. Indeed,

---

[40] Commentaries vol 1, 238. On Blackstone's awkwardness in the face of 1688, see R Willman, 'Blackstone and the "Theoretical Perfection" of English Law in the Reign of Charles II' (1983) 26 *Historical Journal* 39, 55–61.
[41] Ibid 354.

Blackstone conflates the two bodies, arguing that allegiance 'is held to be applicable not only to the political capacity of the king, or regal office, but to his natural person, and blood royal'.[42] That 'not only' signals a surprisingly casual attitude about where loyalty properly belongs.

What looks to be only a minor adjustment has important implications. Blackstone's discussion of the king's perpetuity—part of his chapter on the prerogative—amounts to an examination and exaltation of the king's body politic. 'The law ascribes to him, in his political capacity, an absolute immortality'. This sounds like Coke. But Blackstone continues: 'The king never dies', because when his natural body dies, 'by act of law', the king's dignity 'is vested at once in his heir'. This perpetuity of the 'king's majesty' arises from 'the disunion of the king's body natural from his body politic'.[43] This disunion makes possible perpetuity—the political body's persistence across time—and its 'legal *ubiquity*'—its pervasiveness across space. This is most apparent in the king's role as the reservoir of justice:

> His majesty, in the eye of the law, is always present in all his courts, though he cannot personally distribute justice. His judges are the mirror by which the king's image is reflected. It is the regal office, and not the royal person, that is always present in court, always ready to undertake prosecutions, or pronounce judgment, for the benefit and protection of the subject.[44]

Of course, justices had long reminded their supplicants that they spoke with the king's voice when they provided process and delivered judgments. But Blackstone here reduces the king to an image reflected by others. The political body, in the person of judges—'the regal office, and not the royal person'—pronounces judgment. And all this, 'in the eye of the law'.[45] As Blackstone disembodied the king, he embodied the law, whose gaze now controlled the king.

'[S]o Tender is the law', Blackstone tells us at one point.[46] It is an arresting image: that law should feel as well as see. By his emphasis on sense and sensibility—on seeing and tenderness—Blackstone anthropomorphises law as the king's natural body dissolves from view. Law, instead of the king, possesses mind, heart, soul and body. The law intends and acts. Law 'gives' the prerogatives, even as it 'arm[s] the subject with powers to impel the prerogative'.[47] Using the language of 'constitution', Blackstone explains

---

[42] Ibid 359.
[43] Ibid 242.
[44] Ibid 260.
[45] Ibid 260, 262. Blackstone's approach may be read as being in sympathy with Bolingbroke's *Idea of a Patriot King*. As Bolingbroke put it, 'majesty is not an inherent, but a reflected light': quoted in Clark (n 1) 180. For further discussion, see ibid 179–84.
[46] *Commentaries* vol 1, 242.
[47] Ibid 250.

that law lays down exceptions and boundaries.[48] Law makes suppositions, but only 'in decency'.[49] Law 'acts upon general and extensive principles', and thereby 'gives liberty'.[50]

As we saw in many of the passages quoted above describing the king's capacities, those capacities existed because law 'ascribes' them; the king's capacities operate only 'by act of law'. The king does possess 'the supreme executive power', but only because it is 'vested by our laws' in him, 'in subservience to the law of the land'. The king may be 'sacred', but only 'by law'.[51] Law is the actor, acting upon the king—or on what was left of him.

V THE KING WITHIN THE CROWN

If Blackstone disembodied the king, making him a passive object of law's thinking, feeling and acting, then what is Blackstone's crown? This is no simple question, largely because of Blackstone's occasionally promiscuous use of the words crown and king, as if they are synonyms. But they are not. Slippage between king and crown signals Blackstone's ambivalence about relations among sometimes distinct, sometimes overlapping parts of government. Blackstone is often read as the means by which a Montesquieuan separation of powers was developed; that understanding, we are told, would later come to full flower in the US Constitution.[52] But as we watch Blackstone oscillate between king and crown, we see the extent to which he thought within what we might more properly call an English unification of powers tradition.

This unification of powers, which traditionally occurred in and through the person of the king, had been transposed into 'the crown' by the eighteenth century. The move from embodied king to disembodied crown resulted from historical processes as constructed in Blackstone's historical imagination. This produced an emplotment of the crown rising out of—while still sometimes conflated with—the king.[53] How this worked

---

[48] Ibid 243. I do not mean to suggest here that Blackstone used 'constitution' as a synonym for 'law', but I would suggest that he saw England's and Britain's 'constitution' as something integral to and interpenetrating with the rest of its law rather than hovering above it in a way that set bounds upon law conceived as distinct from the constitution. JW Cairns, 'Blackstone, an English Institutist: Legal Literature and the Rise of the Nation State' (1984) 4 *Oxford Journal of Legal Studies* 318, 346–47.
[49] *Commentaries* vol 3, 255.
[50] Ibid vol 1, 413.
[51] Ibid 183, 235, 242.
[52] This approach to Blackstone is especially common in US constitutional argument. For a recent argument to the same effect from the perspective of political thought, see PO Carrese, *The Cloaking of Power: Montesquieu, Blackstone, and the Rise of Judicial Activism* (Chicago IL, 2003) especially pt 2.
[53] On emplotment, see White, *Metahistory* (n 6) 7: 'Providing the "meaning" of a story by identifying the *kind of story* that has been told is called explanation by emplotment.'

becomes apparent in the many places Blackstone invoked king or crown as the means by which judgment is made and executed. The judicial power is an aspect of the 'executive power of the laws ... vested in the person of the king'.[54] But the transposition of sovereignty into the crown becomes clear in the 'nominat[ation] ... by the crown' of judges.[55] Thus Blackstone described courts as 'the medium by which he [the king] administers the laws', though those same courts 'derived from the power of the crown'.[56]

As the king slipped behind the crown, he or it participated equally in the exercise of 'executive' and 'legislative' authority. Blackstone distinguished these authorities in a number of passages, but this is not to say that even then they correlate neatly with distinct beings called king and parliament. Their entanglement is the key quality of each. For while the executive power 'consist[s] of the king alone', 'happily for us ... the legislature of the kingdom is entrusted to three distinct powers', namely lords, commons and the king. It is *within* this traditionally conceived king-in-parliament that checking occurs, not *between* it and an ostensibly separate king or crown—between a legislature and an executive. Lords and commoners 'check' one another, while 'the king', equally a participant in parliament, 'is a check on both'.[57]

Here we can begin to make sense of a seeming paradox: that Blackstone could declare so powerfully that the 'supreme executive power of these kingdoms is vested by our laws in a single person', after explaining that the 'sovereign and uncontrollable authority in making ... of laws' is parliament, 'the place where that absolute despotic power, which must in all governments reside somewhere, is entrusted by the constitution of these kingdoms'.[58] Parliament, and the king who is a part of it, becomes absorbed into the crown. It is in parliament that 'the whole is prevented from separation, and artificially connected together by the mixed nature of the crown, which is a part of the legislative, and the sole executive magistrate'.[59] Blackstone's crown, not his king, provides the site of and impetus for mixture and thus

---

White developed his thinking about this through critical engagement with RG Collingwood's discussion of history as an act of 'the constructive imagination' of a kind I suggest Blackstone used. In White's terms, we might say that insofar as Blackstone praised the reduction of the prerogative while worrying about the danger of corruption in and through the crown that supplanted the king, he emplotted his history of English law in simultaneous romantic, epic and tragic modes. H White, 'The Historical Text as Literary Artifact' in B Richardson (ed), *Narrative Dynamics: Essays on Time, Plot, Closure, and Frames* (Columbus OH, 2002) 193–94. On the constructive historical imagination, see RG Collingwood, *The Idea of History* (Oxford, 1946, 1993) 231–49, especially 241–46.

[54] *Commentaries* vol 3, 23.
[55] Ibid vol 1, 259.
[56] Ibid vol 3, 23–24.
[57] Ibid vol 1, 50 and 150; more generally, ch 2.
[58] Ibid 156 and 183.
[59] Ibid 151.

acts as the force generating a transformed regal constitution's distinctive unification of powers.

Slippage between the words crown and king signals Blackstone's reduction of the king to a shadow within the crown. 'Crown' is neither synonym nor metaphor for 'king'. It is a metonym, by which crown and king may be associated with one another without their being likened. The metonymical relationship between them is, as Hayden White put it, a relationship of part to part, by which one part 'can effect a *reduction* of one of the parts to the status of an aspect or function of the other'.[60] Blackstone's 'king'—as a disembodied object and an instrument of law's action—becomes an attribute of the crown. Blackstone's crown—embodied in ministers of state, an army, and various agents and officers—is the actor that generates and enforces law.

We might go further by taking up White's suggestion that, by metonym, one manifestation of the reduction one part performs upon the other is to reveal the relationship of cause and effect. Considered this way, Blackstone flips what we might have thought was the right relationship of king to crown. We move from a situation in which the king is the cause of there being a crown—which crown is only a symbol of the king's authority—to the crown being the cause of the king. The crown has become the political-legal order in its entirety: the king is now little but a symbol of the power that is now the crown's. Blackstone's crown produces and sustains the king, a being transformed into little more than a place for locating certain ideas about subjects and their obligations.

Blackstone worried that this inversion of crown and king might produce undesirable results. These worries appeared in the final pages of chapter 8, 'Of the King's Revenue', where he concluded his six chapters concerned with the king's 'rights'. In those chapters, Blackstone had 'chalked out', he tells us, 'all the principal outlines of this vast title of the law, the supreme executive magistrate, or the king's majesty'. Now he concluded with a 'comparative review of the power of the executive magistrate'. This comparative review operates across time as Blackstone takes an explicitly historical turn and applauds the decline of 'the powers of the crown' since the time of James I.[61]

But there was a cloud in this silver lining:

> The instruments of power are not perhaps so open and avowed as they formerly were ... but they are not the weaker upon that account. In short, our national debt and taxes ... [have] thrown such a weight of power into the executive scale of government, as we cannot think was intended by our patriot ancestors, who gloriously struggled for the abolition of the then formidable parts of the prerogative.

---

[60] White, *Metahistory* (n 6) 35 (emphasis in original).
[61] *Commentaries*, vol 1, 322–23.

Greater revenue, 'in the hands of the crown', permitted appointment of 'a multitude' of excise officers, window tax assessors, customs agents, stamp commissioners, soldiers, and more:

> Whatever may have become of the *nominal*, the *real* power of the crown has not been too far weakened by any transactions in the last century ... The stern commands of prerogative have yielded to the milder voice of influence.[62]

As he closed his discussion of king and crown, Blackstone walked up to the place where he might have developed a full critique of corruption and the tyranny it might generate, then walked back. He recognised that the '*real* power of the crown' resided in parliament because the king's chief ministers sit there.[63] It was by their means that the 'mixed nature of the crown' pulled legislative and executive capacities together in dynamic tension. Parliament was a creature of ministers who served the king by serving in parliament; their powers as ministers arose from their ability to command parliamentary majorities. Commanding majorities, who voted to fund the state patronage that sustained ministerial power, expanded crown power. Paraphrasing Montesquieu, Blackstone worried that 'liberty will perish ... whenever the legislative power shall become more corrupt than the executive'.[64] Far from a likeness of the king, Blackstone's crown bound the king in a spiral of political power and corrupting wealth and influence by which ministry and parliament were drawn together.

Once upon a time, the king and his prerogative were things 'too delicate and sacred to be profaned by the pen'.[65] By the 1750s and 1760s, it was parliamentary sovereignty and thus the 'mixed nature of the crown' that proved too embarrassing to discuss fully. As Blackstone put it, these 'instruments of power are not perhaps so open and avowed as they formerly were'.[66] But he would do little more to avow them openly. His silence about how parliament, ministers and patronage constituted the crown spoke as loudly as his words about the king. The sacred had been profaned: prerogative had given way to influence as the king had become hidden within the crown.

---

[62] Ibid 324–26 (emphasis in original).
[63] On the sovereignty of parliament, see Lobban (n 22) 325–27.
[64] *Commentaries* vol 1, 157. Blackstone, quoting Locke, noted that 'breaches of trust in the executive magistrate' occurred when, as Locke put it, the magistrate 'employs the force, treasure, and offices of society to corrupt the representatives': ibid 172. P Laslett (ed), John Locke, *Two Treatises of Government* (Cambridge, 1960) 413. Blackstone continued, in hope and doubt, to write that regulation of election procedures might mean that 'Undue influence [is] thus (I wish the depravity of mankind would permit me to say, effectually) guarded against': *Commentaries* vol 1, 173.
[65] Ibid 230.
[66] Ibid 324.

VI HISTORY'S IRONIES

In ironic mode, the reality of Blackstone's crown negated the unreality of Blackstone's king. In this mode, Blackstone revealed his historical imagination at work, and nowhere more clearly than in the final pages of the *Commentaries*. Here, Blackstone showed how fully he imbibed Enlightenment historiography's ironic consciousness. This consciousness, to return to White, begins

> in an Epic preconfiguration of the historical field ... in the apprehension of a great contest between the powers of reason and unreason, a contest inspired by the hope that history would show the triumph of the heroic powers over the blocking figures that were needed for the tension leading to the movement of the whole.

It remains for us to consider whether Blackstone's 'Epic preconfiguration of the historical field' resolved in 'Comic or Tragic meanings': in the reconciliation of or resignation to the inescapably contrary forces at work in human lives. We must consider whether his narrative arose from the workings of a heroic dogma or of a sombre empiricism.[67]

Blackstone's last paragraph reads as pure triumphal dogma. The Conquest marked the original 'eclipse' of the 'gradual progress' accomplished by Alfred and his Saxon kin before 1066. Thereafter, England's laws were 'every day improving', reaching 'the perfection they now enjoy'. The result was 'a constitution so wisely contrived, so strongly raised, and so highly finished, it is hard to speak [of it] with that praise which is justly and severely its due—the thorough and attentive contemplation of it will furnish its best panegyric'.[68] Heady stuff—the poetry of a dogmatist.

But Blackstone was actually an empiricist; he knew history had not ended in 'perfection'.[69] This he showed in the pages immediately preceding these last flourishes. His ironic negation of king by crown—and the anxieties it raised—is announced in Blackstone's narrative of England's history during the preceding century, which he recounts in the preceding five pages. Historical change—not just Blackstone's rhetorical choices—produced that negation. Charles II's reign brought forth 'the complete restitution of

---

[67] White, *Metahistory* (n 6) 67. In discussing the modes of emplotment, White writes: 'The reconciliations which occur at the end of Comedy are reconciliations of men with men, of men with their world and their society; the condition of society is represented as being purer, saner, and healthier as a result of the conflict among seemingly inalterably opposed elements in the world; these elements are revealed to be, in the long run, harmonizable with one another ... The reconciliations that occur at the end of Tragedy are much more somber; they are more in the nature of resignations of men to the conditions under which they must labor in the world' (ibid 9).

[68] *Commentaries* vol 4, 435–36.

[69] Michael Lobban has emphasised Blackstone's historicism and empiricism. Lobban (n 22), especially 328 and 330.

English liberty for the first time since its total abolition at the conquest'.[70] Since the 1660s, and especially after 1688, 'some invidious, nay dangerous, branches of the prerogative have since been lopped off'. Numerous innovations—for instance, those establishing the independence of the judiciary—had 'reduced the strength of the executive power to a much lower ebb than in the preceding period'.[71]

But Blackstone remained nervous. 'If', he warned,

> we throw into the opposite scale (what perhaps the immoderate reduction of the ancient prerogative may have rendered in some degree necessary) the vast acquisition of force, arising from the riot act, and the annual expenditure of a standing army; and the vast acquisition of personal attachment, arising from the magnitude of the national debt, and the manner of levying those yearly millions that are appropriated to pay the interest, we shall find that the crown has, gradually and imperceptibly, gained almost as much in influence, as it has apparently lost in prerogative.[72]

Blackstone handled the threat gingerly. Once upon a time, one might only discuss the prerogative 'with decency'. Likewise, he suggested in a 1759 letter to Lord Bute, in which he conveyed two lectures on the King's Revenue, that he discussed that delicate matter 'with a Freedom that I hope is decent as well as constitutional'.[73] He wrote with constitutional freedom because it was the 'duty' of 'good subjects ... to reverence the crown, and yet guard against corrupt and servile influence from those who are entrusted with its authority'.[74] Blackstone understood that royal revenues and the influence they bought were to the crown of the 1750s what 'sacred mysteries' had been to the king and his prerogative 150 years earlier: something one discussed in hushed, reverential tones. Nonetheless, the binding of influence, just as the binding of the prerogative, required speech and pen. Blackstone used each unabashedly, attempting to bind the crown just as he had bound the king. But he seemed less sure of himself against such a force. Thus the final paragraph turns out to be little more than an ironic wink to the reader, a nod to the understanding Blackstone and the reader shared that the comic ending to the *Commentaries* did not preclude a tragic future foretold in the pages preceding.

---

[70] Ibid 431. For discussion, see Willman (n 40).
[71] *Commentaries* vol 4, 432, 434.
[72] Ibid 434.
[73] *Commentaries* vol 1, 230 and *Letters* 67. Prest notes Blackstone's 'assertively independent stance' in this letter, and that his lectures were 'in no way self-censored to spare royal susceptibilities'. Prest, *William Blackstone* 163. Bute was tutor to the Prince of Wales at the time.
[74] *Commentaries* vol 1, 326.

VII BLACKSTONE'S REPUBLICAN KING

Blackstone's critique of corruption hanging over the crown was hardly novel. It was a reflection of an Atlantic republican tradition brought to scholarly attention most fully by JGA Pocock four decades ago.[75] It was also a sign of the persistence of what Mark Goldie and Patrick Collinson more recently identified as England's monarchical republic.[76] 'Eighteenth-century commonwealthmen', Quentin Skinner argues, offer 'the spectacle of the monarchical republic finally enthroned'.[77] Blackstone would have agreed.[78] What worried him was whether the republic would remain enthroned in a world where the crown fully covered the king enthroned.

So we must conclude by briefly considering the republican elements in Blackstone's thought. These point to the proximity of his ideas to the patriot ideology of the mid-eighteenth century and to the critical and reformist potential of that ideology.[79] Over and over, Blackstone reminds us that the king and his prerogative exist only for the public good.[80] Thus the king enjoys the privileges of wreck and treasure trove, 'to preserve the peace of the public, as in trust to employ them for the safety and ornament of the commonwealth'. Similarly, property in wild game 'is vested in the king alone ... [for] the benefit of the community'.[81]

The republican aspect of Blackstone's king is most evident in two tightly linked ways. First, and in keeping with the tradition of which Blackstone partook and from which he then departed, king and people are bound by the ligamen of allegiance in the relationship of king and subject. By this

---

[75] *The Machiavellian Moment: Florentine Political Thought and the Atlantic Republican Tradition* (Princeton NJ, 1975).

[76] M Goldie, 'The Unacknowledged Republic: Officeholding in Early Modern England' in T Harris (ed), *The Politics of the Excluded, c. 1500–1850* (New York NY, 2001) 153–94. P Collinson, '*De Republica Anglorum*: Or, History with the Politics Put Back' *Elizabethan Essays* (London, 1994) 1–29.

[77] Q Skinner, 'The Monarchical Republic Enthroned' in JF McDiarmid (ed), *The Monarchical Republic of Early Modern England: Essays in Response to Patrick Collinson* (Aldershot, 2007) 244.

[78] By reading Blackstone as a monarchical republican, we move beyond the juxtaposition too often made between eighteenth-century theories of monarchy and republicanism: *cf* Fisher, 'John Yoo and the Republic' (n 4) 177. Here Fisher argues that John Yoo, former deputy assistant Attorney General of the United States and one of the chief architects of US legal strategy in prosecuting the 'War on Terror' after 2001, was following Blackstone's theory of the king, which the Framers had rejected in their constitutional design. It may be more accurate to say that those Framers were quite Blackstonean in their thinking. Any belief that Blackstone accorded the king unfettered war powers is based on a misreading of the *Commentaries* made possible by reading selected passages in isolation from the whole.

[79] Thus David Armitage has suggested that we need to reassess 'the supposed conservatism' of this tradition: D Armitage, 'A Patriot for Whom? The Afterlives of Bolingbroke's Patriot King' (1997) 36 *Journal of British Studies* 397, 399.

[80] eg *Commentaries* vol 1, 240 and 244; ibid vol 3, 255.

[81] Ibid vol 2, 410–11. Blackstone's extensive use of the language of trust deserves greater attention as an aspect of his monarchical republican thinking.

relationship, the king owes subjects his protection. This obligation justified use of the prerogative, which is 'for the benefit of the people and therefore cannot be exerted to their prejudice'.[82] Second, Blackstone's king is figured as a synecdoche of 'the whole nation'. In the king, 'all the rays of his people are united'.[83] This explains how crime is conceived as 'pleas of the crown': 'because the king, in whom centers the majesty of the whole community, is supposed by the law to be the person injured by every infraction of all the public rights belonging to that community'.[84]

While we would be hard pressed to call Blackstone a contract theorist—witness his embarrassment about the meaning of 1688–89—we may nonetheless call him a consent theorist. In his discussion of criminal law, Blackstone performs a remarkable reworking of St Paul's injunction to obedience in Romans 13. Paul's magistrate bears the sword 'to execute wrath upon him that doeth evil' because the magistrate is ordained of God. But Blackstone's magistrate 'bears the sword of justice by the consent of the whole community'.[85] The community gives consent in order that government—and particularly that of a monarchical republic—might accomplish the ends for which it is created: 'the quiet enjoyment and protection of all our civil rights and liberties'.[86]

Consent is also the basis of English property laws, feudal tenures having been accepted 'by the common consent of the nation'. Blackstone rejected the idea that this meant that 'the king is the universal lord and original proprietor of all the lands in this kingdom'. Instead, his English ancestors consented only 'to put the kingdom in a state of defence by establishing a military system'.[87] Property law resulted from an act of communal consent performed as a manifestation of the fundamental relationship tying subjects and king together in obedience and protection. Historically, the creation of property and the means for its defence—in other words, the creation of society—was a matter of community agreement.

For all that the structure of the *Commentaries*, and especially of Book I, seems to focus our attention on individuals owing to its organisation around 'rights', those rights exist only in community. Blackstone's monarchical republic is thus a manifestation of his fundamentally communitarian commitments.[88] Rights arise from and require duties; duties themselves

---

[82] Ibid vol 1, 239.
[83] Ibid 245.
[84] Ibid vol 4, 2.
[85] Ibid 8.
[86] Ibid vol 1, 56.
[87] Ibid vol 2, 50–51.
[88] I thus agree with Albert W Alschuler when he notes that 'the Enlightenment concept of rights was not merely compatible with communitarianism; it was itself an expression of the communitarian ideals of duty, reciprocity and equality': Alschuler, 'Rediscovering Blackstone' (1996) 145 *University of Pennsylvania Law Review* 1, 51–52, and more generally 44–53.

are 'rights'. Rights are thus 'due *from* every citizen' as well as 'belong[ing] to him'.[89] Such rights are only 'civil', some 'natural liberties' having been relinquished upon entering society. '[C]ivil liberty, rightly understood, consists in protecting the rights of individuals *by the united force of society*: society cannot be maintained, and of course can exert no protection, without obedience to some sovereign power.'[90] The community, rather than the individual, is the core idea in Blackstone's politics and thus the central object of concern to Blackstone's king.

But the crown, not the king, now reigned. Blackstone worried because it was unclear if the community was the central object of concern to the crown. His critique of corruption, insofar as the crown linked king, parliament and ministers through the operation of patronage, focused less on the status of the king than on the king's people and their weal. For there was still a king and they were still his subjects. Blackstone's communitarian, republican commitments were sustained by Blackstone's king. Whether they would be sustained by Blackstone's crown remained to be seen.

VIII BLACKSTONE'S KING, BLACKSTONE'S CROWN

What we have considered here is not *the* king. It was Blackstone's king, a product of Blackstone's poetics. This is not a criticism. Rather, it is a recognition of how all political-legal arguments, like historical arguments, are at bottom imaginative constructions, bodied forth in words. Keenly aware how words might bind the king, Blackstone made a fountain into a reservoir. Having disembodied his king, Blackstone re-embodied the powers once associated with the king in the crown, the being through which law now thought, felt and acted. By containing the prerogative, Blackstone's king yielded to Blackstone's crown. But the result made him nervous. Perhaps Blackstone needed his king after all. That is the most important irony of all.

---

[89] *Commentaries* vol 1, 119 (emphasis in original).
[90] Ibid 244 (emphasis added). And see ibid 254: 'The great end of society is to protect the weakness of individuals by the united strength of the community'.

Modern Blackstone: the King's Two Bodies, the Supreme Court and the President

RUTH PALEY

PAUL HALLIDAY'S CHAPTER aims from the outset 'to focus less on Blackstone's contexts ... than on his text'. He signals very clearly that he intends to consider the text rather than 'contexts in which [Blackstone] wrote and lectured'. Now I have to admit that I have difficulty in considering a text without also considering context. And in this particular case we do not merely need to consider the context in which Blackstone wrote but also the context that motivated Halliday to write about Blackstone's writing. It is abundantly clear that Blackstone's *Commentaries* play a major role in the legal culture of the twenty-first-century United States, where they have effectively been mythologised. Given his attitude to the rebellious American colonists, this is surely somewhat extraordinary. Blackstone voted against the repeal of the Stamp Act in 1766 and then tried to add a clause that would limit the repeal to those colonies 'who expunge out of their Assembly the resolutions ... derogatory from the honour and dignity of the Crown and Parliament'; in one of his last known letters he looked forward to 'a fair prospect of success in America'—a victory over the colonists.[1] To him they were not the lofty founders of a new nation but merely rebels (and rebels without a justifiable cause).

Nevertheless Blackstone seems to have become a sort of honorary member of that peculiarly American pantheon of heroes generally known as the Founding Fathers—a group of men endowed with such extraordinary foresight and clarity of constitutional vision that they seem more like deities than ordinary mortals struggling with the political realities of their day. So godlike are these men that it seems that Americans struggle to come to terms with the heretical suggestion that some had feet of clay; see, for example,

---

[1] LB Namier and J Brooke (ed), *The House of Commons 1754–1790* (Oxford, 1964) vol 2, 97; *Letters* 186.

the exchanges on H-Slavery inspired by Paul Finkelman's recent article in the *New York Times* about 'The Monster of Monticello', which explores the possibility that one of the greatest of those Founding Fathers was actually 'a creepy brutal hypocrite' and a racist bigot with very little interest in the concepts of liberty that he is popularly supposed to have espoused.[2] Thomas Jefferson, it seems, cannot be regarded as an ordinary flawed human being trying to cope with the compromises and expediencies of everyday political life; instead he is conceptualised (rather like women once were) as either on a pedestal or deep down in the pit.

It is clearly part of Halliday's purpose to restore the 'real' Blackstone. Since I am not a lawyer I cannot comment on Blackstone's reception in other parts of the Anglo American world, though my initial reaction is that whilst I recognise that he was influential, I doubt that he is quite as canonical in either the United Kingdom or in any of the old or new Commonwealth countries that have adopted common law traditions. Are there any former British colonies that mythologise their constitutional roots in quite the same way as the Americans? But that having been said, I have been surprised to learn of his significance in Quebec, where one would have expected that the tradition of French law would have excluded him. Perhaps the worldwide significance of the *Commentaries*—and the way its significance changed over time—is something that needs to be studied in more depth.

That Blackstone has become so important in the United States in the twenty-first century has been explained by several writers, yet it remains somewhat puzzling. There is no doubt that Blackstone's *Commentaries* were well received in their day and according to Edmund Burke they were as popular in colonial America as in England.[3] They were nevertheless not without their critics, notably Jeremy Bentham and that self-same Monster of Monticello. To Jefferson the basic legal text for students was not the over simplification offered by Blackstone but the older, more complex and difficult text of *Coke upon Littleton*. In 1822 he told his grandson of a new improved edition of the work produced by John Henry Thomas, who

> has arranged Coke's matter in the method of Blackstone, adding the notes of Lords Hale and Nottingham and Hargrave, adding also his own which are excellent. It is now, beyond question, the first elementary book to be read—as agreeable as Blackstone, and more profound.[4]

---

[2] *New York Times*, 30 November 2012.
[3] WM Elefson and JA Woods (ed), *Writings and Speeches of Edmund Burke. III Party, Parliament and the American War 1774–1780 (Oxford, 1996)* 123.
[4] HS Randall, *The Life of Thomas Jefferson* (New York, 1858) vol 3, 484.

Three years later he wrote with approval (and in almost identical words) of the decision to use Thomas's edition as the basic law text for students at the University of Virginia.[5]

When Robert Ferguson articulated the received wisdom that 'All of our formative documents—the Declaration of Independence, the Constitution, the Federalist Papers, the seminal decisions of the Supreme Court under John Marshall—were drafted by attorneys steeped in Sir William Blackstone's *Commentaries on the Laws of England*' he was quite simply wrong.[6] Jefferson, Adams and the other Founding Fathers (unlike Marshall) were of Blackstone's generation; they, like most other lawyers in the nascent nation, had learned their law without Blackstone's help, by reading and re-reading *Coke upon Littleton*.

Jefferson was most certainly aware of context—particularly political context. He considered the influence of the *Commentaries* on the generation of lawyers that came after him to be to be positively pernicious. As he told Madison in 1826:

> In the selection of our Law Professor, we must be rigorously attentive to his political principles. You will recollect that before the Revolution, Coke Littleton was the universal elementary book of law students, and a sounder Whig never wrote, nor of profounder learning in the orthodox doctrines of the British constitution, or in what were called English liberties ... our lawyers were then all Whigs. But when his black-letter text, and uncouth but cunning learning got out of fashion, and the honeyed Mansfieldism of Blackstone became the students' horn-book, from that moment, that profession (the nursery of our Congress) began to slide into toryism, and nearly all the young brood of lawyers now are of that hue. They suppose themselves, indeed, to be Whigs, because they no longer know what Whiggism or republicanism means. It is in our seminary that that vestal flame is to be kept alive; it is thence it is to spread anew over our own and the sister States.[7]

A few years earlier, Jefferson had written a long letter to the British radical politician Major John Cartwright about the role of the state and federal constitutions. In considering originalist thinking we might note in passing that he made it clear that constitutions were not immutable:

> Can one generation bind another, and all others, in succession forever? I think not. The Creator has made the earth for the living, not the dead ... A generation may bind itself as long as its majority continues in life; when that has disappeared, another majority is in place, holds all the rights and powers their predecessors once held, and may change their laws and institutions to suit themselves.[8]

---

[5] AA Lipscomb et al (ed), *The Writings of Thomas Jefferson* (Washington DC, 1903–04) vol 16, 128–29.
[6] RA Ferguson, *Law and Letters in American Culture* (Cambridge MA, 1984) 11.
[7] Lipscomb (n 5) vol 16, 156.
[8] Ibid 48.

On this at least he was at one with Blackstone. In the second edition of volume 1, as part of a discussion of the union between England and Scotland, Blackstone added a note that 'the bare idea of a state, without a power somewhere vested to alter every part of its laws, is the height of political absurdity'.[9]

But more pertinent to our current topic are his remarks about Blackstone's sloppy thinking. Writing about whether Christianity was part of the common law, he condemned both Blackstone and Mansfield for

> ingulfing Bible, Testament and all into the common law, without citing any authority. And thus we find this chain of authorities hanging link by link, one upon another, and all ultimately on one and the same hook. Finch quotes Prisot; Wingate does the same. Sheppard quotes Prisot, Finch and Wingate. Hale cites nobody. The court in Woolston's case, cites Hale. Wood cites Woolston's case. Blackstone quotes Woolston's case and Hale. And Lord Mansfield, like Hale, ventures it on his own authority ... Here I might defy the best-read lawyer to produce another scrip of authority for this judiciary forgery.[10]

Jefferson was not the only early American to be uncomfortable with Blackstone's *Commentaries*. In 1803 St George Tucker brought out a heavily annotated edition for the American market which attempted to strip Blackstone of those aspects that glorified aristocratic and monarchical ideas, the implications of which he not unnaturally considered to be problematical for a newly born republican nation. Yet the aristocratic and monarchical ideas that were so apparent to Tucker failed to impress Charles Francis Sheridan (member of the Irish Parliament and older brother of the playwright and politician, Richard Brinsley Sheridan). Charles Sheridan was far more worried about what he saw as Blackstone's dubious glorification of 'the uncontrolled, absolute, despotic power of Parliament' which he countered by highlighting the internal contradictions in the *Commentaries*. One example was Blackstone's assertion that the 'absolute despotic power, which must in all governments reside somewhere, is entrusted by the constitution of these kingdoms' to Parliament. Sheridan pointed out that this was an inherent contradiction in terms, 'I need not tell you ... that a despotic, necessarily implies an unlimited power; whereas an entrusted power, must, from the very circumstance of its being a trust, be limited in its exercise, to the objects of that trust'. Sheridan's unease provides another reminder of the importance of context. What worried him was the way in which Blackstone's *Commentaries* could be used to justify the subjugation of the Irish Parliament in Dublin to the British Parliament at Westminster—a situation that he openly likened to what he called 'the American persecution', that is the justification of coercive legislative measures against the American

---

[9] *Commentaries* (2nd edn) vol 1, 97–98.
[10] Lipscomb (n 5) vol 16, 50.

colonies. He also, somewhat uncharitably, invoked a more personal context; Blackstone, he suggested, wished to curry favour with the government in order to secure an appointment as lord chancellor.[11] Sheridan was well aware that the *Commentaries* were not intended to be anything but an elementary introductory text so far as would-be lawyers were concerned, observing that 'from the liberality of the style in which it is written, [it] is perhaps the only one upon the subject of the law which has been generally read by those who do not make the law their profession'. In his opinion this was precisely why bald and apparently authoritative statements about the locus of power in the nation were so dangerous.[12]

Sheridan's point about the intended readership for the *Commentaries* was widely recognised. Tomlin's *Law Dictionary* of 1820, under the heading 'Common Law', surveyed the history of writing about the law and concluded that Blackstone has written 'the best analytic and most methodic system of our laws which ever was published'. But Tomlins went on to point out that the purpose of the *Commentaries* was not to enlighten legal practitioners; rather they were 'the use of students, and of those gentlemen who choose to acquire that knowledge of our laws, which is in fact necessary for everyone'. Indeed shortly after publication of the first edition, Blackstone's *Commentaries* were included in a pamphlet proffering advice on the proper books to form a library for the relatively uneducated gentleman (that is, one who had little or no Latin). They were recommended as 'necessary for gentlemen, who do not intend to study it as a profession'.[13] In other words the *Commentaries* were recognised in England as a useful text for the general reader rather than a manual for lawyers, and certainly not as a reference work for judges. That is scarcely surprising because this was exactly what Blackstone intended.

The idea that gentlemen required some understanding of legal principles had a long history. Sir Thomas Elyot's *Boke Named the Gouernour*, first published in 1531, and regularly reprinted thereafter, addressed the sort of education suitable for elite males and included a knowledge of law via a study of Justinian and the classical orators as a prelude to a study of moral philosophy and full legal training to produce 'worshypfull lawyars' to serve the realm.[14] A more specific demand for a knowledge of the law to form part of a general liberal education was promoted in a pamphlet published in 1708 by Thomas Wood. Wood complained, in a trope that is probably familiar to us all today, irrespective of our countries of origin,

---

[11] CF Sheridan, *Observations on the Doctrine Laid Down by Sir William Blackstone, Respecting the Extent of the Power of the British Parliament*, 2nd edn (London, 1779) 1–3, 5, 11–12, 27, 30, 71.

[12] Ibid 2.

[13] [Anon], *Directions for a Proper Choice of Authors to Form a Library* (London, 1766) 33–34.

[14] [T Elyot], *The Boke Named the Gouernour* (London, 1531) fo 59v.

that a university education left students without the skills they needed for adult life. New graduates quite specifically lacked knowledge of commerce and the law. It was clear to him that those who wished to become legal practitioners had to attend the courts but he was insistent that all students, irrespective of their future vocation, needed 'a general and compendious knowledge of our laws and the reason of them'. Wood went on to publish *The Institutes of the Laws of England* in 1720. This work is something of a precursor to Blackstone's *Commentaries*. Wood prefaced his book with remarks about the difficulty of studying the laws without the aid of a methodical introduction, as there was otherwise

> no way to attain to the knowledge of them, but by a tedious wandering about, or with the greatest application and long attendance on the highest courts of justice ... at present, the way to the knowledge of the laws of our country is dark and rugged, full of turnings and windings.[15]

With what was probably false modesty he hoped that his work might

> sort, or ... put in some order, this heap of good learning; and that a general and methodical distribution, preparatory to a more large and accurate study of our laws, might now be made, as well as an institute of civil or canon law, or of the laws of other nations; which were once too, heap'd up together without beginning or end, before they were unravell'd and rescued from their first confusion and intricacy.[16]

Wood died in or before 1723, but his *Institutes* became a standard work, regularly re-published; the last edition I have traced was issued in 1772. In his biography of Blackstone, Wilfrid Prest notes that Blackstone owned no fewer than four copies of Wood's work, one of which was liberally annotated.[17]

Blackstone shared Wood's attitude to the necessity of teaching law. In volume one of the first edition of the *Commentaries* he introduced the subject as 'a liberal science' that ought to be part of the required education of a gentleman: 'a competent knowledge of the laws of that society in which we live is the proper accomplishment of every gentleman and scholar; a highly useful, I had almost said essential, part of liberal and polite education'. He pointed out that in mainland Europe 'no scholar thinks his education is completed till he has attended a course or two of lectures, both upon the institutes of Justinian and local constitutions of his native soil'. It was much the same in Scotland, 'where it is difficult to meet with a person of liberal education who is destitute of a competent knowledge of that science which is to be the guardian of his natural rights and the rule of his civil conduct'. He was appalled that 'our admirable system of laws' was unknown to all

---

[15] T Wood, *An Institute of the Laws of England* (London, 1720) i.
[16] Ibid ii.
[17] Prest, *William Blackstone* 68.

but practitioners and described his *Commentaries* merely as 'an introductory discourse'.

In other words, what we have in the *Commentaries* is an undergraduate text, and like any undergraduate text it synthesises and organises what was in effect already available in existing literature. Its overwhelming characteristic is Blackstone's ability to organise and categorise what had once seemed a rambling edifice of arcane knowledge. It was a text designed to help gentlemen understand an important part of their society and fit them for a role in life that might require them to serve as unpaid officers of the law, perhaps as a justice of the peace or as a juryman. What it was not meant to do was to train individuals who wished to become lawyers, still less to serve as a reference work for judges, especially in a jurisdiction where the study of the law has become a postgraduate rather than an undergraduate discipline. The reception of Blackstone in the eighteenth-century Atlantic world was very different to his reception in the twenty-first century.

How many people would find it acceptable for postgraduate students to use an undergraduate text as adequate evidence to back up their assertions? Would we not at the very least expect them to treat such a text as a gateway, enabling them to identify and use the sources specified? And in this context 'use' would surely also include checking the accuracy of citations. Yet it appears that in the United States senior, highly trained jurists of the Supreme Court and political theorists discussing the powers and role of the president are deeply—perhaps increasingly—influenced by their perceptions of what Blackstone wrote for undergraduates 250 years ago. Is this not both extraordinary and intellectually lazy? And is there not a certain irony in the realisation that one of the most prominent advocates of originalist thinking and hence of Blackstone's *Commentaries* is Justice Scalia. Blackstone was after all virulently anti-Catholic. Scalia's religion would not only have banned him from office in eighteenth-century Britain; it would also have made him an object of suspicion in colonial America where the British Parliament's decision to grant civil rights to the Catholic Quebecois in 1774 was viewed with such deep distrust that it became a contributory factor to rebellion in 1776.

Moving into closer discussion of Halliday's chapter rather than his motivation for writing it, I still find myself worrying about context. I am reminded of recently reading a letter written by Lord Ashburnham to his agent in the course of a dispute begun in 1695 in which he referred to Parliament being 'so jealous of all oppressions, so ready to redresse'.[18] How am I to know whether that remark should be taken at face value or was meant to be ironic without considering the context not just of the remainder of the

---

[18] Lord Ashburnham to James Mackburney, 22 January 1695/6: East Sussex Record Office, ASH 840.

letter in question but of my general knowledge of the individual based on other correspondence, personal diaries and political profile?

How does the phrase that Halliday quotes early in his essay, 'in the exertion of lawful prerogative, the king is and ought to be absolute' square with the quotation above, that 'absolute despotic power' lies with Parliament? Just as Sheridan identified the inherent contradictions in Blackstone's attitude to the power of Parliament, is there not a similar contradiction in terms in the idea of a 'lawful prerogative', since it is a fundamental maxim of the English common law that 'the king can do no wrong'. Is the maxim to be taken literally—meaning that the king, whether as a person or as a concept, may commit any act and no matter what he does that act is neither wrong nor unlawful? By this definition any exercise of the prerogative must be lawful; in which case why bother to qualify the noun? The literal definition would presumably include a justification for acting contrary to statute. Yet Blackstone also tells us that Parliament wields the supreme power and there are a number of statutes—from the time of Edward II onwards—that purport to limit the royal prerogative. What would be the point of such statutes if they could be overridden? James II's attempt to use the prerogative to suspend the penal laws against non-conformists and Catholics was one of the factors that led to the revolution that toppled him from power. A similar attempt by his brother had after all already been declared illegal by Parliament and overturned. In other words kings who flouted the fuzzy but nevertheless acknowledged limits on the prerogative were considered to be acting unlawfully and if they did so they invited confrontation with their parliaments and their subjects. In this instance at least, kings certainly could do wrong. Perhaps it is a phrase that needs to be interpreted figuratively— or if you like poetically. Thomas Wood wrote in 1720 that

> the common law and the crown law are not two different laws, tho' in almost every case the law for the king is not the law for the subject. The king hath a prerogative in all things that are not injurious to the subject; for the king can do no wrong: his prerogative can never extend so far.[19]

Unlike Blackstone, Wood had no problem with the idea that all property derived from the king. He had no truck with the idea of a social contract (which, certainly in Book 4, though not in other places, appears to be entirely accepted by Blackstone), but Wood's king, like Blackstone's, was nevertheless bound by the law. His king could do no wrong because his king, like Blackstone's, was both a real person and a concept, and the conceptual king was a beneficent figure lacking the capacity to do wrong.

As Halliday notes, the 'mystic fiction' of the king's two bodies as an element in jurisprudence can be identified from at least the reign of Elizabeth I. Its origins were traced back to medieval times by Ernst Kantorowicz

---

[19] Wood (n 15) 35.

in 1957.[20] According to Kantorowicz, Blackstone simply 'conveniently summarises the achievements of several centuries of political thought and legal speculation'.[21] Halliday is probably more accurate in suggesting the sheer complexity of Blackstone's attitude to the king's two bodies. It was a subject full of ambiguities—ambiguities that eighteenth-century commentators still found it hard to contemplate or analyse in detail. Blackstone's *Commentaries* abound with references to the constitutional upheavals of the seventeenth century. In 1649 the doctrine that the monarch was bound by the law was used to justify the trial and execution of Charles I, which was followed by an experiment in republican government. After the restoration of the monarchy in 1660 it became impossible for any serious commentator to treat that particular episode with anything but horror. Yet the revolution that deposed James II in 1688—and which was incited by similar fears about the subversion of the law—was dubbed the 'Glorious Revolution'. The sheer difficulty of justifying the events of 1688 whilst still condemning those of 1649 led to a variety of explanations, including the somewhat bizarre fiction of the baby in the warming pan and the insistence that James II had not been deposed but had abdicated. The reality that the British Isles had been invaded by a foreign power and that the kingship had been usurped was conveniently ignored. A nation that was reluctant to discuss why and how the Dutch stadtholder, William of Orange, had come to be king or why and how the succession could be diverted at the death of Queen Anne to the electoral princes of Hanover, was scarcely likely to wish to add to its constitutional confusion by encouraging rigorous analysis of the conceptual boundaries of the king's two bodies, still less how God's role in appointing a mystical king had been surrendered to Parliament. Blackstone was not the only Englishman to tread warily round a subject fraught with snares. His views need to be teased out precisely because opacity was a deliberate literary—or poetic—strategy. He can have been in no doubt that the king was bound by the law, since the coronation oath required (and still requires) the monarch to undertake to rule according to the customs and laws of the realm, in other words to defend the (unwritten) British constitution. How and why can the oath of office taken by American presidents to preserve, protect and defend the Constitution be construed as anything other than a similar promise to rule according to law?

At the risk of stating the obvious, it is important to remember that Blackstone's poetics extended to his decision about how to title his work. He did not choose to call it *The Institutes of English Law* or *A Philosophical Treatise on the Nature of English Law*. He chose instead to adopt a title that emphasises his purpose: to publish a systematic collection of notes

---

[20] E Kantorowicz, *The King's Two Bodies: A Study in Mediaeval Political Theology* (Princeton NJ, 1957).
[21] Ibid 4.

and comments that helped gentlemen to understand their society and the nature of the laws that underpinned it. What emerges from a study of the *Commentaries* (whether in terms of their poetics or of their socio-political context) is that they are a complex and multi-layered production, full of complexities, ambivalences and contradictions. Blackstone provided us with a thoughtful introductory guide, not an accurate and systematic analysis of eighteenth-century English law and constitutional thought. They may seem to lend themselves to what in the twenty-first century is called the soundbite, but the intricacies of the text make it unsuitable for so simplistic a process. They need to be read as a whole, not cherry-picked for sentences and phrases that seem to support a particular point of view about the state of English law in the second half of the eighteenth century, still less about the ways in which that law was understood by the Founding Fathers (assuming they did have a single agreed understanding, which, given the discussions and compromises that they made, seems unlikely). Using Blackstone in an attempt to provide a definitive explanation of the powers of kings (or presidents) is both impossible and inappropriate because, as Halliday points out so eloquently. Blackstone's king is sometimes a real human being and at others simply a useful but ill-defined concept.

9

Blackstone's Commentaries and the Origins of Modern Constitutionalism

HORST DIPPEL*

ACCORDING TO STANLEY Katz, America's founders rejected the constitutional ideas of William Blackstone; but with the revolution achieved, they happily drew on the *Commentaries* 'for the legal system of a democratic republic'.[1] Yet any close look at the American constitutional debate from the 1760s through the 1790s must cast doubt on this sweeping statement. For Americans of this period showed no reservations about bolstering their constitutional arguments with references to Blackstone. In what follows I first note the wide dissemination of Blackstone's work in colonial America, then give some examples of the range of topics on which he was used as an authority and mention several specific constitutional items on which his text apparently had some bearing. Finally I discuss four principles of modern constitutionalism whose Blackstonian character is evident, even though his name hardly ever appears in specific connection with them.

I

To begin with, it is well known that Edmund Burke drew Parliament's attention to the strong American sales of the first English and colonial editions of the *Commentaries*.[2] A first American edition published in

---

* A previous version of this chapter was read at the Law Schools of the University of Adelaide and of Monash University, Melbourne in March 2010. Special thanks go to Wilf Prest for his helpful comments and suggestions.
[1] SN Katz, 'Introduction to Book I', W Blackstone, *Commentaries on the Laws of England. A Facsimile of the First Edition of 1765–1769* (Chicago IL, 1979) vol 1, xii.
[2] 'I hear that they have sold nearly as many of Blackstone's Commentaries in America as in England' in P Langford (ed), *The Writings and Speeches of Edmund Burke* (Oxford, 1996) vol 3, 123.

Philadelphia in 1771–72 was followed by a second edition in 1773 and further editions for the rest of the century.[3] In 1803 St George Tucker published his Americanised five-volume version as *Blackstone's Commentaries: With Notes of Reference, To the Constitution and Laws, of the Federal Government of the United States; and of the Commonwealth of Virginia*, a title which itself underlines the close connection of Blackstone with American constitutional law. Blackstone's popularity was such that imported copies of the *Commentaries* were to be found in almost every second privately owned eighteenth-century American library.[4] It may be safely assumed that the remainder were happy with an American printed edition, an assumption supported by Max Radin's assurance that 'for many early American lawyers, Blackstone was the Common Law, because, for one thing, they often had no other book'.[5]

While thousands of Americans from the Revolutionary era and the early Republic had studied their Blackstone, there is little indication that they consciously separated the constitutionalist from the common lawyer. Most, it appears, took Blackstone as an undifferentiated whole. One striking example is provided by James Otis, who in his 1765 response[6] to Martin Howard Jr's *Halifax Letter* inserted direct quotations from Blackstone on the rights of individuals,[7] on constitutional arrangements in order to preserve them 'from unlawful Attacks',[8] and on the problem of how the 'supreme Power' in a state should be organised.[9]

---

[3] C Warren, *A History of the American Bar* (New York NY, 1966) 177–80; Lockmiller, 170–71; Eller 37–58.

[4] HA Johnson, *Imported Eighteenth-Century Law Treatises in American Libraries, 1700–1799* (Knoxville TN, 1978) 59 and *passim*.

[5] Quoted in EK Bauer, *Commentaries on the Constitution, 1790–1860* (New York NY, 1952) 18; *cf* M Hoeflich, 'American Blackstones', in Prest (ed) Commentaries 171–84.

[6] J Otis, *A Vindication of the British Colonies, against the Aspersions of the Halifax Gentleman, in His Letter to a Rhode Island Friend* (Boston MA, 1765) in B Bailyn (ed), *Pamphlets of the American Revolution 1750–1776* (Cambridge MA, 1965) vol 1, 545–79. For Howard's *Letter* see ibid 523–44.

[7] W Blackstone, *An Analysis of the Laws of England. To which is prefixed an Introductory Discourse of the Study of the Laws* (Oxford, 1759) 7: 'The absolute Rights of Individuals, regarded by the municipal Laws [(which pay no Attention to Duties of the absolute Kind)] compose what is called political or civil Liberty'. 'The absolute [Rights, or civil] Liberties, of Englishmen, as frequently declared in Parliament, are principally three; the Right of personal Security, [of] personal Liberty, and [of] private Property'. *Cf* Otis in Bailyn (n 6) 558 (square brackets enclose text omitted by Otis).

[8] Blackstone (n 7) 8: 'Besides these three primary Rights, there are others which are secondary and subordinate [; viz.] (to preserve the former from unlawful Attacks) 1. The Constitution and Power of Parliament[s]: 2. The Limitation of the King's Prerogative:—And, (to vindicate them when actually violated) 3. The regular Administration of [public] Justice: 4. The Right of Petitioning for Redress of Grievances: 5. The Right of Having and Using Arms for Self-Defence.' *Cf* Otis in Bailyn (n 6) 558–59 (square brackets enclose text omitted by Otis).

[9] Blackstone (n 7) 2: 'In all States there is [(and must be)] an absolute supreme Power, to which the Right of Legislation belongs; and which, by the singular Constitution of these Kingdoms, is vested in the King, Lords, and Commons'. *Cf* Otis in Bailyn (n 6) 558–59 (square brackets mark an addition by Otis).

Otis's argument has particular interest in the present context. He reproached Howard for misunderstanding Blackstone, although Howard did not even mention the latter directly ('The gentleman seems to have taken this and some other of his distinctions from that excellent treatise very ill understood'[10]); Otis himself defended colonial rights and liberties with express reference to Blackstone. Finally, the Otis–Howard dispute antedated publication of the first volume of the *Commentaries* and so necessarily drew on Blackstone's *Analysis of the Laws of England*, thus demonstrating that his reputation was already well established in America even before the *Commentaries* appeared ('See Mr. Blackstone's accurate and elegant analysis of the laws of England').[11]

Blackstone's authority could only be further enhanced by publication of the *Commentaries*. Given that work's general diffusion, we may safely assume that it often served, especially in the early hours of American constitutionalism, as a benchmark source by reference to which debaters defined their own position. Thus in the Virginia convention ratifying the Federal Constitution, James Madison referred delegates to 'a book which is in every man's hand—Blackstone's Commentaries'.[12] The debates in the ratification conventions of 1787–88 demonstrate that we should take Madison's remark quite literally. Not only did Blackstone's name turn up repeatedly, but he was often quoted verbatim, suggesting that copies of the *Commentaries* were indeed readily at hand.[13]

Some further indication of Blackstone's centrality to early American discussion of constitutions is provided by the request of John Adams, freshly installed as first vice-president, for his wife to send to a house he had newly rented near New York City:

> Hume, Johnson, Priestley, Ainsworths Dictionary, and such other Books as may be most amusing and useful—The great Works and Collections I would not bring on. But Blackstone and De Lolme on the English Constitution and the Collection of American Constitutions I would have.[14]

---

[10] Otis in Bailyn (n 6), 559.

[11] Ibid. G Stourzh, 'William Blackstone: Teacher of Revolution' (1970) 15 *Jahrbuch für Amerikastudien* 184–200, 199 corrected Bailyn's mistaken assumption that Otis was referring to the *Commentaries*.

[12] J Elliot (ed), *The Debates in the Several State Conventions, on the Adoption of the Federal Constitution* (Philadelphia PA, 1836–45) vol 3, 501.

[13] In debate both sides may have been armed with the *Commentaries*, as Wilson was when he argued, 'for Blackstone, in the very volume which the honorable member (Mr. Smilie) had in his hand, and read us several extracts from', in order then to read his own quotation: ibid vol 2, 518 and B Bailyn (ed), *The Debate on the Constitution* (New York NY, 1993) vol 1, 857.

[14] John to Abigail Adams, 24 May 1789, in MA Hogan et al (ed), *Adams Family Correspondence* (Cambridge MA, 2007) vol 8, 358. Presumably Adams owned a copy of the first American edition of the *Commentaries*, as the first reference to the *Commentaries* in his diaries is on 7 June 1771, when he advised someone in Northern Connecticut to restock his two-item law library with it: LH Butterfield (ed), *Diary and Autobiography of John Adams* (Cambridge MA, 1961) vol 2, 27.

II

In assessing Blackstone's impact on modern constitutionalism, neither his common law theories nor the whole range of his constitutional ideas can be analysed here. To what extent he may have been in conformity or at odds with the constitutional reality of Britain during his lifetime is an important question which merits further investigation. But here I focus on those aspects of his ideas which contributed to modern constitutionalism.[15]

Whenever a bill of rights was at stake, 'to secure (what Doctor Blackstone calls) that residuum of human rights which is not intended to be given up to society', due regard to Blackstone's opinions was appropriate.[16] His words in praise of trial by jury, 'so often quoted', were according to Patrick Henry 'more forcible and cogent than any thing I could say'.[17] Samuel Bryan, heavily criticising James Wilson, had argued similarly in October 1787, while Elbridge Gerry, taking Blackstone as his witness, lamented the possibility that 'this inestimable privilege [might] be relinquished in America' for the trial of civil cases.[18] Likewise in the *Pennsylvania Packet* on 18 December 1787, Samuel Bryan abhorred

> the idea of losing the transcendent privilege of trial by jury, with the loss of which, it is remarked by the same learned author [Blackstone], that in Sweden, the liberties of the commons were extinguished by an aristocratic senate: and that *trial by jury* and the liberty of the people went out together.[19]

A closer look at the *Commentaries* might, however, raise questions about Blackstone's position on certain issues. Thus John Dickinson complained that restricting the promulgation of *ex post facto* or retrospective laws in criminal matters alone, as Blackstone appeared to have done, left the door

---

[15] Hence this chapter is not quite what Gerard Stourzh envisaged when he called for closer study of the significance of Blackstone's work for the American Revolutionaries. Stourzh's article (n 11) amply demonstrates how Blackstone's ideas were invoked in the Revolutionary debate without express reference to their author (ibid 187–88).

[16] Richard Henry Lee to Edmund Randolph, 16 October 1787 in Elliot (ed) (n 12) vol 1, 503–04; also in PH Smith (ed), *Letters of Delegates to Congress, 1774–1789* (Washington DC, 1976–2000) vol 24, 482–83.

[17] Elliot (ed) (n 12) vol 3, 544.

[18] *Freeman's Journal* (Philadelphia) 24 October 1787 ('Reply to Wilson's Speech: 'Centinel' II'), in Bailyn (ed) (n 13) vol 1, 84; cf 'Theophrastus', 'A Short History of the Trial by Jury' in CS Hyneman and DS Lutz (ed), *American Political Writing during the Founding Era, 1760–1805* (Indianapolis IN, 1983) vol 1, 698. [E Gerry,] *Observations on the new Constitution, and on the Federal and State Convention* [1788] in PL Ford (ed), *Pamphlets on the Constitution of the United States, Published during Its Discussion by the People, 1787–1788* (Brooklyn NY, 1888) 10.

[19] JP Kaminski and R Leffler (ed), *Federalists and Antifederalists: The Debate Over the Ratification of the Constitution* (Madison WI, 1998) 135. The latter part of the sentence was quoted again, with due reference to Blackstone and 'his excellent commentaries on the laws of England', by Mercy Otis Warren in LH Cohen (ed), *History of the Rise, Progress and Termination of the American Revolution, interspersed with Biographical, Political and Moral Observations* [1805] (Indianapolis IN, 1988) vol 2, 630.

open to undue state interference with the civil rights of citizens, so 'some further provision for this purpose would be requisite'.[20] But brushing aside such criticism, in the *Federalist No 84* Alexander Hamilton singled out for special praise Blackstone's stance against arbitrary imprisonment and his reference to the Habeas Corpus Act as 'the bulwark of the British constitution'.[21]

Securing human rights was one constitutional domain where the *Commentaries* could be drawn on for a wealth of arguments. Another field was power generally, in particular the relative powers of executive and legislature. Blackstone was quoted approvingly even on the core questions of political rights, limited government and sovereignty, so fundamental to a federal structure. Joseph Story had done so in his *Commentaries on the Constitution*, from which the following passage was prefixed by Elliot to his *Debates*:

> It is in the same sense that Blackstone says, 'the law ascribes to the king of England the attribute of sovereignty or pre-eminence', because, in respect to the powers confided to him, he is dependent on no man, and accountable to no man, and subjected to no superior jurisdiction. Yet the king of England cannot make a law; and his acts, beyond the powers assigned to him by the constitution are utterly void.[22]

It is as if the words of John Marshall in *McCulloch v Maryland* were resounding in Justice Story's ears: '[T]he government of the Union, though limited in its powers, is supreme within its sphere of action'.[23]

In the Virginia ratifying convention, debate on relations between executive and legislature focused on the treaty-making power, with several speakers drawing extensively on Blackstone. But while supporters of the Federal Constitution relied on Blackstone to support their case, the anti-federalists also appealed to his ideas. So Patrick Henry made abundantly clear in advancing an argument that Joseph Story would take up again, several decades later:

> I ask, how are the state rights, individual rights, and national rights, secured? Not as in England; for the authority quoted from Blackstone would, if stated right, prove, in a thousand instances, that, if the king of England attempted to take away the rights of individuals, the law would stand against him. The acts of Parliament would stand in his way. The bill and declaration of rights would be against him. The common law is fortified by the bill of rights. The rights of the people cannot be destroyed.

---

[20] Elliot (ed) (n 12) vol 5, 488. Mercy Otis Warren ('A Columbian Patriot') also made this point in her 'Observations on the Constitution': Bailyn (ed) (n 13) vol 2, 290–91.
[21] JC Cooke (ed), *The Federalist* (Middletown CT, 1961) 577; cf *Commentaries* vol 4, 431.
[22] Elliot (ed) (n 12) vol 1, 64.
[23] *McCulloch v Maryland* 4 Wheaton 316 (1819) 405.

Henry concluded

> that there was real responsibility in the British government, and sufficient security arising from the common law, declaration of rights, &c.; whereas, in this government, there was no barrier to stop their mad career. He hoped to obtain the amendments which his honorable friend had proposed.[24]

Whatever the value of Henry's case (one which Madison would immediately and vehemently reject), the pattern is clear. Whether in the affirmative or negative, when the debate turned to the British constitution, it was safe to rely on Blackstone, for everyone could be assumed to be familiar with his *Commentaries*.[25]

It is true that some seem to have rejected Blackstone on principle. James Wilson was among them when he classified the commentator as 'an antirepublican lawyer'.[26] Political responsibility was not a feature of the British system, according to Wilson; on the contrary:

> Sir William Blackstone will tell you, that in Britain the power is lodged in the British Parliament; but the Parliament may alter the form of the government; and that its power is absolute, without control. The idea of a constitution, limiting and superintending the operations of legislative authority, seems not to have been accurately understood in Britain.[27]

Archibald Maclaine of North Carolina appears to have shared this opinion, likewise Alexander Hamilton.[28] But Hamilton was not as rigorous as Wilson in rejecting Blackstone. Indeed he thought that arguments some colonists had used against Blackstone might now be employed by some of the states against the rest, while a year later in the *Federalist*[29] he quoted Blackstone approvingly on the constitutional protection of civil rights.[30]

So in 1787–88 Blackstone was as much an authority on constitutional matters as he had been in the years of outright conflict with Britain. Then, following the Boston Tea Party, the attempt to rule Massachusetts with a royal governor and a submissive council was opposed with direct reference to 'the learned author of the commentaries on the Laws of England ... the

---

[24] Elliot (ed) (n 12) vol 3, 513, 514, 506–14 *passim*.

[25] *Cf* 'A Freeman', 'To the Freeholders and Freemen of Rhode Island', *Newport Herald*, 20 March 1788, in Bailyn (ed) (n 13) vol 2, 368–71 (contrasting provisions of the proposed Federal Constitution with those of the British constitution 'impartially selected from the celebrated Judge Blackstone').

[26] RG McCloskey (ed), *The Works of James Wilson* (Cambridge MA, 1967) vol 1, 79. For Wilson's critical discussion of Blackstone in ch v of his *On Municipal Law* of the mid 1790s, *cf* Hyneman and Lutz (ed) (n 18) vol 1, 1264–98.

[27] Elliot (ed) (n 12) vol 2, 432; *cf* also Wilson's remarks of 24 November 1787 in Bailyn (ed) (n 13) vol 1, 801.

[28] Elliot (ed) (n 12) vol 4, 63.

[29] *Cf* Cooke (ed) (n 21) 577.

[30] M Farrand (ed), *The Records of the Federal Convention of 1787* (New Haven CT, 1911) vol 1, 472–73.

authority of whom I presume you will hardly be disposed to dispute'.[31] The pseudonymous 'Monitor' repeatedly quoted Blackstone directly, including his well-known assertion that 'In a free state, every man, who is supposed a free agent, ought to be, in some measure, his own governor; and therefore a branch at least of the legislative power should reside in the whole body of the people'.[32] So America's liberty would be gone, should the people be excluded from its government.[33] Or as John Adams was some years later to argue, 'there can be no constitutional liberty, no free state, no right constitution of a commonwealth, where the people are excluded from the government'.[34]

In the late 1760s John McKenzie had referred to Blackstone in a similar fashion.[35] This was part of an early shift from direct quotation of Blackstone to the adoption of his ideas without explicit acknowledgement. The subtle infiltration of Blackstonian constitutionalism induced David A Lockmiller to conclude that:

> When the Constitutional Convention met in Philadelphia in 1787 most of the members of that body were familiar with and they were no doubt greatly influenced by Blackstone's analysis of the English governmental system. Such terms in the Constitution as 'crimes and misdemeanors,' 'ex post facto laws,' 'judicial power,' 'due process,' 'levying war,' were used in a sense in which the Commentator had employed them. In like manner most of the early state constitutions were influenced by the *Commentaries* and these in turn were copied in part by the newer states of the Union.[36]

A specific example of this infusion of Blackstonian ideas is provided by article II, section 2, clause 1 of the Federal Constitution on the pardoning power of the president, 'except in Cases of Impeachment'.[37] This provision had previously appeared only in the constitutions of Pennsylvania (1776), of Vermont (1777 and 1786), of Massachusetts (1780), in the failed constitutions of New Hampshire of 1781 and 1782, and in the adopted constitution of 1784.[38] It echoed what Blackstone had written in the first edition of his *Commentaries*: 'in parliamentary impeachments, the king has no prerogative

---

[31] 'Monitor', 'To the New Appointed Councellors, of the Province of Massachusetts-Bay' *Massachusetts Spy*, 18 August 1774, in Hyneman and Lutz (ed) (n 18) vol 1, 277–78.
[32] W Blackstone, *Commentaries on the Laws of England. In Four Books, Re-Printed from the British Copy, Page for Page with the Last Edition* (Philadelphia PA, 1771–72) vol 1, 158; *cf* 'Monitor' (n 31) 278.
[33] Ibid 277–80.
[34] J Adams, *A Defence of the Constitutions of Government of the United States of America, Against the Attack of M. Turgot in His Letter to Dr. Price, Dated the Twenty-second Day of March, 1778*, 3rd edn (Philadelphia PA, 1797; Aalen, 1979) vol 3, 361; *cf* ibid vol 1, x.
[35] *Cf* Stourzh (n 11) 140–45.
[36] Lockmiller 174.
[37] H Dippel (ed), *Constitutional Documents of the United States of America* (Berlin, 2006–2011) vol 1, 57.
[38] Ibid vol 5, 334; vol 7, 16, 29; vol 4, 30, 334, 351, 369.

of pardoning'.[39] This statement was missing in all later English and American editions.[40] But it is perhaps more important to note that when the issue was first debated in the Federal Convention, the wording used in the notes, 'his pardon shall not, however, be pleadable to an Impeachm[e]nt', was seemingly taken directly from Blackstone: 'that no pardon under the great seal shall be pleadable to an impeachment by the commons of Great-Britain in parliament'.[41] This tacit reliance on Blackstone shines even through Hamilton's argument on the same issue in the *Federalist No 69*.[42]

III

Blackstone's language had not only infiltrated early American constitutions, including the Federal Constitution. His impact on modern constitutionalism was far more than merely semantic and thus substantially greater than scholars have so far identified. This second strain of Blackstonian influence led to some of his ideas finding their way into modern constitutionalism without ever being directly associated with his name. Besides specific constitutional provisions, Blackstone's influence indeed extended to several of the core principles of modern constitutionalism itself.

When in 1776 Americans adopted the first Declarations of Rights in Virginia, Delaware, Pennsylvania, Maryland and North Carolina, followed by other states, and in 1791 by the Bill of Rights incorporated into the Federal Constitution, they did more than merely emulate the 1689 original. For these early declarations included a firmly entrenched catalogue of principles said to be established by natural right and reason. Some of these notions Blackstone had set forth in his *Commentaries*. Thus he had declared that 'the principal aim of society is to protect individuals in the enjoyment of those absolute rights, which were vested in them by the immutable laws of nature'.[43] Such rights were not privileges conferred by the state, but 'that *residuum* of natural liberty, which is not required by the laws of society to be sacrificed to public convenience'.[44] This liberty could only 'be lost or destroyed by the folly or demerits of ... the legislature'.[45] In this spirit the constitution of Pennsylvania concluded: 'To guard against transgressions of the high powers, which we have delegated, we declare, that every thing in

---

[39] *Commentaries* vol 1, 259.
[40] *Cf* Blackstone (n 32) vol 1, 269. Bell's Philadelphia edition of 1771 was printed from the fourth English edition of 1770: Eller 37.
[41] Farrand (ed), (n 30) vol 2, 146; Blackstone, *Commentaries* (n 35) vol 4, 258.
[42] *Cf* Cooke (ed) (n 21) 466.
[43] *Commentaries* vol 1, 124.
[44] Ibid 129.
[45] Ibid 127.

this article is excepted out of the general powers of government, and shall for ever remain inviolate'.[46]

When Americans in the late eighteenth and the first half of the nineteenth centuries spoke in elevated terms of 'certain natural inherent and unalienable rights' or 'certain natural, essential, and unalienable rights,' or 'certain unalienable rights' or 'certain inherent and indefeasible rights' Blackstone always loomed large in the background.[47] He, more than anyone else, had insisted on ascertaining human rights and classifying them, like the Americans from 1776 on, as natural rather than granted, as 'the indelible rights of mankind', associating them with 'the dictates of truth and justice, the feelings of humanity'.[48] Perhaps not as capable a philosopher as Aristotle, James Harrington, John Milton, Algernon Sidney, John Locke, or Montesquieu, Blackstone relied on historical experience and common legal knowledge imported into the American political creed, and thereby into modern constitutionalism, the insistence that the rights of man as his natural property must be ascertained and secured against any encroachments by those in power.[49] It was he who convinced them that the birthrights of freeborn Englishmen, which they had claimed for more than a century as colonists, were indeed nothing less than the rights of man.

The separation of powers is a doctrine usually ascribed to Montesquieu. But Blackstone enriched this doctrine with the theory of 'checks and balances'.[50] Blackstone was familiar with Montesquieu's ideas and readily adopted them in distinguishing between executive and legislative powers.

---

[46] Constitution of Pennsylvania (1790), art IX, sec 26 in Dippel (n 37) vol 5, 369. The clause originating from the Pennsylvania document was subsequently adopted by numerous state constitutions, including the 1845 constitution of Texas. The last time it appeared before the Civil War was in the Lecompton constitution of Kansas of 1857.

[47] Dippel (n 37) vol 5, 321 (Constitution of Pennsylvania 1776, ch I, sec 1), ibid vol 7, 11, 25, 39 (Vermont, 1777, 1786, 1793, ch I, sec 1); ibid, vol 5, 13 (failed American Constitution of New Ireland of 1780, Decl of Rights, sec 1); ibid vol 5, 200 (Ohio 1802, art VIII, sec 1); ibid vol 2, 173 (Indiana 1816, art I, sec 1); ibid, vol 3, 2013 (Maine 1819, art I, sec 1); ibid, vol 5, 364–65 (Constitution of Pennsylvania 1790, art IX, sec 1). The same wording appeared in the Constitutions of Illinois of 1818, art VIII, sec 1 (ibid vol 2, 130) and of 1848, art XIII, sec 1 (ibid 163), of Pennsylvania of 1838, art IX, sec 1 (ibid vol 5, 399), and of Florida of 1839, art I, sec 1 (ibid vol 1, 307).

[48] Blackstone (n 32) vol 4, 3.

[49] On Blackstone and rights, see PO Carrese, *The Cloaking of Power. Montesquieu, Blackstone, and the Rise of Judicial Activism* (Chicago IL, 2003) 105–77; also G Anastaplo, *Reflections on Freedom of Speech and the First Amendment* (Lexington KY, 2007) 26–35.

[50] *Cf* MJC Vile, *Constitutionalism and the Separation of Powers* (Indianapolis IN, 1998), esp 58–82, quoting several British authors of the first half of the eighteenth century on the 'balanced constitution'. Their scattered ideas, however, appear not to have taken root. Unlike these early authors, Blackstone developed a genuine theoretical approach to the 'balanced constitution' and 'checks and balances', concepts which made their first appearance in the American constitutional debate only in 1767–68 and again in 1771, two dates closely associated with the publication history of the *Commentaries*.

He also agreed with Montesquieu that in separating these powers one should prevent the other from wrongdoing.

> To hinder therefore any such encroachments, the king is himself a part of the parliament: and, as this is the reason of his being so, very properly therefore the share of legislation, which the constitution has placed in the crown, consists in the power of *rejecting*, rather than *resolving*; this being sufficient to answer the end proposed.[51]

Blackstone's comments may remind us of at least part of the role the president plays in the legislative process of the United States. But Blackstone developed his position in a manner which significantly elaborated on Montesquieu, and which points directly to the American constitutions, completing and not merely reiterating the doctrine of the separation of powers.[52] For he not only supposed the king to provide a check on Parliament, but presented the entire British constitution as permeated with checks. Parliamentary impeachment was a check against ministerial wrongdoing.[53] In a broader sense, the gentry and nobility 'representing their country in parliament' was in the terms of the constitution a check:

> They are the guardians of the English constitution; the makers, repealers, and interpreters of the English laws; delegated to watch, to check, and to avert every dangerous innovation, to propose, to adopt, and to cherish any solid and well-weighed improvement; bound by every tie of nature, of honour, and of religion, to transmit that constitution and those laws to their posterity, amended if possible, at least without any derogation.[54]

John Adams might have liked this passage, and certainly was convinced of the unassailable validity of the subsequent statement for any well-established constitutional order:

> The crown cannot begin of itself any alterations in the present established law; but it may approve or disapprove of the alterations suggested and consented to by the two houses. The legislative therefore cannot abridge the executive power of any rights which it now has by law, without its own consent ... And herein indeed consists the true excellence of the English government, that all the parts of it form a mutual check upon each other. In the legislature, the people are a check upon the nobility, and the nobility a check upon the people; by the mutual privilege of rejecting what the other has resolved: while the king is a check upon both, which preserves the executive power from encroachments. And this very executive power is again checked and kept within due bounds by the two houses,

---

[51] Blackstone (n 32) vol 1, 154.
[52] The classical example of a constitution based on separation of powers without including checks and balances is that of the second French Republic of 1848.
[53] Blackstone (n 32) vol 1, 257–58.
[54] Ibid vol 1, 9.

through the privilege they have of enquiring into, impeaching, and punishing the conduct ... of its evil and pernicious counsellors.[55]

The rationale of the whole complex structure was to 'preserv[e] the ballance of the constitution'.[56] This balance had a double meaning. On the one hand, it should prevent an abuse of power which would 'dissolve the constitution, and subvert the fundamentals of government'. If one branch had the power to set itself above the others 'the ballance of the constitution would be overturned'.[57] Thus, on the other hand,

> in every branch of this large and extensive dominion, our free constitution has interposed such seasonable checks and restrictions, as may curb it from trampling on those liberties, which it was meant to secure and establish. The enormous weight of prerogative (if left to itself, as in arbitrary government it is) spreads havoc and destruction among all the inferior movements: but, when ballanced and bridled (as with us) by it's proper counterpoise, timely and judiciously applied, it's operations are then equable and regular, it invigorates the whole machine, and enables every part to answer the end of it's construction.[58]

There is no need to quote Blackstone further on the idea and the importance of checks and balances to preserve the constitution and with it the liberties of the people. Nugent, in his translation of *L'Esprit des lois*, had used both terms, 'checks' and 'balance'. But Montesquieu had not elaborated on these words as Blackstone was subsequently to do. In his most important chapter on the English constitution, the word 'check' appears only twice and 'balance' not at all.[59] No author other than Blackstone contributed so much to their widespread usage in America. It was in this Blackstonian sense that the *Essex Result* of 1778 had insisted 'that these three powers ought to be in different hands, and independent of one another, and so ballanced, and each having that check upon the other, that their independence shall be preserved'.[60] Even before the Federal Constitution was drafted, John Adams had joined in praising the 'checks and balances of a free government' as the foundations of liberty.[61] A few years later Noah Webster insisted that the transformation of the Blackstonian principles into the American constitutions was happily achieved, as 'we have all the advantages of checks

---

[55] Ibid vol 1, 154–55.
[56] Ibid vol 1, 154.
[57] Ibid vol 1, 244.
[58] Ibid vol 1, 240.
[59] [Montesquieu], *The Spirit of Laws, translated from the French by Thomas Nugent*, 4th edn (London, 1766) vol 1, 228, 234. That this term was less central to Montesquieu is indicated by the fact that he did not use a coherent French expression for it, speaking in the first case of the '*droit d'arrêter*' and in the second case of '*enchaînera*': Montesquieu, *De L'Esprit des lois*, in R Caillois (ed), *Oeuvres complètes* (Paris, 1949–51) vol 2, 401, 405.
[60] O Handlin and M Handlin (ed), *The Popular Sources of Political Authority. Documents on the Massachusetts Constitution of 1780* (Cambridge MA, 1966) 337.
[61] Adams (n 34) vol 1, iii.

and balances, without the danger which may arise from a superior and independent order of men'.[62]

The *locus classicus* for the independence of the judiciary is the Act of Settlement of 1701, whereby what was a major concern of the Glorious Revolution, albeit unobtainable in 1689, finally became enshrined in law.[63] But once again it was Blackstone, rather than Montesquieu, who provided the theoretical rationale of judicial independence within a system characterised by the separation of powers. According to Blackstone 'one main preservative of the public liberty' was that the Crown appointed judges but could not remove them at will.[64]

> Were it [the judicial power] joined with the legislative, the life, liberty, and property of the subject would be in the hands of arbitrary judges, whose decisions would be then regulated only by their own opinions, and not by any fundamental principles of law; which though legislators may depart from, yet judges are bound to observe. Were it joined with the executive, this union might soon be an overballance for the legislative ... Nothing therefore is more to be avoided, in a free constitution, than uniting the provinces of a judge and a minister of state.[65]

Blackstone supported this position by referring to the reasons given for abolishing in 1641 the Court of Star Chamber, an event deeply engraved on the cultural memory of America's political elite. Only an independent judiciary could transform the courts into 'the grand depositary of the fundamental laws of the kingdom [thus having] gained a known and stated jurisdiction, regulated by certain and established rules, which the crown itself cannot now alter but by act of parliament'.[66]

True, the limits of Blackstone's impact become visible as soon as we look beyond the elite. In the Federal Constitution as well as in a number of state constitutions, this strict separation of the judiciary from the other branches of government was established in conformity with the reasons provided by Blackstone. But from the drafting of the constitution of Pennsylvania in 1776 onwards, and especially under the onslaught of Jacksonian democracy in the 1820s and after, this principle commanded less support in the United States than most other essentials of modern constitutionalism, even though the Federal Constitution resisted all demands for its abandonment

---

[62] 'A Citizen of America' [ie Noah Webster], 'An Examination into the Leading Principles of the Federal Constitution' (Philadelphia, 1787) in CA Sheehan and GL McDowell (ed), *Friends of the Constitution. Writings of the 'Other' Federalists 1787–1788* (Indianapolis IN, 1998) 378.
[63] 12 and 13 Will III c 2.
[64] Blackstone (n 32) vol 1, 269.
[65] Ibid.
[66] Ibid 267.

or modification.[67] Yet Americans were ready to follow Blackstone on one of its significant consequences, in relation to the process of impeachment:

> For, though in general the union of the legislative and judicial powers ought to be most carefully avoided, yet it may happen that a subject, intrusted with the administration of public affairs, may infringe the rights of the people, and be guilty of such crimes, as the ordinary magistrate either dares not or cannot punish. Of these the representatives of the people, or house of commons, cannot properly *judge*; because their constituents are the parties injured: and can therefore only *impeach*.

Adapted to American republican institutions, and in conformity with the common law principle that, in contrast to ancient Greece, the people cannot be accuser and judge at the same time, 'It is proper that the nobility should judge, to insure justice to the accused; as it is proper that the people should accuse, to insure justice to the commonwealth'.[68]

A second consequence of Blackstone's position on the judiciary was no more self-evident. Supporting legislative supremacy, Blackstone vehemently rejected any suggestion that judges were at liberty to disregard or put aside parliamentary legislation, 'for that were to set the judicial power above that of the legislature, which would be subversive of all government'.[69] Judicial review, as it came to be understood in America, was inadmissible for Blackstone. His strong words on the subject still had some sway on the Federal Convention in 1787, which debated but failed to embrace judicial review. When discussing how the legislature might be checked, all the Blackstonian arguments came up again, about the separation of powers and whether or not the executive and judiciary should unite in order to fend off attacks from the legislature.[70] Against those ready to consider the practice of some states where judges could 'set aside laws as being ag[ain]st the Constitution', others warned vehemently against 'Judges meddling in politics and parties'.[71] Similarly Hamilton used Blackstonian language

---

[67] *Cf* KL Manning, 'The Massachusetts Constitution: Liberty and Equality in the Commonwealth' in GE Connor and CW Hammons (ed), *The Constitutionalism of American States* (Columbia MO, 2008) 44. Tucker admitted American deficits, 'the inconveniences of which are subjects of daily observation': St G Tucker, *Blackstone's Commentaries: With Notes of Reference, To the Constitution and Laws, of the Federal Government of the United States; and of the Commonwealth of Virginia* (Philadelphia PA, 1803; Union NJ, 1996) vol 2, 269 and n. On the federal level Tucker was, however, unequivocal about what he called the 'absolute independence of the judiciary': ibid vol 1, app 353–61. *Cf* HV Ames, *The Proposed Amendments to the Constitution of the United States During the First Century of Its History* (Washington DC, 1897) esp 144–64.
[68] Blackstone (n 32) vol 4, 258.
[69] Ibid vol 1, 91.
[70] Farrand (ed) (n 30) vol 1, 97–98, 109–10, 139, 144 and vol 2, 73–83, 298–301.
[71] Ibid vol 1, 97 (Elbridge Gerry); vol 2, 300 (Roger Sherman). See also ES Corwin, *The Doctrine of Judicial Review. Its Legal and Historical Basis and Other Essays* (Princeton NJ, 1914) 10–11 and 1–78 *passim*. The practice Gerry referred to is partly documented by Corwin. The 1777 constitution of Georgia was the first to contain a provision that 'The House

in the *Federalist* to reject the idea that judicial review 'would imply a superiority of the judiciary to the legislative power'.[72] This Blackstonian ambivalence, on the one hand insisting on a strict separation of powers with an independent judiciary as a third branch of government, but on the other hand subordinating its role to the principle of parliamentary supremacy, left American constitutionalism without a clear guideline for, and thus contributed to a future ambivalent course in, pursuing the principle of judicial independence in a democratic society with its new challenges.

It is the conventional wisdom that Blackstone elaborated on Montesquieu's exposition of the British constitution, just as de Lolme was to do a few years later. But Blackstone gave his interpretation a particular twist by its incorporation of natural law ideas, which enabled him to claim universal validity for some of that constitution's core elements. Due to this approach Blackstone became one of the main exponents of the universalism associated with modern constitutionalism. When Rudolf von Gneist later insisted that the British constitution proclaimed 'no general constitutional truths', Blackstone would certainly have contradicted him.[73] Unlike Gneist, Blackstone was convinced that justice rested on 'natural foundations'. All human laws depended on 'two foundations, the law of nature and the law of revelation'. '[H]uman laws are only declaratory of, and act in subordination to, the former'.[74] This natural law controlling human law Blackstone equated with 'ethics', and more generally with 'reason'.[75]

From this broad perspective, directed by the universal category of reason, Blackstone was able to give his sweeping definition of the common law as 'nothing else but custom, arising from the universal agreement of the whole community' a pronouncement for which Bentham would shortly afterwards criticise him so severely.[76] For Blackstone the common law was identical with the 'universal law of society', as also with the 'law of nations', the latter being an integral part of English law.[77]

---

of Assembly shall have Power to make such Laws and Regulations, as may be conducive to the good order and well being of the State; provided such Laws and Regulations be not repugnant to the true Intent and Meaning of any Rule or Regulation contained in this Constitution': Dippel (n 37) vol 2, 14. But like subsequent similar provisions there is no indication that this provision was meant to confer the power of judicial review on the courts. The Pennsylvania constitution of 1776 established a 'Council of Censors' empowered 'to recommend to the Legislature the repealing such Laws as appear to them to have been Enacted contrary to the principles of the Constitution' (ibid, vol 5, 343).

[72] Cooke (ed) (n 21) 524; cf 521–30.
[73] R Gneist, *Englische Verfassungsgeschichte* (Berlin, 1882) 688.
[74] Blackstone (n 32) vol 1, 32, 42.
[75] Ibid vol 1, 41, 423, 424; vol 2, 3; vol 4, 67.
[76] Ibid vol 1, 472; cf JH Burns and HLA Hart (ed), J Bentham, *A Comment on the Commentaries and A Fragment on Government* (London 1977).
[77] Blackstone (n 32) vol 4, 66.

[S]ince in England no royal power can introduce a new law, or suspend the execution of the old, therefore the law of nations ... is here adopted in its full extent by the common law, and is held to be a part of the law of the land. And those acts of parliament, which have from time to time been made to enforce this universal law, or to facilitate the execution of its decisions, are not to be considered as introductive of any new rule, but merely as declaratory of the old fundamental constitutions of the kingdom; without which it must cease to be a part of the civilized world.[78]

From this perspective it is not hard to see why Blackstone was convinced that English law was 'founded upon principles that are permanent, uniform, and universal; and always conformable to the dictates of truth and justice, the feelings of humanity, and the indelible rights of mankind'.[79] The general conclusion of this argument could only be that law, as long as it was wise and just, was an expression of this conformity and founded on universal principles of natural law, reason and justice. So a constitution was not restricted to the expression of any particular governmental arrangements, and its legitimacy could not be derived from a spirit of localism. If it was to be accepted and respected its principles had to be universally true. In the same sense the people of Stoughton, Massachusetts, in May 1780, had insisted on 'natural right ... as a principle [sic] corner-stone in the foundation for the frame of government to stand on'.[80] Though only the people could sanction a constitution, Blackstone had helped Americans to see that its contents needed to be founded on universal principles in order to claim legitimacy, a principle modern constitutionalism has insisted on ever since.[81]

IV

To sum up: I do not suggest that Blackstone delivered a blueprint for writing human rights, separation of powers, judicial independence and universal principles into the constitutions of modern constitutionalism. But when Americans came to decide that they needed written constitutions and sought to determine the essentials these documents should contain, Blackstone proved a tremendous source of inspiration. Thanks to the fact that, from around 1770 onwards, almost everyone who read or practised

---

[78] Ibid 67.
[79] Ibid vol 4, 3.
[80] Handlin and Handlin (ed) (n 60) 795.
[81] On Blackstone, 'conflating common law and natural law' thus giving common law a 'seeming universality', *cf* JH Langbein, R Lettow Lerner and BP Smith, *History of the Common Law. The Development of Anglo-American Legal Institutions* (Austin TX, 2009) 842. Blackstone's natural law philosophy, obviously, referred back to Vattel who was widely read in Revolutionary America. But it may be that Blackstone by taking up Vattel's ideas gave them added weight in the evolving constitutional debate.

law in the colonies was familiar with Blackstone's *Commentaries*, his ideas were able to exert a resounding influence both on the legal profession and far beyond it. Hence Daniel Boorstin's comment: 'In the history of American institutions, no other book—except the Bible—has played so great a role as Blackstone's *Commentaries on the Laws of England*'.[82] Blackstone was consulted throughout the colonies and states whenever specific constitutional solutions could be legitimised, or indeed rejected, by referring to his text. But much more than a convenient and authoritative work of reference, the *Commentaries* helped to implant several constitutional truths which sank so deep into the common mind and appeared to be so self-evident that it was no longer necessary to invoke Blackstone's *Commentaries* to confer legitimacy upon them. Many Americans speaking in the late eighteenth century of declarations of rights, of checks and balances, of judicial independence or universal principles might no longer be aware that they were using Blackstonian language. But as written into the early American constitutions, it became part of the constitutional identity of the country, and thus the vehicle and catalyst to ensure that these principles became essentials of modern constitutionalism.

---

[82] DJ Boorstin, *The Mysterious Science of the Law* (Gloucester MA, 1973) iii.

10

Reading Blackstone in the Twenty-First Century and the Twenty-First Century through Blackstone

JESSIE ALLEN*

> On the one hand, a myth always refers to events alleged to have taken place long ago. But what gives the myth an operational value is that the specific pattern described is timeless; it explains the present and the past as well as the future.**
>
> Claude Levi-Strauss

BLACKSTONE'S *COMMENTARIES* IS a legendary fount of learning for lawyers and statesmen in American history, but who actually reads it anymore? And who would use it to answer questions about twenty-first-century American law? The justices of the United States Supreme Court, that's who.

The *Commentaries* is undergoing a renaissance at the Supreme Court. In recent years the Court has cited Blackstone at rates not seen since the early nineteenth century. In some of those references, Blackstone's work supplies historical evidence about aspects of the British legal system that the American colonists both rejected and perpetuated. Some of the Court's uses of Blackstone, however, are more mythical than historical. One technique stands out. Identifying the *Commentaries* as the 'preeminent legal authority' for the 'founding generation', the Court sometimes proceeds as if the United States founders understood the Constitution to silently enact Blackstone's *Commentaries* in between or underneath the constitutional text.[1]

---

* Thanks are due to Bernard J Hibbitts and to participants in the University of Adelaide symposium, 'Re-Interpreting Blackstone's Commentaries', and the Three School Colloquium at the University of Pittsburgh for thoughtful comments that improved the paper. Caroline Hall and McArdle Booker provided research assistance without which there would be no paper.
** C Lévi-Strauss, *Structural Anthropology* (tr) C Jacobson (New York NY, 2004) 209.
[1] See eg *District of Columbia v Heller* 554 US 570, 593–94 (2008).

I BLACKSTONE IN THE UNITED STATES SUPREME COURT

The *Commentaries* is off most lawyers' reading lists these days, and that is hardly surprising. After all, it is not as though we spend much time perusing law books from previous centuries—even those that were once highly influential. But there is a strange wrinkle in Blackstone's obsolescence. Recently, references to Blackstone in the US Supreme Court's opinions have increased dramatically.

Blackstone has been cited often in US courts of all jurisdictions since the country's founding. That does not mean that Blackstone ever appeared in most, or even a large minority of, American judicial opinions. Dennis Nolan's study of a random sample of 471 cases from state and federal courts in the late eighteenth and early nineteenth centuries found that about 7 per cent cited Blackstone, and many of those were in the arguments of counsel, not the final opinions of judges.[2] However that 7 per cent—a reference in approximately one in every 14 cases—was enough to make Blackstone's *Commentaries* the single most cited work in those early opinions.[3]

A closer look at citations to Blackstone in early US Supreme Court cases confirms the basic picture Nolan provided. Between 1801 and 1830 there were 856 Supreme Court decisions issued with signed opinions. Of those decisions, 16, or 2 per cent, included at least one reference to Blackstone by a Supreme Court justice, and 68, or 8 per cent, carried references to Blackstone in the arguments of counsel that the early reporters reproduced.[4] The reason it makes sense to count both of these numbers when gauging Blackstone's importance as a source of authority is that the justices' opinions from those early days are relatively free of citations to *any* authorities, as compared with today's Supreme Court opinions. Scanning the early printed reports, one finds in the arguments of counsel the kind of citation patterns seen in both advocates' briefs and the Court's opinions today. The early justices' opinions, however, which are often just a few

---

[2] D Nolan, 'Sir William Blackstone and the New American Republic: A Study of Intellectual Impact', 51 *NYU Law Review* 731, 753 (1976).

[3] Ibid. Donald S Lutz examined the citation frequency of a number of well-known authorities in the work of various founding political figures in America from 1760 to 1800. DS Lutz, *The Origins of American Constitutionalism* (Baton Rouge LA, 1988) 142–46. Among secular authorities, Blackstone was second only to Montesquieu, with Montesquieu being cited 8.3% of the time and Blackstone 7.9%; the next closest was Locke at 2.9%.

[4] Frequency of citation was determined by dividing the total number of signed opinions of the Court by the number of cases that carried Blackstone mentions by justices or counsel. The number of signed opinions for the term years 1801–1830 comes from A Blaustein and R Mersky, *The First Hundred Justices: Statistical Studies on the Supreme Court of the United States* (Hamden CT, 1978) 137–41. Blackstone citations were compiled through a *Westlaw Next* search '(Blackstone bl england)/s (com commentaries comm tucker)', followed by a case-by-case review to remove false positives (eg references to Kent's *Commentaries* in relation to the law of England).

pages or paragraphs long, for the most part include only the occasional reference. It seems worthwhile, then, to consider the citation rates in both counsels' arguments and justices' opinions as baselines for comparison with the rates of citation in today's Supreme Court opinions. On both of these measures, there is no question that Blackstone's presence in twenty-first-century Supreme Court cases is comparable to what it was in the Court's early days.

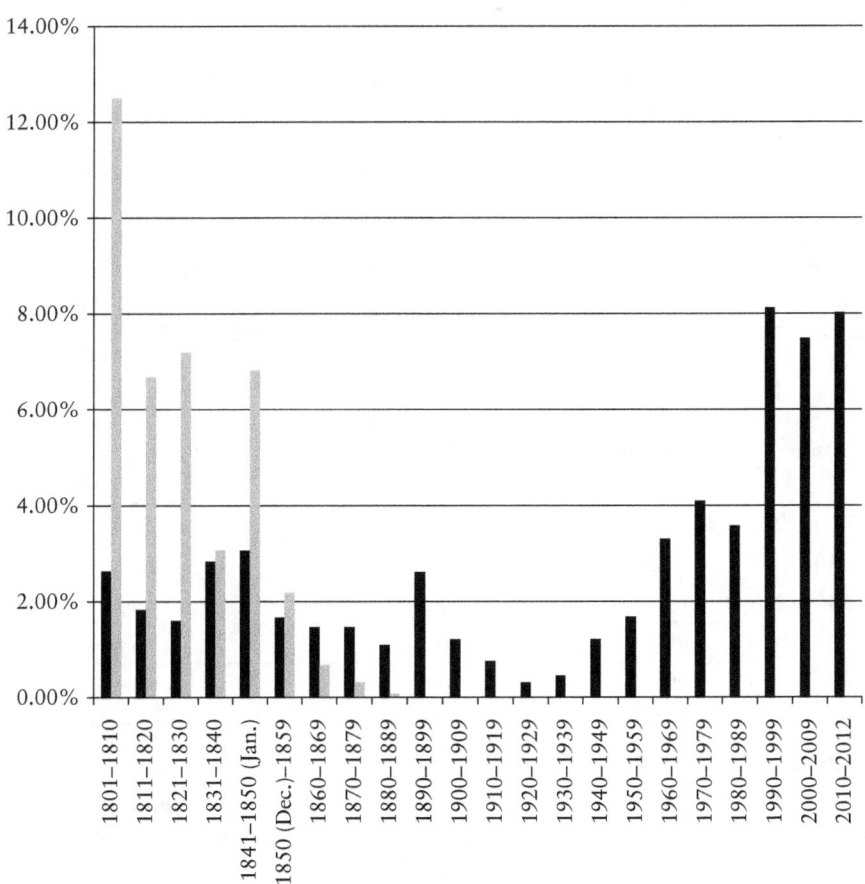

Figure 1. Counsels' and Justices' Citations of Blackstone's Commentaries *in US Supreme Court 1801–2012**

* See footnote on pp 218–19.

Since 1990, Blackstone has appeared in 8 per cent of the US Supreme Court's signed opinions. That citation rate is higher than the rates of either Supreme Court justices or counsel at any time since 1810. Only Blackstone's appearance in 13 per cent of counsels' arguments between 1801 and 1810 outstrips his current popularity now as a source of authority in the Supreme Court.[5] Moreover, Blackstone has not always maintained such a strong presence in the Court's opinions. Figure 1 shows that in the mid-nineteenth century, the Court's Blackstone references began to diminish. Then, after an upsurge at the turn of the century, citations to the *Commentaries* dropped. In the 1920s and 1930s there were quite a few years in which the Supreme Court failed to mention Blackstone at all.

After almost disappearing from Supreme Court opinions in the early twentieth century, however, Blackstone experienced a resurgence. Figure 1 shows that the Court's citations to Blackstone began increasing gradually through mid-century and then rose precipitously from the 1990s to the current rate of about one in every 13 decisions. Remarkably, in every one of the past 60 annual court terms, the justices have pointed to Blackstone's eighteenth-century treatise in at least one of their published opinions. It seems worth noting, moreover, that during Blackstone's previous period of popularity in the nineteenth century, there were considerably fewer authoritative legal sources of any kind. When the Supreme Court cites Blackstone now, his work is being chosen from a much wider range of potential reference points.

Table 1. Blackstone Citations in Opinions of US Supreme Court 1920–2012

Decade	Decisions by signed opinions[*]	Decisions citing Blackstone	Frequency of Blackstone citation
1920–1929	1906	6	1 for every 318
1930–1939	1521	7	1 for every 216
1940–1949	1314	16	1 for every 82
1950–1959	890	15	1 for every 59
1960–1969	998	33	1 for every 30
1970–1979	1294	53	1 for every 24
1980–1989	1397	50	1 for every 28
1990–1999	887	72	1 for every 12
2000–2009	721	54	1 for every 13
2010–2012	212	17	1 for every 13

[5] The calculations begin in 1801 because in the Court's first decade, 1790–1800, the decisions issued are so few and the opinions reported so different in form from the current Court's practice that comparisons seem inappropriate.

[*] Signed opinions for the term years 1801–1972 are taken from Albert P Blaustein and Roy M Mersky, *The First Hundred Justices: Statistical Studies on the Supreme Court of the United*

Table 1 shows the dramatic increase in citations to Blackstone's *Commentaries* in the Court's opinions between 1920 and the present, from a rate of 1 in 318 to 1 in 13 decisions. From 2000 to 2009 the justices of the Supreme Court issued less than half the number of decisions the Court produced from 1930 to 1939; but the number of decisions with citations to Blackstone increased more than sevenfold—from 7 to 54, producing a 1 in 13 or 8 per cent citation rate in 2000–09.

Why so? Or, in a less overtly functionalist mode, what trends in US jurisprudence and in legal culture coincide with that increase that might help us understand its meaning? Without ruling out many other possible contributing factors, it is at least causally suggestive that Blackstone's Supreme Court renaissance coincides with the rise of 'originalism', a mode of constitutional interpretation that looks to the 'original' meaning of the text. In particular, the figure shows a sharp spike in Blackstone citations soon after the arrival in 1986 of the Court's most vehement originalist, Justice Antonin Scalia. But which way does the causal arrow run? We should be cautious about ascribing Blackstone's recent popularity to the work of a single legal interpreter, even one as influential as Justice Scalia.[6]

Both Figure 1 and Table 1 show a steady increase in citations to Blackstone taking place over the half century *preceding* Justice Scalia's appointment. After the long lull in the early twentieth century, including

---

States 137–41 (Hamden CT, Shoe String 1978). Signed opinions for the term years 1973–2009 are taken from L Epstein, J Segal, H Spaeth and T Walker, *The Supreme Court Compendium* 89–90 (Los Angeles CA, 2012). Signed opinions for the term years 2010 and 2011 are taken from the Chief Justice's Year-End Reports on the Federal Judiciary. *2011 Year-End Report on the Federal Judiciary* (31 December 2011), *available at* http://www.supremecourt.gov/publicinfo/year-end/2011year-endreport.pdf; *2012 Year-End Report on the Federal Judiciary* (December 31, 2012), *available at* http://www.supremecourt.gov/publicinfo/year-end/2012year-endreport.pdf. Signed opinions for term year 2012 are taken from a count of 2012 Slip Opinions on the Supreme Court Website. *2012 Term Opinions of the Court*, http://www.supremecourt.gov/opinions/slipopinions.aspx?Term=12, last visited 26 September, 2013. Blackstone mentions were compiled with a Westlaw Next search using search term, '(Blackstone bl england)/s (com commentaries comm tucker)', removing false positives (for instance, references to Kent's commentaries and the effects of same on the law of England) and case-by case categorization of type. The year 1850 appears twice on the figure. In that year, the Court moved the start of its term from January to December, resulting in two full terms identified as 1850. Since that time, Supreme Court terms have started late in the year, and extended into the following calendar year. The result is that now most decisions identified with a particular term year are issued in the following calendar year.

[6] Of course there could be many reasons for the fall and rise of Supreme Court citations to Blackstone. It is possible, for instance, that the low rates in Blackstone citations through the early twentieth century are part of a more general practice of avoiding citations to 'secondary' legal sources. It is also possible that the recent rise of Blackstone citations is part of a broader trend toward citing 'classical' common law sources, including not only Blackstone, but also, eg, Coke and Bracton. Do the justices think it is rhetorically advantageous to demonstrate a mastery of such arcane authorities? Is the Court becoming more academic in its analyses? Does the shift have something to do with the late-twentieth-century practice of employing recent law-school graduates as clerks to the justices? More work needs to be done to understand the significance of the citation trends.

quite a few years with no Blackstone citations at all, the citation rate begins to edge up—from less than 1 percent in the 1930s to just under 2 per cent in the 1950s to around 4 per cent in the 1970s and 1980s. Indeed, looking at the growth of Blackstone citations through the mid-twentieth century you might even say that you were watching the birth of Justice Scalia, or at least the preparation of the ground from which his fertile originalist jurisprudence later appeared. It is really quite striking to see how the Court's citations to 'the preeminent authority on English law for the founding generation' grew slowly but surely, decade by decade, and then shot up shortly after the appointment of the judge who most militantly insists on interpreting the Constitution according to that founding generation's original understanding.[7]

II THE COURT'S BLACKSTONE MYTHOLOGY

> Myth tells how, through the deeds of Supernatural Beings, a reality came into existence.
>
> Mircea Eliade[8]

Part of Blackstone's appeal as an authoritative source is the extraordinary range of legal issues and structures covered in the *Commentaries*. In just the 2012–13 term, the US Supreme Court cited Blackstone for (among other things) the privacy protection accorded houses and surrounding fields, the content of the law of nations, the doctrine of equitable tolling, the definition of extortion, and the historical role of judicial discretion in criminal sentencing.[9] Across their multifarious subject matter, however, the Court's Blackstone citations can generally be grouped into two categories: (1) evidence of facts about legal history, and (2) evidence of the way

---

[7] See eg *Heller* 554 US at 593–94. Although Justice Scalia has the highest rate of Blackstone citations on the current Court, he is not the only justice citing Blackstone. For instance, in the 2012–13 term Blackstone appears in 4 of the 24 (or 1 in 6) opinions Justice Scalia wrote. Justices Thomas and Roberts ran a close second, having cited Blackstone in 3 of 25 and 2 of 17 opinions respectively, a rate of approximately 1 in 8. Justice Alito cited Blackstone in 2 of his 21 opinions (1 in 10) and Justice Breyer used Blackstone in 1 of 18 opinions. Justices Ginsburg, Kennedy, and Sotomayor did not cite Blackstone this term, but they all have done so in the past (although Justice Ginsburg's citations to Blackstone are very few and far between). Indeed the only member of the current court who has never referred to Blackstone in an opinion is Justice Kagan, who joined the Court in 2010.

[8] M Eliade, *Myth and Reality* (tr) W Trask (New York NY, 1975) 5.

[9] Privacy: *Florida v Jardines* 133 S Ct 1409 (2013) (Scalia J); law of nations: *Kiobel v Royal Dutch Petroleum* 133 S Ct 1659 (2013) (Breyer J, concurring); equitable tolling: *McQuiggen v Perkins* 133 S Ct 1924 (2013) (Scalia J, dissenting); extortion: *Sekhar v United States* 133 S Ct 2720 (2013) (Alito J, concurring); sentencing: *Alleyne v United States* 133 S Ct 2151 (2013) (Thomas J).

eighteenth-century Americans understood the legal principles, doctrines and structures implicitly incorporated in the US Constitution. Both uses are susceptible to a problematic shift from factual reference to mythic narrative.[10]

Obviously, an eighteenth-century text on the 'laws of England' can provide historical evidence about eighteenth-century English law. The trouble is that the Supreme Court's ostensibly historical references to Blackstone sometimes slip into ahistorical assertions of timeless legal principle. And while there is wide agreement that American lawyers at the time of the founding were generally familiar with the *Commentaries*, references that equate Blackstone's text with the 'founding generation's' view of common law are problematic because they ignore contemporary criticisms of Blackstone that were undoubtedly familiar to at least some of the men who wrote, ratified and produced the first judicial interpretations of the US Constitution.

Justices of the Court do sometimes use Blackstone to support narrowly contextualised statements of legal-historical fact. For example, Justice Scalia recently cited the *Commentaries*' chapter on corporations, first published in 1765, as proof that corporations were a familiar legal structure when the First Amendment to the Constitution was adopted in 1791. To be sure, this careful legal-historical use of Blackstone is a building block in a larger argument. The reference is part of Justice Scalia's concurrence in the notorious *Citizens United* decision, which struck down limits on corporate spending for political advertisements as a violation of the First Amendment's free speech guarantee.[11] Blackstone's discussion of corporations means the 'lack of a textual exception for speech by corporations cannot be explained on the ground that corporations did not exist or did not speak' when the Amendment was written.[12] Justice Scalia concludes that the Amendment's silence on the subject should be taken to mean that its guarantee of free speech extends to corporate speech. Ultimately, then, this reference to the *Commentaries*' authority does not remain limited to history. Nevertheless, the actual proposition Blackstone is called upon to authorise is a factual claim about law within a specific historical context. As a matter of judicial practice, that seems unexceptionable—the standard

---

[10] The diversity of subject matter for which Blackstone has been cited recently does not, of course, mean that there are no patterns to be found in the content of the Court's use of his authority. Future analysis may reveal more about the way the doctrinal and political content of references to the *Commentaries* have changed over time.
[11] *Citizens United v Federal Election Commission* 558 US 310, 385–93 (2010).
[12] Ibid 388.

lawyer's inferential technique of using multiple limited authorities to build an argument that is rhetorically greater than the sum of its parts.[13]

At other times the Court has cited Blackstone to contrast an old doctrine with the current trend,[14] or made use of Blackstone's own accounts of historical changes in the common law. In the famous case of *Roe v Wade* in the 1970s, for example, Justice Blackmun noted Blackstone's assertion that 'while abortion after quickening had once been considered manslaughter (though not murder), "modern law" took a less severe view'.[15] There are even (rare) cases in which a justice has been willing to contradict Blackstone on his own eighteenth-century terrain. So, for instance, in a 1947 case Justice Rutledge argued that Blackstone was wrong to assert that contempt of court cases were dealt with summarily without the usual procedural safeguards of a criminal trial. Rutledge, citing secondary sources, attributes what he considers Blackstone's mistaken understanding of contempt procedure to 'private communication' with Chief Justice Sir John Eardley Wilmot. According to Rutledge, Wilmot's erroneous views on the subject thereby 'found their way ... into the four volumes of the famous Commentaries'.[16]

Some of the Court's references to the *Commentaries*, however, are not so rigorously contextualised. Instead of building a case that law maintains some eighteenth-century aspect noted by Blackstone, the Court sometimes uses Blackstone as an authority on law *both* then and now. Citations that ostensibly anchor factual propositions about legal history slip over into ahistorical assertions of truths about the nature of law that justify current legal structures. This dual relationship to time is characteristic of myths. The great structuralist anthropologist Claude Lévi-Strauss was perhaps the first to articulate the way mythic narratives merge two opposing temporal perspectives. He observed that across cultures myths refer to specific events

---

[13] See also *Vermont Agency of Natural Resources v United States* 529 US 765, 768 (2000) ('The phrase [*qui tam*] dates from at least the time of Blackstone', citing *Commentaries* vol 3, 160).

[14] See eg *Clark v Arizona* 548 US 735, 766 (2006), citing Blackstone for the proposition that *mens rea* was once defined generally as 'malice', but noting that modern definitions are more specific. Also *McMillian v Monroe County, Alabama* 520 US 781, 804 (1997) (Ginsberg J, dissenting, disputing the majority's reliance on Blackstone for the state, as opposed to local, identity of Alabama sheriffs because 'the English sheriff, as Blackstone described him, was far closer to the crown than his contemporary counterpart is to the central state government') and *New York Central & Hudson River Railroad Company v United States* 212 US 481, 492 (1909) ('In Blackstone's Commentaries, chapter 18, S 12, we find it stated: "A corporation cannot commit treason, or felony, or other crime in its corporate capacity, though its members may, in their distinct individual capacities." The modern authority, universally, so far as we know, is the other way.')

[15] *Roe v Wade* 410 US 113, 135 (1973).

[16] *United States v United Mine Workers of America* 330 US 258, 366 n 32 (1947) (Rutledge J, dissenting).

that are said to have occurred in the historic past but that somehow remain endlessly, timelessly present. Just so the Court treats the *Commentaries* as simultaneously 'belonging to the past', describing law at a specific time and place in history, and yet revealing 'a timeless pattern which can be detected in contemporary' law.[17]

Consider a 2012 majority opinion by Justice Roberts citing Blackstone for the claim that 'Sheriffs executing a warrant were empowered by the common law to enlist the aid of able-bodied men of the community in doing so'.[18] The reference comes in a decision holding that a private attorney who participated in a public corruption investigation is entitled to the same immunity government officials enjoy under the relevant federal statute, which was enacted in the late nineteenth century. Justice Roberts begins by locating a historic context that is admirably specific: 'Under our precedent, the inquiry begins with the common law as it existed when Congress passed Section 1983 in 1871'.[19] The problem is that the nineteenth-century American context he identifies is a hundred years and an ocean away from Blackstone's eighteenth-century English text. And Justice Roberts offers no explanation for how the *Commentaries* fits into the historical framework he has set up.[20] Without that explanation, it appears that 'the common law' of the *Commentaries* is a matter of static, universally applicable, principles.

Anyone even slightly familiar with the section of the *Commentaries* being used to authorise this view will recognise how much at odds that timeless perspective is with Blackstone's own approach. The *Commentaries*' discussion of sheriffs is both historical and attentive to differences from county to county, let alone across countries. So, for instance, Blackstone begins by noting that originally sheriffs were the deputies of earls, but 'the earls in process of time, by reason of their high employments and attendance on the king's person, not being able to transact the business of the county, were delivered of that burden' so that now the sheriff is an independent officer of the king.[21] Blackstone also traces at length the development of the practice of electing sheriffs, from ancient custom and early statute, noting, however, that in some places, including Scotland, the county of Westmoreland, and the city of London, the sheriffdom was an hereditary

---

[17] C Lévi-Strauss, *Structural Anthropology* (tr) C Jacobson (New York NY, 2004) 209.
[18] *Filarsky v Delia* 132 S Ct 1657, 1664 (2012).
[19] Ibid 1662.
[20] One possible explanation would be that at the time the statute was passed, American lawmakers continued to read the *Commentaries* as an authoritative legal text. There is certainly plenty of evidence that late-nineteenth-century American lawyers read Blackstone. What is missing is the argument and evidence that they were reading Blackstone as an authoritative source of nineteenth-century American law.
[21] *Commentaries* vol 1, 328.

office.²² In the process he points to the influence of various specific events, individuals and statutes and also notes disagreements among 'some of our writers' about those practices.²³ It seems quite strange, then, to interpret Blackstone's present-tense description of the English sheriff's power to deputise civilians as referring to a universal practice with relevance to the law of immunity a hundred years later in the United States.

To be sure, the Court does not rely on Blackstone's authority alone to support its ruling. Justice Roberts cited contemporary US cases to support the claim that in the late nineteenth century, when the relevant civil rights statute was passed, civilian deputies were entitled to the same immunity as sheriffs. But why, if relevant contemporary authorities are available, does the Court think it necessary, or desirable, to cite Blackstone at all? Why add the eighteenth-century *Commentaries* to a ruling that a twenty-first-century civilian investigator is immune to prosecution under a nineteenth-century statute?²⁴ The implication seems to be that the *Commentaries* is a work so universally accepted that it adds authority to practically any legal argument.

Sometimes Blackstone is cited by the Court not as direct authority for the content of common law, eighteenth-century or otherwise, but rather for the way the 'founding generation' of the United States *understood* the common law at the time the Constitution was adopted.²⁵ For instance, the *Commentaries* have been cited to support, inter alia, claims about the American founders' views on the existence of an individual right to bear arms, the correct approach to statutory interpretation, whether at the time the United States was founded courts had any power of eminent domain, and parental control of children (and thus whether 'freedom of speech' includes an unqualified right to speak to minors).²⁶ The basic idea behind all these references is that the Constitution should be understood according to its 'original meaning' and that meaning incorporates Blackstone's views of the 'common law', because Blackstone was the 'pre-eminent authority' on common law at the time of the founding.²⁷

---

²² Ibid 328–29.
²³ Ibid 330.
²⁴ Other recent examples of this kind of temporally transcendent use of the *Commentaries* include a dissent by Justice Sotomayor, offering Blackstone as authority for the proposition that the bar on retrial after acquittal is 'the most fundamental rule in the history of double jeopardy jurisprudence': *Blueford v Arkansas* 132 S Ct 2044, 2053–54 (2012), and the majority opinion by Justice Scalia in *Stop the Beach Renourishment, Inc. v Florida Department of Environmental Protection* 130 S Ct 2592, 2598 (2010), which uses Blackstone to define coastal property rights 'at common law'.
²⁵ *District of Columbia v Heller* 554 US 570, 594 (2008).
²⁶ *Heller* 554 US at 593–95 (Scalia J, arms); ibid 665 (Stevens J, dissenting, statutory interpretation); *Stop the Beach Renourishment, Inc. v Florida Department of Environmental Protection* 130 S Ct 2592, 2616 (2010) (Kennedy J, concurring, eminent domain); *Brown v Entertainment Merchants Association* 131 S Ct 2729, 2757–59 (2011) (Thomas J, dissenting, speech).
²⁷ *Heller* 554 US at 593.

For instance, Justice Thomas explains that Blackstone's 100-page discussion of the 'regular and ordinary method of proceeding in the courts of criminal jurisdiction' not only informs but practically defines, and limits, the 'original meaning' of the words 'criminal prosecution' in the Sixth Amendment.[28] Likewise, Justice Scalia, in his dissent in *Hamdi v Rumsfeld*, quoted Blackstone at length to argue that the Due Process and Suspension Clauses express the 'two ideas central to Blackstone's understanding—due process as the right secured, and habeas corpus as the instrument by which due process could be insisted upon by a citizen illegally imprisoned'.[29] Again, I do not mean to claim that the Court cites only Blackstone for the legal interpretations of the constitutional founders. Other sources are also employed—the Federalist Papers, English and colonial case law and early Supreme Court opinions, the founders' own papers, and other classic legal texts (including Bracton, Coke and Kent). But the frequency of citations to Blackstone and the unqualified way the Court's opinions often link Blackstone's view and those of the founders makes his role as a reference extraordinary, if not unique.

Beyond explaining that a specific section of the *Commentaries* was 'well known to the Founders',[30] the Court has repeatedly affirmed that Blackstone's work 'constituted the preeminent authority on English law for the founding generation'.[31] Occasionally justices even go further. In a rather startling assertion of the creative power of Blackstone's text, Justice Scalia has claimed that 'the Framers ... were formed by Blackstone'.[32]

That formative influence is rarely questioned by anyone on the twenty-first-century Supreme Court. The justices may sometimes criticise a particular reference to Blackstone, but usually not by attacking the idea that Blackstone's text shapes the meaning of the particular constitutional principle at stake. Instead, the opposing opinion writer reinterprets the *Commentaries*' quotation, or chooses a different section of the *Commentaries* on which to rely. So, for example, Justice Stevens criticised Justice Scalia's use of Blackstone to interpret the rights conferred by the Second Amendment, contending that Blackstone's assertion of 'the right of bearing and using arms for self-protection and defence' refers specifically to Article VII in the English Bill of Rights and is inapplicable to 'interpreting the very differently

---

[28] *Rothgery v Gillespie County, Texas* 554 US 191, 219–22 (2008) (Thomas J, dissenting).
[29] *Hamdi v Rumsfeld* 542 US 507, 554–56 (2004).
[30] Ibid 555 (noting that 'Hamilton quoted from this very passage in The Federalist No. 84').
[31] *Heller* 554 US at 593–94, quoting *Alden v Maine* 527 US 706, 715 (1999).
[32] *Rogers v Tennessee* 532 US 451, 477 (2001). See also *Brown v Entertainment Merchants Association* 131 S Ct 2729, 2757 (2011) ('Blackstone's Commentaries was 'a primary legal authority for 18th and 19th-century American lawyers', quoting *Washington v Glucksberg* 521 US 702, 712 (1997)); *Green v United States* 355 US 184, 187 (1957) (Blackstone's Commentaries 'greatly influenced the generation that adopted the Constitution').

worded and differently historically situated Second Amendment'.[33] Justice Stevens, however, put forward a different passage from the *Commentaries* to illuminate the meaning of the Second Amendment: 'What *is* important about Blackstone is the instruction he provided on reading the sort of text' at issue, including the fact that Blackstone's interpretive approach 'gave far more weight to preambles than the Court allows'.[34] Rather than question the role of the *Commentaries* in the original meaning of the Constitution, the justices generally prefer to fight Blackstone with Blackstone.

There are certainly reasons to consider Blackstone's text uniquely important for lawyers in the early days of the United States. There is an unchallenged historical consensus that the *Commentaries* was the most widely read law book in late eighteenth-century America.[35] Moreover, while Blackstone was widely available to lawyers, judges and law students, case reports from British and colonial American courts were scarce. Even if Blackstone was not always right about the structure and content of eighteenth-century common law, so the argument goes, he was 'the oracle of the common law in the mind of the American Founders'.[36] Therefore, to the extent that the founding generation understood the Constitution to be predicated on English common law, the Constitution reflects Blackstone's representation of that law.[37]

But the extraordinary popularity and influence of the *Commentaries* does not mean the US founders understood the Constitution to uncritically enact Blackstone's version of every common law structure not explicitly contradicted in the constitutional text. Beyond the kinds of difficulties frequently associated with the pursuit of the 'original meaning' of constitutional rights and structures, there is a particular problem about equating Blackstone's text with that meaning, which again relates to the Court's mythic treatment of the text. That problem is the assumption that eighteenth-century lawyers, judges, legislators, voters and constitution framers viewed Blackstone's text as an objective, politically neutral description of the common law of their time.

---

[33] *Heller* 554 US at 665 (Stevens J, dissenting).
[34] Ibid.
[35] A thousand copies of the *Commentaries* had sold in the American colonies before the first American edition was published in 1772: A Alschuler, 'Rediscovering Blackstone' (1996) 145 *University of Pennsylvania Law Review* 1, 5. On a list of 1,400 subscribers to the first American edition, Dennis Nolan found 16 signers of the Declaration of Independence, 6 delegates to the 1787 Constitutional Convention, a president (John Adams) and an early chief justice of the Supreme Court (John Jay): Nolan, 743–44.
[36] *Gertz v Robert Welch, Inc.* 418 US 323, 381 (1974).
[37] See *Schick v United States* 195 US 65, 69 (1904) ('Blackstone's Commentaries are accepted as the most satisfactory exposition of the common law of England. At the time of the adoption of the Federal Constitution, it had been published about twenty years, and it has been said that more copies of the work had been sold in this country than in England; so that undoubtedly, the framers of the Constitution were familiar with it').

Even if we believe that the founding generation—broadly or narrowly defined—was familiar with the *Commentaries*, on what basis can we assume that they took Blackstone's work as accurately describing a universally applicable common law, or even as an objective rendering of eighteenth-century English law? In the first place, the title announces something quite different. The work is not called, 'The Laws of England', but *Blackstone's* Commentaries *on the Laws of England*. What part of 'commentaries' do the originalists not understand? In the second place, some vehement eighteenth-century critiques of the *Commentaries* were doubtless well known to those US founders who were familiar with Blackstone. Jeremy Bentham published the most famous of these attacks in 1776—the year the United States declared independence.[38] What is more, records of some founders' views of Blackstone's work include both praise and criticism, and, unsurprisingly, indicate that they understood the *Commentaries* to be shaped by Blackstone's political perspective, which they identified as antagonistic to their own.

Thomas Jefferson, for one, did not receive Blackstone's work as an objective account. To the contrary, he found the *Commentaries* politically tendentious: it was 'making Tories of these young Americans whose native feelings of independence do not place them above the wily sophistries of a Hume or a Blackstone'.[39] Jefferson explicitly rejected the idea that Blackstone's work captured all the ins and outs of the common law. He conceded that the *Commentaries* were 'the most elegant and best digested of our law catalogue'. But as a source for deep legal understanding, the work was insufficient. He complained that '[a] student finds there a smattering of everything, and his indolence easily persuades him that if he understands that book, he is master of the whole body of the law'.[40] Moreover, according to Jefferson, the inadequacy of lawyers who relied on Blackstone was 'well understood even by the unlettered common people, who', he pointed out, 'apply the appellation of Blackstone lawyers to these ephemeral insects of the law'.[41] So much for the notion that Blackstone was the legal be-all and end-all for every member of the 'founding generation'.

Nor was Jefferson the only influential founder to criticise Blackstone in print. Justice James Wilson's opinion in *Chisholm v Georgia* (1793) rejected Blackstone's views on sovereign immunity and made it plain that the legal principles set out in the *Commentaries* were politically objectionable, jurisprudentially wrong and incompatible with the legal structures adopted

---

[38] See R Posner, 'Blackstone and Bentham' (1976) 19 *Journal of Law, Economics and Policy* 569, 569–70.
[39] Quoted in Alschuler (n 35) 11 from JS Waterman, 'Thomas Jefferson and Blackstone's Commentaries' (1932–33) 27 *Illinois Law Review* 629, 634–35.
[40] Ibid 634.
[41] Ibid.

by the US Constitution.[42] According to Wilson, Blackstone's common law doctrines of immunity cannot be part of the Constitution because they are underwritten by the principle 'that all human law must be prescribed by a superior', a principle Wilson found contrary to 'the basis of sound and genuine jurisprudence'. Moreover, the theory of sovereign immunity explicated by Blackstone was part of a larger legal scheme, 'upon which a plan of systematic despotism has been lately formed in England ...'.[43] For Wilson, Blackstone was not merely the reporter of that despotic system, but an active proponent: 'Of this plan, the author of the Commentaries was, if not the introducer, at least the great supporter'.[44]

Sceptical views of Blackstone in eighteenth-century America were not restricted to presidents and Supreme Court justices. The report of a 1788 case from the Pennsylvania Supreme Court contains a description of an argument by one Mr Lewis, a lawyer and member of the Pennsylvania General Assembly, in support of a prison sentence meted out to a newspaper publisher for libel.[45] Lewis's speech 'referred to the celebrated Commentaries in support and illustration of his sentiments upon liberty'.[46] But apparently he could not presume that his audience would share his own good opinion of Blackstone's work. Before drawing on that authority, he first 'rescued Sir William Blackstone from the stigma of being a courtly writer, by showing the enthusiasm of that author in favor of the trial by jury'.[47]

The Court's avowals of the US founders' uncritical faith in the *Commentaries* is mythmaking, not only in the sense that it conflicts with parts of the historical record but in another more interesting sense as well. Rather than treating the *Commentaries* as no more than a source of information about past legal practices, the Court treats the text as a venerable but still-active legal influence. I am not claiming that Blackstone's text exerts a causal effect on the Supreme Court's legal determinations. It may—or it may be that the justices go to Blackstone to support outcomes they have already chosen for altogether other reasons. Either way, in the legal culture that emerges from the Court's opinions, Blackstone lives on as a powerful legal ancestor. You might even say that as the 'preeminent' source of the American founders' legal understanding, Blackstone is not just a secondary authority but in a sense the author of a host of legal constructs that the Court reads between the lines of the Constitution. Blackstone's text indeed takes on a constitutive quality not unlike that of the Constitution itself.

---

[42] *Chisholm v Georgia* 2 US 419, 458 (1793); cf Alschuler (n 35) 10.
[43] Ibid.
[44] Ibid.
[45] *Respublica v Oswald* 1 US 319, n* (1788).
[46] Ibid.
[47] Ibid.

If the Court's use of Blackstone exemplifies the dual temporal quality that Lévi-Strauss observed of mythic narratives, the presentation of the *Commentaries* as the founders' legal gospel recalls another of Levi-Strauss's teachings. The focus of this observation is not myths per se, but the relationship between 'primitive' myths and the modern scholars who analyse them. A fundamental insight of critical and structural anthropology has been that portraying other cultures as credulous believers in myths that appear obviously fictional to modern eyes is a way of establishing the triumphant sophistication of modern cultures. Thus Levi-Strauss explained that to regard 'primitive' people as believing in a direct, natural relationship between clans and their animal totems was to 'project[] outside our own universe, as though by a kind of exorcism ... mental attitudes' judged incompatible with modern thought.[48] From this perspective, theories about totemism in aboriginal cultures revealed less about the cultures being interpreted than the interpreting scholars, who sought 'consciously or unconsciously, and under the guise of scientific objectivity', to make the people studied 'more *different* than they really are'.[49]

A related phenomenon seems to be at work when the Court presents Blackstone as the 'oracle of the law in the mind of the American framers'.[50] By presenting mythmaking cultures as naïve believers in those myths, anthropologists distanced themselves from the cultures they studied and highlighted their own critical rationality. Likewise, when the Court today portrays the eighteenth-century originators of the Constitution as uncritical adherents of Blackstone's version of the common law, the founders' simple faith in Blackstone's authority contrasts with the sophisticated legal analyses of the modern Court's opinions. This contrast allows the justices citing Blackstone for the original meaning of the Constitution to have their cake and eat it too. The Court's analysis gains the kind of rule-of-law certainty that comes from relying on the *Commentaries* as a canonical text. But presenting that text as authoritative through the eyes of the 'founding generation' avoids the accusations of legal primitivism that would certainly accompany avowals that the current justices themselves viewed Blackstone's text as *the* definitive source of all common law structures implicitly incorporated in the Constitution.

The irony, of course, is that taken seriously, the Court's approach turns the legendarily sagacious American founders into legal simpletons. Or rather, that would be the result if the Court's view of Blackstone's role for the founders were taken as *fact*. But that must not be what the Court really means. For one thing it would be too much at odds with another American legal myth—namely, the view of the US founders as visionary

---

[48] C Lévi-Strauss, *Totemism* (tr) R Needham (Boston MA, 1963) 3.
[49] Ibid 1.
[50] *Gertz v Robert Welch, Inc.* 418 US 323, 381 (1974).

ancestors whose extraordinary legal and political wisdom remains a continuing resource through the constitutional text. In addition, insisting on the founders' uncritical belief in Blackstone is at odds with the political and historical context. It is hard to believe that, having just fought a war for independence from Britain, the revolutionary American generation would approach uncritically a text written by a man avowedly opposed to American independence. And as we have seen, that view conflicts with some of the founders' own expressed views. Then there is the text itself. Whatever one's view of Blackstone's project, it is hardly debatable that he sometimes minimised legal contradictions and rationalised legal history in order to argue for the continuing legitimacy of the English common law system.[51] Moreover, it seems eighteenth-century readers were less likely than we are today just to dip into Blackstone here and there to confirm some particular point about legal doctrine. Lawyers of the 'founding generation' apparently absorbed Blackstone's four-volume work as a whole, sometimes more than once. John Marshall, the early influential Chief Justice of the United States is said to have read the *Commentaries* four times.[52] That kind of extended familiarity with the work tends to bring out Blackstone's distinctive authorial voice and projects. Cover-to-cover readers would be far less likely to adopt an uncritical belief in the revealed truth of a text as manifestly creative as the *Commentaries*.

In my own reading of the *Commentaries*, I have been struck by the way Blackstone's individual voice comes through, much more clearly than I expected in such a canonical academic work. At times his tone is almost personal, and quite different from the distanced voice of legal advocacy and scholarship today. In his introduction, Blackstone uses the first person. He says 'I think' and 'I hope' and 'Far be it from me'.[53] Although much of the work is more formal, the voice seems to come out when Blackstone wants to emphasise his affiliation with his subject. So, for instance, in a discussion of future estates, Blackstone expresses his admiration for the craft on display in this notoriously intricate doctrinal area: 'the student will observe how much nicety is required in creating and securing a remainder'. Then he shifts into the first person: 'I trust he will in some measure see the general reasons upon which this nicety is founded'.[54] At other times the voice is

---

[51] On some earlier occasions, Supreme Court justices have taken advantage of Blackstone's legitimising approach to give special credibility to Blackstone's *criticism* of traditional English common law structures. For instance, upholding the return of forfeited property, Justice Harlan observed, 'Even Blackstone, who is not known as a biting critic of the English legal tradition, condemned the seizure of the property of the innocent as based upon a 'superstition' inherited from the 'blind days' of feudalism', *United States v United States Coin and Currency* 401 US 715, 720–21 (1971).
[52] Nolan 757.
[53] *Commentaries* vol 1, 5.
[54] Ibid vol 2, 172.

critical. In one passage of likely interest for eighteenth-century American readers, Blackstone observes dryly that England's 'American plantations' were acquired by treaty, conquest 'and driving out the natives (with what natural justice I shall not at present inquire)'.[55]

III BLACKSTONE THE MYTHMAKER

In substance as well as style, Blackstone's work bears his personal stamp. Extended readers can hardly fail to notice that Blackstone has some stories to tell, and, reading these stories, it is practically impossible to see Blackstone as the neutral reporter of an objective view of English common law. Indeed, if the Supreme Court mythologises Blackstone, it is equally true that Blackstone himself was engaged in something of a mythmaking project.

For instance, the *Commentaries* includes a creative retelling of the Norman Conquest, in which an apparently disruptive historical event winds up being the link that connects present-day legal structures with an ancient past. Without this revision, the Conquest would pose real problems for Blackstone's overarching account of common law's evolution from ancient English origins. If, as Blackstone asserts, modern English property law is built on feudal foundations, and if European feudalism was imposed on a defeated English people by William the Conqueror, that hardly seems to validate Blackstone's story of the ancient and uniquely British origins of common law property rights. How can a legal system whose *sine qua non* is *private* property be squared with the 'grand and fundamental maxim of all feudal tenure' that 'all lands were originally granted out by the sovereign, and are therefore holden, either mediately or immediately, of the crown'?[56] Responding to this challenge, Blackstone sets out to show that the received view of feudalism in England is all a 'strange historical mistake.'[57]

Blackstone weaves a tale of a threatened Danish invasion some years after the Conquest, against which, 'the military constitution of the Saxons being then laid aside, and no other introduced in its stead, the kingdom was wholly defenceless'.[58] The foreign army the king brought over to repel the Danes made apparent the advantages of a feudal system for raising a domestic army. Accordingly, 'all the principal landholders submitted their lands to the yoke of military tenure, became the king's vassals, and did homage and fealty to his person' and feudal land tenures were formally

---

[55] Ibid vol 1, 105.
[56] Ibid vol 2, 53.
[57] Ibid 48.
[58] Ibid 49.

introduced into English law.[59] Theirs was a formal agreement, however, that at the time 'probably meant no more than to put the kingdom in a state of defence' by obliging themselves to defend the king's territory *'as if* they had received their lands from his bounty upon these express conditions'.[60] The whole deal was fictional, and thus becomes the basis of a canny claim based on contract law principles. Because the nobles already owned the land the king was ostensibly granting to them, they were 'by no means beneficiaries' and so could not be expected to *really* provide everything they promised in exchange.[61]

So, in Blackstone's version of the story, when eventually the English landholders 'rise up in arms' against the 'rigours of the feudal doctrines', they have the law on their side.[62] They do not fight for 'mere infringements of the king's prerogative' but to restore the rights of Englishmen under the ancient Saxon law that predated the Conquest and were never revoked under the legally correct interpretation of the gentlemen's agreement that the Normans misconstrued.[63] They fight, as it were, *inside* the law.

Here is a legal myth if ever there was one—the story of the hero law. In Blackstone's Conquest, the twists and turns in the descent of property law from ancient norms take place *within* the legal system. Legal rituals, not force, accomplish the evolution from ancient Saxon law through feudalism up to contemporary property structures. Even when property rights were corrupted, during the bad old feudal days, it was not so much the fault of a megalomaniac king or bloodthirsty soldiers, but of those crafty *lawyers* who can make and remake rights and obligations in the forms they choose. Law is by far the most effective, powerful and socially influential actor on this stage. For better or worse, in Blackstone's world a well-crafted legal argument is mightier than the sword.

IV BLACKSTONE EXPLAINS THE FUTURE

I do not mean to suggest that because of his mythologising tendencies, we cannot gain real insight from Blackstone. It might be problematic to present the *Commentaries* as an untroubled universal source of eighteenth-century American legal norms, and still possible to find in this storied text harbingers of twenty-first-century legal and social structures. But before I offer an example of how the *Commentaries* might be read to illuminate law and society in the United States today, let me point out an obstacle to this kind

---

[59] Ibid.
[60] Ibid 51.
[61] Ibid.
[62] Ibid 52.
[63] Ibid.

of reading. I have criticised the Supreme Court for presenting eighteenth-century American readers of Blackstone as less legally sophisticated than the current Court—in effect, 'totemising' the American founders. If the current Court tends to flatten and oversimplify the attitudes of Blackstone's eighteenth-century American audience, however, it is easy to adopt a similar attitude regarding Blackstone's eighteenth-century English subject matter. We may be too quick to view Blackstone's text as depicting a world—and ways of thinking about that world—too different from our own to shed any light on twenty-first-century legal culture.

With that problem in mind, consider chapter 12 of the *Commentaries'* first volume, the subject of which is 'the civil state' or, 'That part of the nation which ... includes all orders of men, from the highest nobleman to the meanest peasant'.[64] Blackstone's method here of representing civil society is strikingly categorical and status bound. It consists of listing the hierarchy of titles and ranks available in eighteenth-century Britain, along with brief descriptions of their origins, privileges and customary duties. Initially, Blackstone's typology of British civil society, with its emphasis on ritual and formal hierarchy, struck me as stilted and wholly at odds with fluid twenty-first-century Western relations. Indeed Blackstone's 'degrees of nobility and honour'[65] at first seemed so different from the social structure of my own world that it put me in mind of the elaborate clan and kinship diagrams reproduced in ethnographies—earls and marquesses as the turtle and kingfisher totems of the British monarchy!

Moreover, I was quick to ascribe to the practitioners of this 'traditional' social hierarchy an inability to look beyond or through its internal boundaries. Just as the Supreme Court's references sometimes obscure the critical faculties of Blackstone's eighteenth-century American audience, I was discounting Blackstone's own sceptical intelligence and that of his subjects. When I read Blackstone's descriptions of the formal degrees of nobility that articulated the eighteenth-century British state, I imagined that the citizens who either were or were not the dukes, earls, knights and peasants would not perceive the contingency of those categories. I imagined that their society was at once more artificial than ours and more natural from the perspective of the people who composed it. But on second thoughts, I could see the totemism at work in my first impressions of Blackstone's world.

Levi-Strauss read the patterns inscribed in myth as expressions of a common structure across cultures. Approaching the *Commentaries* as a potential source of familiar social patterns, how exotic really is the place-for-everyone-and-everyone-in-his-place approach Blackstone describes? Consider, for example, the way academic credentials denominate the different ranks of

---

[64] Ibid vol 1, 384.
[65] Ibid 385.

professional life in the United States today. We may think academic letters stand for more substantial, experiential differences than the degrees of nobility Blackstone describes. After all, university degrees are not inherited. But a glance at the demographics of those who receive JDs, LLMs, BAs, MBAs, PhDs and MDs in the United States reveals that family history plays a large part. About 8 in 10 Americans whose parents hold college degrees enrol in college after high school, compared with only about half of those whose parents did not finish college and fewer than 4 in 10 whose parents who did not finish high school.[66] Of course that does not mean that the divide in the United States today between those with and without college education is strictly comparable to the traditional British system of aristocrats and commoners. But viewing the *Commentaries*' civil ranks as a system that might have analogues in my own time and place makes it possible to see the persistence of hereditary status in our avowedly egalitarian world.

Unlike the ranks Blackstone describes, the marks of status created by education in the United States today are not formally reflected in legal doctrine. But that does not mean they are without legal significance. For instance, as Paul Butler has pointed out, there is a strong correlation in the United States today between educational attainment and criminal incarceration.[67] Put bluntly, prison is largely reserved for those who are academically untitled. Butler reports that only 13 per cent of incarcerated Americans have any post-secondary education, and among state prisoners, 70 per cent never graduated from high school. On the other hand, a college degree has a remarkable immunising effect against the criminal law: Only 0.1 per cent of those with bachelor's degrees are incarcerated, compared with 6.3 per cent of high school drop outs.[68]

Another familiar structure in the United States today that recalls Blackstone's social ranks is the hierarchy embodied in a dizzying array of plastic credit cards. The combinations of gold, platinum and black cards and familiar graphics and designations—'preferred rewards' 'centurion'—even oddly recall aristocratic family crests and mottos. If you doubt that credit cards meaningfully structure social mobility beyond an individual's access to cash, consider that most hotels will not accept guests who do not present credit cards. Ostensibly a way to protect against guests who raid the minibar and then abscond without paying for those exorbitantly over-priced smoked almonds, the hotel credit card prerequisite serves as a de facto

---

[66] SP Choy, 'Students Whose Parents Did not Go to College: Post-Secondary Access, Persistence and Attainment' in [National Center for Education Statistics, US Department of Education], *The Condition of Education* (Washington DC, 2001) 3.

[67] P Butler, 'Poor People Lose: Gideon and the Critique of Rights' (2013) 122 *Yale Law Journal* 2176, 2181–82.

[68] Ibid 2182.

social filter. Americans without credit cards are categorically excluded from a particular, legally recognised relationship to real property—that of being a hotel guest. Lacking this visible sign of 'personal credit', one lacks access to public accommodation, not because of an inability to pay, but for want of a crucial badge of identity conferring access to that 'estate'. This was brought forcefully home to me when a national organisation I worked for held a conference to which we invited community organisers, some of whom had no credit cards. It was quite an undertaking to get the hotel to accept these effectively untitled folks, even with an organisation willing to guarantee any excess room charges with its own AmEx gold card. They might leave home without it, but they certainly were not going to be staying in any major hotel chain overnight. Credit status, and the cards that enact it, thus confers and withholds access to liberty and property in ways that recall the 'original ... several degrees of nobility' and 'names of *dignity*' that structured eighteenth-century British subjects' legal rights and privileges.[69]

Recognising the *Commentaries*' reflections in twenty-first-century American culture can reflect back on one's reading of Blackstone's text. Once we give up the notion that the eighteenth-century British subjects Blackstone describes had a radically different approach to social hierarchy than we do, it is possible to imagine that, like us, they were sceptical about the way law structured their society. Blackstone certainly suggests that he regarded the categorical assignments of British social status as something other than transparent indicia of intrinsic nobility. In the *Commentaries*, the designations of nobility sound decidedly positivistic, not to say completely arbitrary. Blackstone explains, for instance, that new peers are created by formal acts and documents and that existing nobles 'must suppose either a writ or a patent made to their ancestors; though by length of time it is lost'.[70] There is also a discussion of the relative merits of acquiring a peerage by writ (which includes heirs 'without any words to that purport') as against patent (whereby the subject is ennobled even if he never takes his seat in the House of Lords).[71]

Reading this chapter with an eye towards its contemporary relevance draws attention to Blackstone's decidedly realistic tone about the hierarchy he describes. One gets the impression that Blackstone views British titles as reflecting innate or essential superiority of character to about the same extent that we believe modern academic credentials reflect pure intellectual meritocracy or think that offers of new credit cards are a sign of one's objective creditworthiness. Indeed, if critiquing the Supreme Court's story of the founding generation's credulous faith in Blackstone's neutrality brings out

---

[69] *Commentaries* vol 1, 388, 393.
[70] Ibid 388.
[71] Ibid 388–89.

his text's mythic qualities, considering how his text can illuminate current legal culture tends to highlight the pragmatic aspects of his approach.

If the Supreme Court treats Blackstone as an immortal ancestor whose legal ideas continue to shape the US Constitution, others see him as a legal primitive, a fussy antiquarian too firmly embedded in a distant time and place to have real relevance today. But Blackstone's work is neither a timeless source of universal legal norms nor an archaic relic of an exotic legal culture. Blackstone argues for the role of common law in modern society both through valorising myths—for instance, the story of how ancient English property rights outsmarted and eventually prevailed over foreign military force—and by modelling with his own sceptical, historical approach how traditional legal structures might be understood to influence and be influenced by changing social structures. In contrast, the Supreme Court's recent references advance a less convincing account of Blackstone's continued relevance in US law. The Court offers the *Commentaries* as an untroubled source of practically every aspect of the eighteenth-century founders' legal understandings and thus of law today to the extent the Constitution perpetuates those original understandings. That is not a legal myth we can take seriously. It too blatantly ignores the political context of Blackstone's work in the early United States and the critical perspectives some of the US founders expressed towards Blackstone's project. Moreover, the Court's insistence on the founding generation's credulous acceptance of the *Commentaries* as timeless legal truth is in tension with the text itself. It both ignores some obviously mythical aspects of Blackstone's legal account and denies his consciously historical method.

Let me end by suggesting another mythic role for Blackstone as a cultural ancestor. What I have in mind seems at once truer to Blackstone's authorial vision and no less expansively imaginative—if considerably more antic—than the Supreme Court's treatment of the *Commentaries*. Consider how Blackstone's vision of the common law prefigures current idealised visions of the Internet. The common law Blackstone describes is a system of great complexity, flexibility and responsiveness which, despite its lack of top-down order, is mysteriously capable of promoting certain virtues and values instead of breaking down into a cacophony of competing individual interests. For all the references to God and natural rights, the common law of the *Commentaries* is an almost accidental creation—an amazingly complex and resilient bulwark of human liberty that developed through the contingencies of history, not because of some divine, or human, plan.

There is no question that to some extent this vision is a fantasy. The cumulative results of so many unconnected individual judgments must be either far less organised than the picture Blackstone presents or far more driven by political and economic interests. Doubtless both are true of the common law—and the Internet. Yet in both institutions there remains an organisational and communicative power that seems to escape at once the noise of randomness and the deliberate control of powerful individual interests.

Blackstone celebrates common law as a quintessentially social creation with great potential for liberal political development. If the Internet is, or ever can become, such a thing, I dare say Blackstone will be partly responsible. After all, he did as much as anyone to popularise the dream of a massive, intricate, evolving network of ideas that achieves coherence without the control of a single sovereign intelligence, a truly common system that both mirrors and drives the culture that produced it.

Index

abortion, 222
Act of Settlement (1701), 164, 210
Act of Union (1707), 60
actio de effusis vel deiectis, 86
Adams, John, 201, 205, 208, 209
Agier, Jean-Louis, 110
Ainsworth, Robert, 201
Alfred of Wessex, King, 183
Allen, Jessie, 18, 167–8
Amhoerst, Jeffery, 105–6
ancient Greece, 211
ancient Rome, 56
Anne, Queen, 196
Archbold on Criminal Pleadings, 138, 162
architecture, 31–44, 54, 56–7
Argou, Gabriel, 113
aristocracy, 233–4, 235
Aristotle, 51, 146, 207
Armstrong, John, 59, 60
arson, 137
art, 31–44, 51–3
Ashburnham, Lord, 194–5
Ashburton, Lord, 64
Atkins, Richard, 149
The Attorneys Compleat Pocket-Book, 149
Austin, John, 155, 156, 157, 158, 160, 162
Australia:
    Aborigines, 152, 163, 164
    Commentaries and, 145, 146–58
        assessment, 160–5
        colonial jurisdiction, 152, 163
        contemporary citations, 161–3
        criminal cases, 150–2
        legal education, 154–8
    colonial occupation, 151, 152, 163
    Rum Rebellion (1808), 149
    terra nullius, 163

Bacon, Francis, 146
Badger, George, 126–7
Bancas, Louis de, comte de Lauranguais, 109
Batiza, Rodolfo, 74, 85–6, 90, 101
Battle, Kemp Plummer, 127
Beaumont, Jean-Baptiste Jacques Élie de, 110–11
Beccaria, Cesare, 123
Beckett, Gilbert, 133
Bédard, Thomas, 114–15
Bedford, Edward Henslowe, 154
Bentham, Jeremy:
    Australia and, 155, 156, 157, 164
    on Blackstone's oral style, 5

    on *Commentaries*, 4, 61, 67, 68–9, 161, 189
    on equity, 51
    legal structure, 56–7
    New Zealand and, 159
    on publicity and justice, 8
Bibaud, Maximilien, 120–1, 123
bigamy, 57
Bill of Rights (1689), 165, 225
Binney, Horace, 25
Black, Joseph, 146
Blackmun, Harry, 222
Blackstone, Henry, 124
Blackstone, William:
    'Abridgement of Architecture', 32, 39, 41, 42
    Analysis of the Laws of England
        American response, 201
        classification, 44
        French translation, 109
        Preface, 38–9, 46
        'Table of Descents', 48, 50
        tabulation, 39, 43, 46, 48
    American colonies and, 188, 191–2
    anti-Catholicism, 105, 194
    architecture and, 31–44, 54, 56–7
    bookish knowledge, 12–13
    Commentaries see Blackstone's *Commentaries*
    dominance of print, 19–20
    drawing, 33–40
    dying words, 17–18
    early life, 6
    'Elements of Architecture', 32–40, 56
    firmness of opinion, 17–18
    freedom of the press, 150
    judge, 8, 14, 27–9
    lectures, 3, 6, 134
    loyalty to principle, 17
    loyalty to text, 17
    natural law, 7, 73, 85, 94, 96, 156, 174
    optimism, 134
    oral style, 1, 5–20
        anti-performance, 10–11, 12, 18
        embarrassment, 6–7, 13, 15
        Onslow v Horne, 12, 13–16, 27–9
        performance, 7, 14–15
        pressures, 9–10
        repetition, 16
    piety, 176
    poetry of, 4–5, 59–69, 170–1
    Toryism, 125, 134, 169, 227

Blackstone's *Commentaries*:
  affective terms, 3–4
  classical tradition, 68
  colonialism, 151, 152, 163, 164–5
  contemporary comments, 45
  'Countries Subject to the Laws of England', 151–2
  elegance, 4–5
  equity, 51–5
  historical context, 167–8, 223
  iconic cultural monument, 19
  imagination, 65
  intended readership, 192–4
  international influence, 71–2
    18th century accessible texts, 81–4, 113–14, 199–200
    Australia, 145, 146–58, 160–5
    British empire, 154
    Canada, 119
    Louisiana *see* Louisiana
    New Zealand, 145, 158–65
    North America, 75, 153, 160, 164
    North Carolina, 125–43
    pre-revolutionary France, 108–10
    Quebec *see* Quebec
    United States *see* United States
  kingship, 167, 169–87
  law reports citations *see* law reports
  literary work, 59–69
  master and servant, 94, 101, 131
  metaphors, 62, 66, 67, 170
  mythmaking
    explaining the future, 232–7
    feudalism, 231–2
  nobility, 233–4, 235
  objectives, 45
  obsolescence, 153, 216
  picturing the law, 31–58
  political ideology, 164
  pre-revolutionary France and, 108–10
  property law, 132, 186, 195, 231
  pursuit of totality, 60–6, 68–9
  Quebec and *see* Quebec
  reasons for success, 1, 3
  slavery, 93
  source text, 69
  structure, 27, 45, 55, 94
  'Table of Consanguinity,' 46–7
  'Table of Descents,' 48, 49
  tabulation, 46–8, 57–8
  taxonomy, 88–91
    public wrongs, 136
    rights and wrongs, 132
  title, 196–7
  translations, 72, 73–4, 82–4, 109, 111, 113–18, 123–4
Bligh, William, 149
Bodin, Jean, 5

Boileau, René, 114
Boorstin, Daniel, 3, 54, 214
Bounty mutiny, 149
Bracton, Henry de, 13, 225
Brazil: slavery, 93
Bright, Thomas, 154
Broom, Herbert, 161
Brown, James, 80–1, 88, 93, 96, 97
Brown, Jethro, 157
Brown, John, 97
Bryan, Samuel, 202
Buller, Francis, 26, 27
Burgh, James, 9, 23, 126
burglary, 137
Burke, Edmund, 27, 116, 189, 199
Burn, Richard, 149
Burton, William Westbrooke, 151
Bute, Lord, 184
Butler, Paul, 234

Cairns, John W, 95, 96–7, 101, 102
A Calm Examination into the Causes of the Present Alarm in the Empire, 44–5
Campbell, Colen, 32
Campbell, R, 33
Canada:
  Blackstone's *Commentaries* and, 113–14, 119
  Constitutional Act (1791), 107, 123
  Quebec *see* Quebec
  rebellions (1837–8), 107
Cartier, George Étienne, 119
Cartwright, John, 190
Castles, Alex C, 146, 163
Catherine II of Russia, 73
Chalker, John, 60n2
Chapman, Frederick, 158
Chapman, Henry Samuel, 155, 158, 159
Charles I, 196
Charles II, 183–4
Cheshire, Joseph Blount, 128–9
Chesterfield, Lord, 32
children: freedom of speech, 224
Chompré, Nicholas Maurice, 82, 109, 114, 123–4
Christian, Edward, 81, 82, 99, 109, 123, 149, 153
Christian, Fletcher, 149
Cicero, 61
civil society, 187, 233
Claiborne, William CC, 77, 78, 79–80, 97
Clayton and Bell, 146, 147
Clitherow, James, 5, 21
Cobbett, Pitt, 156–7
Cohen, Morris, 101
Coke, Edward:
  Australia and, 146
  Blackstone and, 13, 45

Calvin's Case (1609), 173, 177
concept of legal system, 56
diagrams, 48
influence, 37
Institutes of the Laws of England, 45, 130, 138, 189, 190
on kingship, 173, 177–8
unsystematic approach, 32, 45
US Supreme Court and, 225
Coleridge, Samuel Taylor, 67–8
Collier, John Payne, 26
Collins, David, 148
Collinson, Patrick, 185
Colman, George, 7n25
colonialism:
  Blackstone and, 151, 152, 163, 164–5
  France *see* Louisiana; Quebec
Condorcet, Nicolas de, 110
constitutionalism
  see also kingship
  ambiguities, 195–6
  concept of state, 191
  despotism of parliament, 191–2, 195
  parliamentary supremacy, 191–2, 194–5, 204, 211–13
  separation of powers, 207–13
  United States *see* United States
contempt of court, 222
Cook, James, 145, 146
Cooley, Thomas McIntyre, 99
copyright, 29
Corelli, Arcangelo, 37
Coyer, Gabriel-François, 73–4, 109, 114
credit cards, 234–5
Crémazie, Jacques, 118
Cross, Rupert, *Evidence*, 162
Crossley, George, 149
Cugnet, François-Joseph, 111–13, 123
Culler, Jonathan, 54

Dargo, George, 101
Darling, Ralph, 150
Davies, John, 172–3
de Bonne, Pierre-Amable, 114
de donis conditionalibus (1285), 133
de Lolme, Jean-Louis, 110, 114, 115–16, 116, 118, 201
Derrida, Jacques, 54
di Giorgio, Francesco, 46
Dicey, Albert Venn, 134
Dickinson, John, 202–3
Diderot, Denis, 31
Dippel, Horst, 167
Doddridge, John, 172
Dodsley, Robert, 59
Dodson, Michael, 164
Domat, Jean, 80, 89–90, 93, 94, 113, 119, 122
Donaldson v Beckett (1774), 29

Dore, Richard, 149
double jeopardy, 224n24
Douct, Nicolas Benjamin, 118
Dowling, James, 151
drawing, 33–44, 46–51, 54
due process, 205, 225
Dunning, John, 126
Dyer, John, 59, 61

Edward II, 173, 195
Ehrlich, Jacob W, 130
Eliade, Mircea, 220
Élie de Beaumont, Jean-Baptiste Jacques, 110–11
Elizabeth I, 176, 195
Elliot, J, 203
Elyot, Thomas, 192
Emerson, John, 108, 109
eminent domain, 224
Enlightenment, 3, 5, 68, 73–4, 94, 169, 183
Epstein, James, 24
equitable tolling, 220
equity:
  Bentham on, 51
  Blackstone on, 32, 51–5
  courtroom style, 26
  definitions, 51
Erskine, Thomas, 24
Ewell, Marshall Davis, 129, 130
extortion, 220

Federalist Papers, The, 190, 202–3, 204, 212, 225
fee simple, 133
Ferguson, Robert, 25, 190
Ferrière, Claude Joseph de, 113, 119, 120
feudalism, 56, 114, 121, 186, 231–2
Field, Barron, 149–50
Finch, Henry, 40, 44
Finkelman, Paul, 189
Fleming, Thomas, 173
Fliegelman, Jay, 9, 10, 12
Fontainebleau, Treaty of (1762), 75–6
Foote, Samuel, 7, 11–12, 22
Forbes, Francis, 150, 151–2
Foster, Charles, 158
Founding Fathers, US, 188–9, 197, 199–214, 215, 225, 226–30, 233
Fox, Charles James, 116
France:
  cahiers de doléances, 110
  Civil Code: corporations, 90–1
  colonial slavery, 75, 91
  Coutume de Paris, 75, 120
  Louisiana colony, 74, 75–7
  Napoleonic code, 74, 123, 153
  pre-Revolution and Blackstone, 108–10
  Quebec colony, 105–6
  Quebec legal tradition and, 189

Fréart de Chambray, Roland, 33
free speech, 224
Frobisher, Benjamin, 114

Garran, Robert, 162
Garrick, David, 9
Garrow, William, 24, 26
Gellibrand, Joseph Tice, 150
genius, 51–3, 54
George III, 171
Gerbier, Balthazar, 32
Gerry, Elbridge, 202
Gibson, Albert, 154
Girard, Philip, 119
Glorious Revolution, The (1688–9), 60, 177, 184, 186, 195, 196, 210
Gneist, Rudolf von, 212
Goldie, Mark, 185
Gomicourt, Auguste Pierre Damiens de, 73, 108–9, 113–14, 117, 123
Grainger, James, 59, 60
Graunt, John, 149
Graves, Richard, 5
Grotius, Hugo, 51, 85
Gurney, Joseph, 14, 27–9
Guzmán Brito, Alejandro, 75, 81, 82, 85, 88

habeas corpus, 110, 165, 203, 225
Haiti, 91
Hale, Matthew, 37, 40, 44, 189
Halliday, Paul, 167, 188, 189, 195–6, 197
Hamilton, Alexander, 204, 206, 211–12
Hammond, William, 130, 160
Hargrave, Francis, 189
Hargrave, John Fletcher, 157
Harrington, James, 207
Hastings, Warren, 8, 24
Hearn, William Edward, 155, 156
Helvetius, Claude Adrien, 115
Henry, Patrick, 202, 203–4
Hibbins, Thomas, 148
Hibbitts, Bernard, 3, 17, 19–20
Hindmarsh, John, 152–3
Hobbes, Thomas, 146
Hoeflich, Michael, 99
Holdsworth, William Searle, 53
Holland, Thomas Erskine, 156, 161
Holmes, Oliver Wendell, 137
Hope, Henry, 115
Howard, Martin, 200–1
Howe, William Wirt, 101
human rights, 202–4, 206–7, 213
Hume, David, 61, 201, 227
Hunter, John, 148

impeachment, 211
Iredell, James, 125–6

Ireland, 165, 191
irony, 171

James I, 176, 181
James II, 177, 195, 196
Jefferson, Thomas, 78, 189–91, 227
Jenks, Edward, 155, 161
Johnson, Charles: *The Successful Pyrate*, 22
Johnson, Samuel, 19, 27, 131, 201
Jones, Inigo, 32
Jones, William, 62, 67
judicial review, 211–12
judiciary:
    independence, 210–12, 213
    myth making, 167–8, 220–31
    sentencing discretion, 220
    US Supreme Court, 216–31
juries:
    histrionics and, 25
    trial by jury, 150, 202
justice:
    harmonic justice, 5, 7, 10
    king as fountain of justice, 175–6
    law, reason and, 3–4
Justice of the Peace and Parish Officer, 149
Justinian: *Institutes*, 55, 94, 120, 192

Kadens, Emily, 6, 12–14, 17
Kantorowicz, Ernst, 195–6
Katz, Stanley, 199
Kent, James: *Commentaries*, 98, 158, 225
Kercher, Bruce, 146–8, 150, 161
Kerr, Lewis, 79, 81, 84, 85, 159, 161
Kerr, Robert Malcolm, 159
kingship:
    ambiguities, 197
    consent, 186
    despotism, 172n14, 195
    embodiment, 177–9
    fountain, 175–6
    Glorious Revolution, 177, 196
    historical change, 183–4
    king within the crown, 179–82
    king's person and prerogative, 172–4
    limits of powers, 175–7, 187, 203, 213
    miracles, 173, 176
    pardons, 205–6
    republican kingship, 185–7
    treason, 173
    two bodies theory, 173, 178, 195–6
    US presidential power and, 167
Kingston, Duchess of, 8, 57

La Fontaine, Louis-Hippolyte, 118
Labrie, Jacques, 117–18
law reports: Blackstone citations:
    Australia, 161–3
    Louisiana, 98–9, 100–1, 102–3

New Zealand, 162
  United States, 99–100, 104
    Supreme Court, 216–31
Legrand, Thérèse, 114
Leigh, Richard, 14–15
Leonardo da Vinci, 37
Lévi-Strauss, Claude, 215, 222–3, 229, 233
Lewis, William Draper, 99
libel, 13–14, 17, 97
Locke, John, 33, 115, 116, 207
Lockmiller, David, 160, 205
Lord, Simeon, 149
Louisiana:
  1803 US purchase of, 74, 77
  accessible Blackstone texts, 81–4
  Blackstone citations, 98–9, 100–1, 102–3
  Civil Code *see* Louisiana Civil Code
  cultural mix, 95
  Digest of Orleans see Louisiana Civil Code
  French colony, 74, 75–7
  libel, 97
  slavery law
    Black Code (1806), 92
    Civil Code, 90, 91–3, 96
    post-1803, 78–9
    Spain and France, 75–7
  Spain and, 75–7
  sugar industry, 91
  Territory of Orleans, 71, 74, 76–9, 91, 97
Louisiana Civil Code:
  Blackstone's *Commentaries* and
    argument, 81–94
    claims, 74–5
    counterargument, 95–104
    reasons for using, 84–8
  Blackstone's taxonomy, 88–91
  communities and corporations, 84, 86–7, 90
  exceptionalism, 101
  husband and wife, 89
  jambalaya, 95–103
  master and servant, 84, 85–6, 101
  move to codify, 77–80
  parent and child, 84, 85, 89
  partnership, 98
  persons, 88–90, 93–4
  slavery, 90, 91–3, 96
Lysnar, Douglas, 159

Macarthur, John, 149
Mackay, Jean, 117
Maclaine, Archibald, 204
Madison, James, 190, 201, 204
Magna Carta, 165
Manning, John, 129–31, 134, 135
Mansfield, William Murray, Lord, 4, 8, 14, 53, 61

Marshall, John, 190, 203, 230
Marx, Karl, 54
Matthews, Carol, 32
McArthur, Dr, 158
McKenzie, John, 205
Meehan, Michael, 163
metaphors, 62, 66, 67, 170
Miller, Henry Knight, 68
Milsom, Stroud F C, 46
Milton, John, 19, 207
Mirabeau, Honoré de, 109
Montesquieu, Charles de, 115, 116, 123, 150, 179, 182, 207–8, 209, 210, 212
Moore, William Harrison, 155–6
Mordecai, Samuel, 130, 131–7, 138, 140, 141–3
Moreau-Lislet, Louis, 80–1, 82, 84, 88, 93, 96, 97
Morgan, Lewis Henry, 46–8
Murdoch, Beamish, 119
Murphy, Mary C, 11
myth, 215, 220–37

Napoleon I, 77, 91, 101
natural law, 7, 12, 73, 85, 88, 89–90, 94, 96, 156, 174
New Zealand:
  Blackstone and, 145, 158–65
    contemporary citations, 162
  federation with Australia, 145
  political ideology, 165
  Treaty of Waitangi (1840), 164–5
nobility, 233–4, 235
Nolan, Dennis, 216
Norman Conquest, 183, 231–2
North Carolina:
  Bar applicants' reading lists, 139
  Blackstone and, 125–43
Nottingham, Lord, 189
Nugent, Thomas, 209
Nussbaum, Martha, 4

Onslow v Horne (1770), 12, 13–16, 27–9
O'Reilly, Alejandro, 76, 78
Otis, James, 200–1

Paley, Ruth, 167
Palladio, Andrea, 37, 55, 56
Palmer, Vernon, 92, 93
Palmer, W, 6
pardons, 205–6
parental control, 224
parliamentary supremacy, 191–2, 194–5, 204, 211–13
partnership, 98
Patrat, Joseph: *Jacques Splin*, 7
patriotism, 60, 62
Peacham, Henry, 33

Pennefather, Frederick W, 156
Perrault, Claude, 33
Perrault, François Joseph, 116–17
Perrault, Jacques Nicolas, 115, 117
Petit, Emilien, 109
Petrow, Stefan, 150
Phillips, Edward: *The Mock Lawyer*, 22
Phillips, John, 59
Piggott, Arthur, 26
Pinckney's Treaty (1795), 76
Planté, Joseph Bernard, 114
Pocock, John G A, 185
Pope, Alexander, 9, 18–19, 59, 63
positivism, 94, 157, 160, 164, 235
Pothier, Robert Joseph, 113, 119, 120, 122
prerogative powers:
  despotism, 172n14, 195
  fountain of justice, 175–6
  historical change, 183–4
  king within the crown, 179–81
  king's person and, 172–4
  limits, 175–7, 187, 203, 213
  meaning, 169
  pardons, 205–6
  republican kingship, 185–7
Prest, Wilfrid, 6, 29, 193
Prevost, John, 79, 98
professional hierarchies, 233
property law, 132, 186, 195, 231
Prost de Royer, François, 109
Pufendorf, Samuel, 85, 88, 115

Quebec:
  Blackstone's *Commentaries* and, 108
    1774–1867 debate, 113–16
    1774–1867 legal culture, 116–23
    assessment, 123–4
    French tradition and, 189
    pre-1774, 110–13
  Catholic emancipation, 106–8, 194
  Civil Code
    corporations, 90–1
    sources, 123
  French capitulation, 105–6
  post-1763 legal order, 105–8
  Quebec Act (1774), 106–7, 108, 112, 113, 123
  Royal Proclamation (1764), 108, 110
Quick, John, 162

Radin, Max, 200
repetitive speech, 11–12
Reynolds, Henry, 163
Reynolds, Joshua, 32, 51–3, 54
Richardson, Jonathan, 33
Rigaud, Pierre de, marquis de Vaudreuil de Cavagnal, 105
Roach, Joseph, 18

Roberts, John G, 223, 224
Robinson, Henry Crabb, 25
Roman Law, 80, 86, 122
Romanticism, 68
Roof, Judith, 63–4, 66
Rowlandson, Thomas, 57, 58
Ruffin, Thomas, 127, 128–9, 134
Ruffin, William Kirkland, 128–9
Rutledge, John, 222

St Domingue: slave rebellion (1794), 81, 91
Saint-Joseph, A de, 90
St Paul, 186
St Paul's Cathedral (London), 37, 38
Salmond, John W, 157
San Lorenzo, Treaty of (1795), 76
Scalia, Antonin, 194, 219–20, 221, 225, 225–6
Scotland:
  18th century education, 193
  sheriffs, 223–4
Scott, John, 26
Sedgwick, James, 4
Selden, John, 37
sentencing, 220
separation of powers, 179, 207–13
Seven Years War, 75–6
Sewell, Richard, 155
Sharswood, George, 99
Sheridan, Charles Francis, 191–2, 195
Sheridan, Richard Brinsley, 191
Sheridan, Thomas, 10, 11, 24
sheriffs' powers, 223–4
Shute, John, 32
Sidney, Algernon, 207
Skinner, Quentin, 171, 185
slavery:
  Blackstone's *Commentaries*, 93
  Brazil, 93
  France, 75, 91
  Louisiana code, 90, 91–3, 96
  Spanish colonial law, 76
  St Domingue slave rebellion (1794), 81, 91
  US slave rebellions, 92–3
Smart, Christopher, 59
Smith, Adam, 27, 134
Smith, Seth, 158
Smyth, Russell, 162
social contract, 195
Socrates, 146
Solon, 115
Sotomayor, Sonia, 224n24
Spain: Louisiana and, 75–7
Star Chamber, 210
Steele, Richard: *The Conscious Lovers*, 22
Stephen, Alfred, 150–1
Stephen, Henry John, 122, 153–4, 156, 157, 158, 159

Stephen, Sidney, 159
Stern, Simon, 15, 21–9
Stevens, John Paul, 225–6
Stewart, James, 153
Story, Joseph, 203
Stourzh, Gerard, 202n15
Sweden, 202

Taylor, John Louis, 126
Temple, Kathryn, 21
theatre:
   18th century theatricality of law, 8–11, 21
   18th century trials, 23–5
   English culture, 3
   naturalistic drama, 18
Thomas, Clarence, 225
Thomas, John Henry, 189–90
Thomson, James, 63
Thurlow, Edward, 112
Tillet, Edouard, 109
Todd, Stephen, 162
Tomlin, Thomas, 192
Torrance, William, 120
Toryism, 125, 134, 169, 227
Townshend, Thomas, 111
treason, 149, 173
treasure trove, 185
The Tree of Legal Knowledge, 127, 128, 132, 135, 136
Tucker, St George, 82, 85, 86, 99, 191, 200
Tucker, Thomas, 74
Tudor, Owen Davies, 161
Turner and Hughes, 127

Ulloa, Antonio de, 76
United States of America:
   19th century courtroom performances, 25
   abortion, 222
   Blackstone's *Commentaries* and
     19th century, 160
     21st century, 188, 189, 194, 215, 225–31, 232–7
     explaining the future, 232–7
     Founding Fathers, 188–9, 190, 197, 199–214, 215, 225, 226–30, 233
     historical context, 167–8, 194, 197
     law reports citations, 99–100, 104
     Louisiana, 81–103
     North Carolina, 125–43
     prerogative powers, 169–70
     reasons for influence, 164
     Supreme Court, 215–31
   Constitution
     Bill of Rights, 206
     civil rights, 202–4, 206–7, 213
     due process, 225
     formative documents, 190
     free speech, 224
     habeas corpus, 225
     mythologising, 189, 220–31, 236
     right to bear arms, 224, 225–6
     separation of powers, 179, 207–13
   criminal demography, 234
   eminent domain, 224
   fellow servant rule, 131
   impeachment, 211
   parental control, 224
   political advertising, 221
   presidential power, 167
     Blackstone justification, 194
     pardons, 205–6
     rule of law, 196
   professional hierarchies, 233
   slave rebellions, 92–3
   Stamp Act (1765), 151, 188
   Supreme Court
     Blackstone citations, 216–20
     Blackstone mythology, 220–31
   Treaty of San Lorenzo (1795), 76
utilitarianism, 155 *see also* Bentham, Jeremy

Vasari, Giorgio, 37
Viner, Charles, 64
Virgil, 59, 62, 68
Voltaire, François Marie Arouet de, 116

Way, Samuel, 156, 160
Webb, Beatrice and Sidney, 160
Webster, Daniel, 25
Webster, James, 135
Webster, Noah, 209–10
White, Hayden, 170, 171, 181, 183
Wild, Jonathan, 15
wild animals, 185
Wilkins, John, 44
Wilkinson, James, 77
William of Orange, 196
William the Conqueror, 231
Wilmot, John Eardley, 222
Wilson, James, 202, 204, 227–8
Winde, William, 32
Windeyer, WJ Victor, 157–8
Winter, Steven, 170
Wood, Denis, 48, 51
Wood, Thomas, 64, 67, 94, 192–3, 195
Wordsworth, William, 67–8
Wotton, Henry, 32
wreck, 185
Wren, Christopher, 32, 56

Yoo, John, 172n15

www.ingramcontent.com/pod-product-compliance
Lightning Source LLC
Chambersburg PA
CBHW070029010526
44117CB00011B/1761